THE SWORD AND THE SHIELD

ALSO BY PENIEL E. JOSEPH

THE SWORD AND THE SHIELD

THE REVOLUTIONARY LIVES OF MALCOLM X AND MARTIN LUTHER KING JR.

PENIEL E. JOSEPH

BASIC BOOKS

New York

Basic Books
Hachette Book Group
1290 Avenue of the Americas, New York, NY 10104
www.basicbooks.com

Printed in the United States of America

First Edition: April 2020

Published by Basic Books, an imprint of Perseus Books, LLC, a subsidiary of Hachette
Book Group, Inc. The Basic Books name and logo is a trademark of the Hachette Book
Group.

The Hachette Speakers Bureau provides a wide range of authors for speaking events. To
find out more, go to www.hachettespeakersbureau.com or call (866) 376-6591.

The publisher is not responsible for websites (or their content) that are not owned by
the publisher.

Print book interior design by Trish Wilkinson.

Library of Congress Cataloging-in-Publication Data
Names: Joseph, Peniel E., author.
Title: The sword and the shield : the revolutionary lives of Malcolm X and Martin
    Luther King Jr. / Peniel E. Joseph.
Description: New York : Basic Books, 2020. | Includes bibliographical references and
    index. | Summary: "The Sword and the Shield is a dual biography of Malcolm X
    and Martin Luther King that transforms our understanding of the twentieth
    century's most iconic African American leaders. Peniel E. Joseph reveals a nuanced
    portrait of two men who, despite markedly different backgrounds, inspired and
    pushed each other throughout their adult lives. This is a strikingly revisionist
    biography, not only of Malcolm and Martin, but also of the movement and era they
    came to define"—Provided by publisher.
Identifiers: LCCN 2019051608 | ISBN 9781541617865 (hardback) | ISBN
    9781541617858 (epub)
Subjects: LCSH: King, Martin Luther, Jr., 1929-1968. | X, Malcolm, 1925-1965.
Classification: LCC E185.97.K5 J67 2020 | DDC 323.092 [B]—dc23
LC record available at https://lccn.loc.gov/2019051608

ISBNs: 978-1-5416-1786-5 (hardcover), 978-1-5416-1785-8 (ebook)

LSC-C

10 9 8 7 6 5 4 3 2 1

For Laura and Ayelet

Contents

Contents

Beyond Dreams and Nightmares

On Thursday, March 26, 1964, Malcolm X and Martin Luther King Jr. descended, separately, on the United States Senate building. Each dressed in a suit and tie, their similar sartorial choices reflecting a shared status as religious ministers and political leaders who paid sharp attention to their physical appearance. That day, the Senate debated the pending civil rights bill, with opponents of racial justice conducting a filibuster designed to prevent its passage. Their unplanned joint appearance recognized the US Senate's deliberations as one of history's hinge points. The Senate debate centered on the fate of the bill, already passed by the House of Representatives, which was designed to end racial discrimination in public life. The Civil Rights Act of 1964 promised to bring the nation closer to multiracial democracy through the end of racial segregation. The proposed law guaranteed that restaurants, movie theaters, swimming pools, libraries, and amusement parks would no longer serve as markers of shame, humiliation, and unequal citizenship for black Americans. President

Lyndon Johnson championed passage of the legislation in honor of the martyred John F. Kennedy, who had urged the nation and Congress to embrace civil rights as a "moral issue" in the months before his November 22, 1963, assassination in Dallas, Texas.

Malcolm and Martin attended the filibuster as participant observers in the nation's unfolding civil rights saga. In a sense, they both sought to serve as witnesses to an ongoing historical drama they had actively shaped in their respective roles as national political leaders and mobilizers.

King's presence among the spectator's gallery added a buzz of excitement to the proceedings. He arrived in Washington as the single most influential civil rights leader in the nation. His "I Have a Dream" speech during the previous summer's March on Washington catapulted him into the ranks of America's unelected, yet no less official, moral and political leaders. *Time* magazine named him "Man of the Year" for 1963 and, unbeknownst to King at that moment, he stood on the cusp of being announced as a Nobel Prize recipient. King emerged as the most well-known leader of the "Big Six" national civil rights organizations, which included the NAACP's Roy Wilkins, James Farmer of the Congress of Racial Equality (CORE), the National Urban League's Whitney Young, A. Philip Randolph of the Brotherhood of Sleeping Car Porters, and Student Non-violent Coordinating Committee (SNCC, pronounced "snick") chairman and future Georgia congressman John Lewis.

King's Southern Christian Leadership Conference (SCLC) served primarily as a national mobilizer of local freedom struggles. The NAACP, the nation's oldest civil rights group, marshaled its resources toward eradicating racism in law through a series of court cases that culminated in the 1954 *Brown v. Board of Education* Supreme Court decision, which outlawed racial segregation in public schools, and local efforts to end discrimination in public accommodations and voting rights. Wilkins's measured approach to racial justice reflected his decades of operating in political terrain that waxed and waned between robust political progress and tragic setbacks. CORE's roots in the radical pacifism of the Second World War found new life in the direct-action demonstrations of the early 1960s. The avuncular, baritone-voiced Farmer endured stints in jail alongside young student activists and was confident enough to debate anyone who couched his militant nonviolence as passive or weak. The Urban League defined racial justice as opening the doors of economic opportunity within a system of American capitalism that Young fervently believed held the key to black freedom. A. Philip Randolph served as the dean of the black freedom struggle. Tall, courtly, and intelligent, Randolph began his ascent into black politics as a radical socialist during the First World War, before adopting a militant pragmatism as a labor leader bold enough to threaten a march of ten thousand black men on Washington—a march that was halted only after Franklin Delano Roosevelt signed an executive order banning discrimination in the military. SNCC was the wild card within the Big Six. Organized by Ella Baker, a King colleague and ally turned political adversary, SNCC helped to radicalize the entire movement through its courageous activism in the most dangerous parts of the South, exemplified by Chairman John Lewis's willful insistence of putting his body on the line and receiving the battle scars to prove it. In the American political imagination—and to the chagrin of his colleagues—King was the one who personified the struggle for racial justice, civil rights, and black citizenship around the nation.

Malcolm X's presence in the Senate gallery, on the other hand, stoked fear, surprise, and bewilderment among journalists and spectators. From 1957 to 1963, Malcolm served as the "national representative" of the Nation of Islam (NOI), the controversial religious group whose defiant resistance against white supremacy gained them both a large following in the black community and fear and suspicion among white Americans. The NOI forbade its members from actively engaging in political demonstrations, but Malcolm rejected these rules and inserted himself into the black freedom struggle on his own terms. He arrived in Washington on a mission to establish his political independence after a dramatic departure from the NOI.

Malcolm's reputation as perhaps the most vocal critic of white supremacy ever produced by black America preceded him. As NOI spokesperson, he became Harlem's hero in the fight against racial oppression. He debated journalists, civil rights leaders, and politicians on subjects ranging from police brutality to unemployment, crime, and social justice, and in the process cultivated a personal reputation as the most militant racial-justice advocate in America. Malcolm's critics called him dangerous, but his supporters, both in and outside the NOI, embraced him as black America's prosecuting attorney—unafraid to charge America with crimes against black humanity. To them, he had inspired a long-overdue political revolution. "I have always loved verbal battle, and challenge," Malcolm said. He set his political sights on eradicating "the racist cancer that is malignant in the body of America," a fight that would take him to the corridors of national power. Even as Malcolm sought to influence the center of American government alongside Martin Luther King Jr., he remained a political maverick whose bold truths upset some of the very civil rights forces he now sought an alliance with. Malcolm was a political renegade, unafraid to identify racial injustice in America as a systemic illness that required nothing less than the radical transformation of the political and racial status quo.[1]

Malcolm stalked the corridors of the Senate throughout the day, accompanied by five aides and holding impromptu press conferences in between watching, from the visitors gallery, a debate to decide the fate of millions. He declared that he wanted the bill to pass "exactly as it is, with no changes." But he predicted that, even if the legislation passed, the struggle for black equality would continue: "You can't legislate goodwill," he said. "That comes about only by education." Malcolm informed reporters that he flew in from New York to observe the lay of the land and "see whether we should conduct any demonstrations, and, if so, what form they should take." It was the first time he had ever visited the Senate.[2]

Martin Luther King Jr. exited the visitors gallery in the afternoon to speak to reporters in a conference room, where Malcolm sat like a spectral figure on a rear sofa. Lately, King had been preoccupied with Malcolm. During a recent interview with author Robert Penn Warren, King took umbrage with Malcolm labeling him as "soft." Just eight days later, he now stood for the first time in the same room as a man many considered to be his evil twin. King ignored Malcolm and announced plans for a national "direct action" campaign scheduled to begin in May. "We will not be content at all even if this bill is passed," warned King, in a comment that mirrored Malcolm's skepticism about the possibilities of effectively legislating racial justice.[3]

But in the Senate building, Malcolm offered full-throated support for the pending legislation. The *New York Times* announced, "Malcolm X Backs Rights Bill" in a short article that introduced him as "the 'black nationalist' leader." By 1964, Malcolm X had turned black nationalism—a historic blend of cultural pride, racial unity, and political self-determination—into a bracing declaration of political independence for himself and large swaths of black folk. This shift recognized mainstream democratic institutions, including the right to vote, as crucial weapons in the struggle for black dignity and citizenship. Malcolm X, the racial separatist who routinely attacked civil rights demonstrations as wrongheaded, had pivoted into an embrace of politics as the means to produce radical ends. Malcolm wanted to spread word of what he was witnessing in the nation's capital back to Harlem residents who, he explained, "are beginning to feel black"—describing the restive mood among a population that not too long ago insisted on being called Negro.[4]

King, on the other hand, warned of escalating racial tensions if the bill was not passed. His rising stature in the aftermath of the March on Washington afforded him special privileges in the nation's capital, including private meetings with supportive politicians such as Minnesota senator Hubert Humphrey. King's access to senators and the president allowed critics, including Malcolm X, to identify him as a political insider captured by reformist impulses. In truth, King's conciliatory image masked the beating heart of a political radical who believed in social democracy, privately railed against economic injustice, and viewed nonviolence as a muscular and coercive tactic with world-changing potential. Vowing to convince the nation with "words" and "deeds" of the importance of the civil rights bill, King threatened to organize civil disobedience in the face of "stubborn" opposition to the goal of black citizenship. He candidly discussed the shadow of racial upheaval that simmered beneath the Senate debate and the wider national conversation about black equality in America. Failure to pass the bill, King suggested, would thrust "our nation" into a "dark night of social disruption." King's warning about violence echoed Malcolm's prediction that civil rights legislation, even if passed, could not prevent a violent and long overdue reckoning on racial justice in America.[5]

Martin and Malcolm both recognized the pivotal role violence played in maintaining America's racial caste system, a system that defined white violence against black bodies as legitimate, legal, and morally just and that regarded black violence—even in defense of black humanity—as criminal, dangerous, and a threat to law and order. Malcolm, who cultivated a well-earned reputation for deploying words of fire, arrived in Washington chastened by his recent and acrimonious departure from the Nation of Islam. He avoided his usually blunt language, even as he characterized the entire debate as a "con game" that threatened to provoke a "race war" if the government was not serious about civil rights enforcement. King spoke of violence as an evil that lurked within a Pandora's box that the nation might, if civil rights legislation was passed, still avoid. "I hate to discuss violence, but realism impels me to admit that if this bill is not passed in strength, it will be harder to keep the struggle disciplined," King confessed to reporters. In Washington, Malcolm and Martin found their usual political identities inverted. Malcolm addressed reporters as a budding statesman—an unelected dignitary who identified his moral authority in the thousands of black faces in Harlem, "the black capital of America." King made no such public claims of leadership; instead, he surveyed a tense national racial climate and declared the passage of the civil rights bill to be the only plausible mechanism that might prevent larger racial storms from engulfing the nation.[6]

After watching King's press conference, Malcolm slipped out a side door, where an assistant made certain he would bump into King in full view of the press. Malcolm, six foot three, handsome and smiling, stood eight inches taller than King, who stretched out his hand. For a brief moment, they sized each other up.

"Well, Malcolm, good to see you," King offered.

"Good to see you," Malcolm responded. For the next few minutes, they made history by chatting amiably. Malcolm expressed interest in joining civil rights demonstrations while his assistant snapped photos and United Press International and Associated Press cameras flashed. Both men smiled broadly in the AP photo and were caught in more serious reflection by UPI.[7]

The initial awkwardness of their meeting gave way to a rapport aided by a mutual understanding of black culture, their shared role as political leaders who doubled as preachers, and the rhythms of a common love for black humanity and yearning for black citizenship. Martin and Malcolm would never develop a personal friendship, but their political visions would grow closer together throughout their lives. A mythology surrounds the legacies of Martin and Malcolm. King is most comfortably portrayed as the nonviolent insider, while Malcolm is characterized as a by-any-means-necessary political renegade. But their relationship, even in that short meeting, defies the myths about their politics and activism.

By March 1964, both men were experiencing remarkable political transitions. Malcolm pivoted into lobbying, protesting, threatening, and cajoling democratic institutions, with the goal of achieving black dignity. His appearance in Washington amplified his quest to wed formal political maneuvers—such as voting rights and policy advocacy—to more maverick and controversial notions of political self-determination—such as gun clubs, self-defense groups, and a black-nationalist political party. Malcolm engaged with American democratic institutions in a manner that allowed him to not only participate in the civil rights struggle but reframe it as global movement for human rights, one that connected civil rights activism in America with movements for political self-determination in Indonesia and Nigeria.[8]

Meanwhile, King's political reputation swelled as the movement he came to personify expanded beyond his full comprehension and control. His long-standing appreciation of the relationship between racial equality and economic justice, what the March on Washington had knowingly called "jobs and freedom," remained thwarted by a nation that refused to contemplate the high price of racial justice—and especially who might pay that cost in privilege, power, standing, wealth, and prestige. King's candid discussion of violence, what he called "realism," would rapidly escalate after his meeting with Malcolm. For King, realism produced the sweet spot between aspirations of racial justice and a contemporary reality scarred by Jim Crow.

Over the course of the next three months, Malcolm and Martin organized in the shadow of a national political debate over civil rights whose momentum grew as spring turned to summer. King responded to this rapidly transforming political landscape by making plans to secure voting rights. Malcolm embarked on a five-week tour of the Middle East, where he took the hajj pilgrimage to Mecca and became an orthodox Muslim. The two men would not live to see their shared vision come to fruition.

The passage of the Civil Rights Act on July 2, 1964, announced the legal end of racial discrimination in public accommodations and publicly owned property. The bill also ended the practice of diverting federal funds toward segregated facilities, including schools. Enforcement in certain parts of the nation would take years. Greenwood, Mississippi, a site where King and the movement confronted great resistance, drained its public pools rather than integrating them.[9]

The assassination of Malcolm X on February 21, 1965, broke the secret hearts of millions of African Americans who had quietly claimed him as their unspoken champion, alongside the tens of thousands who publicly did so. Malcolm inspired blacks to unapologetically love themselves. He set a fearless example in this regard, offering his story of individual triumph against racism and poverty as a chance at collective redemption for the entire black community. Malcolm's death arrived before the public acknowledgment of Black Power—a movement birthed from his activism and which would spur King to greater radicalism, more forceful political rhetoric, and an embrace of radical black dignity.

Martin Luther King Jr.'s assassination on April 4, 1968, was a global tragedy. His untimely death indelibly altered American history, evoking a national trauma that we have yet to recover from. A troubling shadow haunts King's legacy, blunting his impact on American democracy. Over one hundred million Americans watched King's funeral on television as major cities convulsed in anger, violence, and mourning in the immediate hours and days after his death. Lyndon Johnson's passage of the Fair Housing Act is usually regarded as a final policy tribute to the racial-justice efforts spearheaded by King. Today, more than fifty years after King's death, the struggle for racial justice continues in ways that are both historically recognizable and disconcertingly new.

In many ways, racial segregation in America has worsened since King's death. National progress has been stalled, indeed reversed, by local, state, and federal policies—from gentrification and zoning laws to tax codes—that have made dreams of racial integration as distant as an unseen horizon. Shortly after the passage of fair housing legislation in 1968, Congress passed a national crime bill that planted the seeds for the contemporary crisis of mass incarceration. The Safe Streets Act of 1968 successfully helped to reimagine the nation's domestic priorities over the next half century, diverting tens of billions of dollars from anti-poverty, housing, and educational programs into the world's largest prison system. America's criminal justice system warehouses, exploits, punishes, and executes the same brown and black faces King challenged the entire world to embrace in love. It is no accident that Richard Nixon's rhetoric of "law and order" during the 1968 presidential campaign season flourished in the wake of King's assassination: Malcolm X and Martin Luther King Jr. had warned against the specter of massive racial uprisings if the nation remained unwilling to commit to guaranteeing black dignity and black citizenship.[10]

King's death roiled national politics generationally. His assassination turned him into much more than a martyr. He became one of the founding fathers of postwar American democracy, a social-movement leader whose memory reinforced both the grandeur and travails of the nation's racial history. Yet, King's posthumous celebration in contemporary American popular culture remains incomplete. He is recognized as perhaps the nation's most famous advocate of nonviolence and celebrated as a prophet whose stirring example unleashed the racial progress that culminated in Barack Obama's presidency. He balanced his critique of America's complicity in promoting materialism, militarism, and racism with a defiant optimism about democracy's enormous potential to achieve a more hopeful and humane world. But the more incendiary of King's politics are still too often ignored, discounted, or unmentioned. The radical King identified racism, poverty, and war as threats against the entire planet, but this aspect of his legacy remains sidelined because of the discomfort his words of fire continue to cause.

In the popular imagination, Malcolm is the political sword of the black radicalism that found its stride during the heroic years of the civil rights era and fully flowered during the Black Power movement. King stands in contrast as the nonviolent guardian of a nation; his shield prevented a blood-soaked era from being more violent. Their respective worldviews antagonized, infuriated, and inspired each other. In many ways, Malcolm might best be considered black America's prosecuting attorney, a political leader who condemned white institutions and citizens for historic and contemporary racial crimes. The sight of Malcolm regaling Harlem audiences, reporters, and television cameras with the era's boldest analysis of institutional racism—always laced with biting humor—remains an indelible image of the period. His sternly handsome face conjures up "a space of myth and mourning." He forged personal intimacy with a mass audience by boldly confronting America's brutal history of racial trauma, and his uncanny ability to recognize the revolutionary potential found in the distillation of black pain proved transformative. Over time, he convinced large swaths of the black community that the very source of their oppression—their blackness—held the key to liberation. Malcolm believed in the intrinsic value of black life even when many African Americans did not. In the early days of the civil rights movement, this made him a man ahead of his time. After his death, his unyielding faith in the beauty of black struggle made him an icon.[11]

While Malcolm inspired black folk on urban street corners from Los Angeles to Harlem, King captivated the centers of American power. The image of the thirty-four-year-old Georgia preacher addressing the nation on August 28, 1963, from the National Mall in Washington, DC, transformed him from a protest leader into a statesman respected by American presidents and world leaders. Whereas Malcolm bonded with audiences through confessional admissions of his youthful moral failings and righteous anger over the indignities of Jim Crow, King displayed a passionate empathy for both sides of the nation's racial divide. He raised the philosophy of nonviolence as shield against the humiliation, poverty, and violence of America's Jim Crow system. Martin Luther King Jr., contrasting Malcolm X's prosecutorial zeal, became the nation's chief defense attorney on both sides of the color line. He defended black humanity to whites and convinced African American audiences that embracing the architects of racial oppression could lead to a transformed world, contoured by racial justice.

Malcolm and Martin achieved political maturity in a revolutionary age that fundamentally transformed race relations in the Global North and South. In the 1950s, a time when Jim Crow laws in the United States diminished black citizenship nationally and virtually obliterated it in the South, the two leaders emerged as internationally recognized advocates for racial justice. Their supple intelligence, political courage, and dazzling oratory set them apart as the quintessential activists of not only their generation, but all subsequent ones that followed. They innovated radical political activism as an enduring vocation capable of eliciting respect from opponents, gaining devotion from supporters, and inspiring lasting political change globally.

Malcolm's formal political activism outside of prison, which spanned the years 1952 to 1965, overlapped with King's, which occurred from 1955 to 1968. While Malcolm embraced political activism as a vocation three years before King, his time as a national figure arrived in 1959, three years after King's emergence as the public face of the epic Montgomery, Alabama, bus boycott. The mythology presents King as a hopeful optimist whose soaring "I Have a Dream" speech at the March on Washington is contrasted with Malcolm X's unapologetic declaration that black citizenship would only be achieved through "The Ballot or the Bullet."

Contemporary depictions of both men have left us with indelible icons more than flesh-and-blood human beings. Too often, our complex and messy national civil rights history has been related to the general public like a children's bedtime story, one that requires—indeed, mandates—a happy ending. Civil rights are now largely recognized as a political and moral good, the movement's demands for citizenship and equality retrospectively considered unassailable parts of our democracy. The era's combative militancy, even among advocates of nonviolence, is obscured in this telling or, at times, forgotten. The real Malcolm and Martin offer a more complex portrait of the era. Braiding their political lives together provides a new, difficult, and challenging, but ultimately more satisfying, understanding of these men and the times they shaped.

Malcolm and Martin, in life and death, retained sharp differences. They disagreed on the role of violence in organizing a political revolution. Early on, they diverged on the source of racial oppression, with Malcolm focused on systemic patterns of racial injustice and King attuned to racism's invidious damage on hearts, minds, and souls. Cultivated in the black Christian church, King deployed religious language in political sermons that elevated the struggle for racial justice into the moral issue of the twentieth century. Malcolm found his religious faith in two distinct forms of Islam that gave him the personal strength to match his political convictions. He embraced the language of street speakers—from learned griots and intellectuals to corner-store hustlers—to offer an unvarnished portrait of institutional racism, white supremacy, and racial violence.

But a binary understanding of Malcolm and Martin is incomplete. Two-dimensional characterizations of their activism, relationship, and influence obscure how the substantive differences between them were often complimentary. It underestimates the way they influenced each other. And it shortchanges the political radicalism always inherent in each, even when they seemed to be reformist or reactionary. This book examines the political lives of two social-movement leaders who assumed divergent but crucially similar roles. Over time, each persuaded the other to become more like himself. Reexamining Malcolm and Martin alongside each other highlights the debt contemporary racial-justice struggles owe them both.

Malcolm and Martin were considered two of the most dangerous activists of their generation. A wide range of politicians (including presidents), Justice Department officials (most notably FBI director J. Edgar Hoover), and police and intelligence agencies marked them as subversives capable of fomenting civil unrest and racial disorder. FBI agents placed illegal wiretap surveillance on King courtesy of the sitting attorney general, garnering compromising information that threatened to derail him and the movement. Malcolm attracted both federal surveillance and a branch of the New York Police Department, the Bureau of Special Services, which served as the NYPD's version of the secret police and tracked him from the early years of the Cold War until his death.

In what follows, I argue that Malcolm X and Martin Luther King Jr. represent two black revolutionaries whose lives, activism, and political and intellectual thinking became blueprints for racial and economic justice advocacy around the world. At the height of their international visibility and political power, they recognized in each other a kindred spirit whose very presence helped them fulfill their respective roles. Their dual strategies, in retrospect, amplified and built each other up. Malcolm's envelope-pushing militancy offered Martin leverage against allegations that he was a communist or worse. Martin's aura of political moderation aided Malcolm's quest to galvanize America's black underdogs: the street-corner hustlers, artists, prisoners, formerly incarcerated, and drug addicted who became his family before his religious conversion in prison.

Malcolm X and Martin Luther King Jr. bestride the postwar global age of decolonization alongside icons such as Mahatma Gandhi, Winston Churchill, and Franklin Roosevelt. America's domestic racial crisis, with its attendant political impact around the world, shaped their professional and political careers. Organizing struggles for black dignity and radical black citizenship became their métier. Malcolm's quest to connect domestic freedom struggles to international human rights battles amplified and internationalized the radical democracy that Martin envisioned at the March on Washington. Similarly, Martin's anti-war activism and anti-poverty campaigns unleashed a stinging critique against racism, militarism, and materialism that echoed Malcolm's strident anti-colonialism. As young men, Malcolm and Martin pursued their political activism through religious institutions: the Nation of Islam and the African American church. While religious faith steadied them, both held larger, radically secular dreams of black liberation. Malcolm and Martin were the two most ambitious, creative, and courageous activists of the generation that forever changed American race relations. Both men confronted American presidents over issues of racial justice and pointed out the political hypocrisy that allowed racial apartheid to flourish in a democratic nation. Martin assaulted democracy's rear flank in speeches and demonstrations that sought to compel the government, institutions, and political leaders to reconcile, at long last, the sacred words enshrined in the founding documents with actual deeds. Malcolm orchestrated a direct attack by confronting democracy's jagged edges of police brutality, economic injustice, and antiblack racism.

Malcolm and King's births, in 1925 and 1929 respectively, meant they came of political age at the dawn of the Cold War. Racial politics of the moment informed their respective birthrights, offering a bittersweet inheritance that would help catapult them to undreamed-of heights as young men. Alive, the two became permanently bound in the public imagination as the Janus-faced symbol of a black freedom struggle that might decide America's political fate. In death, they became sanctified political martyrs, fallen historical icons, and saints whose followers called them simply Martin and Malcolm.

They became the two most visible and important leaders of the civil rights movement's heroic period. This period covers the era from the end of legal segregation in 1954 to the civil- and voting-rights victories won a decade later. Marked by the rise of massive civil disobedience, demonstrations, sit-ins, political assassination, and racial violence, this era has become enshrined in our national memory as a searing test that the country passed, to its credit, by ending segregation and guaranteeing black citizenship. King's presence buttresses a narrative of inexorable racial progress, from bus boycotts and sit-ins to the March on Washington and voting legislation. Malcolm's activism disrupts such a linear tale, forcing us to gaze into the hidden bowels of black America that shaped him and his worldview. Malcolm identified antiblack racism as an institutional dilemma that required the kind of public truth telling that many whites, and some blacks, did not want to hear. But he pushed for a reckoning on the issue of black dignity with blunt language that contrasted with King's search for black citizenship capable of allaying white fear and black anger.

Martin Luther King Jr.'s most enduring legacy is the commitment to and introduction of what I call *radical black citizenship*. For King, radical black citizenship encompassed more than just voting rights. Urban violence in the Los Angeles neighborhood of Watts erupted in August 1965, less than a week after the passage of the Voting Rights Act. The result of an encounter between a local resident and police, the conflict escalated into a sprawling, citywide riot that shocked and frightened the nation. After the urban rebellion of Watts, King came to realize that in addition to voting, true citizenship included a good job, living wage, decent housing, quality education, health care, and nourishment. That is to say that citizenship meant, according to King, more than the absence of the negative structures of oppression he spent his life fighting. His legacy of radical black citizenship—one that continues in the work of Moral Mondays, March for Our Lives, #MeToo, and Black Lives Matter—encompassed his revolutionary life, fearless love of the poor, and uncompromising stance against war and violence, all of which offers hope for a better future. His life also provides a framework for resistance against rising levels of inhumanity, racism, and injustice that he would find all too familiar today.

Malcolm X too often remains primarily remembered for what he was not: Martin Luther King Jr. But in reality, Malcolm was a brilliant activist, organizer, and intellectual whose life reminds us of the possibilities of a liberated future in America and beyond. His unapologetic insistency on what I call *radical black dignity* marked him as a prophetic visionary in the eyes of a global black community and as a dangerous subversive to the American government. Malcolm defined black dignity as a collective goal that required bold leadership and the ability to confront America's tragic racial history. The embrace of black identity, history, and beauty served as the first step in organizing a revolutionary movement for political self-determination, empowered by Africa's presence on the world stage and the courage of ordinary black people in insisting that their lives, traditions, culture, and histories mattered in the face of archipelagoes of racial terror that stretched from Brooklyn to Birmingham to Bandung. Malcolm's searing description of the pain, trauma, and violence of America's racial wilderness became the crux of his political debate with King. King fully acknowledged the panoramic nature of racial oppression— in essence the existence of the American racial wilderness—only after Malcolm's death.

America's civil rights struggle in the twentieth century, now remembered as a virtually seamless march toward racial progress, unfolded in violent fits and starts. The signal events of the heroic period—1954's *Brown* Supreme Court decision; the August 1955 lynching of Emmett Till, followed that December by the Montgomery bus boycott; 1957's Little Rock Central High School crisis; the 1960 sit-in demonstrations that spurred the creation of the Student Non-violent Coordinating Committee and the 1961 Freedom Rides; James Meredith's 1962 integration of the University of Mississippi; Birmingham, Alabama's, racial crisis in the spring of 1963, followed by the March on Washington, the Sixteenth Street Baptist Church bombing, and the Kennedy assassination; the Freedom Summer and the passage of the 1964 Civil Rights Act; and Bloody Sunday in Selma and the passage of the Voting Rights Act—continue to frame the popular conception of the era at the expense of a more nuanced and historically complex understanding. This limited vision of the period constrains our ability to appreciate the personal and political contradictions that enveloped Malcolm X and Martin Luther King Jr. during this era.

In the years immediately following the First World War, Marcus Garvey's jaw-dropping call for political and racial self-determination transformed black identity, paving the way for the emergence of Malcolm X and the Nation of Islam. King's political ascent rested on the central role of the black church and interracial groups like CORE and the Fellowship of Reconciliation, which created new political spaces where radical democracy briefly thrived during the Great Depression and Second World War. The immediate postwar years featured daring interracial alliances, robust movements for black political self-determination, and potential for black equality that briefly aligned political and ideological radicals, moderates, militants, and conservatives in a struggle for dignity and democracy. Cold War liberalism blunted freedom dreams, turning former allies into informers, decimating a budding labor and civil rights alliance, and smearing advocates of interracial democracy as communists and worse.[12]

Malcolm X and Martin Luther King Jr. came of age in an American political landscape that crushed dreams of black dignity and openly rejected the idea of black citizenship. Yet they also inherited a political and historical legacy that offered a revolutionary vision for social and political change. Racial violence scarred black life daily, culminating in well-publicized sexual assaults against black women that, although subsequently airbrushed from history, helped to shape the political activism of vital segments of the African American community.[13]

Conventional narratives of the civil rights era's heroic period also obscure discussion of black people residing on the lower frequencies of American political life. Malcolm X thrived in these spaces, cultivating prisoners, the formerly incarcerated, and the black working class in an effort to reach a mass audience of disenfranchised Negroes.[14]

Malcolm X helped to internationalize black political radicalism. He defined the struggle for black citizenship through global events that made him black America's unofficial prime minister. Black radicals, aware of the racial conflicts that made national headlines, looked toward anti-colonial struggles in the Third World for inspiration in their own domestic racial justice struggles. Malcolm toured African nation-states, Middle East capitals, and European cities in an effort to link domestic black politics to the larger world of anti-colonial and Third World liberation movements. He engaged in international affairs from the start of his career and not, as is popularly imagined, during his final year. These events abroad, which paralleled and at times intersected with the mainstream civil rights demonstrations, remain largely hidden from the public. Understanding the ways in which Malcolm and Martin both shaped and were shaped by the local, domestic, and global currents of the civil rights and Black Power movements offers us a better appreciation of the movements and their legacies.

Malcolm X came to embody and amplify the ferment of radical black political self-determination both domestically and around the world. With increasing intellectual and political agility, he traveled beyond cultural and political borders, attracting a coterie of supporters that included civil rights activists, white leftists, African intellectuals, and Third World revolutionaries.

Malcolm's most profound influence on the civil rights era after his death came from a most unexpected place. Martin Luther King Jr.'s political activism following the passage of the 1965 Voting Rights Act directly reflects the influence of Malcolm X and Black Power radicals. During the last three years of his life, King evolved from a national political mobilizer on friendly personal terms with American presidents into a revolutionary. King's travails in America's searing political battlefield during these years is overwhelmingly overlooked; the nation's collective gaze is instead kept on the triumphant passage of civil rights and voting rights legislation. But King's August 1965 visit to Los Angeles in the wake of the rebellion stirred in him the seeds of revolutionary discontent. His April 4, 1967, Riverside Church speech in New York City braided racial injustice, economic inequality, and the

Vietnam War into a brilliant critique of American empire, institutional racism, and violence. A year later in Memphis, Tennessee, King found his reputation among white Americans in decline as he recruited a multiracial army of the poor to come to Washington and demand radical legislation that would provide a living wage, guaranteed income, and an end to poverty in the world's richest nation. The revolutionary King, who pushed America to become a redistributive social democracy that embraced racial justice and black citizenship, is largely missing from our national understanding of the era.

Politics—ranging from racial segregation in public accommodations in the South to police brutality and unemployment in the North—preoccupied Malcolm X's and Martin Luther King Jr.'s early activism. Martin and Malcolm's claims to national leadership rested on relationships initially cultivated at the neighborhood level, and their sensitivity to racism's local manifestations proved to be foundational to their collective political development. King's rhetorical genius helped turn a local boycott in Montgomery, Alabama, into a national referendum on racial dignity and American citizenship. Against the backdrop of a Cold War that identified civil rights activists as domestic subversives influenced by communists or worse, King identified racial justice as the hidden key to reimagining American democracy. Malcolm turned Harlem into his local political headquarters for a grassroots movement for social justice. He mirrored this success in cities such as Detroit, Boston, and Los Angeles, where black nationalists came to view him as the leader of a movement for black political power that paralleled civil rights struggles.

Malcolm X's national leadership ascended upon a torrent of blunt words that simultaneously punished and inspired. His scathing critique of institutional racism and white supremacy made him a folk hero. Malcolm's words were oracular. His searing image of impending racial conflict, the fecklessness of white liberals, and the failure of black leadership accurately predicted the dawning age of national political rebellion.

Malcolm and Martin found common ground in an understanding of the global nature of racial struggle. They both fervently believed in the moral and political rightness of anti-colonial movements and in the right of self-determination for indigenous people. King called the personal and political ties that bound humanity together the "world house," where the fates of individual nation-states, cities, towns, and hamlets were inextricably linked. Malcolm satisfied his own search for international political inspiration in the 1955 Afro-Asian Conference in Bandung, Indonesia, an event that symbolized the Third World's political coming of age. Malcolm and Martin's political activism took place against the backdrop of the decolonization struggle, an epic fight where political revolutionaries challenged the prevailing social and political order of the last century.[15]

Yet each leader drew distinctive, at times contrasting, lessons from his worldliness. Revolutions raging across the Third World generally, and in Africa specifically, inspired Malcolm's personal imagination and political ambition. For him, black solidarity on a global scale might achieve what many thought to be impossible: a political revolution that brought genuine freedom, dignity, and liberation to black people the world over. He often criticized American democracy, blasting the United States in domestic and international speeches as an unrepentant empire—the proverbial "wolf," he often remarked in homespun allegories, disguised as humankind's liberator.

King, on the other hand, transformed American democracy by placing the civil rights struggle at the center of the nation's origin story. On this score, King's "dream" implicitly acknowledged democracy's jagged edges, what Malcolm called a "nightmare" of political and economic oppression made worse by the nation's perpetual state of racial denial.

Complex legacies of black political, cultural, intellectual, and religious activism shaped Malcolm and Martin. Malcolm found his religious and political calling in prison, but he traced his political lineage back to the Jamaican-born Pan-Africanist Marcus Garvey and his own Baptist preacher father, Earl Little. Garvey's Universal Negro Improvement Association (UNIA) captivated millions of blacks around the world with a defiant call for political self-determination that attracted a wide range of followers, including working-class entrepreneurs, black intellectuals, and professional revolutionaries. The Nation of Islam partially owed its existence to the Garvey movement, which for a time attracted both Malcolm's biological father and his political mentor, a young Elijah Muhammad (born Elijah Poole), to its burgeoning flock. Black nationalism would rise from the ashes of the Garvey movement and steadily grow in the postwar era, buoyed by movements for self-determination abroad and Malcolm's interpretation of a philosophy that had inspired his own father at home.

King grew up in the black church, enrolled at Morehouse College at fifteen, found his passion for the theological underpinnings of social justice in seminary, and finished a doctorate at Boston University, where his work contained seeds of the religious and philosophical interpretation of racial justice that would animate his political activism. King's intellectual genealogy emanated from the political ferment of the war years, particularly the interracial, social democratic, labor, and religious groups that characterized Jim Crow as a moral and political catastrophe.

The political afterlives of Malcolm X and Martin Luther King Jr. continue to shape American democracy. Their shared history offers up new ways to view the struggle for racial justice in America and around the world, from the postwar era to the present. America in the Martin Luther King Jr. and Malcolm X years found itself irrevocably transformed by their galvanizing political rhetoric and activism. The iconography surrounding these historical titans has produced a national holiday and memorial, postage stamps, movies, and Pulitzer Prize–winning biographies and books. In death, their symbolic power has launched a cottage industry trumpeting the superficial myth of the two men as opposites, which often obscures their actual political accomplishments, failures, and shortcomings. A full appreciation of Malcolm and Martin and the historical epoch that shaped them requires taking them down from the lofty heights of sainthood and rescuing both of these men from the suffocating mythology that surrounds them.

Throughout this book I use the metaphor of the sword and the shield to argue for a new interpretation of Malcolm X and Martin Luther King Jr. Conventional depictions of Malcolm wielding a sword in pursuit of black dignity while King carried a shield for the defense of black humanity tell only part of the story. *The Sword and the Shield* argues that Martin and Malcolm, after beginning as rivals, developed a political partnership more clearly illuminated by examining the destinations they, respectively, reached toward the end of their lives. The personas they comfortably assumed at the start of their political careers grew as they matured. In the halls of the United States Senate during their sole meeting, Malcolm and Martin traveled down a shared revolutionary path in search of black dignity, citizenship, and human rights that would trigger national and global political reckonings around issues of race and democracy that still reverberate today.

Malcolm X and Martin Luther King Jr. transformed the aesthetics of American democracy through social justice advocacy that altered national conceptions of race, citizenship, and democracy. By illuminating the relationship between black oppression and white supremacy, Malcolm and Martin permanently altered America's racial landscape. Their words both persuaded and coerced. Malcolm's and Martin's shared rhetorical genius and organizing skills compelled large audiences to freedom's cause and attracted praise, controversy, and condemnation. In popular culture they represent opposing visions of racial equality; where King dreamed of carving a stone of hope from a mountain of racial despair, Malcolm forcefully identified a growing nightmare of racial injustice, Jim Crow segregation, and simmering rage. This neat juxtaposition obscures more than it reveals, erasing the profound ways in which their politics and activism overlapped and intersected, and often-times helped to transform national and global debates over racial and economic justice, the role of the criminal justice system, the use of violence, and the resilience of American democracy.

CHAPTER 1

The Radical Dignity
of Malcolm X

Malcolm X inherited the legacy of his parents, Earl Little and Louise Norton Little, proud disciples of the legendary Jamaican organizer Marcus Garvey. Malcolm grew up in a home that celebrated black pride, boldly proclaimed black dignity, and brandished political activism as practically a familial birthright. The members of the Little family were pioneer black nationalists who endeavored to follow Garvey's dictum of establishing black political power across urban and rural American landscapes. Garvey tapped into deep currents of black political radicalism swirling in a newly reconfigured urban American landscape, one populated by black southern migrants and Caribbean immigrants. The Great Migration, which started between the world wars and crested in the immediate years after blacks won the right to vote, dispersed millions of southern migrants across the nation's vast expanse, in the process creating archipelagoes of black cultural and political power in small and large cities. Inspired by the bootstrap racial uplift politics of Booker T. Washington and intrigued by anti-colonial rhetoric, Garvey promoted a philosophy of black nationalism that he offered, like Promethean fire, to any black person courageous enough to take it.

Millions passionately embraced black nationalism, turning "Garveyism" into a global movement for self-determination. As a political philosophy, black nationalism promoted racial solidarity, the recognition of black history, culture, and beauty, and the right for black people to define solutions to their own problems as the keys to individual freedom, collective liberation, and political and economic power. Garvey's personal stature grew until his 1924 arrest on charges of mail fraud related to his efforts to establish a Black Star Line of ships. The shipping line was to be funded by stock certificates purchased by the black community and facilitate the trade of black-owned goods between North America, the Caribbean, and Africa. The project faltered, hampered by mismanagement, corruption, and negligence on the part of Garvey and Universal Negro Improvement Association officials. J. Edgar Hoover, the youthfully dynamic head of the Bureau of Investigations, the forerunner of the FBI, orchestrated the investigation into Garvey, which reinterpreted his financial mismanagement as outright fraud. Federal officials used the charge to imprison and later deport him. Garvey's exit from the American political stage dimmed but did not extinguish the burning embers of the movement he helped found.[1]

Following Garvey's deportation, Garveyism did not so much decline as transform into diminished versions of his movement, scattered around the nation. Malcolm Little grew up the child of racial-justice pioneers daring enough to promote the radical philosophy of black self-determination in the far reaches of the Midwest: first, in Omaha, Nebraska, where Malcolm arrived on May 19, 1925, and then in Lansing, Michigan. There, the Little family formed a tiny star in the constellation of racial uplift that stretched from major cities swelled by black migration to more distant outposts in southern rural hamlets. Earl Little was a dark-skinned, barrel-chested carpenter from Georgia who had moved to Montreal, where he met Louise Norton, who traced her roots to Grenada and was light enough to pass for white. Earl Little became an organizer for the Garvey movement, bolstered by Louise's support.[2]

Earl and Louise's shared love for social justice bound them in pursuit of an itinerant existence made predictable only by the frequency of childbirth and relocation. Black political activism in parts of the Midwest attracted white attention, disapproval, and threats that frequently escalated into physical violence and terror. Earl's passionate commitment to racial justice triggered a backlash in Nebraska that forced the family to flee under threat from local Klansmen. Following brief stints in Milwaukee, Wisconsin, and East Chicago, Indiana, the Littles settled in Lansing, Michigan, where Earl resumed his efforts to recruit local blacks into the UNIA. The Little household's financial and emotional hardships were exacerbated by Earl's violent behavior toward his wife and children, which Malcolm largely escaped; Malcolm remembered his dark-skinned father favoring him because of his light complexion. Earl Little established himself as one of the leaders of the fifteen UNIA chapters scattered across Michigan. He frequently led Garveyite caravans to Detroit, the city that a teenage Malcolm would derive his nickname from. Although he was only five or six years old at the time, Malcolm later vividly remembered his father leading UNIA meetings where members chanted the group's slogan, derived from Garvey himself: "Up, you mighty race, you can accomplish what you will!"[3]

Earl's political tutelage of young Malcolm ended abruptly on September 8, 1931. That evening, Earl left the house to pick up money from the sale of some chickens. He never returned. The police arrived with the news late at night that Earl lay in a hospital, severely injured in what authorities described as a streetcar accident. Police surmised that Earl had slipped and fallen beneath a moving streetcar's back wheels. The family immediately suspected racist violence by the Black Legion, the area's version of the Ku Klux Klan. Malcolm believed so too. Over thirty years later, he could still visualize it: "The house filled up with people crying, saying bitterly that the white Black Legion had finally gotten him."[4]

For the remainder of his life, Malcolm would try to re-create the familial structure shattered by Earl's death. Malcolm's mother, Louise, found herself a widow taking care of seven children, including three-month-old infant Wesley. Louise's commitment to Kalamazoo State Hospital in 1938 for mental illness, just after the birth of Malcolm's half brother Robert, further disrupted Malcolm's childhood. Louise remained institutionalized for the next twenty-four years. For three years after his mother was committed, Malcolm shuttled between foster care and juvenile facilities. In later life, he would find a replacement father figure in Nation of Islam leader Elijah Muhammad. But even then, Earl Little's unapologetic commitment to racial justice and political organizing—even at the expense of spending time with his wife and children—would frame Malcolm's behavior. Memories of Earl presiding over sparsely attended but vigorously energetic UNIA meetings resonated deeply with Malcolm, and he held up Earl as his political hero. Malcolm had attended political meetings with his father, read black newspapers at home as a child, and listened to his father teach the entire family about the importance of faraway happenings in Africa and the Caribbean. He fervently admired Earl's rugged political determination in the face of white racism. Earl cast a shadow in death better than he had alive, bequeathing his young son with a model of itinerant political organizing that Malcolm would adopt for the rest of his life.[5]

Earl's death hastened Malcolm's departure from a Michigan public school system he found to be incorrigibly racist. Malcolm recalled his time at Mason Junior High School as an abject lesson in racism, where white teachers referred to him as "nigger" and even friendly white students thought of him as little more than a mascot. "I was unique in my class, like a pink poodle," he remembered. He had a natural affinity for reading, debating, and social engagement, and early on he was touted as a charismatic leader.

His predominantly white classmates voted him class president, an honor later blunted by a white teacher's dismissal of his dreams of being a lawyer. At fifteen, he dropped out of school and entered a sordid world of hustling—one populated by young black men with little education and even fewer prospects. The bowels of black urban American neighborhoods in New York City and Boston became a proving ground for a teenage Malcolm. He came of age in those cities during the 1940s, learning to rely on his intelligence, quick wit, and charisma to survive the streets.[6]

In February 1941, Malcolm departed Lansing by bus to move in with his twenty-seven-year-old, Georgia-born half sister, Ella Mae Collins. A formidable woman whose obsidian skin, sharp intelligence, and outspoken manner reminded Malcolm of Earl, Ella offered the closest example of parental love that the fifteen-year-old had ever received. They lived in the Hill neighborhood of Boston, where small groups of working-class black families thrived during the war years, enjoying job opportunities as blue-collar and, at times, white-collar professionals. Ella fit neither of these categories. Despite a veneer of middle-class respectability, Malcolm's sister was a habitual thief, one whose criminal exploits included arrests for shoplifting and assault and battery. In 1942, Ella married her third husband, and Malcolm became fast friends with Malcolm "Shorty" Jarvis, who schooled him in the ways of Boston's black underworld.

Malcolm dived into Boston's nightlife; he learned to drink liquor, smoke marijuana, and romance women. He shined shoes at Roseland State Ballroom, where he encountered some of the era's great jazz musicians, including Count Basie and Duke Ellington. He purchased a zoot suit, with its large lapels, balloon pants, and wide-brimmed hat, and completed the look by styling his hair in the fashionable "conk" style of the 1940s, which straightened his hair with chemicals. Malcolm, whose light skin and auburn hair at times made him feel self-conscious, now went by the nickname Red, danced the Lindy Hop, and searched for ways to make fast money and spend time with easy women. Red personified the black hipster archetype: young black men who lacked formal education determined to find autonomy, freedom, and pleasure in urban cities against the backdrop of war, violence, and racial segregation.

As Red, Malcolm rebelled against the conventions of black and white middle-class ambitions. He possessed neither the education nor the ambition to be allowed entrée into black respectability—the assumption by elites, repeatedly proven wrong by racial violence and Jim Crow, that racial progress could be steadily measured through black achievement. Such a perspective denied racism's uncanny power to shape black life and denigrated the poor, unlettered, and unemployed as the root of white people's racial animus. In Boston, Malcolm joined a generation of young black men who refused to work dead-end jobs and resisted military induction. They endeavored to enjoy a life constrained by Jim Crow to the fullest, embracing the bebop style of jazz that came to be identified with young musicians such as Charlie Parker, Dizzy Gillespie, and Thelonious Monk and pursuing sensory pleasures whenever and wherever they could find them. Red dated black and white women in Boston—including Bea Caragulian, blonde haired and of Armenian descent, who became his steady girlfriend.[7]

In May 1942, at age seventeen, Malcolm relocated to Harlem, where he frequented Smalls' Paradise and the Cotton Club, venues that made the nightlife in Roxbury and Boston seem provincial. Red lived a double life in Harlem, holding a series of working-class jobs while hustling after hours, hanging out in nightclubs, and consuming illicit drugs and alcohol. He became known as Detroit Red, after the big city closest to Lansing, to distinguish him from a redhead from Chicago, John Sanford, who became legendary black comedian Redd Foxx. For a few months in 1942, Malcolm enjoyed a brief stint as a Pullman porter serving sandwiches, where he was nicknamed Sandwich Red.[8]

The war nearly interrupted Detroit Red's sporting life. He escaped the draft by arriving at his draft board "costumed like an actor," purposefully styling his "hair into a reddish bush of a conk" and promising to mobilize black soldiers to "kill us some crackers!" The military psychiatrist promptly categorized him as 4-F: not fit for duty. Detroit Red drifted deeper into the hustler's life, selling marijuana and steering prostitutes toward interested customers.[9]

In 1944, Malcolm return to Boston to be reunited with Ella and his girlfriend Bea. He had a cocaine habit, picked up in Harlem, and plans to make easy money robbing homes with Shorty Jarvis, Bea, and three others. They robbed numerous homes in the Boston suburbs in December 1945, only to have their criminal pursuits unravel in the early New Year. Malcolm's later description of himself as a hard-core gangster in his autobiography obscured some harsh truths: he turned in his entire crew after police caught him selling a stolen watch to a pawnbroker while carrying a loaded handgun. Malcolm pleaded guilty after being promised less time, only to receive a sentence of eight to ten years—hard time based, at least in part, on Malcolm and Shorty "associating with white women." To add insult to injury, Bea, the white woman in question, testified against him to save herself.[10]

In Charlestown State Prison, Malcolm found himself mentored by a fellow prisoner, John Elton Bembry, a man Malcolm would immortalize as "Bimbi." Malcolm arrived in prison as an ill-tempered "fish," the term used to describe new inmates, who labored to kick a drug habit and displayed an evil enough temper that other prisoners initially called him Satan. A generation older than Malcolm, Bembry took the young Malcolm—who turned twenty-one while in Charlestown and who had yet to begin shaving regularly—under his wing. Bembry, serving time for burglary, impressed Malcolm with his intellectual erudition and ability to hold court publicly. He routinely lectured convicts and white prison guards about politics, history, and current affairs. Bembry's height and skin complexion favored Malcolm's, and he was a self-taught intellectual with a wide range of interests, including history and literature. He encouraged Malcolm to read and study in prison. Malcolm did just that, devouring books from the prison's modest library, discovering new words through careful study of the dictionary, taking university correspondence courses, and becoming a better public speaker.[11]

Malcolm retained part of his Detroit Red persona, setting up a sports-betting ring at Charlestown "on fights and ballgames." The breaking of Major League Baseball's color line mesmerized him. "Jackie Robinson," Malcolm recalled, "had, then, his most fanatic fan in me." Malcolm longed to be transferred to Norfolk Prison Colony, a facility that looked more like a college campus than a prison, but settled for a move to the Massachusetts Reformatory at Concord in 1947.[12]

It was there that Malcolm first encountered the Nation of Islam. The NOI personalized the history of racial oppression in America as the product of white supremacy and the loss of black power, racial pride, and personal dignity. This black-nationalist perspective dovetailed with a patriarchal-historical view that interpreted slavery, lynching, and Jim Crow as assaults on the black community rooted in the emasculation of black men, who, due to institutional racism, could neither protect nor provide for their families. Malcolm learned of Elijah Muhammad and the Nation of Islam when his brother Reginald visited and regaled him with dramatic stories of the Nation's exploits. Through Reginald, Malcolm discovered that three more of his siblings—Philbert, Wesley, and Hilda—had joined the group. Malcolm's sister Ella knew Elijah Muhammad and his wife Clara from her time in Georgia, where the couple had resided before joining the Nation. For the Little family, politics was a family affair, and Malcolm soon joined the NOI while still in prison.[13]

In jail, twenty-one-year-old Malcolm found his first intimate positive male role models since Earl's death. The most important of these came through the Nation of Islam, which had come of age in the political space created by the decline of Garveyism. The Nation innovated a messianic vision of racial pride, dignity, and self-determination that had found a beachhead in the economic misery of the Great Depression. Elijah Poole, a semiliterate former Georgia sharecropper, refashioned himself as the Honorable Elijah Muhammad, Allah's messenger, who held the key to black liberation. The Nation's eclectic philosophy combined aspects of black nationalism, Pan-Africanism, and religious mythology to preach a version of Islam that identified whites as the creation of a misguided black scientist named Yacub. Blacks were not Negroes but "Asiatic-African" people who once ruled civilization. The group's tiny membership of several hundred followers recognized Elijah Muhammad as Allah's handpicked messenger, capable of uplifting the black underclass from the depths of poverty, imprisonment, and death.[14]

Garvey's promotion of black history and culture found new energies in the Nation, but with a twist. Muhammad promoted black political self-determination as part of God's design to restore black people to their former glory. In this sense, the NOI's teachings represented the opposite of the Protestant Social Gospel, which insisted that religious faith be tied to worldly deeds. The Messenger predicted doom for whites, who were characterized as "devils" for crimes against blacks that stretched from slavery to the present. Malcolm Little's jailhouse conversion in Massachusetts transformed the group. Malcolm's intelligence, wit, and devotion shone through in his correspondence with the Messenger, who began to write to him regularly. Over time, Muhammad treated Malcolm as a son, protégé, and heir apparent. Malcolm, in turn, credited the Messenger for his rehabilitation, editing out Earl Little's role in shaping his political consciousness.

Members of the NOI abstained from drugs, alcohol, and extramarital sex. Muhammad's "laborers" worked multiple jobs, including in NOI businesses, to pay tithes, fees, and special collections to support the Messenger's rising standard of living and the group's increasingly grand ambitions. Located primarily in Detroit and Chicago, the Nation recruited from the depths of black

America's poor: prisoners, ex-convicts, and drug addicts. After his release from prison, Malcolm quickly traversed the organization's hierarchy through hard work and dogged commitment, rising in a short time to assistant minister and then head minister. In time, Malcolm proved to be Muhammad's most outstanding laborer. He distilled rough truths about racial slavery, black identity, and white supremacy to local temples, black newspapers, and increasingly curious sectors of the black middle class. But he truly excelled as an organizer. If Elijah Muhammad offered a program designed for racial uplift, it would take Malcolm's presence to recruit the flock.

The Nation of Islam offered Malcolm his first chance to establish a family since his father's death, but Elijah Muhammad became more than a surrogate father. The NOI's religious iteration of Garvey-styled black nationalism struck a personal chord for Malcolm and his siblings. The organization's strict moral rectitude, regimented behavioral framework, and rigid code of conduct mirrored Earl Little's efforts to politicize his family during their itinerant sojourns through the Midwest. As a child, Malcolm had overlooked Earl's personal transgressions and found strength in the certitude his father displayed when presiding over UNIA political meetings. He searched for most of his life for a black father figure who could replace Earl. Elijah Muhammad became that surrogate father, entering his life at his exact moment of need. Malcolm's projection of black masculinity would be culled from his memories of Earl, his time as a street hustler, and his conversion to Islam. Elijah Muhammad positioned himself as both Allah's messenger on earth and a literal embodiment of the patriarch that, in the eyes of believers, the black community sorely lacked. Malcolm, in turn, revered Muhammad as a surrogate for Earl.

Malcolm used his time in Massachusetts state prison as a religious seminary, a period that became the rough equivalent of Martin Luther King Jr.'s three-year experience at Crozer Theological Seminary in Chester, Pennsylvania. At Charlestown, Malcolm began to reinvent himself by taking educational classes, reading any book he could find in the small prison library, and generally attending to his intellectual development. Malcolm's siblings frequently visited him, introducing him to the teachings of the Nation of Islam. For Malcolm's extended family, which included three children from Earl's first marriage, the NOI offered a chance to restore kinship ties and emotional stability ruptured by divorce, distance, and death.[15]

Through the assistance of his sister Ella, Malcolm secured a transfer to the Norfolk Prison Colony in March 1948. Norfolk was more focused on rehabilitation than punishment, providing inmates with open access to books, a debate club, and a newspaper published by prisoners called the *Colony*. Malcolm devoured the increased educational opportunities afforded him. He began to seriously study black history through the works of African American historians and scholars such as Carter G. Woodson and W. E. B. Du Bois. Their focus on the lost history of black Americans, the reclamation of a proud African identity, and narratives of racial solidarity and political self-determination brought Malcolm closer to Earl's teachings than he had been since he was a child. Malcolm also joined the debate team, quickly earning a reputation as a bold, versatile, and erudite verbal combatant. His favorite subject— criticizing the racial oppression that black people experienced— emerged from reading and personal experience.[16]

Malcolm balanced intellectual pursuits with a search for religious conviction. He embraced the Islamic faith as defined by Elijah Muhammad and the Nation with a zeal and energy that surpassed that of the siblings who had introduced him to the religious teachings. Beginning in 1950, Malcolm became adept enough to convert fellow inmates to Islam and emerged as a faith leader and religious activist within the prison. At the start of his third year in Norfolk, he stirred controversy by requesting (in some instances successfully) that officials allow Muslims to follow special dietary restrictions, including no pork, and to relocate to cells in the prison's eastern wing so they could pray in the direction of

Mecca. Malcolm, citing religious reasons, also refused to receive a typhoid inoculation, a decision that the deputy superintendent used to facilitate his return to state prison. He would spend just over two years back in Charlestown before being paroled on August 7, 1952.[17]

After being released, Malcolm set out to become a full-time minister. It would be a short apprenticeship marked by the dazzling organizing and rhetorical skills he had displayed from the start. By becoming a minister, Malcolm was a rarity in Jim Crow America: a black man who found an enduring profession outside of labor unions, universities, professional schools, or the criminal underworld. Malcolm, like the majority of black men at the time, struggled to find meaningful work until he discovered his passion for the ministry. On parole, he divided his time between his religious training and employment as a dockworker, assembly-line laborer, and furniture salesman. Malcolm's prison record listed his past occupations as a dozen working-class jobs. Short stints as a waiter, packer, dishwasher, porter, and shoe-shine boy alternated with time as a bartender, warehouse man, and mattress maker. Even after he became a full-time minister, Malcolm remained staunchly opposed to the drudgery and humiliation that often accompanied the lives of black workers who lacked formal education in America. The Nation of Islam had offered him a way out, with the added bonus that he could further develop his precocious intellect. Becoming a minister, for Malcolm, created an avenue to live the life of the mind. Norfolk had served as Malcolm's entrée into higher education, and his time on parole became a unique kind of postgraduate work.[18]

After prison, Malcolm wanted to make sense of his past. He crafted a narrative, later published in his autobiography, rooted in the truth as he remembered it. The memories that were most distressing revolved around his mistreatment of women. Detroit Red's romantic life, from the perspective of the newly reborn Malcolm X, was littered with emotionally abusive relationships.

Malcolm's new surname, X, represented his official entrée into the Nation of Islam, which gave members that last name as a symbol of having been stripped of their identity during racial slavery. Malcolm chose to embrace the NOI's rigid gender roles as a balm to heal the childhood wounds caused by the dual traumas of Earl's death and Louise's virtual disappearance from his life. These past hurts were compounded by the ghost of Detroit Red, which he tried to exorcise by becoming the most personally disciplined member to ever join the NOI. He attributed much of the pain he experienced in childhood and as a young man to the failure of morally, economically, or spiritually compromised women. Bea's betrayal made him publicly disparage the morality of white women. "I got my first schooling about the cesspool morals of the white man from the best possible source, from his own women," he remembered. The Nation of Islam's focus on the restoration of a patriarchal black family, whose loss Malcolm still mourned, resonated deeply. The group's insistence that black women adopt roles as caretakers, teachers, and nurturers of black families and helpmates of black men shaped Malcolm's reinterpretation of his past and his plans for his future.[19]

The Nation of Islam served as Malcolm's de facto reentry program. After Malcolm completed his training as a minister, the NOI provided the former convict with a full-time job, a living wage, a car, and a modest home. His position offered him a vocation and the chance for continuing education. He had found his métier. "It was right there in prison," Malcolm recalled years later, "that I made up my mind to devote the rest of my life to telling the white man about himself—or die." His emerging intellectual and political framework identified America as the perpetrator of history's greatest crime, racial slavery, made more heinous by the ongoing denial of black humanity. His personal experience gave him an unsentimental yet intimate portrait of black working-class life as an ex-convict, the criminal underworld as a teenage hustler, and the underclass as an adolescent who lived in a series of foster homes. As he gained fame as a minister, Malcolm became a working-class hero. His iconic political career took him from Harlem soapboxes to Ivy League campuses; from pilgrimages in the Middle East to meetings with African and Caribbean revolutionaries. Along the way, Malcolm transformed the local, national, and international civil rights landscape by boldly attacking white supremacy, linking contemporary racial injustice to racial slavery, and arguing that only black political self-determination could lead to freedom.[20]

Malcolm created new, urgent language that pushed the boundaries of black identity and reimagined American racism as structural, institutional, and global. His rhetoric drew links between domestic civil rights struggles and global anti-colonial movements. Where civil rights activists embraced American democracy, Malcolm explicitly rejected it. "Whenever a Negro fights for 'democracy,' he is fighting for something he has not got, never had and never will have," Malcolm observed in one of his signature denunciations.[21]

When Malcolm X walked out of prison, after nearly seven years, on Thursday, August 7, 1952, he entered a Turkish bath to remove the "physical feeling of prison-taint" from his body. He would dedicate the rest of his life to the soul-cleansing work of political activism. He cleansed his body as well, eating only once a day, refraining from pork, and following the diet recommend by the Nation's teachings. He moved in with his brother, Wilfred, in Inkster, a majority-black suburb of Detroit. He took a series of odd jobs but spent every spare moment working in the Nation's Detroit temple. Over the next two years, he would help recruit hundreds of new members. Malcolm met Elijah Muhammad in person for the first time in Chicago three weeks after his release, one of two hundred laborers who gathered to hear the Messenger speak. In front of a relatively small crowd, the Messenger praised Malcolm as a true believer whose daily letters from prison reminded him of the biblical prophet Job. Afterward, Muhammad hosted the

Little family at his newly purchased Hyde Park mansion, where he instructed his newest follower to focus on recruiting the young, reasoning that older generations would "follow through shame."[22]

Malcolm X became skilled at "fishing" for new members, lost souls living in racially segregated ghettos whom he captivated with lectures combining history, politics, and the Nation's religious teachings. He recruited black churchgoers, the formerly incarcerated, young people, the unemployed, and people with good jobs who were still dissatisfied with the pace of racial progress. Malcolm refashioned black-nationalist teachings on African pride, black culture, and racial solidarity through a searing critique of white supremacy. "We didn't land on Plymouth Rock, my brothers and sisters," he would regale a crowd. "Plymouth Rock landed on us!" The NOI's admonishment that ministers "make it plain" enough for ordinary and semiliterate black folk, the "originals" who lived on the margins of urban America, reached new depths in Malcolm's penetrating voice.[23]

Malcolm observed his first black Muslim service in Detroit, where he served as an assistant minister. Makeup-less women wore ankle-length dresses with white scarves covering their hair, men dressed in simple suits with bow ties, and children seemed unusually well-behaved. "I had never dreamed of anything like that atmosphere among black people who had learned to be proud they were black," he remembered, "who had learned to love other black people instead of being jealous and suspicious." A typical NOI service included the Islamic flag, depicting a crescent and a star that symbolized the power of the religious faith, which believers equated with "Freedom, Justice, and Equality"—words emblazoned in chalk beneath the flag at temples. This contrasted with the presentation of the American flag, with the words "Christianity, Slavery, Suffering, and Death" written below. Muslims sang no religious hymns but could listen to jazz before a service.[24]

Members of the Fruit of Islam (FOI), the Nation's security force rumored to have training in the martial arts and other self-defense techniques, searched all who entered the temple, stood as sentries during services, led the congregation in call-and-response chants with the minister, and guaranteed an exacting measure of disciplined behavior. At larger gatherings, signs proclaiming "We Must Protect Our Most Valuable Property Our Women" exemplified the patriarchal gender roles that the Nation embraced. Muslim women and men were forbidden to engage in unmarried sex. Women were represented in temple leadership as captains of the Muslim Girls Training and General Civilization Class (MGT-GCC), the all-female counterpart of the FOI. Women in the MGT-GCC were taught how to become upstanding Muslims through a fifteen-point program that banned alcohol, smoking, provocative clothes, pork, and adultery. The Nation provided the kind of rigorous physical, intellectual, and spiritual regimen that Malcolm had lost with Earl Little's passing.[25]

Malcolm framed black poverty, racial injustice, police brutality, and other social ills politically. On Detroit street corners, the young minister delivered searing public seminars that linked contemporary Jim Crow to the nation's original sin of slavery. He often highlighted sexual violence directed against black women. Rape, to Malcolm, represented an assault, both physical and psychological, that black women endured and that men were helpless to prevent. In vivid, dramatic detail, Malcolm portrayed white society as a criminal syndicate whose antiblack racial violence shaped the twentieth century. From the perspective of both Malcolm and black nationalists, black political self-determination meant black men assuming the kind of power over businesses, communities, and families that white supremacy had historically denied them. "I would become so choked up sometimes I would walk in the streets until late into the night," he remembered. "Sometimes I would speak to no one for hours, thinking to myself about what the white man had done to our poor people here in America." Potential recruits felt his passion. He articulated Elijah Muhammad and the Nation's message and, in making it his own, innovated a new stream of black political thought and consciousness. Muhammad promoted Malcolm to full-time minister near the end of 1953 and charged his young protégé with opening up a new temple in Boston. He completed this task and was transferred to Philadelphia within a few months. In Philadelphia, Malcolm served as the Nation's chief political organizer, a position that brought him regional and national visibility. But black Muslims were not the only ones watching.[26]

An FBI informant attended one of Malcolm's recruiting meetings in Boston in 1954, the start of the surveillance campaign that would continue for the rest of Malcolm's life. Malcolm spent this time as a roving minister, organizer, and publicist for the NOI—the beginning of his successful rise as a political celebrity who would garner the attention of law enforcement. The bureau identified Malcolm's reach as transcending domestic racial politics and emanating out into the larger world. In his speeches, Malcolm argued that indigenous Afro-Asiatic peoples were driving out colonial oppressors, noting that "English devils" were fleeing even as "French devils" were being forcibly removed from what was then called Indochina. Not yet thirty years old, Malcolm was sketching out an anti-imperialist critique of American global power, one that reverberated from distant Cold War beachheads to the gritty inner cities of Detroit, Boston, and Philadelphia. Although 1954 was the start of surveillance, the FBI's interest in Malcolm extended back to 1950, when, from prison, he wrote a letter to President Harry Truman opposing the Korean War and reminding the commander in chief of his efforts "to enlist in the Japanese Army" during World War II. In 1953, FBI agents personally questioned Malcolm about his failure to register for the selective service (he registered shortly after their visit).[27]

In the early 1950s, Malcolm looked toward anti-colonial movements in Kenya and Indochina as the dawn of a new age. By the middle of that decade, his position had crystallized. The treatment of African Americans, he said, was "the yardstick by which all

Dark Nations of earth" measured white American attitudes toward race. According to Malcolm, America's treatment of people of color—both national and global—reverberated, offering powerful ammunition to the struggles at home and abroad. Throughout the 1950s and '60s, Malcolm's audience grew beyond the confines of the Northeast, bursting into the South and across international borders. Malcolm carried a message wide and deep enough to attract a global constituency that dwarfed the relatively small number of black Muslims he converted.[28]

Malcolm X arrived in Harlem in June 1954, just weeks after the watershed *Brown v. Board of Education* Supreme Court decision formally outlawed racial segregation. Harlem both benefited from and contributed to the political stirrings of the moment, via a rich history of activism that the youthful Malcolm Little had caught only glimpses of during the war years. In Harlem, Malcolm became minister of Temple No. 7 on West 116th Street. He found himself competing with veteran street speakers, seasoned black nationalists, venerable Garveyites, and long-admired radicals of various ideological backgrounds. Beyond grassroots activists celebrating black pride was a class of powerful elected officials, including Manhattan borough president Hulan Jack and the legendary congressman Adam Clayton Powell Jr., who presided over the fifteen-thousand-strong Abyssinian Baptist Church. Powell and Malcolm became allies and occasional adversaries, jockeying for Harlem's attention—but whereas one translated tough talk on racial justice into votes that could be leveraged in Congress, the other set out to win hearts and minds.

Powell had a well-deserved reputation for late-night carousing and outspoken candor against racial injustice. He was a hero among his Harlem constituents. The most well-known black elected official in America, Powell represented a militant yet pragmatic brand of black politics. More established than Malcolm and the Nation, Powell embraced the aspects of their rhetoric that touched the beating heart of black ghettos around the nation. Malcolm and

Powell both identified themselves as authentic representatives of the black community, and Powell instantly recognized the younger activist as an emerging talent and cultivated him as a potential rival for political leadership. He invited Malcolm to speak at Abyssinian Baptist, fully aware of his public criticism of Christianity. Malcolm denied rumors that he wanted Powell's congressional seat with measured support, noting that while the Harlem congressman "has done a good job, he could do a much better job." He later confided to Powell, "You don't get any money from white people—it's all black money. . . . That's it, Adam, that's why I love you."[29]

Malcolm's sermons indicted Christianity as culpable in America's original sin of racial slavery and its continued perpetuation, by another name, under Jim Crow. He personalized this denunciation by resurrecting the ghost of Detroit Red. "I was a typical 'Christian Negro' . . . buried up to my neck in the mud of this filthy world: with very little hope, desire, or intention of amounting to anything." Malcolm imagined Christianity as a religion invented and practiced by white people who enslaved his ancestors and used the Bible to justify centuries of racial oppression.[30]

The Islamic flag and the contrasting American flag lent visual power to Malcolm's denunciation of America as a searing wilderness of racial turmoil, oppression, and injustice. Malcolm's speaking style—which combined the fervor of a Baptist preacher with the brio of a Harlem street speaker—helped mold a new generation of ministers, the most exceptional being Louis Eugene Walcott, a college graduate and calypso singer whose parents, like Malcolm's, had been disciples of Marcus Garvey. Louis X, as he would be known before rising to fame as Louis Farrakhan, first encountered Malcolm in Boston and quickly became one of his most fervent admirers.[31]

The Nation of Islam attracted black artists, intellectuals, and performers who felt stymied by Jim Crow, impatient with the pace of racial change, and disillusioned with the Christian beliefs espoused in mainstream black churches. Malcolm's youthful love of jazz and bebop and friendships with popular artists and musicians of the 1940s made him comfortable around cultural and literary figures. His outreach to New York City's leading black artists and intellectuals stretched the limits of acceptable behavior within the Nation, which disdained entertainers. James Baldwin became one of Malcolm's biggest supporters. Less than a year older than Malcolm, the Harlem-born Baldwin joined America's civil rights front after years living in a self-imposed Parisian exile, trying to escape the specter of racial discrimination. After a detour through postwar literary circles, Baldwin finally came to the racial-justice struggle back in Harlem. He reinvented himself as a literary firebrand, prolific essayist, and civil rights champion whose wide circle of politically active friends included both Martin Luther King Jr. and Malcolm X.

Malcolm also purposefully established alliances with influential black journalists. James Hicks of the *New York Amsterdam News*, William Worthy of the *Baltimore Afro-American*, and reporter Louis Lomax were some of his key interlocutors. The black press, populated by important outlets such as the *Los Angeles Herald-Dispatch*, *Pittsburgh Courier*, and *Chicago Defender*, shaped sympathetic coverage of the Nation of Islam in a way that white periodicals never could. These newspapers did not condemn the group as hate-mongers or reverse racists. Instead they approached the Nation of Islam as part of the wide spectrum of black religious and political organizations that historically sought to carve a space of autonomy within an unrepentantly racist nation. In a historical environment indelibly shaped by Jim Crow, black newspapers framed African American public opinion in a manner unseen before or since.[32]

Malcolm's growing fame placed him within a long history of black radicalism in Harlem. Harlem radicalism stretched back to the days of the passionately erudite socialist street speaker and organizer Hubert Harrison, who helped introduce Marcus Garvey to new audiences. The neighborhood's legendary renaissance promoted artistic rebellion as the cultural arm of a political revolution that seemed to sputter just as it began to truly soar. Glimpses of the glorious days of the New Negroes, whose literary exploits briefly turned Harlem into an avant-garde paradise of interracial bonhomie, could be seen in the scattered remnants of black writers and artists who would reclaim an identity once thought to be lost by befriending Malcolm X. From Muslim mosques in Harlem and Philadelphia, Malcolm articulated the disillusionment of these intellectuals by comparing the violence and degradation of Jim Crow to slavery. A keen observer of the civil rights struggle, he held up photos of black activists being brutalized in Mississippi as proof of the depths of white supremacy. Malcolm confided to NOI members that he resisted fighting in World War II and the Korean War as a "conscientious objector," noting the irony in blacks willing "to go all over the world and fight" on behalf of whites, while refusing "to go around the corner to fight for their own people."[33]

The April 1955 Afro-Asian Conference in Bandung, Indonesia, introduced the nonaligned movement, a powerful alternative to the claustrophobic dictates of the Cold War. Led by Indonesian president Sukarno and the prime ministers of India, Pakistan, Burma, and Ceylon, the conference framed Asian and African nations as independent. They made history by refusing to join Western democracies or communist blocs, opting instead for a nonaligned movement where indigenous people would shape their own future. Representatives from majority-Muslim countries including Saudi Arabia, Syria, Lebanon, Afghanistan, Iran, and Iraq attended. The gathering, which featured twenty-nine world leaders representing over one billion people, reimagined the Global North and South, elevating what would be called the Third World as a major player in world affairs. Malcolm read about Bandung in the press and drew instant inspiration.[34]

Immediately after the conference, Malcolm began touting the gathering and its importance to black power. Malcolm's expansive definition of black unity, forged through a shared history of racial oppression, took shape through the prism of Bandung's reimagining of the Third World. He conceived of radical black dignity as a kind of global citizenship based on a daring combination of human rights and political self-determination, backed by the collective power of billions. Malcolm insisted that black people were part of a larger group of darker nations capable of transforming the world if they were brave enough to identify with his vision.

Malcolm X saw, in Bandung's display of political unity, a vision of a liberated future stretching from Africa to America. Racial oppression within the United States, from Harlem to Los Angeles, would continue as long as black political activists remained divided over strategies, tactics, and ideology. The NOI, Malcolm surely knew, contributed to these divisions with its talk of racial Armageddon, dire predictions of the fall of American empire, and racially provocative allegations that whites were predisposed toward antiblack violence. To combat this, Malcolm dreamed of convening "a Bandung Conference in Harlem." He was convinced that a conference of his own could unify black leaders toward the creation of a militant movement for racial justice. Bandung helped Malcolm to appreciate the global dimensions of political oppression and the necessity of solidarity that transcended religious and political differences in service of liberation. He championed the gathering's willingness to convene across ideological and political differences, an example he yearned to follow in his own organizing.[35]

Malcolm's success in modernizing the Nation of Islam impressed Elijah Muhammad. In 1956, Muhammad approved the purchase of a brand-new Chevrolet for Malcolm's personal use. Malcolm estimated that in five months he drove that car thirty thousand miles across the nation during fishing expeditions. The gift of a car proved to be a prelude for a far more significant promotion. In 1957, Muhammad named Malcolm the NOI's national representative. Muhammad recognized that Malcolm's impact grew as more people were exposed to his particular message. His ability to win converts, build new temples, fundraise, and extol the power of Muhammad made him the Nation's most important recruit since the Messenger himself.[36]

As the NOI's national representative, Malcolm X became the public face of the organization. He projected an image of almost superhuman vitality, masking the effects of a punishing, around-the-clock travel and work schedule, which came to a head in October. That month, Malcolm entered Sydenham Hospital in Harlem after experiencing chest pains that mimicked a heart attack. Doctors diagnosed Malcolm with stress and released him after two days, but his hectic pace would only increase with the passage of time. The stress of becoming Malcolm X, advocate and champion of radical black dignity, took a private toll not witnessed by the public during these years.[37]

Malcolm joined the Nation's inner circle while courting twenty-three-year-old Betty X (formerly Sanders), a nurse who attended Temple No. 7, but their relationship faced several considerable obstacles. The year before they met, Malcolm experienced a brief engagement to Evelyn Williams, a past love from his Detroit Red days who joined the Nation after he did. He broke this engagement under pressure from the Messenger to remain unencumbered from a family, to better devote his energies to building the Nation. Many friends thought that Malcolm loved Evelyn and never truly recovered from her loss, but Malcolm also considered the prospect of marriage to be a potential liability. He often generalized women as treacherous, disloyal, and selfish. He wanted a wife who would conform to the instructions set forth in MGT-GCC classes.

He found this in Betty. During fishing expeditions, he gave panoramic seminars about the black community's inability to defend the family, and Malcolm promised to protect "beautiful black women" from racist abuse within the secure confines of the Nation. He charged white society with denigrating black women during slavery, where "pregnant women were forced to work in the fields almost to the point of delivery, and the women who did not keep up their work, were whipped." But a duality existed in Malcolm's understanding of gendered violence. He viewed historic assaults against women as illustrating a shameful lack of patriarchal authority and black male power in America. While he blamed white men for these crimes, he also held black women accountable for what he saw as their willingness to imbibe the worst aspects of Western society, a world that mocked black men's intelligence, power, and authority. From this perspective, the perceived dysfunction of the black family could be attributed to black women who became unwitting tools of white supremacy by resisting the teachings of the Nation of Islam. Steeped in these views, Malcolm was unprepared for the kind of deep intimacy that represented the hallmark of a strong marital relationship. After his 1958 wedding to Betty, Malcolm tended to see her as an extension of his political work, expecting her to be dutiful, loyal, and an attentive mother and homemaker. It was an often-painful union, and Malcolm, like his father, was frequently absent, devoting much more to professional ambitions than home life.[38]

While Malcolm would struggle to establish a happy familial life, he excelled at projecting black solidarity publicly. As national representative, he reached out to Harlem's most important black church and its most powerful elected official. From Congressman Powell's pulpit at Abyssinian Baptist, Malcolm facilitated "an unprecedented display of religious unity," proclaiming the Nation's solidarity with a black Christian community it had previously denounced. Referring to Muslims and Christians alike as "brothers," Malcolm challenged Abyssinian parishioners to recognize a shared political and racial solidarity. Black unity, Malcolm argued, meant black power, citing Harlem as "the key spot to elect a governor or mayor or anyone you want"—an admission of the power of black voting rights.[39]

On the last Friday of April 1957, NOI member Johnson X Hinton witnessed police officers beating a black man on 125th Street and Lenox Avenue in Harlem. Hinton and a group of NOI members intervened. "You're not in Alabama," they reportedly told police. "This is New York." Police arrested Hinton and then brutally beat his face, head, and shins with nightsticks. A series of standoffs occurred between police and almost two thousand community activists outraged at Hinton's brutal treatment. Battle lines shifted between the 123rd Street police station and Harlem Hospital, where Hinton was treated for a fractured skull, head lacerations, and blood clots in his brain. Coverage of the events labeled Malcolm X as the group's "spiritual leader," a turn of phrase that anticipated the emerging competition between the Messenger and his protégé and further catapulted Malcolm from local activist to national political figure within the black community.[40]

Hospital officials transferred the gravely injured Hinton back to the 123rd Street police station. Malcolm and thousands of others followed. Standing outside the police station, dressed in suits, overcoats, and hats, the NOI projected the appearance of an unarmed military unit awaiting orders. Behind the men were rows of Muslim women, heads covered, standing erect and impassive. The scene outside 123rd Street was cinematic, and the few dozen NOI members were joined by thousands of Harlem residents murmuring about the latest case of police brutality. Malcolm successfully pressured police officials into letting him see Hinton. Blood cascaded from the top of his head down his shoulders. "That man belongs in the hospital," Malcolm said to the lieutenant in charge. Dressed elegantly in a two-piece suit, camel-hair coat, fedora, and glasses, Malcolm led tense negotiations with police officials in an effort to save Hinton's life and calm the crowd outside, which was simmering with rage over a long history of police violence.

New York's deputy police commissioner agreed to transfer Hinton back to the hospital for treatment. The crowd followed. Rows of Muslims walked along Lenox Avenue, one of Harlem's main boulevards, and stood vigil outside of Harlem Hospital. Police officials approached Malcolm for the second time that evening, asking him to help defuse another standoff threatening to erupt in violence. Malcolm demurred, telling police that Muslims "were standing peacefully, disciplined perfectly, and harming no one." The police conceded as much but expressed fear of the hundreds who gathered behind the Muslims, unsupervised Harlem residents who answered to no one. "I politely told him those others were his problem," Malcolm recalled. When Malcolm was allowed into the hospital to see Hinton, he turned to the crowd and, with a single wave of his hand, dispersed the Muslim battalion, with bystanders soon following. *New York Amsterdam News* editor James Hicks stood next to a deputy police inspector as the scene unfolded. "Mr. Hicks," the inspector reportedly said, "that's too much power for one man to have."[41]

Police released Hinton the next day, sixteen hours after sustaining the original injuries. A group of NOI members rushed him to Harlem's Sydenham Hospital. Doctors gave him even odds of recovering. Four hundred NOI members, from as far as Baltimore, Boston, Hartford, Wilmington, and Washington, DC, stood vigil at a nearby park awaiting word. On the Monday that followed, April 29, as Hinton's life hung in the balance, Malcolm negotiated with police officials. Police agreed to investigate allegations of brutality in exchange for a promise that the NOI would not retaliate in the streets. Hinton survived and a grand jury declined to indict him on charges of disorderly conduct and resisting arrest, but the ordeal involved multiple surgeries that left Hinton with a metal plate in his head and physical and psychological wounds that never fully healed.[42]

In the aftermath of the Hinton incident, Malcolm served as the quasi spokesperson for black New Yorkers abused by the criminal justice system. The New York Police Department's tense relationship with the black community tested Malcolm's hypothesis about the merits of racial solidarity. Malcolm thought that if black New Yorkers were unified politically they could forge a power base strong enough to end police brutality and mistreatment forever. He now viewed the fight to eradicate police brutality and gain equal treatment from the justice system as an extension of the Nation's prison ministry, a mission he had actively benefited from and joined while incarcerated. The fervor over Hinton's treatment created a buzz that amplified the profile of Elijah Muhammad and the NOI. The Nation's message of political self-determination, dignity, and self-help put the organization forth as an all-black alternative to local civil rights groups. Malcolm fervently believed this, while the Messenger most certainly did not. Muhammad remained committed to the religious, rather than political, aspects of the group, but enjoyed the benefits of Malcolm's growing success. This tension was manageable so long as Malcolm's skirmishes into racial-justice politics provided more benefits than liabilities.

The beating of Johnson X Hinton and the vigils and negotiations that followed were important demonstrations of Malcolm X's political leadership. Without ever acknowledging as much, Malcolm led a nonviolent demonstration that amplified the Nation of Islam's power in New York City and showcased the potential for Muslims to work as power brokers and political players in Harlem, especially in work related to the criminal justice system's treatment of black Americans. During the incident, a police officer had pointed at Malcolm and said, "We should break that bastard's head because he is their leader." Indeed, Malcolm's work during that critical weekend in April elevated his standing from the sectarian confines of the NOI to the wider arena of racial struggle that marked black life in Harlem. Malcolm became a folk hero on the same streets where he had once run wild in his youth.[43]

Malcolm's relationship with the black press proved to be key here. "Most important, in Harlem, the world's most heavily populated black ghetto, the *New York Amsterdam News* made the whole story headline news," Malcolm recalled, "and for the first time the black man, woman, and child in the streets were discussing 'those Muslims.'" So were the police, who took keen interest in the group's activities. During the first week of May, NYPD officers conducted a warrantless search of Temple No. 7, and Malcolm spotted officers filming NOI members as they entered religious services. He accused police of attempting to "embarrass and intimidate" congregants in retaliation for standing up for their dignity in the Hinton case.[44]

Malcolm's knack for public relations was transformative. Five years after Malcolm's release from prison, the Nation of Islam had grown from a marginal group of roughly four hundred, primarily in Chicago and Detroit, into a small but formidable part of the political and cultural landscape in major American cities, with membership numbering in the thousands. By 1957, Malcolm was authoring a weekly column, "God's Angry Men," for the *New York Amsterdam News* and had facilitated the Messenger publishing a weekly column in the same paper. Malcolm's column, friendships with black journalists, and networks within the national black press inspired him to start planning for an NOI newspaper, *Muhammad Speaks*, which he envisioned being "filled with Nation of Islam news."[45]

Malcolm oversaw the Nation's growth through his recruiting efforts, oversight of new temples, and identification and cultivation of a new generation of Muslim leaders, including Joseph X Gravitt, a military veteran rescued from alcoholism and a volatile temper by Malcolm and Louis X. Joseph would serve alongside of Malcolm in the Nation's Harlem mosque as captain of the Fruit of Islam, the group's paramilitary security force. FOI sentries guarded against internal and external forces, policing the boundaries of the Nation's mosques for violations of protocol as minor as failing to pay regular dues or as major as drinking alcohol or taking drugs; punishments ranged from verbal warnings and temporary suspensions to physical violence and expulsion. Louis X became the minister of the Boston temple and one of Malcolm's closest confidantes, a devoted acolyte driven by a sincere belief in the Messenger, deep admiration of Malcolm, and personal ambition to make his mark within the organization. Ella Mae Collins returned to the NOI fold via the Boston temple, a circumstance that both pleased and surprised Malcolm, who considered his sister to be perhaps the most formidable person, besides Earl, he had ever met.[46]

In practical effect, Malcolm X modernized the Nation of Islam. By 1955, NOI membership had increased to almost six thousand members; by 1961, it had surged to over fifty thousand. With the glaring exception of Elijah Muhammad's family, positions of leadership were based on talent and hard work. Malcolm possessed a jeweler's eye for spotting potential within neglected parts of the black community. He utilized the media to build a personal and organizational following. At his core, Malcolm X was a diplomat, even as he cultivated a public following as a bold oracle of racial militancy. Behind the scenes, he could chat amiably with political adversaries as if they were close supporters and friends.[47]

Malcolm's organizing abilities buttressed his rhetorical swagger, and his reach extended as far south as Georgia. During a southern campaign trip as part of a national speaking tour in the summer of 1957, Malcolm founded Atlanta's Temple No. 15. In the summer of 1958, thirteen thousand people listened to Elijah Muhammad at Uline Arena in Washington, DC, the crowd overflowing into a nearby park, a vacant lot, and the streets. It was a display of organizational strength and political power that would have been unimaginable before Malcolm joined the NOI. In Washington, Malcolm's description of Muhammad as the one man capable of "bringing black people together" obscured his own indispensable role in such triumphant moments. The Messenger entrusted Malcolm with mounting organizational responsibilities, even as members of his family began smearing the young prince as a potential usurper and Muhammad's inner circle remained fearful that Malcolm might grow too powerful.[48]

Malcolm's organizing prowess solidified his position within the NOI and helped to shape the public identity of both the Nation and himself. He defined his religious beliefs through political commentary and analysis of racial injustice in America and around the world. He came to view radical dignity as a political and ideological platform that could organize global black power against the pervasive forces of white supremacy. Ultimately, his aims of confronting American democracy's jagged edges, challenging police brutality, advocating for self-defense and racial pride, and calling out the use of American power internationally would loom even larger than the thousands of new recruits who poured into the Nation. Malcolm's words of fire inspired black activists outside of the group, serving to radicalize mainstream civil rights discourse. Black leaders critical of Malcolm's position privately conceded that he correctly diagnosed America's racial illness, even as they attacked his cure as perhaps worse than the disease.

CHAPTER 2

The Radical Citizenship
of Martin Luther King

Throughout the late 1950s, Malcolm X found himself responding to a political landscape shaped by Martin Luther King Jr. King's political mobilization of southern Negroes in Montgomery, Alabama, reverberated nationally. While Malcolm made inroads in the South through the establishment of Muslim mosques in Atlanta and Florida, King took command from the pulpit of the Dexter Avenue Baptist Church in Montgomery. Dexter represented the church of "big" Negroes: college-educated professionals, doctors, lawyers, and entrepreneurs flocked to the church and its twenty-six-year-old Negro preacher with a doctoral degree from Boston University.

Born on January 15, 1929, in Atlanta, Georgia, as Michael Luther King Jr., King grew up safely ensconced in the world of the black elite, his childhood free of the tragedy that would shape Malcolm X. By the time Mike, as friends called him, turned five years old, his father, Michael, changed both of their names following a trip to the Baptist World Alliance in Berlin. King Sr., the highest-paid black minister in Atlanta, toured Europe and the Middle East and returned to Georgia to a welcome featured on the front page of the *Atlanta Daily World*.[1]

Martin Luther King Sr. came from humble sharecropping origins around Stockbridge, Georgia. Daddy King, as he came to be known to friends and family, reinvented himself as preacher, marrying Alberta Williams, the daughter of one of Atlanta's most successful black pastors, A. D. Williams. After Williams's death, King Sr. presided over his congregation at Ebenezer Baptist, becoming a leading "race-man," the affectionate name for black leaders who advocated racial uplift against the backdrop of white supremacy. King Jr., along with his younger brother A. D. and older sister Christine, grew up in Atlanta's segregated black elite. Public accommodations were rigidly policed, and even the children of the black bourgeoisie encountered racial assaults. King's awareness of racial inequality came at an early age: when he was eight years old, he received a sharp slap in the face from a white woman who accused him of stepping on her foot.[2]

Daddy King forcefully resisted the indignities of Atlanta's Jim Crow system, something that young Martin witnessed and admired. King Sr. refused to ride Atlanta's segregated buses, he never answered to the denigrating term "boy" that whites used to refer to adult black men, and, in King's recollection, he once stood up to a police officer after a traffic stop by pointedly identifying himself as "Reverend King." Like Malcolm X, King revered his Baptist preaching father, a man comfortable enough to tell black parishioners to embrace political self-determination. "I am going to move forward toward freedom, and I'm hoping everybody here today joins me," King Sr. declared before one thousand people attending a 1939 rally at Ebenezer. Young M. L., as friends called him, worshipped Daddy King as "a man of real integrity, deeply committed to moral and ethical principles," an image that shaped his professional and intellectual aspirations.[3]

As the son of a preacher, King wrestled with his own faith. He experienced doubts about God's beneficence following the unexpected death of his grandmother. And Atlanta's race relations filled him with resentment for whites throughout his youth. At ten, King watched in horror and fascination at the city's Christmastime showing of the film *Gone with the Wind*. The festivities included a downtown parade, replete with Confederate flags, and thousands of Atlanta's white residents crammed into Loew's Grand Theater to enjoy the film's romantic depiction of antebellum slavery. King's discomfort with the film's nostalgic portrayal of white supremacy—which included Academy Award–winning actress Hattie McDaniel's role as Scarlett O'Hara's black "mammie" caretaker and Butterfly McQueen's performance as the anxious, loud, and not-too-intelligent house servant Prissy—mirrored that of fourteen-year-old Malcolm Little, who watched the film in Mason, Michigan. "I was the only Negro in the theater," Malcolm remembered, "and when Butterfly McQueen went into her act, I felt like crawling under the rug."[4]

King's encounters with racism in popular culture were mediated through his personal experience. He was acutely aware of the ways that blacks were forced to degrade themselves. At six, he lost his white best friend to the harsh discipline of racial segregation. At fourteen, he was forced to remain standing on a ninety-mile bus trip from Atlanta to Dublin, Georgia—black passengers were forced to move once white passengers boarded. "It was the angriest I have ever been in my life," King recalled.[5]

King both admired and feared his father, whose discipline included whippings until King turned fifteen. He spent the summer before college working on a tobacco farm in Simsbury, Connecticut, which allowed him access to integrated travel between New York and Washington, an experience he came to relish. After that summer, when he returned to the Jim Crow South, "the very idea of separation did something to my sense of dignity and self-respect," he later remembered.[6]

He enrolled at the historically black Morehouse College, the most prestigious four-year men's school in the nation. King matched a precocious intellect with a burgeoning sense of himself as a potential agent of social change. Dr. Benjamin Mays, Morehouse's distinguished president and a friend of Daddy King, was an intellectual who believed in social justice and helped imbue an ethic of leadership as service. He became one of King's mentors and role models. Religious classes with Dr. George Kelsey offered a scholarly entrée into the study of Christianity, which King longed for as an antidote to what he regarded as the emotionalism—kicking, stomping, and verbally praising the Lord—that he encountered in the black Baptist church (a tradition that Daddy King exemplified). King dressed well, and his love of fine clothes earned him the nickname Tweedy. He pursued romantic relationships with the daughters of Atlanta's black elite. Despite his average height, King presented as a good catch, with his baritone voice making him stand out as mature beyond his years. At Morehouse, King's reputation as a ladies' man earned him great admiration from male students, who called King and his friend Larry Williams "the Wreckers" in honor of their dating exploits.[7]

King's plans to study medicine and then law were scuttled by a growing interest in the intersection of race, religion, and justice. On August 6, 1946, while Malcolm X spent his first year as a "fish" in Charlestown State Prison, King wrote a letter, "Kick Up Dust," published in the *Atlanta Constitution*. He wrote the letter against the backdrop of the murders of two black couples and one black man, Maceo Snipes, by whites in Georgia. Both cases made national news. Snipes's killing especially galled King. Snipes had cast the sole black vote in Taylor County and was killed the next day for his courage. "We want and are entitled to the basic rights and opportunities of American citizens," wrote seventeen-year-old King. He accused white racists of bringing up interracial intimacy as an excuse to deny black citizenship. "We aren't eager to marry white girls, and we would like to have our own girls left alone by both white toughs and white aristocrats." The letter exemplified young King's racial militancy and a pride and confidence in black history rooted in the political example he saw at home, encountered at Morehouse, and dreamed of carrying forth into the world.

He spent his first three years at Morehouse resisting Daddy King's pleas to join the ministry. In 1947, he finally relented. At eighteen, King passed his trial sermon at Ebenezer Baptist Church.[8]

That same year, King wrote an essay in the Morehouse newspaper chiding his classmates for aspiring to be middle-class black elites who used their education to "forever trample upon the masses." It proved to be an early example of King's criticism of the capitalist economic system. In his final year in college, he served as Daddy King's assistant pastor, something that pleased his father to no end. He also penned a campus newspaper article, "The Purpose of Education," that criticized Georgia's former governor Eugene Talmadge for his segregationist views. King took further steps into the public arena by joining, over Daddy King's objections, a council of interracial students from area colleges. His budding relationships across the color line made him view "many white persons as allies, particularly among the younger generation." Morehouse president Benjamin Mays chose King as class speaker for the senior sermon, where he dazzled his classmates during the mandatory chapel service.[9]

After graduating from Morehouse, King spent three years at Crozer Theological Seminary in Chester, Pennsylvania. The school's location, close to Philadelphia and removed from the domineering Daddy King, drew him closer to crafting a personal religious philosophy that connected with his interest in social justice. He joined nine other black students in a class of thirty-two, a surprising diversity for a prestigious, typically white school. The surprises didn't end there: a poolroom beneath the seminary chapel became a fixture where certain students, including King, congregated.

At Crozer, King discovered, analyzed, and came to embrace the Social Gospel through reading the work of Walter Rauschenbusch, the theologian and author of *Christianity and the Social Crisis*. The Social Gospel interpreted Christ's teachings as a vehicle for social justice on earth, not just in heaven. Rauschenbusch examined

Christianity through the prism of social ethics, arguing that social justice on earth reflected the greatest manifestation of God's love, and King immediately gravitated toward this perspective.[10]

Crozer attracted an eclectic faculty of religious scholars, intellectuals, and free thinkers who challenged, fascinated, and inspired King. He studied the writings of Mahatma Gandhi and Karl Marx, and although he was more intrigued by Marx, he would come to be permanently associated with Gandhi. King rejected the "evils" of communism—which he defined as the ideology's "metaphysical materialism, an ethical relativism, and a strangulating totalitarianism"—while paying close attention to its critique of economic injustice and social inequality. When King read Gandhi, the philosophical concept of satyagraha, roughly translated to "truth force or love force," held particular appeal for him, as his experiences with Jim Crow had previously convinced him that nothing short of "an armed revolt" would bring about racial justice. King regarded Gandhi's nonviolent movement against British colonialism in India as the collective application of Jesus's love, one capable of inspiring "a powerful and effective social force on a large scale." As he studied these thinkers, King was seeking a religious and political philosophy that deplored poverty while recognizing love, democracy, and justice as sacred principles.[11]

In his first term at Crozer, King wrote a paper outlining the obligation he felt to personally address "unemployment," ghettos, "and economic insecurity." King felt that preachers "should possess profundity of conviction" and spellbinding oratory—one absent the other produced spiritual impoverishment. He viewed the role of preaching ministry as "a dual process," wherein he labored to inspire his flock to transform society "so that the individual soul will have a change."[12]

King applied himself to his seminary studies, reporting to his mother, "I never go anywhere much but these books." Although he was more serious about academics at seminary than he had been at Morehouse, King slightly overstated his dedication. He found plenty of time to cultivate a new community of friends, colleagues, and mentors that extended from Chester to Philadelphia to New York. He attended regular dinners at the home of pastor J. Pius Barbour, a King family friend and Crozer's first black graduate. Reverend Barbour served many roles for King: a confidant about romantic entanglements, a debating partner on racial-justice issues, and a mentor whose family became a second home for King throughout his time at Crozer. King also took advantage of the natural beauty that surrounded the seminary. Each afternoon, he enjoyed long walks to the edge of campus, where a tributary from the Delaware River ran. His efforts to commune with nature reflected a deeply meditative side of his personality that he would struggle to cultivate alongside growing demands on his time.[13]

King discovered Reinhold Niebuhr's 1932 classic, *Moral Man and Immoral Society*, during his final year at Crozer, and the book offered him a blueprint for his transition from a preacher with intellectual ambitions to a faith leader and public intellectual undergirded by a belief that "justice is love's message for the collective mind." Niebuhr turned King inside out. The theologian's skepticism toward the Social Gospel, Marxism, and liberalism forced King to reexamine his own views. Niebuhr identified power as the necessary adjunct to moral transformation. He judged nonviolent methods as more important for their ability to alter oppressive regimes than for their romantic interpretations, such as those associated with Gandhi. The study of Niebuhr gave King the tools to confront evil that existed beyond intellectual comprehension in service of challenging political problems that required moral courage.[14]

In 1950, while Malcolm X made intellectual strides at Norfolk Prison Colony and fomented protests for better prison conditions, King came into his own at Crozer as a budding scholar, precocious speaker, and student leader of weekly devotionals. He was elected student body president during his second year, making him the first black person to win that honor. King's time in Chester exposed him to both the opportunities and the limits of integration. He socialized with white students and fell in love with Betty Moitz, the white daughter of Crozer's dietician. He dated Betty while seeing other women in Chester, Philadelphia, and New York, continuing a pattern of womanizing that began at Morehouse. He toyed with the possibility of marrying Betty, until the pressure from friends and mentors, who insisted that the relationship would place too great a burden on his future ambitions, convinced him not to. His dating life wasn't the only troubled aspect of his time at Crozer. As a young seminarian, his essays illustrated a sharp mind but sloppy writing. He unevenly credited the source of his work, only occasionally attributed the words of others, and produced papers that would have constituted plagiarism if checked more thoroughly. These problems would continue to haunt him throughout his academic career. But both the secret romance with Betty and his plagiarism would remain undiscovered during his lifetime.[15]

King grew more intellectually ambitious and politically confident during his years at Crozer. He delivered dozens of lectures in churches in Chester and Philadelphia and audited a graduate seminar on Ethics and Philosophy of History at the University of Pennsylvania. The importance of Gandhi was reinforced for him after listening to a speech by Howard University president Mordecai Johnson in Philadelphia in 1950. Fresh from a trip to India the previous year, the outspoken Johnson railed against Christianity's complicity with Jim Crow and compared the British treatment of Indians to the way America "treated colored citizens in Alabama and Mississippi." King also continued to develop a skepticism toward American capitalism. "I am convinced," King wrote in early 1951, "that capitalism has seen its best days." His disapproval stemmed from his deepening empathy for the poor and political underdogs. Since capitalism "has failed to meet the needs of the masses," he reasoned, it would be replaced by an "unconscious" move toward social democracy. His embrace of a socialist model contrasted with Daddy King, a fervid capitalist who blanched at his son's leftward political drift. Father and son discussed, debated, and argued about economic justice. Daddy King found himself talking to a young man repudiating "the basics of capitalism and Western democracy" in favor of a more redistributive social and economic system.[16]

King, in contrast to Malcolm, continuously encountered black men who served as professional and intellectual mentors: Morehouse president Mays, Reverend Barbour in Chester, and Daddy King, who remained his son's North Star and primary source of inspiration. But despite his deep love for his father, King found his own political, theological, and personal voice during his years at seminary. When his father came to visit, King played pool and smoked cigarettes in front of him, behavior that would previously have drawn harsh rebuke. In sermons at Ebenezer during the summers, King tested out political themes he had encountered at Crozer. He used his deep baritone, crisp diction, and southern drawl to find a rhetorical middle ground between the fire-and-brimstone Baptist preachers, like his father, and the white ministers, including some of his professors, whose academic preaching style left him cold.

King graduated from Crozer on May 15, 1951. He received a $1,200 fellowship to pursue graduate studies, as well as another honor given to the school's equivalent of a valedictorian. Named the most outstanding student out of his class of ten seminarians, King left Crozer with a deeper sense of his intellectual identity and a clearer idea of the kind of preacher he longed to be. If Malcolm X found intellectual, religious, and personal validation in a New England prison, King found similar affirmation in a northern seminary, where he studied a wide range of thinkers and befriended white students and professors. He left Chester with plans to move temporarily further north, rather than return to Atlanta. Instead, he secured a scholarship to Boston University to pursue of doctorate in the philosophy of religion.

With no steady girlfriend, King had continued to cultivate a reputation as a ladies' man. But in Boston, he met and fell in love with Coretta Scott, a classically trained singer, two years older than the twenty-two-year-old doctoral student, on scholarship at the city's New England Conservatory of Music. King bluntly informed Coretta that he was seeking a wife who possessed "character, intelligence, personality and beauty." "You have them all," he told her. He called her Corrie and she called him Martin. They married in her native Alabama, just outside of Selma, less than eighteen months after their first date. Coretta proved to be far more of a match than King could have imagined or anticipated. But even as he cast harsh judgment on Daddy King's unrepentant capitalism and the moral evil that gripped much of the world, King personally reveled in the masculine privileges of his social class. He expected a sexual fidelity and loyalty from Coretta that he would never offer in exchange. It was a complicated relationship, and their early romance eventually flowered into a marriage that became an intellectual and political partnership that bound them in a whirlwind of experiences, public and private, that drew them closer with each passing year.[17]

In January 1954, King's coursework was completed and he sought a steady income for his new family. He received an invitation to preach at Dexter Avenue Baptist Church in Montgomery, Alabama. Two months later, the church offered him the position of pastor with a salary of over $4,000, making him the highest-paid black minister in the city. He preached his first sermon as Dexter's full-time pastor in May, the same month as the *Brown* Supreme Court decision and shortly before Malcolm X arrived in Harlem to preside over Temple No. 7.

Not long after arriving in Montgomery, King found his professional trajectory altered by local activists and their struggle to end segregation on the city's buses. Rosa Parks, a forty-two-year-old NAACP organizer who had attended classes at the radical Highlander Folk School in Tennessee, emerged as the symbol of quiet dissent against Jim Crow after her arrest for refusing to give up her seat to a white passenger on December 1, 1955. Parks's arrest set the stage for a planned bus boycott, organized by some of Montgomery's leading labor and civil rights activists. The 381-day action thrust King into the national spotlight as the president and chief spokesperson for the Montgomery Improvement Association (MIA). King's election to the position had represented a compromise choice. As a relative newcomer to Montgomery, he had not had time to make the kind of political enemies that blocked the ascent of more well-known activists. Through the MIA, King learned enduring political and organizational lessons from seasoned activists more familiar with grassroots organizing for racial justice. Over the course of the boycott, he survived death threats, a house bombing, and arrest to emerge as a national civil rights leader with a moral and political vision rooted as much in the Social Gospel and Christian faith as in the nation's founding documents.[18]

In the year leading up to the boycott, King developed a deep friendship with Ralph Abernathy, the charismatic black pastor of First Baptist Church. Abernathy was born in Alabama's black belt and was gifted with a pragmatic intelligence. He admired King's elite social background as much as King delighted in Abernathy's deep country roots. The two enjoyed a shared sense of humor, private jokes, and teasing in a way that made them more brothers than friends.[19]

Martin and Coretta welcomed their first child, Yolanda (called Yoki), weeks before the start of the boycott. The young husband and father briefly hesitated before diving into his role as chief spokesperson of a local movement that captured the national imagination. As MIA president and pastor of Dexter, King presided over twice-weekly mass meetings. There, he outlined a political philosophy arguing that the combined power of Christian love and nonviolent protest could challenge the evils of Jim Crow. "One of the great glories of American democracy is that we have the right to protest for rights," King noted at one meeting. The protests were organized by some of Montgomery's leading labor, women's, and civil rights activists and organizers. The Women's Political Council, led by Alabama State University English professor Jo Ann Robinson, used Parks's arrest to organize a citywide boycott its members had been discussing for several years. E. D. Nixon, past leader of Montgomery's NAACP, Pullman porter, and proud member of A. Philip Randolph's Brotherhood of Sleeping Car Porters, knew Parks and represented the defiant voice of black workers. The boycott relied on the deep well of knowledge such activists brought to organizing carpools, leafleting Montgomery's population of fifty thousand black folk, and sustaining the racial solidarity that transcended the class tension within the MIA— where E. D. Nixon chafed at the increasing attention directed at the young Martin Luther King Jr.[20]

King's place at the forefront of the Montgomery bus boycott made him a lightning rod for threats from law enforcement and racial terrorists. On January 26, 1956, almost two months into the boycott, Montgomery police arrested King for speeding, a pretext designed to intimidate and disrupt the movement. King's brief incarceration had the opposite effect, galvanizing blacks who came to the city jail in a show of support that compelled his release that evening. Four days later, racists bombed King's home. Coretta and Yoki escaped injury, but the violence directed at King and his family amplified the stakes of his involvement in the movement.[21]

Bayard Rustin's appearance in Montgomery less than a month after the bombing helped King make sense of the incomprehensible. A brilliant organizer, pacifist, and raconteur, Rustin had helped to mobilize some of the most effective interracial anti-racist movements of the 1940s, but his activism was overshadowed by a complicated personal history that included past ties to communists and a stint in jail as a conscientious objector. Rustin's political ambitions were also thwarted by his homosexuality. But he shared his experience as a professional organizer with King, exposing him to the intricacies of nonviolence as a way of life, which would disallow the use of armed bodyguards. Tall and courtly with a shock of gray hair, Rustin would emerge in this pivotal moment as one of King's closest advisors.[22]

A Montgomery grand jury's decision to indict nearly one hundred MIA members for violating an Alabama state law prohibiting boycotts brought the movement, and King, even more attention. He was ready for prime time. Journalists who flocked to Alabama found him to be a bracing combination of intelligence, erudition, and humility. The *New York Times* praised him as a religious scholar and preacher "well read in Kant and Hegel." In King, the black press in particular discovered a new hero. "Alabama's Modern Moses," proclaimed *Jet* magazine. It was the first time King appeared on the cover of a national black publication.[23]

The more legal troubles King incurred, the more his support, celebrity, and influence grew. On March 22, 1956, a judge found King guilty of leading an illegal boycott and sentenced him to serve 386 days in jail or pay court costs and a $500 fine. Released on an appeal bond, he went on the offensive, traveling to Brooklyn to speak at a fundraiser and announcing plans to help organize the black vote in Montgomery.[24] Daddy King's ties to the sprawling National Baptist Convention, USA, Inc., helped to bolster Martin's support among professional black preachers, their congregants, and the vast network of faith-based organizations. Racial-justice activists who combined Christian faith with a fervent belief in the integration of America sought King out, including members of the Fellowship of Reconciliation (FOR) and the Congress of Racial Equality—groups founded during the Second World War, when segregation's end seemed tantalizingly close amid wartime talk of interracial democracy and anti-fascism.[25]

King proved to be a dynamic and active listener, with an uncanny ability to absorb the ideas of a generation of veteran activists, including Rustin, Glenn Smiley, A. J. Muste, James Farmer, and the black feminist organizer Ella Baker. King's deft political instincts made him appealing to a wide group of at times competing interests. Supporters of Gandhi pointed out similarities between

King and the anti-colonial leader. Over time, King embraced the portrait of himself as the American Gandhi. Conversely, in front of dedicated Baptists, he cast himself as a humble and observant Christian servant who preached against the evil of segregation. Journalists covering the boycott found King unique enough to be intriguing, and international reporters, in addition to the black press and correspondents from major dailies, began writing about King as his fame grew throughout 1956. The black press hailed him as the symbol of a dynamic movement, one that combined militancy, patriotism, and religious faith—sacrosanct qualities in Negro communities. The *Baltimore Afro-American* named King the "Top American" of 1956, the first of many such honorifics that he would receive.[26]

By the spring of 1956, the Montgomery bus boycott emerged as one battleground in a larger movement for racial justice. King's travels outside of the city—giving major speeches, attending fundraising events, and sitting for interviews with an international contingent of journalists—galvanized support for the movement. Civil rights luminaries, most notably W. E. B. Du Bois, the first black Harvard PhD, NAACP organizer, and scholar-activist whose 1903 classic, *The Souls of Black Folk*, remained required reading among the African American intelligentsia, corresponded with King.

On the second anniversary of the *Brown* decision, King addressed a New York audience of twelve thousand. His sermon, "The Death of Evil upon the Seashore," made the struggle for black citizenship analogous to the Old Testament story of the Israelites escaping Egypt. He characterized Europe's colonization of Africa as one of history's worst tragedies. "The great struggle of the twentieth century has been between these exploited masses questing for freedom and the colonial powers seeking to maintain their domination," King observed in a line that might have made Malcolm X proud. That same evening, King spoke at the NAACP Legal Defense Fund dinner, describing events in Montgomery as the actions of a "new Negro" in the South who refused to live under Jim Crow's oppressive regime a moment longer. "The tension which we are witnessing in race relations in the South today" explained King, illustrated "the revolutionary change in the Negro's evaluation of himself and his determination to struggle and sacrifice until the walls of injustice crumble."[27]

King, without identifying himself as such, represented the generation of new Negroes he lauded. Civil rights elders recognized his efforts to distinguish the MIA and Montgomery's movement from an earlier generation of activists even as he culled their support. King's celebrity placed him and the MIA as fundraising competitors with the NAACP, whose Legal Defense Fund covered the Montgomery movement but received a large boost thanks to the infusion of new energy orchestrated by the young preacher.

Montgomery city officials trafficked in legal threats, delay, and denial after a federal court panel ruled on June 4 against the city's segregated bus statutes. As the state of Alabama tried to prevent the inevitable, King narrated the story of the bus boycott to rapturous crowds across the nation. On June 27, he delivered one of two keynotes at the NAACP convention in San Francisco alongside the grizzled veteran A. Philip Randolph. King's speech emphasized nonviolence as a political method that effectively challenged racial segregation and white supremacy and love as "the regulating ideal" that allowed blacks to resist the evil of Jim Crow without bitterness or strife. The movement for black equality transcended race, King argued to an applauding crowd of one thousand delegates. "The struggle is at bottom a tension between justice and injustice." The movement to bring about "full citizenship" for black Americans had entered a new phase, one that linked racial equality to America's national destiny. For "if democracy is to live, segregation must die."[28]

King's hectic schedule increasingly resembled that of an elected political leader, and, on August 11, he testified before the platform and resolutions committee at the Democratic National Convention in Chicago, in hopes of getting the party to officially endorse the *Brown* decision. He introduced himself modestly as the representative of black Montgomery. But by that time, his reach extended both nationally and globally. Racial justice, King explained, meant not only a victory "for 16,000,000 Negroes, but a victory for justice and democracy."[29]

The Supreme Court's November ruling upholding the federal panel's Montgomery decision hastened Jim Crow's death. On December 3, King addressed the MIA's first annual Institute on Nonviolence and Social Change. The institute sought to mobilize the energies unleashed in Montgomery on a national scale, offering seminars on nonviolent civil disobedience, voter registration, and civics education. In his speech, King acknowledged the many groups, organizations, and people who had allowed the boycott to flourish. "I would like to express my deepest appreciation to each of you for following my leadership," he explained, recognizing that despite public shows of humility, his individual talents were integral to freedom's cause. King touched upon global histories of "colonialism and imperialism" by noting that the "vast majority" of indigenous people living under oppressive regimes were "colored" and beginning to struggle for freedom.[30]

King compared domestic struggles for racial justice to anticolonial movements sweeping across the world. "The old order is passing away," he said. "And the new order is coming into being." This new order required black leaders capable of occupying a creatively militant middle ground between what King called "the extremes of 'hot-headedness' and 'Uncle Tomism.'" On December 21, Montgomery finally complied with the nation's highest court. King, surrounded by MIA colleagues and a caravan of reporters, climbed aboard a city bus for a hard-earned victory lap.[31]

King's world grew larger as events in Montgomery faded from the national spotlight. Shortly after his twenty-eighth birthday, he appeared on the cover of *Time* magazine. A striking drawing of a determinedly handsome King staring into the distance, silhouetted on the top right by a smaller sketch of him preaching and on the bottom left by an image of blacks triumphantly entering a bus, powerfully depicted his growing national stature. On March 3, the *New York Times* Sunday edition profiled King in a story that noted his sharp mind, penchant for quoting Western philosophers and theologians, and extensive vocabulary. King had cultivated the persona of a religious scholar for the story; when the reporter visited him at home, Beethoven played in the background. But despite King's extensive education, blacks of all class backgrounds embraced him. "He knows how to speak to the Ph.D.'s and the No D.'s," locals in Montgomery were fond of saying. The coverage framed King as a salt-of-the-earth family man, an intellectually driven scholar, and religious leader whose humility made ordinary black people embrace him as one of their own.[32]

Like Malcolm X, King fostered a deep interest in the potential for global affairs to inform domestic freedom struggles, especially in Africa, which he and Coretta visited for the first time in early March. In Ghana, formerly the Gold Coast, King observed the pomp and circumstance of the formal end of British colonialism. He marveled at Ghana's post-independence euphoria, enjoyed a private lunch with Prime Minister Kwame Nkrumah, and chatted about American race relations with then vice president Richard Nixon. King arrived in Ghana in order to witness "the birth of this new nation with my own eyes." He found strength in comparing African liberation movements with black freedom struggles back home. King, in contrast to Malcolm, viewed Ghanaian independence with a sense of optimism that made him believe that domestic freedom could be won through a nonviolent revolution. He personally marveled at the fact that Nkrumah dressed in the same cap and clothes he wore while in prison for sedition. Ghana offered King a lesson in the ultimate victory of sacrifice over violence: shared witness against injustice could marshal triumphs that wars never could. After Ghana, King traveled to London to meet with C. L. R. James, the itinerant Trinidadian Marxist and author of *The Black Jacobins*, a classic account of the Haitian Revolution.

James listened to King's description of the Montgomery struggle with keen interest, writing to friends afterward that nonviolence represented "a technique of revolutionary struggle characteristic of our age."[33]

King's Ghanaian sojourn confirmed his status as the leader of an internationally recognized social movement. He started receiving letters from African students and Algerian revolutionaries. He returned to Alabama preaching a radical message of anti-colonialism. "The Birth of a New Nation," a speech delivered from the pulpit of Dexter Avenue Baptist Church on the first Sunday in April, positioned Ghana's long journey into the community of free nations as a metaphor for the black freedom struggle. King framed a discussion of the travails of African countries since the trans-Atlantic slave trade around the book of Exodus, which found the prophet Moses leading his people out of bondage. As an appendage to the British Empire, the Gold Coast had experienced "all of the injustices, all of the exploitation, all of the humiliation" of colonial domination. King recounted how political oppression had been unable to diminish the thirst for freedom that remained humanity's birthright and, in Ghana's case, became personified by Nkrumah, a native son educated at historically black Lincoln University, the University of Pennsylvania, and the London School of Economics. Like Malcolm X, King revered Nkrumah as one of history's most remarkable underdogs, a boy of humble origins who grew into an African leader capable of toppling an empire.[34]

Elected prime minister from a jail cell, Nkrumah had turned prison walls into a political kingdom. "The road to freedom is difficult, but finally, Ghana tells us that the forces of the universe are on the side of justice," observed King. King's speech boldly proclaimed the coming end of Western imperialism and colonial domination as part of a divine plan of justice for oppressed peoples on both sides of the Atlantic. King retained his commitment to the principles of nonviolence, even as he offered a radical critique of global power relations and linked domestic civil rights struggles in America to anti-colonial insurgency around the world.[35]

King's visit to Ghana and Europe, where he marveled at the resilience of ordinary Africans and paused to consider the vastness of a rapidly crumbling British Empire, found him firmly in the camp of black internationalism, a political philosophy shared by Malcolm X. Malcolm's thirst for radical black dignity and King's quest for radical black citizenship most comfortably met on the world stage. Both men recognized the systemic nature of racial oppression, one that transcended boundaries of nation-states to impact what King characterized as the "world-house," humanity's mutual interconnectedness. King's historical knowledge of Gandhi and Nkrumah and his personal experience in Montgomery—where he survived a litany of death threats and assassination attempts that only increased after the bus boycott—buoyed his faith in the political, philosophical, and strategic use of nonviolence, which he deployed as a shield against oppression both visible and unseen. Malcolm X might have found common ground with much of what King said in Montgomery that Sunday, especially King's visceral love of African people, the stinging indictment of colonialism and imperialism, and his professed belief that the world's "Asian-African bloc" would determine history's future. For Malcolm, however, defending black lives against racial terror remained a sacred right of citizenship and a necessary tactic for a people still living in bondage almost a century after slavery's formal end.[36]

The press largely ignored the radical pronouncements in King's discussion of Ghana in favor of a more polished narrative of quietly determined moral leadership. In 1957, King publicly called on the federal government to robustly oppose racial segregation, an implicit rebuke of the Eisenhower administration's foot-dragging in the aftermath of the Supreme Court's virtually unenforced integration of public schools. While Malcolm X organized Muslim temples throughout the Northeast, Midwest, and strategic parts of the South and West, King spent the year searching for a vehicle to continue the stalled momentum of Montgomery. King's intellectual, political, and moral vision leaned toward a radical interpretation of social justice, but his personal instincts remained fundamentally cautious. Behind the scenes, he pushed for a private meeting with Eisenhower, something civil rights leaders had been trying to do since the president's first year in office.[37]

Bayard Rustin's assistance during the bus boycott proved to be invaluable, and he became a close friend and advisor to King. He introduced King to his vast network of social justice activists, some of whom would also form political associations with Malcolm X. Two of the most important would be Ella Baker—an NAACP organizer, labor activist, and feminist from North Carolina who butted heads with the relatively inexperienced King and his largely male coterie of preachers—and Stanley Levison, a radical lawyer and social justice philanthropist who would find an easy rapport with the young civil rights leader and emerge as a trusted advisor. The Southern Christian Leadership Conference, headed by King, administered by Baker, and with Rustin serving as chief counselor, became the vehicle for expanding Montgomery's success on a national scale.

The SCLC's national agenda included registering millions of black voters across the South and forming a national clearinghouse to provide direction, attention, and resources to local movements in Montgomery's aftermath. King's most visible effort after returning from Ghana revolved around the Prayer Pilgrimage for Freedom at the Lincoln Memorial, an effort to shame and cajole the nation toward racial progress on the third anniversary of *Brown*. Planning for the event brought King further into the orbit of NAACP executive Roy Wilkins, a key ally during the bus boycott but a rival for claims of national leadership. Privately, Wilkins remained convinced that the NAACP's Legal Defense Fund offered the best avenue to end racial segregation, yet he recognized the power of the burgeoning social movement flourishing alongside King. A. Philip

Randolph, the ex-socialist turned labor leader who adopted Rustin as an organizer after his own heart, viewed the event as a continuation of his 1941 March on Washington Movement, a signature effort of the "double V" campaigns to end racism at home and fascism abroad that pressured President Roosevelt into signing an executive order desegregating the military under the threat of thousands of black men descending upon the nation's capital.[38]

Aspects of the pilgrimage seemed like a dress rehearsal for the 1963 March on Washington, with entertainment featuring prominent cultural supporters of the movement such as singer Mahalia Jackson and entertainer and King confidant Harry Belafonte. King addressed the rally last, speaking to the biggest audience of his life. The moment was a generational passing of the torch from A. Philip Randolph to the young King as the movement's crown prince. King's speech, "Give Us the Ballot," called for voting-rights legislation as a means of promoting black citizenship. Judging Democrats and Republicans alike as having "betrayed the cause of justice," King described the president as "silent and apathetic" in the face of racial terror and Congress as "stagnant and hypocritical" amid escalating national crises. The black movement required "soul force" to combat segregationist violence. Parts of the speech warned against rumblings of "black supremacy" and bitterness against racial oppression, anticipating King's public response to the Nation of Islam and Malcolm X's national rise. But still, shades of King's talk veered toward the militant, especially when he characterized the US Congress as "hypocritical," perhaps Malcolm X's favorite description of American democracy. In contrast to Malcolm's words of fire attacking white supremacy, though, King gently criticized white liberals as "so bent on seeing all sides" they failed to commit to anything.[39]

The passage of the Civil Rights Act of 1957 in September was anticlimactic, falling far short of ending Jim Crow in public accommodations. The legislation created a civil rights commission and granted the Justice Department the ability to file lawsuits against discriminatory voting registrars in the South, but it lacked broad enforcement powers and robust support from the president. The nation's first civil rights legislation since 1875, the new law provided hope for better days to come and burnished the reputation of then Senate majority leader Lyndon Johnson, a Texan with presidential ambitions who found enough common ground with liberals and conservatives to craft what one newspaper characterized as a "masterpiece." Civil rights activists interpreted the law as merely an encouraging first step.[40]

As summer turned to fall, King publicly confronted American democracy's racial demons, which gripped the nation during a crisis at the Little Rock Central High School. Arkansas governor Orval Faubus's decision to use the National Guard to prevent the enrollment of nine black students at the high school triggered a slow-motion crisis that produced some of the iconic images of the era, complete with angry mobs of white men, women, children, and teenagers screaming in unrepentant anger at the stoically dignified black faces attempting to reverse a century of racial apartheid. President Eisenhower spent three weeks negotiating a failed compromise before ordering the army's 101st Airborne Division to restore order and peace to Little Rock. Fantastic images of American soldiers escorting nine black students into the previously segregated school instantly became the stuff of legend, offering the movement its modern parallel to the Reconstruction era—the last time federal troops occupied the South.[41]

On September 25, King sent a telegram praising Eisenhower "for the stand you have taken to restore law and order in Little Rock, Arkansas." King's encouragement of federal intervention in local racial struggles would become the linchpin of his future political mobilizing, shaping the tenor of cooperation and conflict with the Kennedy and Johnson administrations. But for now, King was flailing, disconnected from the northern grassroots communities that galvanized Malcolm X and unable to transform Montgomery's righteous discontent into a national movement. Instead, he primarily served as America's most celebrated conduit for discussing the contours of racial oppression in a shared language that resonated with black and white audiences.[42]

During a nationally televised October 27 interview on NBC's *Look Here* program, King spoke of racial oppression as a moral evil that required "massive non-cooperation." He characterized nonviolence as the most powerful weapon against global regimes of political oppression and authoritarianism and traced his own "pilgrimage to non-violence" through his reading and personal experience in seminary. Nonviolence, King explained, required courage and fearlessness; the term "passive resistance" obscured, rather than illuminated, the strategy's profoundly disruptive impact on society. King's concept of nonviolence as "dynamically active" was in contrast with Malcolm X's withering description of the movement as simply organizing black victims to be brutalized by racial terrorists in the South.[43]

King psychologized the "folkways of white supremacy," acknowledging how the civil rights movement negotiated a minefield that included the enduring paradox of liberal white guilt over racial discrimination juxtaposed against conservative white bitterness over blacks asserting their long-denied humanity. He ended the interview by optimistically detailing how the promise of shared economic prosperity, greater religious and civic courage, black political self-determination, international support for civil rights, and the hope of robust federal action made him confident that Jim Crow would soon end. Framing America's system of racial segregation as a moral evil allowed King to speak in the common biblical language of churchgoing citizens, even as his distillation of Gandhian principles of nonviolence combined with Christian ethics of love revealed the complex thinking of an intellectual.

As Malcolm X ascended to the pinnacle of black radical militancy in Harlem, King became the face of national civil rights protest. King's success in Montgomery made him a larger-than-life symbol of the movement. A comic book, *Martin Luther King and the Montgomery Story*, was released, and King's ghostwritten (by Alabama State professor L. D. Reddick) narrative of the boycott would be published in 1958 as *Stride toward Freedom*. But on the ground, King's projects lacked momentum. Competitive tension between the SCLC and the NAACP hampered some of his organizing efforts. An additional problem was his failure to embrace the SCLC's new interim director, Ella Baker, whose organizing tenacity and brilliance should have made her indispensable to King but did not. King's political compass on gender matters hewed closely to established hierarchies that placed women, no matter how talented, in subordinate positions.[44]

King's leadership energized the national civil rights movement and placed the black church and faith leaders at the forefront of the struggle for racial justice in ways that reverberated across black politics. His time in Montgomery introduced him to veteran labor, peace, and civil rights activists, who found renewed inspiration in the bus boycott and King's embrace of Gandhian principles of nonviolence. His relationship with Baker, who would run the SCLC's Atlanta office for three years, might have helped him to better recognize the importance of collective, rather than top-down, decision-making and leadership. But, as a product of the black church's clearly established hierarchies, King took no such lesson. While he admired a measure of political militancy, he embraced traditional leadership roles that placed power in the hands of privileged men. In other words, he remained a work in progress. Baker pushed King to acknowledge black women in the movement as intellectual and political equals, challenging him to expand the scale of his vision and the depth of his personal commitment to freedom for all people. King, always uncomfortable with personal conflict, deflected these challenges by avoiding Baker and excluding her from his inner circle. His lack of professional chemistry with her was rooted in his reluctance to take seriously the organizing expertise of a veteran activist twenty-five years older than him. He found Baker's criticism of SCLC top-down leadership structure too harsh and her distaste for charismatic preachers offensive. His personal sexism, imbibed at home, in the black church, and in the larger society, precluded him from acknowledging black women as more than political surrogates.[45]

On the tenth anniversary of Mahatma Gandhi's death, King published an editorial arguing that humanity faced a choice between "non-violence and non-existence." He was confident in the ability of Christianity's love ethic to spur social transformation across whole societies, regions, nation-states, and, eventually, the entire world. He would begin by confronting southern racial mores that viewed black subjugation as the divine right of whites, who blissfully attended segregated churches, wept at Billy Graham's religious crusades, and prayed to God to maintain a way of life based on black misery.[46]

King also took a month-long tour of India in early 1959, and the trip moved him closer to becoming the kind of leader Baker longed for. Bayard Rustin arranged for meetings with key associates of Gandhi, and King returned to America with amplified respect for the suffering of local justice movements. After leaving India, he visited the Middle East, where he toured Lebanon and Jerusalem. Brief stops in London and Paris during the trip gave King the opportunity to meet with Richard Wright, the radical black novelist and expatriate whose literary masterpiece *Native Son* inspired generations of radical African American writers and activists. Over dinner, King and Wright developed a familial rapport. King marveled at the writer's abilities as a raconteur, which sparked a warm friendship that would be cut short by Wright's premature death the next year. Four days after that meeting, King dined with Jawaharlal Nehru, India's first prime minister and a dashing international hero of anti-colonialism. Over four hours, they discussed Nehru's practical efforts to eliminate poverty and caste discrimination and his role as head of state in a world buffeted by violence. Having never been invited to dinner at the White House, Nehru honored King as a visiting head of state.

Locals followed suit in their embrace, especially India's marginalized class of "untouchables," who greeted King as a brother in the south Indian state of Kerala.[47]

King's sojourn to India found him basking, like Malcolm X, in the burgeoning political strength of the Third World. King encountered India as both a faith leader and political mobilizer. The American Gandhi praised Mahatma in speeches and books for facilitating a practical strategy to institutionalize a vision of the beloved community based on Christian teachings of love, peace, and self-sacrifice. Politically, King took full advantage of his Third World moment, characterizing himself as a "pilgrim" coming to pay homage to a nation liberated from colonial oppression against seemingly insurmountable odds. Before Malcolm X stepped foot in Africa, King proudly claimed the Third World as an integral part of a worldwide social justice movement.[48]

King narrated his trip in the July issue of *Ebony* magazine, the popular monthly enjoyed by the black middle class. "My Trip to the Land of Gandhi" announced King as a global figure whose connection with the nonviolent movement's most sacred historical figure went beyond soaring rhetoric—now he had been in Gandhi's homeland. King compared India's caste system to American Jim Crow. He claimed India enjoyed more racial progress than the United States and contrasted Nehru's public opposition to discrimination with a lack of moral courage by America's political leaders.[49]

King's taste of the world further refined his civil rights activism and expanded his empathy for the poverty-stricken masses, whom he now personalized through his trip to India. Travel abroad introduced him to the ways in which problems of race, poverty, and violence flourished around the world, echoing the civil rights conflicts at home. The world stage bolstered King's personal conviction that a movement for achieving black citizenship could reshape not only American democracy but human rights struggles that spanned the globe. He returned to America's domestic civil rights front more aware than ever of the movement's international dimensions.

CHAPTER 3

The World Stage

I n 1959, Malcolm X, like King, explored the international contours of the black freedom struggle. Malcolm's first trip abroad
expanded his political vision, organizational ambitions, and intellectual yearnings. Touring parts of the Middle East gave him a
new appreciation for the expansiveness of the struggle for black
dignity. He identified with Muslims and the larger pan-Arab world
through a shared religion and understood anti-colonial struggles
as part of his own freedom quest. Malcolm's sojourn abroad also
gave him the opportunity to flex new political muscles. He comfortably took on the role of both NOI surrogate and international
diplomat eager to negotiate stronger ties between the Messenger
and the larger Arab world.

The Messenger and his followers were sensitive to allegations
that their religious practices fell outside the boundaries of orthodox Islam. But, as the Nation of Islam's financial resources grew,
so did Elijah Muhammad's efforts to be considered a part of the
global Islamic community. Muhammad began a correspondence
with Egyptian leader Gamal Abdel Nasser by congratulating
him on the successful Afro-Asian Peoples' Solidarity Conference
in Cairo that convened December 26, 1957, to January 1, 1958.
This initiated a cordial relationship that resulted in the Egyptian
government inviting Muhammad to make the hajj to Mecca, an

invitation that he delayed in accepting, opting to send Malcolm as his envoy instead. Malcolm applied for his first US passport one week after turning thirty-five. In the Middle East, he became a freelance diplomat who courted the heads of newly liberated Third World nations.[1]

Malcolm arrived in Cairo on Saturday, July 4, 1959. Like King's glorious reception in India, the Egyptian government received him as a visiting dignitary, housed him in an elegant hotel, and placed Vice President Anwar Sadat at his disposal. Malcolm's first encounter with the Arab world was eye-opening, as he fumbled through prayers with little knowledge of Arabic. But he conversed intently with diplomats, clerics, and official emissaries about the fight for racial justice in America, and he grew excited upon finding that the people in the Middle East reminded him of home. These kindred spirits pushed Malcolm to expand his political imagination. He encountered light-skinned and near-white Muslims who shared his thirst for the political liberation of all oppressed people. "99 per cent of them (Arabs) would be Jim-crowed in the United States of America," Malcolm noted. They "would be right at home in Harlem." From Cairo, where a case of dysentery left him incapacitated for three days in his hotel room, Malcolm traveled to Saudi Arabia. The warm treatment he received from both light- and dark-skinned people in Saudi Arabia proved to be transformative. "There is no color prejudice among Moslems," he wrote in a column published by the *Pittsburgh Courier*, "for Islam teaches that all mortals are equal and brothers." Malcolm reported back to the black press that Arabs and Africans were "more concerned" about the civil rights struggle in the United States than "their own status right here in Africa." Malcolm used personal reportage to build and promote a pan-African solidarity between black Americans and the Middle East.[2]

In Sudan, from Khartoum's Grand Hotel, Malcolm reveled in the role of the radical statesman, praising "intelligent Africans" who questioned why millions of blacks lived "without freedom,

without public school rights," only to be "relegated to slums, ghettoes, and other social imprisonment" in America, a nation that
touted its "democracy" all over the world. He accepted the gracious
hospitality of local officials during his eleven-day stay in Khartoum. The prominence of dark-skinned officials, such as Egypt's
Sadat, impressed Malcolm, who came to better understand the
nuances of racial identity outside of America. He discovered that
light-skinned politicians in the Middle East could be just as radical as their darker-skinned counterparts. Tours of Cairo, Saudi
Arabia, and Sudan convinced him that "Africa is the New World,"
in whose bright future "Negroes are destined to play a key role."[3]

Malcolm's trip drew him closer to the world of countries battling for political autonomy outside of Western domination. His
wish to feel the "pulse of as many of the African masses as possible" before returning home made him an eager student and careful observer. As he surveyed the breadth of US global influence,
Malcolm dared Americans to confront racial injustice back home.
Africans, Malcolm wrote from Sudan, "are asking why so many
American Negroes suffer unemployment, bad housing, slum conditions, and poverty." He sought to wield the power of international opinion as a sword in the struggle for racial justice. "Here in
Africa, the all-seeing eye of the African masses is upon America,"
he concluded.[4]

Malcolm returned to New York City on Wednesday, July 22,
1959, a few days after the airing of *The Hate That Hate Produced*, a
nationally broadcast five-part documentary series that turned the
Nation of Islam into a genuine phenomenon. The documentary
was the brainchild of Louis Lomax, one of Malcolm's favorite reporters. A savvy journalist who refused to let a five-year prison
stint derail his professional ambitions, Lomax parlayed his inside
access with the Nation into a documentary hosted by local journalist Mike Wallace, who would make his name from the controversy
generated by the film. *The Hate That Hate Produced* premiered over
five consecutive nights, but it was such an immediate sensation

that CBS rebroadcast it as a one-hour special the day Malcolm returned from Africa. Wallace breathlessly narrated footage of the Messenger and Malcolm speaking to thousands of followers in Washington, DC. "Here you see their Minister Malcolm X displaying five of the biggest Negro papers in America," observed Wallace. "Papers published in Los Angeles, New York, Pittsburgh, Detroit and Newark and Negro politicians, regardless of their private beliefs, respectfully listen when the leaders of the black supremacy movement speak." A one-sided indictment of the group designed to scare white liberals, outrage conservatives, and shame the civil rights establishment, the documentary had the unintended consequence of turning Malcolm and Elijah Muhammad into folk heroes within the black community. Nonetheless, mainstream media and civil rights leaders would repeat the film's characterization of the Nation as "black supremacists" preaching racial hatred. Six weeks later, Martin Luther King Jr. followed suit, describing the NOI as advocates of "black supremacy."[5]

Malcolm's instincts for public relations inspired the Nation to assume control of a narrative shaped by the white media. As civil rights leaders vilified the group by echoing the film's simple reverse-racism thesis, the Messenger headlined a massive rally in Harlem. Over six thousand supporters packed St. Nicholas Arena to hear Muhammad deliver a combative speech. He praised the Nation as part of a global Islamic community, which Malcolm's recent trip to the Middle East had resoundingly solidified. *The Hate That Hate Produced* had transported the NOI from the margins of the national civil rights movement to its center. The Nation's steadily increasing membership virtually exploded, from six thousand to over fifty thousand by 1961. The footage of all-black rallies designed to frighten whites energized portions of the black community that had only dim memories of the New Negro and Marcus Garvey, reinvigorating a strand of black radicalism that had been pushed to the sidelines of the American political and cultural mainstream. But while the press attention spurred unprecedented growth for the Nation, it also introduced new doubts, fears, and anxieties within the group's cloistered ranks. Skepticism and envy of Malcolm within the organization grew, as did rumors that he, and not Elijah Muhammad, exerted the most control. As the NOI flourished, Muhammad's genuine paternal love for Malcolm slowly curdled into deep suspicion and resentment.[6]

Martin Luther King Jr. confronted the controversy directly during an August 20 speech at the National Bar Association in Milwaukee. A week earlier, he had sent a telegram to President Eisenhower unsuccessfully urging him to issue a proclamation in support of school integration ahead of Soviet premier Nikita Khrushchev's visit to the States. In Milwaukee, King claimed that Eisenhower was on the wrong side of history's sweeping momentum for racial justice, characterizing the White House as "too silent and apathetic" in the midst of an epic freedom movement. "I fear that future historians will have to record that when America came to its most progressive moment of creative fulfillment in the area of human relations," said King, "it was temporarily held back by a chief executive who refused to make a strong positive statement morally condemning segregation."[7]

King condemned both major political parties in his speech. Accusing southern racists and right-wing northerners of unleashing toxic anti-democratic energies into the Democratic and Republican parties, King mockingly praised segregationists such as Mississippi senator James Eastland "because he airs his vicious prejudice all the time," in contrast with politicians who pretended to support black citizenship during election time, only to abandon black folk and "democracy itself" once in office. Near the end of the speech, without explicitly mentioning Malcolm X and the Nation, King decried the rise of black hate groups. "Black supremacy is as bad as white supremacy," he proclaimed, providing a phrase that continued the simple analogy between the Klan and black Muslims. This allegation overwhelmed his pungent criticisms of the Eisenhower administration, the Washington political establishment, and American democratic culture. King had misinterpreted Malcolm's call for radical black dignity as simply the continuation of racial oppression, with black folk assuming the negative role historically adopted by whites. What King referred to as "black supremacy," Malcolm defined as radical political self-determination—an affirming act that acknowledged the humanity long denied African Americans.[8]

Although King publicly repudiated the ideas of racial violence and separatism increasingly associated with the Nation and Malcolm X, he never engaged with Malcolm directly. Instead, King's biggest adversary on the subject of black militancy came from a recent outcast from the NAACP. In the pages of the pacifist magazine *Liberation*, Robert F. Williams channeled Malcolm's call for self-defense against white supremacy in an essay titled "Can Negroes Afford to Be Pacifists?" Williams turned a rash statement that "we must fight back" into a clarion call for black political action, arguing that nonviolent boycotts in Montgomery could not root out the evils that plagued Monroe, North Carolina, where he lived. Williams, a proud Marine who had enlisted the year the Supreme Court ordered school desegregation, noted that his own country taught him to fight and that "nowhere in the annals of history does the record show a people delivered from bondage by patience alone." Williams concluded his essay by accusing King of hypocritically supporting American violence during the Second World War as a moral good to defeat fascism but preventing defenseless Negroes from doing the same at home. Williams took particular umbrage with King's July 17 address at the fiftieth annual NAACP convention, where delegates debated and affirmed Williams's suspension from the organization. King had also condemned him during a speech to an NAACP youth contingent that evening but had praised black participation in the global struggle for democracy during the day, a contradiction the Monroe leader pounced on.[9]

Williams did characterize King as an effective leader in the civil rights struggle, but he contrasted the experiences of black people in rural hamlets like Monroe, where blacks confronted "savage violence," with the struggles of those whom King had led in Montgomery. "There is more power in socially organized masses on the march," countered King, "than there is in guns in the hands of a few desperate men." King blamed debates within the movement between nonviolence and self-defense on external forces who substituted "token integration" for the transformational power of fully integrating the nation's democratic institutions and public, civic, and social spaces. King's essay responding to Williams, "The Social Organization of Nonviolence," urged blacks to place their bodies on the front lines of an enduring nonviolent struggle capable of ridding the world of segregation. To do so, he argued, blacks would need to stop fighting among themselves and innovate new, creative forms of protest. In his public fight with Williams, King confronted Malcolm through a proxy, a pattern that would continue with Malcolm regularly debating Bayard Rustin, one of King's closest advisors, over the next three years.[10]

At the end of the decade, King left Montgomery and Dexter Avenue Baptist Church to return home to Atlanta, where he fulfilled Daddy King's dreams by finally assuming co-pastorship of Ebenezer Baptist Church. Malcolm, meanwhile, responded to the ferment of publicity and energy surrounding his global travels by founding the weekly newspaper *Muhammad Speaks* in 1960. An immediate sensation, the newspaper featured penetrating editorials, reports, and analyses of the unfolding civil rights revolution. Malcolm hired seasoned black reporters and dedicated journalists who covered the fight for black equality at the local, regional, national, and global levels. With a circulation that would grow to over a half million, *Muhammad Speaks* would document the rise of Black Power activism that overlapped with civil rights struggles at home and anti-colonial upheavals around the world. "Aftermath of Birmingham! Worldwide Echoes of U.S. Oppression," blared a typical headline during the early 1960s.[11]

In 1960, Malcolm X was leading a black nationalist movement that critics, including the *New York Times*, characterized as racial extremism. That year, buoyed by national media coverage and Malcolm's exhaustive speaking schedule, the NOI made deeper inroads into New York City's political landscape. Malcolm and the Nation led black nationalists across the five boroughs via mosques, small businesses, and well-attended religious rallies that served as de facto political events. They moved from competing with rival black nationalist sects for access to visiting African dignitaries to commanding the stage with political leaders such as Ghana's Kwame Nkrumah.[12]

The Nation of Islam's embrace of racial separatism and advocacy of self-defense turned them into a group perceived as both dangerous and exotic. Malcolm's rhetoric of racial solidarity against white supremacy found him superficially maintaining the Nation's official policy against formal political involvement; the NOI preferred instead to build up a nation of dedicated followers whose economic resources, religious faith, and personal dignity, they hoped, would shield them from the hardships of Jim Crow racism. As white interest in the Nation grew, so did the group's wish to shape the media narrative that surrounded it. They would do this most successfully through the founding of *Muhammad Speaks*. But the NOI also disallowed whites from attending Muslim religious service, and journalists had been barred from Elijah Muhammad's triumphant visit to Harlem the previous July. The NOI's popularity shifted political alliances in Harlem, turning Malcolm X and the group into power brokers, regularly consulted by black elected officials and religious and civic organizations. Other major civil rights groups, including the NAACP, remained distant but respectful.[13]

Malcolm's insistence on black dignity came alive when four black students from the historically black school North Carolina A&T staged a sit-in on February 1 to protest racial segregation at a Woolworth lunch counter in Greensboro, North Carolina. By peacefully sitting in the area reserved exclusively for white patrons, the students announced themselves as dissidents whose actions incited shock, controversy, and over time violence, arrests, and support. The sit-ins swelled over the following months. They started to include white activists, and they moved from North Carolina to other southern states and then finally to the North, where interracial groups of students organized sympathy demonstrations. With the lunch counter sit-ins, direct confrontation against Jim Crow captured the national imagination.

Although he remained skeptical of their steadfast belief in American democracy, Malcolm admired the boldness of the student activists. He alluded to the "new Negro"—black folk directly challenging white supremacy through demonstrations, pickets, and sit-ins—during a March 10 radio debate with journalist Barry Gray in New York. Malcolm and Gray parried over race, democracy, and social justice during the hour-long program. Malcolm identified himself as "a black man, despite complexion," noting that his fair skin, red hair, and freckles did not exclude him from a community he defined by membership in a shared history of oppression. Radicals "don't clap our hands and say hooray over the few" blacks who've made it, observed Malcolm. "We're thinking of the masses." His critique of American democracy took center stage; he observed that "anytime you have to make new bills or pass new bills to give voting privileges, or give voting rights, to approximately twenty million black people, then you can't just call these people citizens." For Malcolm, citizenship meant dignity, something new laws and legislation could not possibly bestow.[14]

Malcolm's rhetoric matched the tenor of the times. Ella Baker, a longtime critic of Martin Luther King Jr., recognized the sit-ins as a long-awaited opportunity. Baker organized an Easter weekend meeting at Shaw University in Raleigh, North Carolina, aimed to harness the political energies unleashed by the student activists. Time with King had convinced Baker that the movement needed a grassroots leadership that wasn't enmeshed with middle-class preachers. The meeting attracted dozens of the most gifted and dedicated student organizers around the country, many of whom remained impressed by King, who helped to sponsor the event. Baker urged them to turn the insurgent sit-in demonstrations into a permanent organization, one unattached to any existing civil rights group, untethered to any preexisting agenda, and unencumbered by top-down leadership. The Student Non-violent Coordinating Committee was born from these deliberations.

SNCC activists became soldiers on freedom's southern battlegrounds, practicing the tedious, dangerous, and unacknowledged work of organizing poor black sharecroppers in southwest Georgia, Arkansas, Mississippi, Alabama, and throughout the South. But SNCC's reach also extended along both coasts, where "friends of SNCC" groups popped up to organize sympathy demonstrations, hold fundraising events, and help publicize the group's efforts nationally. SNCC's campus affiliates, especially Howard University's Nonviolent Action Group, became effective lobbying organizations, protesting for racial integration in the building trades, testifying before the US Commission on Civil Rights, and lending an edge of northern militancy to the group's southern roots. SNCC also attracted religious students enthralled by King's example. Alabama native John Lewis, South Carolina's brilliantly combative Ruby Doris Smith Robinson, Atlanta's cosmopolitan Brahmin Julian Bond, and New Yorker with Caribbean roots Stokely Carmichael all gravitated toward SNCC.[15]

Many of these activists would come to form close relationships with King. His friend, Vanderbilt University seminarian James Lawson, helped to train student activists based in Nashville on nonviolent tactics and philosophy in the months leading up to the sit-ins. Other SNCC members, most notably Carmichael, deeply admired Malcolm X's criticism of white supremacy and advocacy of black pride. Howard University represented the group within SNCC most comfortable with Malcolm's brand of black radical politics. Two competing tendencies—which roughly paralleled the public arguments and philosophies adopted by Malcolm X and Martin Luther King Jr.—emerged within SNCC. For many, especially already devout Christians raised in the black southern church, nonviolence became a spiritual philosophy, and they looked toward Gandhi for inspiration. Malcolm's insistence on black dignity, on the other hand, appealed to the sensibilities of activists who longed for bold action in the face of white supremacy. The more secular-minded SNCC members adopted nonviolence as a useful tactic but argued for keeping all options open.[16]

King released a statement to reporters on April 15, the first day of the conference at Shaw University, that characterized the sit-in movement as the latest chapter of a global struggle for "dignity and freedom" and explained that the students were wielding the shield of nonviolent civil disobedience and mass protest as a weapon against racial subjugation. During the weekend in Raleigh, King discussed the rise of the student movement on NBC's *Meet the Press*. Moderator Ned Brooks identified King as the leader of a national movement for nonviolence that included the sit-in protests, the exact kind of suggestion that exasperated Baker and, over time, would disappoint some students. King applauded young people for showing the world "the indignities and injustices" blacks faced around the country. He pushed back against former president Harry Truman's assertion that private business had the right to choose whom to serve. He defended the concept of civil disobedience to the roundtable of journalists who questioned the morality of a movement that asked the federal government to enforce desegregation laws while trumpeting a right to civil disobedience. The "direct-action approach," argued King, sought to stir the conscience of the American public on behalf of both recently won civil rights victories and those freedoms that remained unwon.[17]

Malcolm responded to the fervor surrounding the sit-in demonstrations by organizing the Harlem Freedom Rally, an event whose political diversity reflected his continuing dreams of bringing a

Bandung Conference to Harlem. Four thousand people gathered on the last Saturday in May on Seventh Avenue and West 125th Street to hear Malcolm headline a six-hour program on the merits of racial solidarity. The "grave racial crisis confronting America," Malcolm explained, required creating a "diverse-thinking" united front. He promised his full support for "any fearless black leaders who will stand up and help the so-called American Negro get complete and immediate freedom." Roy Wilkins, citing previous commitments, failed to show, as did Martin Luther King Jr. and other civil rights leaders invited to the event. But the Freedom Rally amplified Malcolm's role as a secular political leader, comfortable enough in his own religious truths to preach a transcendent political message directed at "the black people of Harlem, the black people of America, and the black people all over this earth."[18]

Malcolm spent 1961 honing his speaking style for general audiences. He practiced introducing himself for his frequent radio appearances, often bypassing the host's canned remarks about reverse racism and black supremacy in favor of a respectfully succinct introduction: "I represent Mr. Elijah Muhammad, the spiritual head of the fastest-growing group of Muslims in the Western Hemisphere." Malcolm enjoyed debating civil rights moderates and black intellectuals, whom he derisively referred to as "professional Negroes." For Malcolm, such spokesmen were little more than puppets "for the white man." He also relished publicly sparring with racial integrationists, and he participated in two high-profile debates that year, the first with Reverend William James, a Harlem pastor, on WMCA radio, the same station that had carried his Barry Gray debate. The second, at Yale University Law School, featured NAACP youth secretary Herbert Wright. In both instances, Malcolm characterized the NOI's racial separatism as a philosophy based on strength and the realization that America's practice of racial segregation represented the country's core principles. Where civil rights activists, most notably King, argued that racial integration reflected the deepest aspirations of both whites and blacks, Malcolm objected. He defined segregation as the control of Negro bodies by whites—in contrast to separation, which was the voluntary promotion of self-determination for a black community in search of its own place in the world.[19]

That June, as the group prepared for a massive rally in the nation's capital headlined by the Messenger, Malcolm took key steps to politicize the Nation in support of radical black dignity. In the run-up to the event, he compared the Nation's organizing efforts to other civil rights groups, but with a twist. Muslims, he argued, wanted separation from white racism in the form of separate states within the United States so they could flourish and thrive, free from racial oppression. The impracticality of such a plan would prove irrelevant to the Nation's most ardent supporters, who entered into an unspoken agreement, just as the followers of Marcus Garvey's "back to Africa" plans had, that however unlikely physical separation proved to be, the very idea represented the dream of black political autonomy and independence.

Malcolm told reporters that thousands of non-Muslims planned to attend the DC rally. They felt "tired of the slow pace of token integration, too intelligent to submit patiently to continued segregation, and fed up completely with the compromising attitude of Negro leaders," he said. He spread rumors in the black press that the Messenger might go to the White House, backed by thousands of black folk hungry for bold leadership. The rally's theme, "Separation or Death," highlighted the Nation's self-promotion as an uncompromising group who willfully defied the racial integration promoted by civil rights groups in favor of self-determination. Despite the Messenger's absence due to illness, the event attracted between 7,500 and 10,000, a crowd that demonstrated the NOI's growing national appeal. Three thousand Muslims from New York alone attended the event. Wallace Muhammed, one of the Messenger's sons and a protégé of Malcolm's, characterized Muslims as a "peaceful people who can cause a great deal of trouble" and needed to be taken seriously. "Any Negro trying to integrate is actually admitting his inferiority," said Malcolm, "because he is also admitting that he wants to become part of a 'superior' society."[20]

Elijah Muhammad did make it to Harlem for his annual pilgrimage to the 369th Regiment Armory, where for the first time whites were allowed entrance to hear the Messenger speak. That same month, Malcolm attended a reception for Jaja Wachuku, the Speaker of the Nigerian House of Representatives, forging ties with African diplomats that would grow more intimate as the decade progressed.[21]

Fidel Castro's unexpected visit to Harlem in September 1961 confirmed Malcolm's new status. Black America's prosecuting attorney now shifted into a new role as the unofficial prime minister of African American radicalism. Castro, the dynamic young lawyer turned revolutionary guerrilla, led the 1959 Cuban Revolution that deposed the American-backed regime of Fulgencio Batista. A vocal critic of Western-style democracies, capitalism, and imperialism, Castro alarmed American political leaders and anti-communist cold warriors, even as he galvanized supporters of anti-colonial movements around the world. Cuba inspired large swaths of the American Left, including black radicals who toured the island, wrote articles about the new government's efforts to eliminate racial segregation, and touted Castro as an anti-racist leader bold enough to criticize America's Jim Crow policies and offer rhetorical support for liberation movements raging through Africa, the Caribbean, and Latin America.[22]

Malcolm met Fidel Castro during a midnight session that included reporters, photographers, and an interpreter. "I had always wanted to come to Harlem, but I was not sure what kind of welcome I would get," said Castro, holding court in his ninth-floor suite. "When I got news that I would be welcomed in Harlem, I was happy." As photographers took pictures of the two leaders smiling and chatting amiably, Malcolm assured Castro that "We in Harlem are not addicted to the propaganda they put out." The *New York Amsterdam News* gained exclusive access and carried a front-page story of the meeting, which showcased the ties between liberation struggles in black America and in the rest of the world.

During their brief stay at the Shelburne Hotel in Midtown Manhattan, the entire Cuban delegation alleged mistreatment that smacked of racism, while Shelburne staff accused them of obnoxious behavior—unleashing recriminations that left all parties dissatisfied. The Cubans relocated to the Hotel Theresa in Harlem. Castro, dressed in "immaculately creased" green fatigues, sat on the edge of a bed in his suite and invited Malcolm, wearing an overcoat, suit, and tie, to sit next to him. Malcolm greeted Castro, fully aware of the problems the delegation had had at the Shelburne. "Downtown for you, it was ice, uptown it is warm," Malcolm announced, in an opening volley that Castro heartily embraced. "Aahh yes, we feel very warm here," he said in halting, broken English. They discussed racial politics in America and around the world, with Castro remarking that Cuba accomplished in "18 months what you are still trying to do for 400 years." Castro touted efforts to end racial discrimination in Cuba as evidence of the kind of international solidarity that Malcolm had been preaching since he first learned of the Bandung Conference. "We are all brothers," explained Cuba's young leader. "The new nations and we in Latin America are all African Americans," he asserted, pointing to the fourteen African countries newly recognized by the United Nations. Malcolm and Castro bonded over shared reputations as unconventional political mavericks.[23]

The men both recognized the symbolic power of the Cuban delegation's visit to Harlem. Malcolm invited them to dine at the Nation of Islam's restaurant on 116th Street, but Castro declined the offer with his trademark sense of humor. "We want to cause as little trouble as possible," he replied. "We will try to eat all our meals here in the hotel." Malcolm departed with an invitation from Castro to visit Cuba and a renewed sense of the black freedom movement's international possibilities. The *New York Citizen-Call* featured a photo of a beaming Malcolm and Castro on its front cover. The *New York Amsterdam News* splashed a boldfaced headline, "Castro Talks," above its exclusive interview, while secondary headlines "Bars White Press; He Calls Himself 'African American'" played up the novelty of a white-skinned Cuban boldly identifying with Negroes in the language of Malcolm X and the Muslims.[24]

Malcolm's meeting with Castro turned into a public-relations coup, as well as a small rebellion against the Messenger's strict orders to avoid political activism. The high-profile appearance acknowledged that the Nation was more than just a religious group led by a former Georgia sharecropper. It identified the organization as a political force within the United States, important enough to warrant a meeting with the new leader of revolutionary Cuba. As the black press feted Castro as a charismatic political ally, Malcolm defended himself against external charges of subversion in the press and internal grumblings among Muslims who considered his unsanctioned meeting to be reckless. Elijah Muhammad went as far as publicly rebuking his protégé through an interview with *Washington Post* reporter Wallace Terry, saying that if he had known Malcolm planned to meet Castro he "would have prevented it." Muhammad's anger over the meeting was based on several considerations. The sixty-three-year-old Messenger suffered from debilitating pulmonary disease; rumors that Malcolm would take over the Nation after his death increased with each passing day. Also, his alliance with the Messenger's son, Wallace, touched off alarm bells within the royal family. And his unauthorized sit-down with Castro further strengthened the impression, within and outside the group, that Malcolm operated independently of Muhammad's leadership.[25]

Despite the Messenger's disapproval of his freelance diplomacy, Malcolm continued, using the cover of his membership in the Twenty-Eighth Precinct's welcoming committee not only to gain access to a secular world Muhammad insisted was doomed,

but to shape that world politically. Participation in the committee represented Malcolm's assumption of local political leadership
in Harlem. "Fidel Castro has denounced racial discrimination in
Cuba, which is more than President Eisenhower has done here in
America," Malcolm defiantly told reporters from the *Pittsburgh
Courier*. Castro's stance against lynching, a position the president
refused to publicly take, was reason enough to meet with him, even
though Malcolm backpedaled from pro-communist statements.
"I went to see Castro as a Muslim," Malcolm assured reporters.
Still, he remained unapologetic about the meeting, claiming he
preferred to be seen with Castro than with "some prominent white
people here in the United States." He praised Castro as "the only
white person he ever liked."[26]

Ghanaian president Kwame Nkrumah spoke in Harlem one
week later. Nkrumah represented the latest Third World revolutionary to visit Harlem in a fortnight, following appearances
by Castro, Egypt's Gamal Abdel Nasser, and India's Jawaharlal
Nehru. On a stage outside the Hotel Theresa, Nkrumah called
Negroes the "strongest link between the people of North America
and the people of Africa." The speech echoed Malcolm's burgeoning pan-Africanism. "I wanted you to know that my presence in
Harlem would show the solid bond we feel between the people
of Africa and the Afro-Americans in this country," proclaimed
Nkrumah, deploying the descriptive term for blacks favored by
Malcolm X. One thousand people attended an afternoon rally,
made all the more remarkable by the fact that Malcolm's radical
message of pan-African solidarity as the key to black liberation at
home was becoming mainstream. Nkrumah reminisced about his
time spent in Harlem as a young man and invited black America's "artisans, doctors, scientists" to Ghana to aid a revolution that
offered the tantalizing hope of ending colonial rule in Africa and
around the world. Nkrumah's passionate words about the "loss of
dignity for the African people" representing "a loss of dignity for

people of African descent everywhere" would resonate immediately in the New Year, following news of the assassination of Congolese prime minister Patrice Lumumba.[27]

Malcolm X and Martin Luther King Jr. would never meet in a formal debate; however, both were acutely aware of one another. More than that, they were each building—both consciously and unconsciously—a public persona that served as a response to the other. King's stature in mainstream America and around the world was greater than Malcolm's while both men were still alive. But Malcolm bested King among the black quotidian: the unrefined mass of African Americans who, like him, held no college degrees, survived life on the streets, and were unashamed of stints in jail. If King could claim increasing dominion over national civil rights affairs, Malcolm relished his status as Harlem's political hero. He settled for debating a wide array of proxies for King, individuals who advocated nonviolence and racial integration and were simultaneously opposed to black nationalism, self-defense, and racial separatism.

Malcolm debated these high-profile civil rights activists because doing so increased his political notoriety around the nation. Activists such as Bayard Rustin and CORE leader James Farmer participated for the same reason. Malcolm's words of fire gave political cover to civil rights organizers seeking to appear more politically moderate than their personal histories suggested. Rustin fit this description perfectly, since his ties to pacifists and socialists and his barely hidden homosexuality made him a perpetual target within and outside of movement circles.

Paradoxically, these debates drew the movement and Malcolm closer to one another, even as they highlighted stark political and ideological divisions. Fiery debates with Rustin and Farmer developed into more intimate friendships offstage. Farmer admired Malcolm, who returned his affection in the form of humorous banter that papered over their political differences. Farmer's respect illustrated Malcolm's influence among seasoned activists who sharply disagreed with him. Farmer's deep roots in pacifism and racial-justice activism stretched back two decades to the Second World War, when interracial groups of activists embraced Gandhian methods against Jim Crow. But for a younger generation of CORE activists, especially in New York and Chicago, Malcolm's rhetorical eloquence deeply moved them. Farmer himself would concede as much, describing a strong sense of racial pride as a healthy, even necessary, perquisite to justice and equality for black people. Over time, access to Malcolm's defiant vision of black political self-determination would transform CORE from its pacifist roots into an organization that embraced black nationalism.[28]

Malcolm X's rhetoric and the NOI's disciplined presence galvanized black nationalists in Harlem. The death of Congolese prime minister Lumumba on January 17, 1961, compelled them to action. Lumumba was a political activist who had been released from jail to serve as the former Belgian Congo's first democratically elected prime minister the previous summer. Young, handsome, and an outspoken critic of Western colonialism, he became an icon of African independence in 1960. The United Nations called the start of the new decade the "year of Africa," and many black radicals in America considered Lumumba to be the continent's brightest star. But an alliance between Belgian officials and Congolese reactionaries, with the implicit approval of America's State Department, which blanched at the young prime minister's overtures to the Soviet Union, sealed Lumumba's fate. News of his death reached the States in February, and Harlem activists, many with direct ties to Malcolm X, organized an unprecedented demonstration inside the UN building. *New York Amsterdam News* editor James Hicks called Lumumba's death an "international lynching of a black man on the altar of white supremacy." The Congo crisis rescued an earlier generation of black activists from political obscurity, unleashing a torrent of organizing energies that allowed fledgling black nationalists, seasoned Marxists, and anti-colonialists of all stripes to find a unity of purpose. The tragedy also offered an international seminar in world affairs for budding pan-Africanists such as Maya Angelou and literary troublemaker LeRoi Jones, as well as Harlem nationalists poised to bear public witness against a "lynching staged before the world under the auspices of the United Nations."[29]

While not directly involved in organizing the demonstration, Malcolm's political example framed the protest's confrontational posture and militancy. Angelou, Jones, and Rosa Guy were among those who participated in what the *New York Times* called an "invasion" of the UN. While protesters battled security guards inside the organization's Forty-Second Street headquarters, hundreds of demonstrators gathered outside First Avenue and Forty-Third Street in a muscular display of black political radicalism—a scene that would be repeated when groups of black nationalists assembled in Times Square and Harlem to continue protesting Lumumba's murder.[30]

James Baldwin instantly recognized the UN demonstration as the black community's radical political awakening in support of African independence, Third World liberation, and the elimination of Jim Crow. Baldwin's "A Negro Assays the Negro Mood" appeared in the *New York Times* and discussed the ways in which politicians studiously avoided analyzing the roots of the UN protests in favor of blaming communist bogeymen and Muslim agitators. Southerners, Baldwin argued, blamed northern blacks for civil rights protests, while America "blames the Kremlin."[31]

In the aftermath of the protest, reports cast Malcolm as the leader of a secular revolt that threatened to overshadow the Messenger's restrictions against political activism, which created further distance between Elijah Muhammad and his most talented and devoted follower. Malcolm, publicly blamed for the melee inside the UN and protests outside, threatened to sue anyone, including Adlai Stevenson and New York police commissioner Stephen Kennedy, who accused him and the NOI of taking part in the controversial protests. Malcolm neither condemned nor praised the demonstrations, vowing to "permit no one to use me against the nationalists" to discredit a movement after his own heart. At the same time, he balked at media requests to disavow the violence associated with the protests. From the point of view of law enforcement, political officials, and journalists, Malcolm's fingerprints were all over these events. They recognized Malcolm's rhetoric as possessing the unique ability to inspire segments of the black community unaffiliated with the religious teachings he advocated. For a growing corpus of black folk around the nation, Malcolm, rather than any group he represented, inspired both belief and action. His domestic activism dovetailed with his political support for global anti-colonial struggles. His trip to the Middle East, meetings with African diplomats in Harlem, rendezvous with Fidel Castro at the Hotel Theresa, and relationships with the black nationalists who had organized the UN demonstrations had showcased his diplomatic side as black America's unofficial prime minister.[32]

CHAPTER 4

A World on Fire

I n 1960, Martin Luther King was arrested at an Atlanta sit-in alongside of young SNCC activist Julian Bond. The sit-in had come on the heels of an ultimatum from student leader Lonnie King. The activist had admonished Martin Luther King Jr., perhaps the movement's most symbolic leader, for making grand speeches without ever putting his own body in harm's way. King's reluctance to do so would become a running theme over the next several years. For the SNCC contingent at Howard University, his distance from the gritty realities of everyday struggles—the arrests, physical violence, and small and large humiliations—made him a suspect leader. In contrast, John Lewis, a native of Alabama who became part of a group of Nashville activists dedicated to nonviolent protests, typified the students who admired King. Lewis, the future chairman of SNCC, revered King to the point of unconscious imitation, and he adopted nonviolence as a personal philosophy. A smaller faction, including Stokely Carmichael, navigated a middle ground that identified King's uncanny rapport with ordinary black folk as an opportunity for local organizers to shape the movement as they saw fit. King's projection of affable humility and quiet courage attracted the widest spectrum of black humanity—people of all types came to see him, shake his hand, and hear his rich oratory.[1]

King carried himself in an unpretentious manner that rural blacks gravitated toward. In the Mississippi delta, he ate pickled pig's feet right out of the jar, challenged skeptical teenagers to games of pool, and attracted local blacks curious to see in person the man they had heard so much about. King's fame translated into fuel that helped to create a powerful movement on the ground; one that at times benefited student activists and at times diverted attention and resources from them. King's very presence, with its ability to attract thousands who would otherwise remain on the sideline, buoyed activists seeking entrée into some of the nation's most uncultivated political regions.[2]

Martin Luther King Jr. found himself at the center of events that roiled national politics, negotiating between and among several disparate strands of the black freedom struggle. The sit-in movement compelled him to act as a mediator between young activists impatient with a legalistic approach to racial justice and Roy Wilkins, the NAACP's formidable executive director. On the side of the students stood King's friend James Lawson, whose reputation as a nonviolent firebrand was more in tune with the temperature of young civil rights activists during the spring of 1960. Lawson's stature among student radicals grew after his expulsion from Vanderbilt University's Divinity School for helping to organize demonstrations throughout Nashville. Lawson authored parts of SNCC's statement of purpose, noting that nonviolence sought "a social order of justice permeated by love." Roy Wilkins fumed after excerpts from Lawson's talk to students during the initial student conference in North Carolina were leaked to the *New York Times*. Lawson's characterization of the NAACP as "a fundraising agency" and "a legal agency" that failed to leverage the power of the black grassroots sent Wilkins into overdrive. He pointedly reminded King in a letter that the NAACP had "rushed in to help the youngsters," and he seemed mystified by Lawson's anger.[3]

In truth, Lawson's close association with King exacerbated existing tensions between the NAACP and King's organization, the

SCLC. Both groups found themselves competing for a pool of overlapping financial resources. King enjoyed more name recognition and star power, but the NAACP tapped into a far more extensive network of political and cultural resources. King found himself explaining his deep admiration for the NAACP not only to Roy Wilkins, but to Jackie Robinson, the former star athlete turned businessman and civil rights advocate. Robinson parlayed his breaking of Major League Baseball's color line in 1947 into a second act as one of the nation's leading racial-justice advocates. King assured him that "I have never seen conflict" between the NAACP and the SCLC and said he hoped only for "the possibility of the greatest harmony."[4]

Although King had a natural gift for mediating disputes, he largely avoided confronting tensions within the SCLC and the wider movement, at least until they reached a breaking point. He wanted to be liked. This style of leadership infuriated some, puzzled others, and worried his closest advisors, Stanley Levison and Bayard Rustin, who were, more often than not, delegated the hard decisions that King refused to make. From this vantage point, King found himself increasingly buffeted by forces beyond his control. Direct-action protests increased his reputation as a national civil rights leader while also expanding the number of organizations and activists who now held him accountable for mistakes, failures, and shortcomings. King's political skills, for the most part, were deft enough for him to portray himself as a statesman of the movement. He had enough humility to reach out to almost the entire spectrum of black politics in a manner that transcended petty differences, and he inspired civil rights activists to display in action the united front that Malcolm X talked of in theory.[5]

On May 26, 1960, James Baldwin wrote to King, whom he had briefly met two years earlier, requesting time for an extended interview. "If you will permit it, and it is possible, I would simply like to be allowed to follow you about for a day or two, or longer, in order to be made able to convey some dim approximation of what it is like to be in your position," wrote Baldwin. He turned up at Ebenezer and was indeed granted an interview, which ultimately turned into something more. The outcome was an essay in *Harper's* magazine, "The Dangerous Road before Martin Luther King." In *Harper's*, Baldwin expressed open admiration for King's infinite potential to serve as a steadying force during America's tumultuous political maturation. The nation's growing pains included banishing ideas of racial superiority, "for the myth of white supremacy is exploding all over the world, from the Congo to New Orleans." King's unapologetic love for black people made him speak with a bracing candor that traversed fault lines on both sides of America's racial divide. King's awareness that segregation was doomed disturbed the realities of white racists, some black nationalists, and moderates alike. Baldwin recognized unrealized depths in King, just as he did in Malcolm. The essay hinted at the potential for revolutionary transformation that lurked beneath King's political shield. It showcased him as a work in progress whose genuine affection for black folk was only matched by his passion to eradicate all vestiges of racial inequality in American life.[6]

King, as the most recognizable face of civil rights protest, was trying to navigate a national groundswell of organizing that now surpassed the militancy he had injected into the Montgomery protest. At thirty-one, he developed a sober, high-minded, and steadfast image of a political leader that lent him the gravitas of a more mature figure. By this point, his public image displayed the emotional scars of five years in the national spotlight. His reputation had taken a hit during the presidential election, when he faced charges of signing false Alabama tax returns for two of the last four years. Although he was found not guilty in May, the legal distractions, a crushing travel schedule, and a demanding home life that included Coretta pregnant with their third child made it virtually impossible for King to exert the kind of leadership he or his most ardent admirers hoped for.[7]

In 1960, King became friendly with John F. Kennedy, the young senator who eagerly courted his endorsement during a clandestine meeting arranged by Harry Belafonte and Kennedy aide Harris Wofford at the beginning of the summer. King's moral passion for civil rights made the cerebral Kennedy uncomfortable. The candidate was initially cautious on racial-justice matters, careful not to alienate the southern votes he would need in a general election, an attitude of reticence that disappointed King. The two men came away from their initial meeting regarding each other as more necessary professional allies than kindred spirits. Closer personally to Nixon, whom he had met at the White House and in Ghana, King refused to publicly endorse either candidate. But, after King was arrested for the sit-in in Atlanta, Kennedy had worked to secure his freedom, and he released a statement of being "deeply indebted to Senator Kennedy, who served as a great force in making my release possible." Daddy King followed these words with deeds, rallying those within his sphere of influence to support Kennedy with votes. King's unintentionally pivotal role in electing Kennedy president helped him regain his political footing.[8]

The Kennedy campaign strategically benefited from King's Atlanta arrest and subsequent release in October 1960, just weeks before the election. The campaign bombarded black Atlanta with a last-minute pamphlet contrasting the vice president, who remained silent about King's arrest, with the young Massachusetts senator: "'No Comment' Nixon versus a Candidate with a Heart, Senator Kennedy." The pamphlet, and more importantly the actions that inspired it, helped Kennedy win upward of 70 percent of black votes nationally; something that King would spend the next year repeatedly reminding the new president. Kennedy's election thrust King, for the first time, into the position that he would occupy for the rest of his life: the presidential alter ego on race matters and the conscience of the nation with respect to social justice, civil rights, and the conviction that the struggle for black citizenship represented the beating heart of American democracy.[9]

Throughout 1961, King discovered the limits of being bound to rules that Malcolm frequently ignored. The postelection Kennedy transition to the White House proved especially challenging. An exhausted King debated James J. Kilpatrick, the segregationist editor of the *Richmond News Leader*, on the NBC show *The Nation's Future* on Saturday, November 26. The thirty-minute debate left King feeling despondent for having failed to take Kilpatrick to school on the moral rightness of civil disobedience. Kilpatrick's assertion that sit-ins sparked "a great deal of tense pushing and shoving, in an atmosphere that is electric with restrained violence and hostility" placed King on the defensive. King's efforts to explain the "great distinction between the immoral, hateful, violent resistance of many white segregationists" followed the rules of civilized public engagement about race in America, but his equanimity displeased student militants.[10]

During the course of the 1960 presidential campaign, John F. Kennedy had openly supported the civil rights movement, going as far as speaking approvingly of sit-in demonstrations at a lunch with African diplomats. The candidate spoke to thousands of black activists the day before the Democratic National Convention in Los Angeles and promised "no second-class citizenship for any American." During a Harlem appearance less than a month before the election, he vowed to eliminate racial segregation in federal housing "with a stroke of a pen," a campaign promise that thrilled black supporters. But once he reached the White House, Kennedy's famous energy stalled on racial-justice issues. His delay in proposing strong civil rights legislation especially disappointed King, who dreamed of finding with the young president the political chemistry that he lacked with Eisenhower. King approached Kennedy as a fellow statesman; Kennedy intermittently recognized this fact but preferred avoiding confronting racial injustice until crisis engulfed his administration, leaving him no other recourse but to forge an alliance with King. Kennedy's creation of a presidential committee on equal employment opportunity and efforts to add the Justice Department to a list of plaintiffs calling for school desegregation in Prince Edward County, Virginia, proved to be more token gestures of goodwill than comprehensive policy reform.[11]

In the February 4, 1961, issue of the *Nation*, King threw down the gauntlet. In his essay, "Equality Now: The President Has the Power," King pressed Kennedy to publicly support the struggle for black citizenship in word and deed. "The new Administration has the opportunity to be the first in one hundred years of American history to adopt a radically new approach to the question of civil rights," wrote King. He urged Kennedy to embark on a bold plan of promoting racial justice through executive orders and to use the White House as a bully pulpit. Such actions were necessary, since "the federal government is the nation's highest investor in segregation." King demanded that the Kennedy administration take up civil rights as a national cause in the same manner that the Roosevelt administration had enacted the New Deal during the Great Depression. Recalling his trip to India and efforts to aid the "untouchables," King suggested that black disenfranchisement required extraordinary measures to remedy, underscoring his support for affirmative action–style programs that would become federal policy within a decade. He prodded the president to make good on a promise to end housing segregation with the stroke of a pen. Civil rights and the federal government were destined to be allies, he argued, although they would be forever locked in creative tension over the speed of the unfolding political revolution.[12]

In retrospect, King's blunt truths about the Kennedy administration should have caught Malcolm X's attention, since both leaders expressed public disappointment over the political mistreatment of blacks. But if Malcolm ignored King's pointed criticism at the president, Kennedy seemed to distance himself from a movement that helped him get elected. Bowing to pressure from southern senators, Kennedy refused to appoint King's mentor, Morehouse president Benjamin Mays, to the US Commission on Civil Rights. King voiced his displeasure in public, through a telegram to Kennedy printed in the *Atlanta Daily World*, calling efforts to stifle Mays's appointment nothing short of a tragedy. King's efforts to forge an alliance with Kennedy did not preclude him from publicly criticizing what he considered the administration's repeated blunders and missed opportunities on civil rights issues.[13]

While King was attempting in vain to schedule a private meeting with the president, the Atlanta movement reached a settlement with city officials to integrate downtown stores within thirty days of public school desegregation, scheduled for September. The apparent victory left a bad taste in the mouths of students, especially local leader Lonnie King, who threatened to upend the agreement by continuing the protests that black leaders, led by Daddy King, had promised to immediately end. King found himself walking a tightrope between protecting Daddy King's reputation as one of Atlanta's preeminent race men and understanding the simmering impatience of student activists. King watched in silence, at one point his eyes welling with tears, on Friday, March 10, as students denounced the agreement as fool's gold for not immediately ending segregation and attacked Daddy King as some kind of modern-day Uncle Tom.

In response to criticism from student activists, Daddy King touted his three decades in the city as proof of his commitment to justice, only to have one person cry out, "That's what's wrong!" One thousand people had packed Atlanta's Warren Memorial United Methodist Church for the meeting, and tensions rose until a passionately composed King spoke. He defended Daddy King from the humiliating taunts and accusations of betraying black interests to white power brokers downtown. King noted that he would be "terribly hurt if anybody said to me, 'Martin Luther King, Jr., you sold us out!'" King's pleas calmed dissent, producing a united front in the face of political chaos. But although he defended Daddy King publicly, the students' anger resonated within him deeply.

King personally identified with the courage of student demon-strators who, in his mind, did not receive enough support from the black middle class and elites, including his father.[14]

In April 1961, King managed to secure a lunch meeting with Attorney General Robert F. Kennedy, the president's hard-charging younger brother, at the Mayflower Hotel in Washington. King made a good impression on Bobby Kennedy. King's focus on voting rights dovetailed with the Justice Department's efforts to harness the energy of street demonstrations into pragmatic ac-tion. Bobby personally gave King the private telephone numbers of Burke Marshall and John Seigenthaler, two Justice Department officials who would come to regard the civil rights struggle as both a professional responsibility and a personal cause. Harris Wofford, the Kennedy aide who set up the meeting, took King for an im-promptu tour of the White House that same day. "It's good to see you," remarked President Kennedy to King as they shook hands. The two men chatted briefly, but not substantively, about civil rights in general. The president mentioned that he kept up with the movement mainly through his brother Bobby. Both King's substantive meeting with Bobby Kennedy and more informal chat with the president were off the record. Yet they proved critically important as the year progressed. The meetings offered private tribute to the manner in which some of America's most powerful leaders regarded King as a conduit to the civil rights movement's beating heart. King now met with the president and attorney gen-eral as the leading representative of the black freedom struggle, an acknowledgment that no previous administration had offered.[15]

The Freedom Rides, inaugurated the next month by a group of baby-faced students who deeply admired both Kennedy and King, put civil rights squarely on the national agenda by precipitating confrontation between peaceful groups of interracial activists and violent white mobs. For student activists and politicians, King served primarily as a political mobilizer and lightning rod. Rais-ing enough money to maintain the SCLC's annual expenses of

$84,000 required King to conduct grueling speaking tours, sometimes delivering five speeches in one day.[16] But even though King was busy running the SCLC, journalists, politicians, segregationists, and anti-racists alike identified King as the leader of Freedom Rides. The Freedom Riders boarded Greyhound and Trailways buses, two small groups of integrated passengers determined to journey through Dixie's heart to challenge racial segregation in travel facilities. On May 14, ten days after their initial departure from Washington, DC, the Freedom Riders experienced spasms of racial violence in Anniston, Alabama—a vicious assault, fire-bombing, and bloody attack that made front-page news nationally and around the world. White mobs attacked again in Birmingham, and reinforcements from universities around the country rushed to continue demonstrations that now forced a hesitant Kennedy administration into action.[17]

On Sunday, May 21, 1961, King presided over an MIA-sponsored rally in support of the Freedom Riders in Montgomery, Alabama. The massive gathering of one thousand people convened at Ralph Abernathy's First Baptist Church in the city's downtown. In attendance were several Freedom Riders who had experienced the violence in Anniston. Alabama's segregationist governor John Patterson used the presence of the riders to amp up supporters, who interpreted Bobby Kennedy's use of federal marshals to partially escort riders away from conflict zones as government power run amok. Against this emotionally charged backdrop, King spoke to the congregation while a white mob gathered around First Baptist Church, turning a site of refuge into a potential ambush. "We will present our physical bodies as instruments to defeat the unjust system," King preached from the pulpit.[18]

King called Bobby Kennedy just after 10:00 p.m., seeking reassurances that federal marshals could protect those inside the church. Bobby's attempt at gallows humor—asking King "to pray for us" that those inside and outside of First Baptist would be unharmed—fell flat. King forcefully reiterated his fear that the entire church might be burned down and, in the process, managed to convey the sense of personal terror that Bobby's comments had sought to deflect. "The deputy marshals are coming," the attorney general explained, attempting to soothe an agitated King. The awkward exchange revealed the men's lack of personal chemistry and contrasting temperaments. King's raw vulnerability during the crisis exhibited the kind of emotion that made Bobby Kennedy uneasy. Similarly, the attorney general's ability to find dark humor against the backdrop of potential racial violence struck King as unseemly. Despite the rough start, several hours later reinforcements—in the guise of one thousand National Guard troops, promised by Bobby Kennedy and begrudgingly sanctioned by Governor Patterson—arrived and dispersed the mob.[19]

The next day, two busloads of Freedom Riders departed Montgomery for Jackson, Mississippi, under heavy guard. Jackson authorities promised to arrest them on arrival, and Bobby Kennedy hoped to convince the students to accept being bailed out by the Justice Department instead of remaining in jail—and therefore continuing to make national headlines. Before departing, the Freedom Riders, led by Nashville student leader Diane Nash, met with King to request that he accompany them to Jackson. King refused, citing the fact that he remained on probation from a Georgia traffic stop the previous year; a new arrest might plunge him into further legal turmoil. When some riders volunteered that they were pressing on to Jackson despite their own tenuous legal status, King dispatched with his lawyerly defense. He instead asserted the right "to choose the time and place" of his political showdown with the forces of segregation. His admiration for the courageous student activists stopped short of joining them, despite the disappointment it produced within activist circles that stretched far beyond Montgomery. King felt conflicted: the tumult of national events related to civil rights found him juggling multiple roles, at times unsuccessfully. The public, including the White House, considered him to be the singular figure behind demonstrations swirling across the country, even though King knew differently. Authorities credited King, like they had with Malcolm X, as the mastermind behind sprawling protests that he had no direct ties to. This perception granted King considerable power while also jeopardizing his image as an authentic champion of black struggle in the eyes of students and activists. Ultimately, King sought to assume a measure of control over events by refusing to place himself in harm's way for a demonstration that he did not originally organize.[20]

King's role as an intermediary between the Freedom Riders and the Kennedy administration increased after the activists departed Montgomery on Wednesday, May 24. Bobby Kennedy, who hoped to avert another crisis, or at least remove the protests from headlines, was dismayed when police arrested twenty-seven riders attempting to use segregated facilities inside the Jackson bus depot. His efforts to bail out those arrested were thwarted by the Freedom Riders' decision, modeled after Gandhi, to stay in jail as a declaration of conscience against Jim Crow. After releasing a statement to the press advocating "a cooling-off period" from further demonstrations, Bobby Kennedy called King demanding to know why the riders insisted on remaining in jail. King succinctly described the students' thinking as resistance based on "a moral obligation to accept the penalty"—words the attorney general interpreted as a threat. "The fact that they stay in jail is not going to have the slightest effect on me," he responded. "They'll stay," said King, ending the conversation. King's resolve and the Freedom Riders' actions compelled the attorney general to act, which he did the following Monday by ordering the Interstate Commerce Commission (ICC) to end segregation in all travel facilities. Although the rides continued, interest in the spectacles of violence that greeted the first wave waned.[21]

That summer, King, the Justice Department, philanthropic groups, and civil rights organizations convened in secret to organize voter-registration efforts that could be afforded legal protection from the federal government and, the Kennedy administration naively believed, might prove less troublesome than sit-ins and Freedom Rides. The Voter Education Project (VEP) drew from practically the entire civil rights movement, although the SCLC received the largest resources, even as SNCC would provide the bulk of the field workers required to make headway in some of the most dangerous parts of the country. Tensions flared over students' fears that King's presence would divert SNCC money to the SCLC. He denied the charge, but it remained a point of contention. In truth, King's political stature and name recognition did place the SCLC in competition with funds over rival civil rights groups. His celebrity was a constant source of irritation for young activists who believed, correctly as it turned out, that much of their grueling fieldwork in the Deep South would be credited to the Georgia preacher.

King's national profile grew larger in the aftermath of the Freedom Rides. For King, the events of that spring reverberated loudest in official corridors of power. The Kennedy administration, despite its initial concerns, preferred to negotiate directly with King instead of with the students, a position that gave him more leverage than he had enjoyed with the previous administration. King's conversations, debates, and disagreements with Bobby Kennedy planted the seeds of political transformation within the White House on race matters. King prodded the Kennedy brothers in public and private to embrace racial justice as the centerpiece of American democracy and a core national value. The effects of these conversations would be revealed on the centennial of the emancipation of racial slavery.

King's proximity to power drew closer scrutiny from FBI director J. Edgar Hoover. After being privately admonished by the president over the bureau's conspicuously low profile during the Freedom Rides crisis, Hoover immediately recovered by producing a report marking King as a political subversive worthy of deeper investigation. At the same time, King's image as an American Gandhi was taking a hit in the eyes of the student activists who witnessed his caution during the Freedom Rides up close. King found himself shaken by events beyond his control, but he was also buoyed by the new opportunities for constructive engagement with federal officials. After the Freedom Rides, he sought to take greater command of shaping the civil rights movement's agenda, rather than simply reacting to unfolding political dramas.[22]

Since the success of the Montgomery bus boycott, King's primary role had been as the movement's spokesperson, ad hoc behind-the-scenes negotiator, faith leader, and public intellectual. But King had grown weary of entering political campaigns only at the flashpoint of crisis. He sought to change these circumstances by forcing the SCLC to adapt to a shifting national landscape. One of King's biggest talents was his ability to mobilize already motivated populations of black people in search of justice. Now, he looked for the perfect opportunity to do just that: on Monday, October 16, 1961, seven months after King's initial request, President Kennedy finally met with him at the White House.

The meeting came five weeks after King published a *New York Times* essay comparing the activism of the Freedom Riders to liberation movements spreading across Africa. He reported that black students told him that just as "African brothers can break the bonds of colonialism, surely the American Negro can break Jim Crow." Black high school and college students' "extraordinary willingness to fill the jails as if they were honor classes" and their disciplined commitment to nonviolence in the face of brutality exemplified a new kind of political revolution. Following a meeting with Bobby Kennedy, King urged the president to formally announce a "Second Emancipation Proclamation," a gesture he felt would move beyond symbolism by throwing the full weight and prestige of the presidency behind the movement. Kennedy declined to announce a new emancipation proclamation or propose a comprehensive civil rights bill, arguing that political opposition in Congress was too great. He eased the disappointment of this response with an offer to show King his private second-floor residence, a tour led by First Lady Jacqueline Kennedy.[23]

While King found President Kennedy to be an intelligent and skilled leader, he also thought that Kennedy lacked the "moral passion" to truly embrace the cause of racial justice. King's hour-long talk with the president left him disappointed but resolute. Kennedy likewise remained unaffected by King's conviction that the quest for black citizenship held the key to advancing American democracy. An active and attentive listener, Kennedy made for a sympathetic if skeptical audience, one that could, under the right circumstances, rally to the cause of civil rights with the qualities of passion and empathy that signaled politically advanced leadership. King said as much during a press conference with reporters immediately after the meeting.[24]

The time had come, King pleaded, for "an executive order outlawing all forms of segregation" in America. To reporters, King recounted telling Kennedy details about voting-rights efforts being waged by SNCC in tiny and racially volatile McComb, Mississippi. The cordial tone of King's remarks belied their clear political intention. King, the social leader, positioned himself as a black statesman capable of pressuring the Kennedy administration into committing public support for the civil rights movement. King believed that racial justice required more than new laws. The birth of a new American age required the transformation of hearts and minds, a quest that King now embarked on to teach to the president, the attorney general, and the entire nation the depth and breadth of an unfolding "social revolution" that he endeavored to remain at the center of.[25]

Malcolm X debated Bayard Rustin on the subject of "separation or integration" at Howard University two weeks after King's meeting with Kennedy. The event was a watershed moment in the evolving racial consciousness of young black student activists galvanized by the sit-in movement. SNCC's campus affiliate at

Howard, the Nonviolent Action Group, helped to organize the event. Stokely Carmichael, still recovering from over a month spent in Mississippi's Parchman Farm penitentiary for his service as a Freedom Rider, helped to recruit students to attend the debate. Most of the politically active students in attendance expected Rustin to win handily. They knew him as an outspoken organizer, pacifist, and advisor to A. Philip Randolph and, more importantly, Martin Luther King Jr. Rustin also expected to win. In the run-up to the debate, he informed Malcolm that he would attack him for "having no political, social, or economic program for dealing with the problems of blacks." Malcolm was up to the challenge. "I'll take you up on that," he responded.[26]

More than two thousand people turned out for the debate, moderated by the eminent Howard University sociologist E. Franklin Frazier. Rustin characterized Malcolm's proposal of racial separatism as impractical. "If this ship sinks what possible chance do you think your 'separate' state would have?" Rustin asked. Malcolm pushed past the practicalities of the NOI's philosophy and focused on the struggle for black dignity, one he claimed racial integration denied. "The black man in American will never be equal to the white man as long as he attempts to force himself into his house," Malcolm retorted. Both speakers received loud cheers during parts of the debate; however, Malcolm's performance touched students and faculty in a visceral and unexpected way.[27]

"Howard will never be the same," said one professor after listening to the debate. "I feel a reluctance to face my class tomorrow." Carmichael, who sat in the front row in awe of both speakers, remembered the occasion as an inflection point, "when nationalism took its firm root" in SNCC. Malcolm's presence at Howard inspired black students who equated freedom with racial integration to reconsider their position. The Muslim leader's talk of racial pride, political self-determination, and black solidarity motivated a generation of young activists to imbibe large quantities of black history, investigate the significance of African decolonization, and reimagine the meaning of African American identity in Western culture.[28]

Students had organized a dinner for Malcolm just before the debate, where they listened as he drank coffee, smiled, and exhibited a sense of humor and grace they found to be surprisingly endearing. Carmichael especially came away impressed. Malcolm patiently addressed questions from students, "and with every answer his stock rose, as much because of his manner as his answers," Carmichael recalled thirty-five years later.[29]

For Rustin, these events showcased his usefulness to the movement, even as he remained prone to being sidelined from major organizations. Malcolm, too, benefited, his reputation further enhanced every time even a semirespectable Negro leader dared to venture with him into the debating arena. Howard also opened up new points of contact between Malcolm and the black student movement. Exposure to Malcolm forced university students to reconsider the political framework the struggle for racial justice operated in. He introduced them to a new way of fighting for black dignity without apology, offering a critical lens for viewing issues of race, democracy, and citizenship to student activists eager to listen. Malcolm enthralled them by repudiating the idea that black freedom by necessity should rely on proximity to white power. Instead, he suggested an alternative reading of American history, one where black life only mattered to the extent that African Americans themselves recognized their intrinsic value and organized institutions, political movements, and unity around this concept. Black power, according to Malcolm, would be located in the last place that racial integrationists cared to look: in the very heart of the black community.[30]

While Malcolm made small but significant inroads among groups of students dedicated to nonviolent civil disobedience, King's passion for turning local civil rights struggles into a national racial-justice movement drew him, ten days before Christmas, to the tiny southwest Georgia city of Albany (pronounced Al-benny by locals), where SNCC organizers and local activists sparked a movement culled from efforts to test out the ICC's desegregation ruling in the wake of the Freedom Rides. After students protested the maintenance of segregated facilities at the city's Trailways bus station, local activists formed the Albany Movement, which featured members of the NAACP, SNCC, and local civil rights groups. The movement vowed to eradicate racial segregation in every corner of the city, pursue economic justice for its beleaguered African American community, and end police brutality.

Through a combination of youthful exuberance, deft organizing, and bullheaded stubbornness, the activists organized a movement to desegregate facilities and promote voting rights in Albany. The Albany Movement featured mass protests, Freedom Rides, and boycotts to disrupt the city's regime of Jim Crow, tactics that, after officials jailed hundreds, brought the protests national attention. The religiously devout Charles Sherrod and Bernice Johnson Reagon represented a wing of SNCC who were devoted to the nonviolence teachings of James Lawson and mesmerized by the idea of translating King's "beloved community" into an integrated nation where love and justice triumphed over racism and poverty. On this score, they cultivated religiously motivated youth through a nonviolent call to arms that shamed and cajoled more reticent middle-class church leaders into the fold. Albany's movement distinguished itself through urgent actions and ingenious strategies, becoming known in folklore as the "singing movement" and by one historian as the "praying movement." Its legacy continued through spirituals like "We Shall Overcome" and "Eyes on the Prize"— sung by the Freedom Singers and associated specifically with the movement in Albany but destined to become national exemplars of the wider civil rights era's heroic period.[31]

King's arrival in Albany on December 15 briefly turned the town, whose twenty-six thousand black residents made up a third of its population, into the most watched city in the world. That evening, King delivered a rousing address to one thousand at a mass meeting in a local church. "All over the South we must continue to engage in creative protest to break down the system of segregation," he insisted. The next day, King, along with Ralph Abernathy, joined a demonstration, getting arrested and pledging to remain in jail during Christmas if racial justice did not come to Albany. Behind the scenes, negotiations with the local officials resulted in a weekend jail stint in Americus, sixty miles from Albany, for King, who was freed after an agreement that released seven hundred jailed protesters. Promises by Albany's white city officials to desegregate the city were quickly disavowed. Five days before Christmas, Albany turned into a public-relations setback for King, with newspapers praising Albany police chief Laurie Pritchett's successful strategy of mass arrests that, absent violence, lent a civilized air to Jim Crow's continued practice. King returned to Atlanta in time to celebrate the Christmas he had vowed to spend in jail, privately distraught over political circumstances that raged beyond his control.[32]

In early 1962, Malcolm X took the political offensive, touring the country as a racial-justice crusader whose appearances both created and attracted controversy. Malcolm and Bayard Rustin took their Howard University debate on the road, addressing a capacity crowd of 1,300 in New York City on the last Tuesday in January. Malcolm praised Rustin for his willingness to debate before excoriating racial integration as ineffective and hypocritical. A little more than two weeks later, they resumed their performance, this time in Chicago. "Ladies and gentlemen, whenever I talk with Malcolm X, my twenty minutes seems to go so fast and his so slow, so I'd better get to the point," began Rustin, conceding Malcolm's superior debating skills if not the substance of his argument.[33]

Rustin praised the Nation of Islam for injecting "a sense of decency, dignity, and morality" into the civil rights struggle and acknowledged Malcolm X as black America's working-class hero, a champion of Negro constituencies that eluded mainstream civil rights organizations. Rustin's candid assessment of class divisions within the movement was something Malcolm certainly agreed with. On the other hand, Malcolm's passionate analysis of institutional racism struck a chord with Rustin, but he argued that Malcolm's programmatic response of turning inward rather than engaging in mass political struggle relegated blacks to utopian fantasies of racial separatism. "The Muslim movement," remarked Rustin, "is a movement of withdrawal from the real struggle."[34]

In March 1962, Malcolm debated James Farmer, the CORE leader who had spent time in a Mississippi jail. Malcolm denounced the pursuit of racial integration as morally and politically bankrupt. "I'll never take part in a sit-in because if someone forces me with a club or attacks," he said, "I would have to rely on my equality, my God-given rights, and use the same force in retaliation." Malcolm insisted that black people had the right to defend their lives against racial terror. "We don't want to integrate with someone who says one thing and preaches another," he told Farmer. Malcolm conceded that he could support racial integration "if it restored human dignity" for black folk. "But if it doesn't, out the window with integration and let's get another method." Malcolm expressed open skepticism about some black people's "confidence in the white man" and democratic political institutions. Civil rights activists "believe they can change you, they believe there is still hope in the American dream," he objected. Then he unleashed one of his signature phrases: "But what to them is an American dream to us is an American nightmare."[35]

Malcolm counted himself as one of the rare black activists cognizant of the "era of great change" unfolding domestically and internationally. He interpreted this transformation as less dependent on white goodwill than black political strength. "It is not a case of wanting integration or separation," Malcolm argued. "It is a case of wanting freedom, justice, and equality." The goal of the black freedom struggle, he contended, pivoted around the achievement of "human dignity," regardless of method. He characterized the entire world as ablaze with revolutionary insurgencies that pitted the darker denizens against old and new Western empires. Living in an era "where dark mankind wants freedom" required black Americans to reimagine the terrain of struggle from narrowly domestic to expansively international. "The same rebellion, the same impatience, the same anger that exists in the hearts of dark people in Africa and Asia is existing in the hearts and minds of 20 million black people in this country" who remained under a political regime as oppressive as any in the world.[36]

Malcolm shared King's understanding of the importance of anti-colonial struggles to the civil rights movement. But for Malcolm, global struggles for black power required the creation of political alliances that would tap into the domestic movement's revolutionary potential. From this perspective, King was constantly negotiating from a position of weakness, failing to comprehend that black people were in a position to dictate the terms of their freedom if they could only grasp the scope of their global power. Black Americans were "colonized mentally," said Malcolm, operating under the burden of racial inferiority that college degrees and respectability politics could never cure. Black elites were ashamed of their racial identity, black skin, curly hair, and African features. The Nation of Islam, he insisted, "is only trying to undo the white supremacy that you have indoctrinated the entire world with."[37]

Farmer criticized the Nation of Islam as lacking a plan for the collective liberation of black people. "We're not looking for the pie in the sky, but things are being done," said Farmer. "I tell you that we are Americans," he added, challenging Malcolm's assertion that blacks would never achieve equal citizenship. "This is our country as much as it is white Americans'." Black people, thanks to civil rights demonstrations along Route 40, could now eat anywhere "between Wilmington and Baltimore." The CORE leader discussed the impact of the Freedom Riders on American racial attitudes and in combating the "evil of segregation." Racial separatism contributed to this evil, no matter how eloquently Malcolm explained it. "We are working," Farmer said, "for the right of Negroes to enter all fields of activity in American life." He disputed Malcolm's notion that racial integration meant copying white folks and that CORE demonstrators were mostly white. After Malcolm admitted that "no followers of the honorable Elijah Muhammad know what he has in mind" as the ultimate solution for ending racial oppression, Farmer struck back. "Oh, I see," he said, smiling. "You mean Allah hasn't decided yet and it's all a big secret."[38]

Malcolm stood on firmer ground discussing world affairs. "While the white world is getting more quiet, the black world is getting more loud," he observed. "We are living in an era of great change." He offered a capsule history lesson on the lack of moral equivalency between slavery and contemporary symbols of racial progress. "We have been giving slave labor for 400 years and we're not going to get sufficient repayment through any Jackie Robinsons, Marian Andersons or a cup of coffee," said Malcolm, singling out the baseball player who was his hero in prison and the extraordinary black singer who performed at the Lincoln Memorial in 1939 in defiance of Jim Crow as poor substitutes for collective black dignity. Malcolm defiantly claimed to represent a group of people who "don't think that an integrated cup of coffee is sufficient payment for 310 years of slave labor."[39]

The debate with Farmer introduced Malcolm to new constituencies, increasing his celebrity as a draw at elite colleges and universities nationwide. For Farmer, who held his own against Malcolm, the venue offered an opportunity for CORE to display its growing nonviolent militancy in the civil rights arena. Malcolm and Farmer, who had first met a year earlier, went out for coffee after their debate. Mutual respect turned into a budding friendship that pushed beyond their ideological differences to a comfortable offstage personal rapport. The debate showcased Malcolm's brilliant intellect, highlighting his commitment to black freedom by any means necessary. His emphasis on "human dignity" illustrated that he shared core values with civil rights activists, even though he vehemently disagreed about the political tactics necessary to achieve such a goal. For Malcolm, that dignity required a level of power blacks were on the verge of attaining, if only they knew where to look. If King sought to persuade the highest bastions of white power of the worthiness of black citizenship, Malcolm remained convinced that black people needed to recognize the strength of their own humanity before they could rightfully expect others to do so.[40]

On April 27, 1962, Los Angeles police fatally shot NOI member Ronald Stokes. Officers mistook him and a group of Muslims removing clothes from a car outside a Los Angeles mosque for criminals. The conflict quickly escalated to a police raid inside the mosque, leaving a total of seven Muslims shot, one killed, and one paralyzed from a bullet wound to the back. Stokes's death compelled Malcolm to engage in new dimensions of the black freedom struggle. He discovered a new center of political gravity by returning to the arena that had launched him: America's racially scarred criminal justice system. Decades before protests against mass incarceration galvanized the black freedom struggle, Malcolm indicted the entire justice system as racist. His crusade against police brutality and violence against black folk in urban cities paralleled King's mobilization of southern blacks in Montgomery and Albany. Malcolm transformed Stokes's death into a political indictment against American democracy, linking systemic police violence in black Los Angeles to structural inequalities that, he argued, gripped every facet of American society.[41]

The melee in Los Angeles shook Malcolm, who had founded the temple five years earlier and knew Stokes personally. The violence demonstrated the tension between the Nation of Islam and law enforcement, something Malcolm would stress in his public account of the events. The black presence in Los Angeles, like in other major cities, had grown exponentially following the Second World War as southern migrants sought relief from Jim Crow and found new economic opportunities. By the early 1960s, African Americans in Los Angeles and other major cities were experiencing discrimination in housing, public schools, and employment that upended the narratives that claimed Jim Crow as a peculiar problem of the South. Northern-style racial segregation could be seen in poverty-filled urban ghettos and in the tense relationship between law enforcement and those communities. If segregated lunch counters, bus and train stations, and water fountains served as the most glaring symbols of racial discrimination in the South, the police served as the most visible declaration of racial injustice in big cities.[42]

Malcolm exploded upon hearing news of Stokes's death. From New York, he gathered Fruit of Islam soldiers and prepared them for a retaliation mission in Los Angeles. Elijah Muhammad restrained him. "Brother, you don't go to war over provocation," he warned, sensing that any plans for retribution might bring down the full weight of law enforcement upon the Nation. Malcolm listened but chafed at the Messenger's orders and his interpretation of the events leading to Stokes's death. "Every one of those Muslims should have died before they allowed an aggressor to come into their mosque," the Messenger concluded. The decision stunned Malcolm and left him embarrassed by the group's inability to defend itself.[43]

Muhammad's lack of action pushed Malcolm, as the Nation of Islam's national representative, to launch a nationwide speaking tour that turned Ronald Stokes into a martyr of the larger civil rights struggle. Malcolm immediately flew to Los Angeles from New York, where he conducted a press conference describing the Friday-night melee between a group of devout Muslim worshippers, fresh from an evening service, and gun-toting police officers as an act of racist violence. He combatted police chief William Parker's version of events, which cast Stokes and the six other men who were shot as anti-white zealots who gleefully prayed for "the destruction of the Caucasian race." Malcolm elicited support from the NAACP, turning the tragic circumstances into a call for a black united front.[44]

On Friday, May 4, one week after Stokes's death, Malcolm held court at the Statler-Hilton Hotel. His press conference featured a poster-size photo of Stokes, proof, Malcolm claimed, that Stokes had been viciously beaten in the head with a nightstick after he had been shot. "The police went wild—went mad—that night," he claimed. Anticipating a grand jury's ruling of justifiable homicide that would be released eleven days later, Malcolm prosecuted the Los Angeles Police Department and the entire criminal justice system to a wider black public, one that included civil rights activists, concerned citizens, the black working class, and elites.[45]

Malcolm responded to what he characterized as "cold-blooded murder!" with action. He dove into the black freedom struggle with renewed conviction, forming an ad hoc coalition with civil rights groups. The black united front Malcolm often spoke of became a political reality through joint rallies with civil rights leaders, black nationalists, and local activists from everywhere from Boston to Oakland. At his most constructive, Malcolm brought together disparate strands of the black freedom movement, as he did at the Palm Gardens in New York shortly before Stokes's funeral, where he spoke alongside James Farmer and journalist William Worthy. Operating on little sleep, Malcolm blasted white liberals who accused him of being a reverse racist. "If it's racism to know who my enemy is, if it's racism to know that I'm catching hell from White America, that it's condoned and sanctioned and backed and supported by a white government, if that's racism, well I'll take racism above democracy and Americanism and any kind of -ism you can hand me," Malcolm thundered.[46]

Malcolm characterized Stokes's death as the latest murder of a black man by the forces of white supremacy, the common enemy of black people since the bullwhip days of slavery. He compared the LAPD's brutal history of violence against black bodies to the gestapo tactics of Nazi Germany, daring his critics to disagree. And he deployed the briskly selling *Muhammad Speaks* as a political weapon to offer detailed versions of the shooting to hundreds of thousands of readers, most of whom did not belong to the Nation but devoured the paper for its lucid depiction of the wider black world. After Los Angeles, Malcolm ramped up the notion of self-defense as a central element in a global anti-colonial struggle that stretched from the United States to the Third World.[47]

Malcolm X's eulogy of Ronald Stokes doubled as an intellectual seminar on institutional racism in the justice system. He informed the two thousand in attendance that despite religious, political, and ideological differences, they were being "brutalized because we are black people in America." He decried the depiction of black anger against lynching, rape, and murder as violence, noting that the US government "doesn't call it violence when" it "lands troops in South Vietnam." Black communities were living in "a police state," he argued, demonized by law enforcement, the press, and the public. He identified Ronald Stokes as a world citizen, a recognized part of "the dark world" fighting for humanity in the face of white supremacy. In searing language, Malcolm laid out the political vision he would now follow. The death of Ronald Stokes had pushed him to his breaking point with the Nation of Islam's policy of nonengagement in political activism and in his personal relationship with Elijah Muhammad. His departure from the group began in earnest as he eulogized Stokes in language more befitting a political leader than a Muslim minister. His words reverberated through the Nation as well. In Chicago, Muhammad unveiled two manifestos detailing "What the Muslims Want" and "What the Muslims Believe" that included eliminating police brutality and would provide inspiration for a new generation of black activists.[48]

Nine days after Stokes's funeral, the *New York Times* published a front-page story detailing the growing amount of organized student activism, by both liberals and conservatives, on American college campuses. The story traced interest in "political and social issues" back to the sit-in movement in Greensboro, North Carolina, that launched SNCC. While conservative Arizona senator

Barry Goldwater was the most popular campus speaker, two black political leaders were close behind: Malcolm X and Martin Luther King Jr. Malcolm and Martin both attracted controversy and were denied from speaking at some universities because of their political beliefs. The story reductively described Malcolm's appeal to the black working class, well-educated African Americans, and increasing numbers of white college students attracted by the lurid "shock speeches on black segregation and supremacy." As the story noted, Malcolm's political repertoire traveled far beyond religion. His cordial relationship with the venerable black labor leader A. Philip Randolph soon blossomed into an open alliance, and Malcolm forged coalitions with black nationalists on the West Coast, including Donald Warden, a gifted speaker and founder of the influential Afro-American Association, a group whose members included future Black Panther leader Huey P. Newton.[49]

As Malcolm discovered new political strength by venturing beyond the Nation's proving grounds into new worlds of public engagement, King cultivated the southern version of the black working-class communities that helped shape Malcolm in the North. King also arrived in Los Angeles, on the heels of a speaking tour and voter-registration drive that took him to the Mississippi delta, Virginia, and South Carolina.[50]

King stepped up his criticism of the Kennedy administration's reticence on civil rights by publishing a combative essay, "Fumbling on the New Frontier," in the *Nation*, which served as a sequel to his piece a year earlier. The essay forcefully attacked President Kennedy for failing to live up to campaign promises to desegregate federal housing by executive order. It also displayed King's combative side, one that supporters and critics tended to ignore. Malcolm X's criticism of King often failed to acknowledge his militant role within the mainstream civil rights movement. While Roy Wilkins and the NAACP proceeded cautiously in acknowledging disappointment with the slow pace of the Kennedy White

House, King expressed his dissatisfaction in bold strokes, chiding the president for engaging in a "cautious and defensive struggle for civil rights against an unyielding adversary."[51]

On this point—that white supremacy and institutional racism formed unapologetic obstacles to racial progress—Malcolm X undoubtedly agreed. He and King parted ways on solutions, with the southern preacher maintaining an obstinate hope that creative policies, legislative breakthroughs, and legal precedents, combined with spiritual and social transformation, would change hearts and minds while healing deep-seated racial wounds. Kennedy's reluctance to sign the housing executive order especially irked King. He argued that the Kennedy administration's symbolic gesture of Negro cabinet appointees accomplished only the "limited goal of token integration" rather than the sweeping changes required to crush racial discrimination once and for all.[52]

King characterized racism as "the burden of centuries of deprivation and inferior status" carried by blacks, regardless of educational achievement and class background. Kennedy, white liberal allies, and the larger American public ignored the immensity of the so-called Negro problem in favor of symbolic gestures that only stiffened the massive resistance of white southerners and their northern collaborators. King publicly lamented presidential inaction even as he remained defiantly optimistic that mass action would allow Kennedy's intellectual support of the freedom struggle to blossom "into passionate purpose."[53]

The SCLC's annual convention in Birmingham that September foreshadowed the site of King's political redemption and Malcolm's more active engagement in the civil rights struggle. Malcolm's efforts during the year to organize the black poor and working class, while forging a political coalition with the intellectuals and elites who formed much of the civil rights leadership, paralleled King's political travails in Albany. Both men devoted considerable time, energy, and resources to different aspects of racial discrimination but failed to achieve the full measure of victory they had hoped for when their campaigns began.

King acknowledged that re-creating the spectacle of his victory in Montgomery through political forays into unchartered waters was difficult, if not the disaster some journalists asserted. Nine months of active support for the Albany Movement proved unable to end racial segregation in the city. The *New York Times* reported the grim reality that "public life in Albany remains segregated" as if scoring a boxing event, with King designated the loser by a technical knockout. King found such criticism unfair and oblivious to the reality that when segregation won, the entire nation lost—from the Kennedys perched in the White House to sharecroppers toiling in the Mississippi delta. Racial struggle ennobled black people to fight for dignity, King claimed, finding common ground with one of the crucial aspects of Malcolm X's political thought. "The victory of the Albany Movement has already been won," King explained to one reporter. "Thousands of Negroes have won a new sense of dignity and self-respect." Yet he personally vowed to more carefully expend his political energies. "I don't want to be a fireman anymore," he told SCLC staff. He promised to stop trying to extinguish racial fires created by Jim Crow, though he still planned to fan political flames at a time and place of his choosing.[54]

King found time, in the midst of fundraising for the SCLC, to meet in New York with Ahmed Ben Bella, the dashing premier of the new Algerian Republic, which came into being after a bloody guerrilla war against the French. King met with Ben Bella at the Barclay Hotel in New York—a summit that echoed aspects of Malcolm X's meeting with Fidel Castro, but with a twist. Whereas Castro and Malcolm implicitly recognized violence as a tactic for building a new society, King and Ben Bella found common ground in the effectiveness of nonviolence in the US struggle. Over the course of nearly two hours, King found Ben Bella to be unusually well informed about the civil rights struggles taking place in the

States, from the Montgomery bus boycott to the sit-in movement. "The significance of our conversation was Ben Bella's complete familiarity with the progression of events in the Negro struggle for full citizenship," King wrote afterward in an essay published in the *New York Amsterdam News*.

King described battles against colonialism in Algeria and for black citizenship in America as part of "a common struggle" that reflected the global dimensions of the civil rights movement. Ben Bella's assertion that America would lose its "moral and political voice" in world affairs if it failed to end Jim Crow resonated deeply with King and in the black press, which reported the meeting as a major political breakthrough on matters of racial justice. King told reporters that during their conversation, Ben Bella regretted the necessity of violence in forging Algeria's own revolution. The meeting deepened King's appreciation of the impact that unfolding African revolutions might have domestically.

King and Malcolm both shared a deep interest in anti-colonial struggles, but for different reasons. Malcolm regarded Third World revolutionary leaders, especially those who engaged in guerrilla struggles, as glimpses into a liberated political future for black America that would include bloodshed. But King envisioned a world wherein meeting with a revolutionary leader like Ben Bella amplified the power of nonviolent social change, prevented the nation from settling for an "anemic democracy," and inspired radical social change through the realization that "racial segregation in America has international implications."[55]

King toured Alabama in December as part of the same voter-registration drive that had taken him to parts of the South earlier in the year. Fred Shuttlesworth, the leader of Birmingham's local movement and an SCLC member, enjoyed a good relationship with King and invited the group to participate in citywide demonstrations to end racial segregation in the Magic City. In Alabama, King had found a state under siege from racial terror and a black community unapologetically organizing for freedom. When terrorists bombed a black church that housed meetings of Shuttlesworth's Alabama Christian Movement for Human Rights—a name taken after the state banned the NAACP—King telegrammed President Kennedy railing against the racists' "Gestapo like methods," using the same language that Malcolm X had deployed in describing the Stokes killing. Both Malcolm X and Martin Luther King Jr. recognized how deeply institutionalized racism threatened the hopes, dreams, and lives of blacks living in America. They each brilliantly diagnosed flaws within American democracy, yet they embraced different strategies for black liberation at this point—with King maintaining faith in legal and political solutions to combat racial injustice and Malcolm relying on the growing strength, political sophistication, and worldliness of the black community as the true measure of power. In 1963, historic events in Birmingham would inspire each to recognize the value of the other's political personality, racial-justice strategy, and commitment to black freedom.[56]

CHAPTER 5

Birmingham's Radicals

In April 1963, Martin Luther King Jr. and the SCLC began a desegregation campaign that turned Birmingham into the center of the world. Organized rallies, meetings, and a boycott of downtown stores were all deployed as weapons of nonviolent resistance designed to end Jim Crow in the city. King applied seven years of political experience to this local campaign. A genuinely seismic event in American history, the Birmingham protests cleaved the nation in two, forcing citizens of all backgrounds to take honest measure of the intersection between race and democracy in national life. This included Malcolm X, who, despite his public disapproval of King's tactics, grew in stature as a natural leader in a rebellion that could not be quelled by half measures. The campaign radicalized the civil rights movement and galvanized racial-justice discourse at home and abroad. Birmingham also cast a political spell strong enough to transform President Kennedy from an ambivalent bystander into a freedom fighter. King identified Kennedy as a fellow leader and statesman, going as far as accepting the code name "JFK" during the Birmingham campaign. He considered himself the president's black counterpart in the field of race relations, and he studied Kennedy's speeches like only a fellow orator could.[1]

City commissioner Bull Connor, a renowned hard-line racial segregationist, fresh from a stinging mayoral defeat to a moderate segregationist, responded with mass arrests, fire hoses, and police dogs. King's arrest on Good Friday, April 12, made national headlines. Pictures of King being hauled to prison dressed in blue denim overalls dominated the news, with the *Baltimore Afro-American* boiling the struggle down to an epic clash of wills: "Dr. King vs. Bull Connor." King's weekend in solitary confinement was interrupted by a chance to phone Coretta in Atlanta, a courtesy extended by jailers through the personal intervention of President Kennedy. King immediately seized on this gesture of goodwill to leverage more national support for the movement. From his prison cell, King composed "Letter from Birmingham Jail," an elegant refutation of critics who characterized the protests as reckless.[2]

King's Birmingham letter matched intellectual erudition with passionate moral and political advocacy. The moderate tones of its initial paragraphs soon gave way to raw, unvarnished political indignation, an emotion that led King to identify the black freedom struggle as part of larger global movement. "Oppressed people," he reminded the world, "cannot remain oppressed forever." Meticulous efforts to politically justify the struggle for black equality gave way to a wider moral indictment that questioned white moderates for failing to join a human rights struggle rooted in the nation's Judeo-Christian religious traditions. He openly decried the immoral caution of church leaders unwilling to defy laws they personally considered to be unjust. Parts of King's letter paralleled the tone of Malcolm X's critique of Christianity, especially when he observed that "the judgment of God is upon the church as never before." The letter also revealed flashes of Malcolm X's political rage. Like Malcolm, King personalized his message through revealing bits of autobiography, recounting the pain of explaining to seven-year-old Yoki that Atlanta's Funtown amusement park denied entrance to black children. King concluded by celebrating protestors as America's "real heroes": women, men, and schoolchildren risking their freedom and their lives in service of "a majestic sense of purpose" the nation struggled to comprehend. Released after eight days in jail, King narrated the movement's actions as shedding light on the cancerous sore of racism. "We bring it out in the open where it can be seen and dealt with," wrote King.[3]

Addressed to eight clergymen in Birmingham who were pleading with King to halt protests, the "Letter from Birmingham Jail" represented King's most cogent argument to date for radical black citizenship. He defined citizenship transnationally, comparing the slow pace for racial justice in America with the "jet-like speed" of African and Asian nations hurtling toward independence and political self-determination. King's castigation of "the appalling silence of good people" thrust him toward his boldest public repudiation of white Americans—from the clergy to ordinary citizens—unable to empathize with the pain of racial injustice. The letter contrasted King's professed disappointment in white clergy who insisted that black citizenship required infinite patience with his obvious pride in black folk who were "moving with a great sense of urgency toward the promised land of racial justice."[4]

On the first Thursday and Friday in May, hundreds of black elementary and high school students marched from the Sixteenth Street Baptist Church to city hall, only to be arrested by Birmingham police. On Friday, Bull Connor unleashed snarling dogs and fire hoses powerful enough to strip bark off of trees onto demonstrators and innocent bystanders at Kelly Ingram Park in a naked display of brutality. The images of this incident were destined to circulate around the world as gruesomely iconic evidence of American racial terror: pictures of peaceful school-age demonstrators being attacked by German shepherds and baton-wielding police officers, pushed and shoved into paddy wagons, made international news.[5]

John F. Kennedy admitted that the widely circulated photos made him "sick," yet he deflected on procedural grounds that he lacked the federal power to end the chaos. King's efforts in

Birmingham drew the president, whose personal temperature ran cool, toward rising degrees of both anger and indignation. Racial violence in Birmingham stirred his moral passion in a way that meetings with civil rights leaders never could. The activists and city officials reached a negotiated settlement on Friday, May 10—a fragile accord that left neither side completely satisfied. The rest of the spring featured intermittent clashes between protesters and police, threats of racial violence, and lingering tension that made Birmingham the site of a protracted war of attrition. Kennedy's deployment of the National Guard to Birmingham to quell demonstrations—after protests against the planting of bombs by white supremacists turned violent on Mother's Day—earned him the permanent enmity of Malcolm X, who criticized the president for authorizing force only when white property and lives, rather than that of black women and children, hung in the balance. King's pleas for nonviolence did little to ease tensions ratcheted up by racial terror against locals.[6]

King's actions in Birmingham placed new pressure on the Kennedy administration and Malcolm X alike to take bold action. In May, as Birmingham continued to seize domestic and global attention, Malcolm arrived in the nation's capital as a different kind of politician. Under orders from Elijah Muhammad, he was taking over as interim minister of Temple No. 4 while retaining full-time duties in Harlem. He immediately organized weekly meetings to spread a radical message of black political dignity. During a press conference, he directly addressed the nation's growing racial crisis, where he characterized Birmingham as a missed opportunity, an "example of what can happen when the Negroes rely on the whites to solve their problems for them." In contrast, he promised to combat the evils of juvenile delinquency, drug abuse, and crime in Washington by exposing the black community to the discipline and religious beliefs that changed his life. "We don't preach hatred and violence," Malcolm said. "But we believe that if a four-legged or two-legged dog attacks a Negro he should be killed."

Malcolm's words revealed frustration with the Messenger's official policy of nonengagement in political demonstrations. Earlier in the year, after NOI members were arrested on trumped-up charges in Rochester, New York, Malcolm fired off a telegram to President Kennedy expressing outrage and led a six-hundred-strong protest demonstration in the city. Three weeks before arriving in Washington, Malcolm publicly mulled over participating in organized civil rights demonstrations, while warning that Muslims would not "turn the other cheek" if met with violence. Malcolm's political advocacy for radical black dignity ran past the constraints of the Nation of Islam.[7]

Malcolm's rhetorical gauntlet, thrown against the backdrop of Birmingham's horrific racial violence, violated the spirit of Muhammad's repeated warnings to stay out of politics. But in Washington, Malcolm found a deeper, more combative, and unusually resonant voice. He vowed to turn Temple No. 4, located at 1519 Fourth Street in the city's northwest section, into a headquarters of criminal- and racial-justice reform. On just his second day in the city, Malcolm pointedly chided King for sending children into a combat zone, one that endangered their lives and sacrificed black dignity in the process. For Malcolm, the sight of black children being arrested in civil rights demonstrations illustrated the failure of King's leadership. "Real men don't put their children on the firing line," he objected to reporters.

The situation in Birmingham gripped the entire nation, especially Malcolm, who begrudgingly recognized the full measure of King's impressive power to marshal black protest. Malcolm argued, correctly, that events in Birmingham reached a boiling point only after black residents untrained in nonviolence but seething over racial oppression fought back against police brutality in a manner that surprised authorities and politicians. "President Kennedy," observed Malcolm, "did not send troops to Alabama when dogs were biting black babies," revealing what most civil rights leaders dared not say. "He then sent troops after the Negroes demonstrated their ability to defend themselves." President Kennedy's lack of empathy with black suffering, according to Malcolm, forced African Americans to take control of the situation by fighting back. Blacks were unafraid of "white reprisals," he contended, and were now ready to "react today with violence if provoked."[8]

"Kennedy," Malcolm said, "is wrong because his motivation is wrong." He expressed this sentiment at a press conference, fresh from a meeting on race and juvenile crime with Democratic congresswoman from Oregon Edith Green, who chaired the education subcommittee. While Malcolm declined to offer Green specific policy suggestions, he told reporters that until "the image of the black man is changed in the black man's mind," problems of juvenile delinquency that scarred his own youth would persist. Malcolm accused President Kennedy of religious discrimination for suggesting during a meeting with newspaper editors that Muslims represented a potential haven for black extremists. "Instead of attacking the Ku Klux Klan and the White Citizens' Council," Malcolm asserted, "Kennedy attacked Islam, a religion." Malcolm roamed through Washington amid the Birmingham crisis like a man on fire. He resembled a political leader more than a religious one, giving press conferences with reporters, meeting with elected officials, and maintaining a running commentary on the Kennedy administration and a corollary analysis of the failures of King and the larger movement.[9]

But as King was maneuvering for a major strategic victory in Birmingham, Malcolm was experiencing private doubts about his own place in the Nation of Islam. Unfolding crises within the organization diminished Malcolm's power. Malcolm confirmed Elijah Muhammad's sexual affairs with his secretaries after interviewing several of them. Worse, he learned that he was the subject of Muhammad's private scorn, even as the Messenger publicly praised him as his most outstanding follower. A national profile in the *Saturday Evening Post* focused on Malcolm's charisma at the expense of Muhammad, ratcheting up petty jealousies and the envy of Muhammad's family.[10]

This time also saw the publication of a *Playboy* magazine interview of Malcolm by Alex Haley, a collaboration that anticipated their work together on *The Autobiography of Malcolm X*. The high-profile interview pushed Malcolm further into the national spotlight. Although he praised Elijah Muhammad as his leader, the story presented Malcolm as the far more dynamic and charismatic figure. Malcolm's conception of radical black dignity as a vehicle capable of unifying divergent parts of the African American community announced him as creative thinker and visionary political leader. The politically moderate Haley peppered Malcolm with uncomfortable questions, designed to knock the preternaturally poised Muslim leader off-balance, only to be regaled with a seminar on black history, politics, and culture that stretched back from ancient Egypt to the present. When Haley admonished him for praising the honesty of white racists, Malcolm responded with cool precision. "The fact that I prefer the candor of the Southern segregationist to the hypocrisy of the Northern integrationist doesn't alter the basic immorality of white supremacy," he answered.[11]

Malcolm X's stature found him in the process of writing an autobiography at just thirty-eight years old. His national celebrity made his personal journey and rise from a life of crime and hustling into politics one of the most captivating stories of the era; the book would become an instant classic and best seller. Mainstream press coverage of Malcolm helped to spark an interest in black radicalism as a literary commodity. Praising the Messenger for his political transformation, Malcolm succinctly traced his evolution from ex-convict to radical icon through painful memories of confinement. "I often think, sir, that in 1946, I was sentenced to 8 to 10 years in Cambridge, Massachusetts, as a common thief who had never passed the eighth grade," he reminded Haley. "And the next time I went back to Cambridge was in March 1961, as the guest speaker at the Harvard Law School Forum."[12]

As a national reckoning on black dignity in Birmingham ratcheted up, so did Malcolm's assaults on dual targets: Martin Luther King Jr. and John F. Kennedy. Malcolm branded King's political alliance with Kennedy as a failure. Part of Malcolm's harsh words toward King stemmed from his own inability to enter the thick of the civil rights fray and what he considered to be the movement's support for ineffective strategic compromise. Malcolm responded to King's constructive, face-to-face engagement with the president by lobbing rhetorical firebombs that characterized nonviolence as the tool of the weak. Ignoring the movement's undeniable ability to bend public will and political favor toward legal and legislative breakthroughs, Malcolm steadfastly argued that nonviolent tactics would never fully liberate black America. In Washington, he spoke with the confidence of a political leader who required no election to confirm the level of support he enjoyed in America's racially segregated and economically impoverished ghettos. "Our goal is eliminating the frame of mind that makes us turn toward alcohol, dope, gambling and crime," he told reporters. "We will spread a message among our people." Malcolm's provocative talk of political self-determination also received implicit support from the Messenger, who was quoted in the March issue of *Muhammad Speaks* supporting black political candidates.[13]

The angrier Malcolm became, the louder his message resonated. *Newsweek* identified Birmingham as the root of sprawling national unrest on race matters that touched off an archipelago of raucous demonstrations from Nashville, Tennessee, and Greensboro and Raleigh, North Carolina, to Cambridge, Maryland, a border state. Birmingham amplified Malcolm's impact. Six thousand people attended a Harlem rally where Malcolm, surrounded by two huge posters of black victims of police brutality, reimagined the geography of civil rights struggles. "Birmingham is not in the South alone," he insisted. "It is in the North too." President Kennedy took notice, observing to reporters in early June, during a conversation about a minor political furor caused by the TFX fighter jet, that "we have had an interesting six months . . . with TFX and now we are going to have his brother Malcolm for the next six." Malcolm's presence in the nation's capital had reached the White House.[14]

Birmingham pushed Bobby and John F. Kennedy to move proactively in support of racial justice before further crises erupted. After spending years avoiding the problem of racial discrimination, Bobby Kennedy, with the president's approval, now set out to receive a crash course on race relations. At the suggestion of the black comedian and activist Dick Gregory, the attorney general planned to use writer James Baldwin as a sounding board to better understand growing racial unrest around the country. On Friday, May 24, 1963, Baldwin organized a meeting between Bobby Kennedy and black intellectuals and artists, along with some white allies, in an apartment on Central Park South owned by the Kennedy family patriarch, Joseph. It would be the closest that either of the Kennedy brothers would ever come to being in a room with Malcolm X. Boldfaced names in black cultural life joined the meeting: black psychologist Kenneth Clark, the intellectual whose work helped to integrate public schools by documenting the psychological wounds segregation caused black children; playwright Lorraine Hansberry, famous for the award-winning Broadway play *A Raisin in the Sun*; singer Harry Belafonte, who frequently served as a conduit between the Kennedy family and King; and entertainer Lena Horne, one of the first black women to appear in major Hollywood films during the 1940s. Clarence Jones, King's personal attorney and friend, attended, as did a young Freedom Rider named Jerome Smith. Although it was sold to the group as a listening session, Kennedy intended to use the meeting to detail the administration's efforts at ending racial discrimination and guaranteeing black citizenship.[15]

Baldwin, meanwhile, was fresh off the publication of his explosive book *The Fire Next Time*. The two essays that made up the text served as meditations on contemporary American race relations, with Baldwin adopting the role of an Old Testament prophet, issuing words of fire in hopes of saving a doomed land. "Time," he wrote, "catches up with Kingdoms and crushes them." Comfortable in white literary environments as well as chatting with black Muslims who predicted a coming race war, Baldwin both defended whites against Elijah Muhammad's apocalyptic visions of racial conflict and castigated America as an updated Roman Empire hopelessly adrift as racial violence threatened to end its very existence. The book's January release heralded the peak of Baldwin's importance as a public intellectual and civil rights activist.[16]

At the meeting, Bobby pleaded with attendees to recognize the bigger picture of how behind-the-scenes political maneuvers would achieve racial justice. "We have a party in revolt and we have to be somewhat considerate about how to keep them on board if the Democratic Party is going to prevail in the next elections," he reminded them. The attorney general's discussion of intraparty conflict related to the growing discomfort among southern Dixiecrats with the Kennedy administration's support for civil rights. He added a warning about blacks being seduced by the siren song of extremism, mentioning the Muslims without calling Malcolm X by name. Bobby's tone, which mixed a paternalistic view of racial justice with self-righteous bragging about the White House's civil rights record, pushed Jerome Smith past his breaking point. "You don't have no idea what trouble is," Smith explained, his voice growing louder. "Because I'm close to the moment where I'm ready to take up a gun. I've seen what government can do to crush the spirit and lives of people in the South"—perhaps an allusion to Bobby's halting efforts to assist Freedom Riders two years earlier. Stunned, the attorney general looked toward some of the other faces in the room in search of a rescue that never came. Instead, Lorraine Hansberry regarded Smith as the only person in the room "who should be listened to," and Clarence Jones, following King's urgings since 1961, suggested the president sign a new emancipation proclamation on the centennial anniversary of the first.[17]

Baldwin asked Smith if he would take up arms on behalf of America. His answer—"Never! Never! Never!"—struck Bobby Kennedy as unpatriotic. "How can you say that?" he asked, perhaps fueled by the memory of an older brother lost in action in the Second World War, the same conflict that President Kennedy served honorably in as a naval officer. Smith vowed to refuse to fight overseas for a nation that "continued to deny us our rights here." Bobby Kennedy fumed at the raw anger unfolding before him, feeling betrayed by attendees he considered to be friends. No one would depart this meeting unscathed. Jones would be the subject of wiretap surveillance approved by Bobby in the aftermath of the meeting, and surveillance of Baldwin and the other attendees increased as well. Baldwin would leak his version of events to the *New York Times*, which published consecutive front-page accounts on Saturday and Sunday.

Baldwin and a contingent of influential black artists and activists, the paper reported, had warned Bobby Kennedy of the "explosive situation" in northern race relations, a point Malcolm X had been making for years. Baldwin hoped that the attorney general's "naiveté" might jumpstart a "national dialogue" on racial justice around the country. Bobby, who refused official comment about the meeting as Baldwin basked in the attention, was in no mood for such a dialogue. Baldwin viewed Birmingham's recent violence as less of a temporary racial storm than a weather pattern traveling north. He obliquely referenced his recent meeting with Bobby by suggesting to a reporter that the days of individual blacks serving as racial spokespeople were over. "There is no one with whom the white power structure can negotiate a deal that will blind the Negro people," said Baldwin. "There is, therefore, no possibility of a bargain whatsoever." Blacks in the northern ghettos were poised for violent eruptions that could only be contained if whites recognized their inherent humanity, whether they were civil rights workers, sharecroppers, or slum dwellers.[18]

One of the rare public figures of the era close to both King and Malcolm X, Baldwin lamented the way in which events seemed to outpace the SCLC leader's ability to manage them and that, despite his personal disagreements with the Muslims, the NOI remained a reflection of black sentiment at the lower frequencies of American life. Still, Baldwin accorded the ideas of black radicals, such as Malcolm X and the student agitators in SNCC, a space within an American political discourse that regarded them as racial extremists. He considered such activists a crucial part of the larger American story; their uncompromising quest for racial justice exposed hidden truths about the nation's past, present, and future. Yet Baldwin remained defiantly optimistic in his assessment of American race relations. For him, despair remained the ultimate sin. "I believe that. It is easy to be bleak about the human race, but there are people who have proved to me that we can be better than we are."[19]

"It was all emotion, hysteria," Bobby Kennedy angrily lamented immediately after the meeting. He contrasted the anger and sadness that at times had overwhelmed the room with the intellectual and policy expertise of more practical leaders. "They don't know what the laws are," he claimed. "You can't talk to them the way you can talk to Martin Luther King or Roy Wilkins." The black voices at the meeting had adopted Malcolm's outsider's view, warning of coming uprisings that would dwarf Birmingham and grip northern cities with greater urgency than what was currently being seen in the South. Malcolm X's militant denunciation of American democracy as nothing more than hypocrisy in the face of the nation's continued racism hovered over the attorney general's meeting with Baldwin and the other civil rights activists. Just as Birmingham had expanded the reach and power of Martin Luther King Jr., its reverberations now thrust Malcolm X's political thought into the public in an unprecedented manner. Black folk who once could be courted as civil rights moderates were unleashing a profoundly radical critique against the gradualist policies of the Kennedy administration. Malcolm's example provided the courage for black intellectuals and activists to denounce the attorney general to his face. For Bobby Kennedy, the meeting marked a memorably combative entrée into a personal epiphany about America's long-standing racial wounds. He returned to the Justice Department both angry and emboldened, determined to increase job opportunities for blacks in the federal government and strategize with the president about major civil rights legislation.[20]

On Sunday, May 26, two days after the meeting, Martin Luther King Jr. addressed an estimated crowd of more than thirty-five thousand people at Los Angeles's Wrigley Field—one of the three biggest crowds he would speak to that year—reflecting on Birmingham's national reverberations. The rally, in honor of "freedom and human dignity," propelled the movement into new dimensions, allowing Birmingham's national call for racial justice to inspire local freedom struggles. King called the rally, which featured appearances by Hollywood movie stars and entertainers including Sammy Davis Jr., "the largest and most enthusiastic civil rights rally that has ever been held in the history of this nation." The momentum allowed King to take the political offensive, not only against segregationists but against critics within the black freedom struggle. Without mentioning Malcolm X by name, King rejected the idea that nonviolence was a tactic for cowards. "These are the strong people of this land," King argued, noting that thousands of demonstrators brave enough to face "howling and jeering mobs" displayed a tenacious courage worthy of respect and praise. "Let us not laugh at nonviolence," King said. "It is not a weak method as some have tried to say." He described nonviolence as a political art that allowed civil rights activists to transform prisons from "a dungeon of shame into a haven of freedom and human dignity."[21]

"You can help us in Birmingham, Alabama," King told the crowd in Los Angeles, "by getting rid of any segregation and discrimination that exists in Los Angeles, California." Throughout the speech, he repeated that "now is the time" to guarantee black citizenship in word and deed. On this score, he publicly asked the president to sign an executive order declaring segregation illegal based on the equal protection clause of the Fourteenth Amendment. He challenged Kennedy, whom he called a "man of good will," to travel to Tuscaloosa on June 10 to escort a black student to the University of Alabama, in defiance of Governor Wallace's vow to personally block any effort to integrate the state's flagship university. King amplified the movement's credo of physical sacrifice as witness against an evil system, a form of protest that could encompass humble students and sharecroppers as well as the nation's most exalted political leaders.[22]

The movement collected thousands of dollars in donations. Sammy Davis Jr. pledged $20,000—one week's salary from his Las Vegas show—on the spot. "I can only say," he told the crowd, "that my leader is your leader—Martin Luther King." The Los Angeles rally demonstrated the struggle for racial justice's national drawing power and the way in which King asserted his political will to shape the emerging narrative of a Negro revolution. King's reach outpaced Malcolm's, but he still felt the need to address his chief critic within the black movement, with language that described nonviolence as a transcendent display of moral and political fortitude. His muscular call for "Freedom Now!" during the speech, his robust defense of nonviolence as a powerful force for social change, and his willingness to chide President Kennedy implicitly rebuked Malcolm X's efforts to portray him as an unmanly tool of the white power structure.[23]

Birmingham was the most visible example of a cascading series of confrontations, demonstrations, and protests gripping the nation in the spring and early summer of 1963. Over 750 separate civil rights demonstrations erupted in almost two hundred cities nationwide, resulting in almost fifteen thousand arrests. The widespread unrest produced increased attention from a new generation of activists around the country, who tried to make better sense of events through the broad interpretive framework offered by Martin Luther King Jr. and Malcolm X. For King and the SCLC, the uprisings infused new financial resources into the organization and effectively mainstreamed civil rights activism in America. Malcolm, on the other hand, gained access to intellectual, literary, and political circles who viewed him with new eyes in light of Birmingham's racial violence. Anti-black violence in Birmingham and the Kennedy administration's weak response made people reconsider nonviolence as the only acceptable tactic. Birmingham pushed Malcolm to broaden his concept of political engagement and reimagine the terrain of black struggle—a process that black people around the country were experiencing. Individual Muslims now openly engaged in civil rights demonstrations, following Malcolm's lead—a circumstance that led Chicago NOI officials to physically threaten violence against those who joined in protests.[24]

John F. Kennedy responded to America's growing civil rights crisis in the second week of June, in a speech that served as both a national call to arms against racial injustice and a more intimate response to King's activism and Malcolm's outrage. Kennedy linked the moral authority of the civil rights movement to the constitutional and symbolic powers of the presidency. In doing so, he displayed the potential for moral leadership and the passion for racial justice that King had spent almost two and half years lobbying for.

Tuesday, June 11 may not be the most recognized date in the history of America's civil rights struggle, but it would prove to be one of the most important. The drama first erupted in showdowns between segregationist politicians and incoming black students. Alabama's segregationist governor, George Wallace, began the morning with his infamous "stand at the schoolhouse door," vowing to physically block a black student from integrating the

University of Alabama. At the same time, northern segregationists, led by Boston school committee chairwoman Louise Day Hicks, redoubled efforts to keep public schools under racial apartheid—a stance that led the city's NAACP chapter to start a decade-long battle to integrate schools, a struggle that would symbolize the intractability of racial injustice in America. Kennedy addressed the country in an effort to turn civil rights from a political liability into a democratic touchstone that might energize the nation and produce an unexpected legacy for his presidency.[25]

Kennedy directed his staff to request national airtime at 8 p.m. eastern standard time that evening. The order surprised White House officials, who assumed that, because Wallace had peacefully allowed the university to be integrated and the crisis in Alabama had been averted, the president would stay off the air. Instead, Kennedy delivered his most powerful speech as president. After asking Americans to examine their "conscience," Kennedy bluntly announced that the nation, "for all its hopes and all its boasts will not be fully free unless all its citizens are free." He acknowledged how racial oppression denied blacks the measure of full citizenship, the continual denial of which robbed the entire nation of its political and moral standing. Kennedy declared that black students should be able to go to school "without having to be backed up with troops," attend restaurants and shop freely "without being forced to resort to demonstrations on the street," and to exercise voting rights "without interference or fear of reprisal." Kennedy cited higher rates of death for black babies, diminished earning power for blacks, limited educational opportunities, and shorter life expectancy as definitive proof of institutionalized racism's impact in America. Most importantly, the president now recognized black citizenship as fundamental to the larger imperatives of American democracy. "A great change is at hand, and our task, our obligation, is to make that revolution, that change, peaceful and constructive for all," he explained. "Those who do nothing are inviting shame as well as violence. Those who act boldly are recognizing right as well as reality."[26]

Historical events quickly overwhelmed Kennedy's finest moment as president. Medgar Evers, the uncompromising NAACP field secretary in Mississippi, was assassinated outside of his home in Jackson a few hours after the president's speech. The next morning, Kennedy braced himself for the impact of both his speech and Evers's death. Civil rights, Kennedy ruefully observed, "has become everything." He now felt, as a politician and president, the burden of race that King and Malcolm had carried with them from birth.[27]

Two days after Evers's death, Washington, DC, experienced a major racial-justice protest as three thousand demonstrators marched through the nation's capital. The march featured several hundred white participants. Outside the Justice Department building, Bobby Kennedy addressed a raucous crowd through a bullhorn, touting his record of hiring black lawyers, even as he explained the federal government judged applicants on merit and not solely race. By this time, Bobby believed the path to healing racial wounds required constructive engagement with political dissent against the administration's civil rights policies. Bow-tie-wearing Muslims hawked copies of *Muhammad Speaks* as members of the American Nazi Party set up counter pickets across the street, surrounded by local police. "Freedom Now" signs competed with more esoteric calls for "No Federal Funds for Apartheid States" and the poignant "Medgar Shall Not Have Died in Vain." Although Malcolm was "impressed" with the demonstration, he balked at the demands for racial integration. According to him, "Whenever sheep try to integrate with the wolf, then there is a step forward for the wolf, not the sheep"—an elaboration on one of his classic metaphors explaining that fair housing and fair employment acts were meaningless in a nation ruled by Jim Crow.[28]

President Kennedy sent a civil rights bill to Congress on June 19, 1963, designed to reach the goal of racial integration that

Malcolm disparaged. The bill included provisions banning racial discrimination in public accommodations, eliminating funding for federal programs that excluded blacks, and giving the Justice Department broad powers to file lawsuits to desegregate schools. It would be the strongest piece of legislation in support of black equality passed in a century, but its prospects seemed cloudy at best, since southern Democrats were destined to wage war against the bill.

Martin Luther King Jr., A. Philip Randolph, James Farmer, Roy Wilkins, and the Urban League's Whitney Young convened at the White House with the president three days later to strategize, but Kennedy and the group talked past each other. Randolph planned to organize a March on Washington for Jobs and Freedom that would be a peaceful show of support as well as a subtle display of power. The idea first originated in 1941, when a younger Randolph pledged to bring one hundred thousand blacks to Washington to protest racial exclusion in the military and defense firms. President Roosevelt blinked and signed an executive order banning racial discrimination in defense industries, but the notion of the march had percolated through the movement ever since. Kennedy pleaded with the group to "oppose demonstrations which will lead to violence" and to give Congress "a fair chance to work its will," lest a rally antagonize officials willing to vote yes but not while under visible threat.[29]

Vice president and former Senate majority leader Lyndon Johnson agreed with the president, noting that the bill's success hinged on just over two dozen swing votes in the Senate. "To get those votes we have to be careful not to do anything which would give those who are privately opposed a public excuse to appear as martyrs." But black leaders in the room held firm. King reasoned that the march might "serve as a means of dramatizing the issue and mobilizing support in parts of the country which don't know the problems first hand." The meeting ended with President

Kennedy jokingly telling those assembled not to "be totally harsh on Bull Connor," the notorious segregationist who had unleashed mayhem in Birmingham. "After all," said a smiling Kennedy, "he has done more for civil rights than anyone else."[30]

Kennedy had found, however belatedly and at times begrudgingly, common ground with King's political calculus, which believed racial progress required a national crisis to foster the unity necessary for substantive change. After the meeting, Kennedy summoned King for a private chat in the rose garden. The president dropped a bombshell allegation, courtesy of FBI director Hoover, that two of King's aides, Stanley Levison and Jack O'Dell (the black head of the SCLC's New York office), were communists and would need to be immediately dismissed. King asked for proof, but the president continued, "If they shoot you down, they'll shoot us down too." Kennedy now recognized King as a fellow statesman whose political fortunes were closely tied to his own. King left the White House with plans to sever ties with O'Dell but to retain Levison, who in the years since Montgomery had become a close personal friend. The president's suggestion during their private chat that he was under surveillance worried King, who joked with his aides that Kennedy took him out to the rose garden because Hoover had bugged the Oval Office.[31]

The next day, King spoke in Detroit at the largest civil rights demonstration ever assembled. The Walk to Freedom had begun as a demonstration and fundraiser in support of the movement in Birmingham but grew into a national event, one that attracted a crowd of 125,000 people to downtown Detroit. Head of the United Auto Workers Walter Reuther, Mayor Jerome Cavanagh, the Reverend C. L. Franklin (whose daughter Aretha would become an iconic soul singer), and the Reverend Albert Cleage were among the speakers who shared the dais with King. The rally convened at Cobo Arena, where sixteen thousand people filled up the space, with another ten thousand occupying the adjacent

Cobo Hall. One hundred thousand more listened to strategically placed loudspeakers outside. King spoke for nearly an hour, at one point passionately relating his dream that racial justice would be achieved in his lifetime. He called the city's Walk to Freedom "the largest and greatest demonstration for freedom ever held in the United States." The protest drew supporters of King and Malcolm X closer together by rallying them against the racial oppression Birmingham had exposed, while still highlighting divisions on how best to achieve black citizenship. But for now, the walk, like the planned March on Washington, provided a détente from political infighting and offered an example of the racial solidarity Malcolm X longed for—a portrait of the "new Negro" King had lauded since the Montgomery bus boycott.[32]

The day after some his allies cheered King in Detroit, Malcolm appeared on television blasting the movement and its most prominent leader. In the short film *The Negro and the American Promise*, broadcast on June 24, Malcolm excoriated King during a conversation with the black psychologist Kenneth Clark as "the best weapon that the white man, who wants to brutalize Negroes, has ever gotten in this country." Malcolm defined his own political goals as including a "moral reformation" capable of attracting blacks to "God's side," in contrast with white racists unable to participate in the "kingdom of brotherhood." Asked by Clark if blacks were citizens, Malcolm answered bluntly: "If they were citizens you wouldn't have a race problem." He characterized the Thirteenth, Fourteenth, and Fifteenth Amendments that respectively had ended slavery, established citizenship rights, and guaranteed voting rights as little more than "hypocrisy," the same word he used to describe the long-delayed integration of the nation's public schools.[33]

Martin Luther King Jr.'s separate interview with Clark on the same program countered Malcolm's talk of separating from white society with an urgent message to the Kennedy administration.

King suggested that time was "running out" for a peaceful solution to the racial crisis gripping the nation. To Malcolm's charge that his political philosophy "played into the hands of white folks," King defended his advocacy of love as "something strong" that enabled dramatic political change. Citing white violence against peaceful demonstrations across the nation, King proudly claimed that his approach purposefully disturbed white society's conscience and institutions into action. He countered Malcolm's dismissal of nonviolence by detailing a philosophy that required diligent training, personal discipline, and intense, community-wide political commitment, from elementary-age schoolchildren to senior citizens. For King, nonviolence embodied intellectual, physical, and spiritual resistance against social ills that transcended Jim Crow segregation and pushed toward the higher moral ground of eradicating war, ending hunger, and bringing peace to a troubled world. The more Malcolm dismissed his strategy and tactics, the more King reaffirmed the strength of nonviolence as a weapon of peace capable of transforming American democracy.[34]

The Negro and the American Promise received national media attention and firmly established Malcolm X's place as one of the two most important black leaders in America. Malcolm's influence on King, however, was subtler. The more he ridiculed and challenged King publicly, the more pains King took to emphasize the strength, power, and discipline of nonviolent resistance.[35]

Malcolm's appearance alongside King burnished his reputation as King's primary counterpart, an image bolstered by numerous speaking engagements and television and radio interviews, where he continued to blast King as having "more white followers than he has Negroes." But Malcolm displayed a divided mind about King as the year progressed, even inviting his rival to one of his Harlem rallies "to get an idea of the mood of the masses of Negroes"— an invitation King declined. Despite Malcolm's growing celebrity, King's star power remained unsurpassed. The political reckoning with King and the Kennedy administration that Malcolm craved would require traveling away from Harlem to unfamiliar territory. For Malcolm, it proved to be a dangerous gambit that would find him turning one of King's greatest triumphs into the inspiration for his own political future.[36]

CHAPTER 6

"Now Is the Time to Make Real the Promise of Democracy"

Malcolm X, from his perch as head of Muslim Temple No. 4 in Washington, DC, witnessed events leading up to the March on Washington up close. He was also pulled closer to SNCC, his favorite civil rights group. He regaled the young activists with his vision of radical black dignity, igniting fruitful political conversations that would continue in the coming year. Stokely Carmichael, who would emerge as Malcolm's most visible heir within three years, gravitated toward Malcolm's orbit after witnessing his electrifying Howard University appearance in 1961. Conversations with brilliant young activists influenced Malcolm's thinking too. Grassroots voting-rights organizing by SNCC field workers in the Deep South bolstered Malcolm's support for the ballot.[1]

In Washington, Malcolm frequented some of the same places as the Howard University SNCC workers. He loved to eat sweets, and at one point he ran into Carmichael and fellow SNCC member Cleveland Sellers at an ice cream shop. "The students of the movement" greeted Malcolm with a broad smile; since their first meeting, Carmichael and Malcolm's relationship had grown easy and familiar whenever their paths crossed. Malcolm spoke of the upcoming march in parables, claiming that earlier plans to paralyze the city through massive civil disobedience represented a cup of black coffee designed to energize, excite, and wake the nation up, while the current incarnation lacked intensity and thus resembled coffee lightened by cream. Carmichael and Sellers shot back a well-rehearsed defense about the importance of direct-action protest and the power of nonviolence, then departed the shop with the usual exchange of pleasantries and promises of future debate. Throughout the spring and summer, Malcolm haunted SNCC's Washington-based activists. SNCC workers admired Malcolm's political courage, basked in his personal charm, and laughed at his well-timed flashes of humor. For Carmichael, such interactions offered an opportunity to bond with a kindred spirit and represented a peek into his own political future.[2]

Three weeks before the March on Washington, Malcolm used a thirty-five-millimeter camera to snap photos of demonstrators in downtown Brooklyn being brutalized by police. Police used bolt cutters to free protesters chained to the entrance of a construction site. "If there were no captions for these pictures you'd think this was Mississippi or Nazi Germany," Malcolm told reporters. "Only difference between Gestapo and the New York police is that this is 1963." Racial oppression, according to Malcolm, gripped the entire nation, with little distinction between North and South. Malcolm recognized the relationship between institutional racism, legal violence, and law enforcement as a system of structural oppression that required large-scale political transformation—a problem that civil rights leaders, especially King, failed to grasp.[3]

When discussing the upcoming march, Malcolm veered from admiration for the thousands of black people seeking a political reckoning to frustration over perceived white control over the proceedings. On the second Sunday in August 1963, Malcolm renewed his call for a black united front before three thousand in Harlem. Behind the scenes, he had invited King to appear at the rally, since the "present racial crisis" demanded nothing less than political unity within the black community. Although he repeated the charge that President Kennedy's approval of the March on Washington meant that "you're not going to go in the same direction you started in," Malcolm cordially signed the invitation with the words "Your Brother." Malcolm's public comments about Kennedy amplified a secret war with Elijah Muhammad, who personally warned him to refrain from criticizing Kennedy in a private letter at the beginning of the month. Instead of heeding Muhammad's caution, Malcolm increased his criticism of the president and, in doing so, accelerated his own exit from the Nation of Islam. The black masses that Malcolm championed remained on the sidelines while civil rights leaders and white power brokers haggled over their fates. "When the white man found out he couldn't stop it," Malcolm loved to remind everyone, "he joined it."[4]

On August 27, the day before the march, Malcolm entered the thick of the proceedings at DC's Statler-Hilton Hotel. Earlier that month, Malcolm had announced that the Messenger himself might appear at the demonstration to ensure "no sell-out" of black interests at the hands of white power. Now, from the hotel's lobby, Malcolm cracked jokes, warned against co-optation, and sounded off on themes that he would more fully develop in the march's aftermath. That evening, he mingled with dozens of black power brokers in a hotel suite cocktail party that included his friend and sometimes collaborator Louis Lomax. Bayard Rustin had emerged as the principal organizer of the march, coordinating logistics, soothing competing egos among major leaders, and making sure there were enough bathrooms for the expected crowd of tens of thousands.[5]

The most iconic outcome of the march would be Martin Luther King Jr.'s keynote address. King's "I Have a Dream" speech represents a watershed moment in both the history of the black freedom struggle and the larger narrative of American democracy. It also remains one of the most misunderstood addresses in

American history, primarily because many of his words have been forgotten, lost in the rhetorical heights of the "I have a dream" peroration that closes the seventeen-minute speech. King's discussion of blacks occupying "a lonely island of poverty" amid the abundance of American wealth has been ignored, likewise his efforts to discuss reparations by demanding "a check" be cashed on behalf of black America. King discussed the need for the movement to struggle together in order to redeem the nation's soul, hastening a rendezvous with a political destiny that would lead to freedom, justice, and liberty for all. Against the backdrop of the Lincoln Memorial, King spoke of completing democracy's unfinished journey from racial slavery to black citizenship. He appeared in his trademark dark suit and tie before 250,000 people, the biggest crowd he ever addressed, watched by the largest group of reporters, journalists, radio operators, and television cameras assembled in Washington since the Kennedy inauguration.[6]

In the speech, King unveiled an audacious vision of multiracial democracy contoured by an acknowledgment of the frightening realities of racial oppression, publicly denouncing Alabama's "vicious racists" while expressing hope that Dixie's cradle might one day embrace black and white children "as sisters and brothers." But King tempered his robust expression of faith in American democracy with a hard-earned realism about the struggles ahead, noting the need for civil rights activists to "work together, to pray together, to struggle together, to go to jail together" to achieve the expansive dream of freedom he outlined. The speech described the depth and breadth of structural racism as an organizing force in American life, noting that many who traveled to the nation's capital had been "staggered by the winds of police brutality." King charged those in attendance with returning to their cities, towns, and states with a renewed determination that American democracy could be redeemed by "unearned suffering" that creatively dramatized racial and economic injustice. His extemporized conclusion riffed on the themes of justice, equality, and interracial democracy that had been a hallmark of his public oratory and sermons but had never been witnessed on such a grand scale. He juxtaposed the history of slavery, the massive white resistance to racial integration, and the complicity of elected officials against the dream of a future where Georgia, Mississippi, and Alabama exemplified racial justice and radical democracy. Having brought the entire nation as close to a mass church meeting as it would ever get, he ended in an "old Negro spiritual: 'Free at last, free at last; thank God Almighty, we are free at last.'"[7]

The March on Washington successfully made racial justice the core of America's national creed. The turnout of a quarter of a million Americans, including almost one hundred thousand white people, represented a high point in the nation's unfolding civil rights saga; the culmination of decades of political activism that placed racial equality as the key to America's democratic imagination and national political ambition. King's speech painstakingly bridged the divide between those who saw civil rights as solely a political struggle and those who viewed it primarily through a moral, theological, and spiritual lens. Ultimately, the most radical aspects of King's words would be forgotten by supporters, like Kennedy, who marveled at King's speechmaking: "He's damn good."[8]

Malcolm X, meanwhile, turned whatever admiration he had for King's oratory into an attack on the proceedings as stage-managed by the Kennedy administration. He accused the president of trying to hijack the revolutionary potential of the black freedom struggle and shape it into a reformist movement. He viewed the entire affair as missed opportunity thwarted by the Kennedy administration and the burning desire of Negro leaders for political acceptance. Abandoning earlier plans to shut down the capital's roads, bridges, and airports through massive civil disobedience, organizers instead had settled for "marching between two dead presidents."[9]

Although Malcolm didn't attend the march, some of his political surrogates did, most notably journalist William Worthy. Worthy considered Malcolm to be a friend and political exemplar, taking his call for self-determination one step further by forming the Freedom Now Party (FNP), perhaps the earliest effort to organize an independent black political party during the 1960s. During the march, Worthy and other FNP activists passed out leaflets entitled *The Declaration of Washington*, promoting an all-black political party. They argued that blacks, by casting one million votes for the FNP, could alter power relations in Washington and throughout the nation.[10]

The FBI observed FNP activists, hoping to both investigate the group and keep Kennedy out of a potential public-relations disaster. The prospect of such controversy increased the day after the march, when Worthy led eight FNP activists into FBI headquarters for an impromptu sit-in that frightened officials enough to schedule an on-the-spot meeting with J. Edgar Hoover. For an hour, Worthy accused the FBI with dereliction of duty in protecting civil rights workers as Hoover strongly denied the charges. Sensing the entire scenario might be a setup to damage the bureau's reputation, Hoover lauded the goals of the march, publicly telling the assembled that he hoped it might quell "unjustified violence against the Negro." Afterward, both sides claimed victory, with Worthy satisfied that his group had dared to personally confront the FBI director and challenge him to protect black lives, while Hoover and his aides crowed about having stalled a potential race controversy. The larger meaning of the episode lay in the hidden bowels of the black freedom struggle, a world where unsanctioned allies of Malcolm X leveraged King's mobilizing abilities in service of their own radical political ambitions.[11]

The March on Washington's success engineered a rapprochement between King and Kennedy. A visibly impressed Kennedy reunited with King at the White House after the speech like an old friend. "I have a dream," offered the smiling president. His actions were in stark contrast with his attitude from just that spring, when he had warned Bobby Kennedy away from associating too closely with King, noting that "King is so hot these days that it's like Marx coming to the White House." A president with a keen sense of popular sentiment, Kennedy now accepted King with open arms.[12]

One week after the march, Malcolm X and James Baldwin publicly debated the merits of racial integration, the progress of racial justice, and the future of American democracy. "If integration is going to give the black people in America complete freedom, complete justice and complete equality," Malcolm declared, "then it's a worthwhile goal." He pointed out that civil rights struggles were inherently flawed: they operated from a position of weakness rather than strength by begging for citizenship rights. "It's not integration with us until the entire thing is laid on the table, not a hundred years from now, but in the morning and at the rate that the NAACP, CORE, and the Urban League is willing" to wait on white America's forbearance, "we who are Muslim feel we'll be sitting around America for another thousand years, not waiting for civil rights . . . but even waiting to be granted the rights of a human being."[13]

With that, Malcolm threw down a gauntlet that remains as central to his political legacy as it is unrecognized. He viewed civil rights at its best as an assertion of black humanity. Not only did black lives matter, they did not require federal permission to sit at a lunch counter, the protection of troops to attend public schools, or massive demonstrations to guarantee their right to vote. Baldwin remained mesmerized by the sheer audacity of Malcolm's truth telling, but he was skeptical of his ability to lead a political revolution. He considered Malcolm's ability to diagnose American racism to be unparalleled, yet Baldwin chafed at substituting one form of oppression (institutional racism) for another (religious theocracy under Elijah Muhammad). "I think it has a great deal less to do with equality than it had to do with power," suggested Baldwin, anticipating the chief argument deployed by Black Power activists.[14]

Baldwin disputed Malcolm's portrait of white supremacy as irrevocably damaging to black identity. "It is no longer possible," insisted Baldwin, "for a white man in this country to tell a Negro who he is and make the Negro believe this because the controlling image is absolutely gone." Malcolm and Baldwin bonded over a shared skepticism about American democracy's ability to extend citizenship to black people. Both men, in meticulous and exacting ways, relished confronting the brutality of America's racial history. Slavery, Jim Crow, and lynching figured deeply in all of Malcolm's speeches and Baldwin's essays. Each recognized in the other an ability to boldly speak truth to power in a unique voice that matched genuine passion with a rare talent for lucid analysis.[15]

Malcolm used scathing humor to express his disapproval of the March on Washington, comparing it to a sporting event. "I was impressed the same way I would be with the Rose Bowl game, the Kentucky Derby, and the World Series," he recounted to one journalist. He offered the suggestion that President Kennedy "should get Academy Awards for directing the best show of the century." He admitted to reporters that he was "moved" by Mahalia Jackson's stirring singing and King's speech, praise he quickly followed with a line that would become legendary: "While King was having a dream, the rest of us Negroes are having a nightmare."[16]

Then, on Sunday, September 15, a little over two weeks after the March on Washington, the Sixteenth Street Baptist Church in Birmingham was bombed, killing four young girls attending Sunday school. The bombing triggered civil unrest in the city as hundreds gathered in expressions of rage and grief that led to skirmishes, pitting bottle-and-rock-throwing demonstrators against armed police. The death of four innocent girls seemed to justify Malcolm X's withering characterization of the March on Washington as a kind of political theater that allowed the nation to ignore its dark underbelly. While President Kennedy released a statement lamenting "violence which has fallen on the innocent," King preached the joint funeral of three of the girls, Addie Mae Collins, Carol Denise McNair, and Cynthia Wesley. Carole Robertson, the fourth victim, had a separate funeral the day before.

King contemplated several strategies in light of the tragedy, including a nationwide boycott, massive demonstrations of civil disobedience, and a voting-rights campaign. He warmed to the last suggestion but, in the meantime, flew from Birmingham to Washington to meet with Kennedy. King urged the president to dispatch federal troops to Birmingham to restore a sense of dignity and safety to a black community he described as under siege. "There is a great deal of frustration and despair" in Birmingham, he told the president, ticking off the fact that the city's black population had been plagued by over two dozen unsolved terror bombings. Kennedy acknowledged that the long history of black suffering in Birmingham made "this bombing particularly difficult" but balked at federal intervention. Then, in October 1963, Bobby Kennedy approved FBI wiretaps of King's Atlanta office and home. The order represented the culmination of two years of J. Edgar Hoover's prodding, sparked by the president's disappointment with the FBI's lethargic response during the Freedom Rides. Stanley Levison's ties to the Communist Party USA, then long severed, gave Hoover an inroad into marking King as a subversive potentially taking orders from foreign agents.[17]

For Malcolm X, even as he found his strength within the Nation diminishing, the shifting civil rights landscape offered him new opportunities to exert political influence within the larger struggle. Throughout the fall, he positioned himself as a leader suitable for black activists who disagreed with King's tactics and were skeptical of the potential impact of civil rights legislation. He led a parallel black freedom struggle, one that intersected and overlapped with the mainstream movement but yearned for radical measures to achieve black citizenship. Detroit represented one of the key political centers for black radicalism on this score, and Malcolm established deep ties there. In the second week of November, Malcolm's allies, including Reverend Albert Cleage, organized the Grassroots Leadership Conference. The event attracted black militants, some with past and current associations with civil rights groups, who nonetheless longed for more combative leadership in the struggle for racial justice. Many of these activists—including Cleage, James and Grace Lee Boggs, journalist William Worthy, and Cambridge, Maryland, civil rights leader Gloria Richardson—considered Malcolm their political leader. The conference would resonate for a long time: its local character and national ambitions provided the intellectual and political genealogy for future activists who would posthumously take up Malcolm's legacy.[18]

Malcolm's "Message to the Grass Roots," delivered in Detroit on Sunday, November 10, 1963, might be best interpreted as his rejoinder to King's "I Have a Dream" speech. If King's concept of social justice offered the black freedom struggle as a shield against America's worst racial impulses, Malcolm envisioned the black revolution as a sword cutting through centuries of oppression with political self-determination that would upend long-standing injustice.

Over the course of a watershed evening at King Solomon Baptist Church in front of an audience of over two thousand, Malcolm X laid down the political blueprint for a "black revolution," one that required radical black solidarity. He cited the history of violent upheaval in Russia, Latin America, Cuba, Asia, and Africa to challenge the notion that black freedom could be achieved peacefully. "You don't have a turn-the-other-cheek revolution," Malcolm said. "There's no such thing as a nonviolent revolution." He characterized the political struggle being waged within the black community, personified by his increasingly public conflict with King, through the allegory of the House Negro versus the Field Negro. The former was similar to modern integrationists. During slavery, Malcolm argued, House Negroes psychologically and politically identified with America's master class, enjoying better food, clothing, and shelter at the expense of their human dignity. This dynamic of paternalism and tokenism stood in stark contrast to Field Negroes, the black working class Malcolm championed. Field Negroes plotted slave revolts, rebelled against plantation owners, and prayed for the deaths of white slave owners.

"I'm a Field Negro," Malcolm proudly proclaimed, castigating blacks who identified with American democracy at the expense of understanding the inner workings of racial oppression.[19]

Malcolm once again excoriated the March on Washington for diminishing the movement's revolutionary energies. "They didn't integrate it," Malcolm alleged. "They infiltrated it. They joined it, became a part of it, took it over." Consequently, "it ceased to be angry, ceased to be hot, it ceased to be uncompromising." Instead it "became a picnic, a circus." Malcolm later recounted his disappointment with the manner in which the march seemed to be under white control. "They had been told *how* to arrive, *when*, *where* to arrive, *where* to assemble, when to *start* marching, the *route* to march," he remembered. "First-aid stations were strategically located—even where to *faint*!" Malcolm's narrative portrayed King and civil rights leaders as too eager to please the president, unaware of the political resolve they had displayed over the White House's objections to the march. In its own inimitable way, the march represented a militant nonviolent protest against the racial injustice and economic inequality that Malcolm himself railed against. A part of him knew this, and he wrestled with it in public by portraying the march as a missed opportunity to paralyze the entire city.[20]

Malcolm's speech expanded the political, ideological, and geographical horizons of the "black revolution," yet he was describing a struggle that King played a vital role in popularizing. Malcolm now embarked on a mission of organizing a black political revolution with new allies, representatives of at least eleven cities in eight states who vowed to join a national effort to internationalize the black freedom struggle by touring Africa, supporting the all-black Freedom Now Party, and advocating for radical political self-determination that included self-defense. His address altered the landscape of black politics, but its impact would not be felt until two generations of black activists would come together to organize a movement for Black Power.[21]

On November 22 of that same year, John F. Kennedy was assassinated in Dallas, Texas. The event shocked the nation and left King without his most powerful ally. After watching news reports of the president's assassination, King struck a note of fatalism with Coretta. "This is what's going to happen to me," he told her. "This is such a sick society."[22]

On December 1, nine days after Kennedy's assassination, Malcolm X's association with the Nation of Islam formally ended. Although he generally heeded Muhammad's warning not to publicly disparage Kennedy's legacy, he slipped and described Kennedy's death as "chickens coming home to roost," unleashing a metaphor that sparked national controversy. And his speech, "God's Judgment of White America," made the same point. America's wealth, he argued, rested on an empire of slavery that would, just like past kingdoms, topple under the weight of its own misdeeds. "The hour of judgment and doom" were the direct results of "the evil seeds of slavery and hypocrisy" that allowed Americans to forget the horrors of its past while extolling the virtues of democracy and citizenship, which rested on racial oppression and black exploitation. Malcolm linked the decline of Western civilization and America's empire to "the rise of the dark world," whose flourishing anti-colonial movements were toppling kingdoms. "Our present generation," Malcolm observed, "is witnessing the end of colonialism, Europeanism, Westernism," and "white supremacy"—all of which was at the root of global injustices both visible and unseen.[23]

Malcolm parried with reporters after his speech, which was attended by seven hundred people, including representatives of Elijah Muhammad. Malcolm knew as much, at one point joking with reporters that they were looking to bait him into rejoicing over Kennedy's death by saying, "Hooray, hooray! I'm glad he got it!" He turned serious by citing the 1961 murder of Congolese prime minister Patrice Lumumba and the more recent assassinations of Medgar Evers in Mississippi and four black girls in Birmingham as examples of the swirling violence plaguing America. The nation,

Malcolm explained, was in a death spiral precipitated by its own behavior. Why should a sitting president be immune to forces he himself had helped amplify?[24]

Malcolm's speech marked the denouement of his long-running critique of President Kennedy, which was part of a conversation on race and democracy that Malcolm participated in—both as a counterpoint to Martin Luther King Jr. and as a public intellectual offering a radical interpretation of American history and politics—that remains an unappreciated chapter in the racial saga of the 1960s. Indeed, "God's Judgment of White America" focused on the hypocrisy of American democracy and its slain president. Malcolm's verbal denunciations of Kennedy helped to secularize his message of radical black dignity.[25]

The Messenger reacted swiftly, banning Malcolm from speaking publicly for three months. The decision was less of a punishment than a form of exile, since Muhammad knew that Malcolm would be unable to remain silent. Muhammad released a statement proclaiming that Malcolm's sentiments about "our president" were not his own, a stunning public reversal for a man whose teachings predicted nothing less than the destruction of American society. Behind the scenes, the Messenger was using Malcolm's ill-timed comments as a pretext to muzzle his most powerful disciple. Malcolm's discussion of Muhammad's sexual misconduct within the Nation, coupled with his growing national political ambitions, made his presence in the organization untenable.[26]

Malcolm personally chafed against the growing contradictions within the movement, especially the Messenger's failure to sanction retaliation against Muslims who had been killed or assaulted by police, most notably Ronald Stokes, the Los Angeles NOI laborer whom Malcolm had considered a friend. Malcolm also longed to actively participate in, and help shape, local and national civil rights struggles. And his deepening interest in orthodox Islam made him uncomfortable with NOI mythology. He would use the next three months to take a family vacation, but he remained in the media spotlight through the rise of Cassius Clay, one of his Muslim protégés who had become a heavyweight boxing champion, and reemerged in March as an independent political leader. Freed from the NOI's constrictions, Malcolm would be full of surprises, including public and private overtures to former adversaries, most notably Martin Luther King Jr.

Kennedy's assassination upended the lives of both King and Malcolm, but for different reasons. The president's death saddened King as a lost opportunity and example of the culture of violence gripping much of American society. In this sense, King personally felt, but did not publicly express, the larger meaning behind Malcolm X's "chickens coming home to roost" statement. Malcolm recognized, as did King, the corrosive nature of violence in society. But where Malcolm sought to redirect and harness violence as a sword capable of defeating centuries of long-standing racial oppression, King looked upon nonviolence as a balm capable of healing the nation from the specter of violence unleashed by the murder of the president.[27]

Kennedy's death introduced King to his third American president in the span of four years. Two days after Malcolm's suspension from the NOI, King met with Lyndon Johnson at the White House, coming away "impressed" by the president's knowledge and commitment to racial justice. The meeting touched off a relationship that would grow into a fruitful, if at times contentious, partnership. In a nation stunned by Kennedy's death, King emerged with a stature that rivaled the anxious new president. *Time* named King "Man of the Year," an honor that would soon be surpassed by global accolades. On December 21, he expressed aspects of Malcolm's argument that Kennedy's death represented the culmination of an American and global culture of racial hatred and violence in more gentler tones, in an article for the *New York Amsterdam News*. "What Killed JFK?" blamed the president's assassination on "the same climate that murdered Medgar Evers in Mississippi and six innocent Negro children in Birmingham, Alabama."[28]

King diverged from Malcolm X by offering no hints of pleasure at either the circumstances that led to the uptick in national violence or Kennedy's actual death. King implicated the entire nation in the assassination by virtue of a collective betrayal of democratic principles, reflected in "an atmosphere in which violence and hatred have become popular pastimes." His essay attracted far less attention than Malcolm's post-assassination sound bite but explored remarkably similar themes. He interpreted Kennedy's death as a political, cultural, and spiritual crossroads for the nation and challenged elected officials, religious clergy, and ordinary citizens alike to come to terms with the moral and political futility of violence. King agreed with, and even amplified, major aspects of Malcolm's criticism of American violence. Nevertheless, he delivered this message under the cover of a national call to unity that, for the moment, distinguished him from his rival. For now, Malcolm and Martin's parallel vision that located the roots of the Kennedy assassination in racial violence was a shared, although unspoken, political symmetry between them.[29]

CHAPTER 7

"What Is a Dream to You Is a Nightmare to Us"

President Lyndon Johnson's January 8, 1964, State of the Union speech called for "peace and abundance for all," tapping into Martin Luther King Jr.'s most ambitious freedom dreams. Johnson challenged Congress to do "more for civil rights than the last hundred sessions combined." He amplified King's message about economic injustice by calling for "all-out war on human poverty and unemployment" in the nation. For King, the prospect of major anti-poverty legislation lent new credibility to the inroads civil rights activism was making on American political culture.[1]

King, along with several other civil rights leaders, met with Johnson at the White House ten days after the speech. They listened as Johnson announced full-throated support for the Kennedy civil rights bill, "without," the president explained, "a word or comma changed."[2] Johnson, who deeply admired Franklin Delano Roosevelt's New Deal, planned to inaugurate a similar era of progressive legislation by using political momentum from the Kennedy assassination to enact civil rights policy. Johnson viewed racial justice and the war on poverty as an essential part of his imagined

Great Society; a nation that basked in its racial and ethnic diversity, refused to let the poor and elderly reside in squalor, cherished its children, and offered health care to the middle class and the indigent. King, sensing an opportunity, informed reporters after the meeting that Johnson planned to do nothing less than "bring the standards of the Negro up and bring him into the mainstream of life." Black citizenship, King suggested, required not only legislation that would end racial discrimination; it required a massive redistribution of economic resources nationally, which Lyndon Johnson had privately acknowledged during their meeting.[3]

The shadow of the Kennedy assassination and the promise of the war on poverty combined powerfully in the political imaginations of King and Johnson. The political climate engendered by national crisis offered opportunities and perils for the civil rights leader and the new president. King spent the next two months delivering speeches and formulating plans for a major SCLC initiative in Alabama and Florida that would concentrate on voting rights and desegregation. All the while, he remained a target of FBI surveillance. J. Edgar Hoover grew particularly interested in King's extramarital liaisons. He labeled King a "'tom cat' with obsessive degenerate sexual urges." Although King had been previously warned by Kennedy about the bureau's interest in his private life, he seemed unable to change his behavior, instead remaining burdened with guilt over the potentially catastrophic damage exposure of his affairs would have on the civil rights movement.[4]

The FBI also doggedly watched Malcolm and the NOI. In 1957, the same year that Muhammad named Malcolm national representative, J. Edgar Hoover placed a wiretap in the Messenger's Chicago home. FBI agents infiltrated the NOI, monitored the Messenger's movements and phones, read *Muhammad Speaks*, and carefully watched Malcolm X's every move. One report on Malcolm described him as no ordinary agitator. "He neither smokes nor drinks and is of high moral character," wrote the NOI informant. The New York Police Department's investigative unit, the Bureau of Special Services, amplified this surveillance. Malcolm held a defiant awareness of federal and local intrusion on his political activities. "When I was speaking publicly sometimes I'd guess which were F.B.I. faces in the audience or other types of agents," he recalled. "Both the police and the F.B.I. intently and persistently visited and questioned us." But, despite his bravado, Malcolm grew weary of the constant surveillance.[5]

Malcolm, in the midst of wrestling with his own secrets, declared his political independence to the world via a press release on March 8. He now used his public-relations skills to their maximum benefit. He announced plans to leave the NOI, declaring himself loyal to the Messenger and vowing to advance Elijah Muhammad's message of self-determination on his own. In fact, Malcolm had no intention of walking away from an organization he helped to build. He dreamed of recruiting hundreds, if not thousands, of disgruntled Muslims who were fed up with the Messenger's behavior and the growing culture of corruption, violence, and graft that shadowed the NOI. Malcolm privately hoped to recruit his friend, mentee, and newly crowned heavyweight boxing champ Cassius Clay to his cause.

Elijah Muhammad matched his wayward pupil's efforts at public dissemblance. The Messenger wept in front of reporters at his Phoenix home upon hearing the news of Malcolm's official departure. "I am stunned," he told reporters. "I never dreamed this man would deviate from the Nation of Islam." Muhammad failed to mention that he personally authorized Malcolm's ouster and dictated the terms of his exit. The Messenger's recent decision to rename Cassius Clay Muhammad Ali struck the first blow in a political battle that would play out over the course of the next year. The ease with which the Messenger had plucked the young boxer from the celebrity New York minister who personally converted him to Islam demonstrated how Muhammad's organizational strength outmatched Malcolm's charismatic appeal. Muhammad vowed to strip his former disciple of everything and made no effort to quiet the death threats against Malcolm already emerging from inside the NOI.[6]

After reading reports of Muhammad's tearful speech, Malcolm sent a telegram to reporters blaming his separation from the group on NOI officials jealous of his fame and political integrity. The statement and telegram highlighted the internal conflicts that led to the split. Within the Nation, soldiers were already making plans to assassinate Malcolm, who was positioned as an apostate and a traitor to the Messenger and Islam. Malcolm, on the other hand, navigated a treacherous exit from the group that had nurtured him and provided his first taste of personal and professional dignity.[7]

On Thursday, March 12, 1964, just over three months after his suspension, Malcolm held a press conference where he verbally joined the civil rights struggle and openly courted figures he once castigated as "modern Negro magicians." In essence, this press conference represented his first real effort at a rapprochement with Martin Luther King Jr. Malcolm's talk of forming a "black nationalist party" inspired at least one black newspaper to call him a "politician." He now vowed to aid the black freedom struggle, including advocates of racial integration, by injecting a new revolutionary voice into the movement. He claimed that no special education or expertise gave him the right to lead a movement, "but I am sincere," he said, "and my sincerity are my credentials." He called himself a leader in the "struggle for Human Rights" and discussed a wide range of political issues, including independent black politics, rifle clubs promoting self-defense of black communities, and the use of black electoral power to ensure political accountability in a presidential election year. Malcolm sounded a clear warning that echoed his "Message to the Grass Roots" address in Detroit: "There can be no revolution without bloodshed," he thundered, "and it is nonsense to describe the civil rights movement in America as a revolution." He counseled blacks to boycott the US military. "Whenever a Negro fights for 'democracy,'" he quipped, "he's fighting for something he has not got, never had, and never will have."[8]

"I have no plans to run for office," Malcolm explained coyly, before noting that black people "who can't be bought out" should mount political campaigns. Instead, he expressed a keen interest in challenging public policies that furthered black oppression, most notably New York City's recent stop-and-frisk and no-knock laws, which gave police more power at the expense of black civil liberties. "This is an anti-Negro law," Malcolm observed, and he called on civil rights organizations to "wipe it out or wipe out the politicians who passed it." He proposed self-defense as the simple recognition of black people's constitutional rights—actions that were within the bounds of the law. "If the government thinks that I'm wrong for saying this," Malcolm said, anticipating a torrent of criticism that would redefine his statement as a call for "violence" against whites, "then let the government start doing its job." Malcolm spent the spring lobbying civil rights activists, ordinary black Americans, and grassroots political organizers on behalf of a revolutionary political agenda, one that he explicitly tied to transforming American democracy through the legal and legislative arena. Privately, he made plans to make the hajj, the pilgrimage to Mecca that had eluded him during his visit to the Middle East five years earlier.[9]

Already considered in some quarters to be black America's unelected prime minister, Malcolm now dove into secular politics with the same zeal that had helped him turn the NOI into a phenomenon. Critics interpreted the self-defense posturing as a declaration of war, characterizing him as a dangerous pied piper for racial violence, his fame built around "charm and guns." *Muhammad Speaks*, the NOI newspaper that Malcolm helped to build from scratch, now publicly identified him as a blood enemy, recruiting ex-friends, old protégés, and family members to offer negative testimonials that ensured his exile would be permanent. The same organ that Malcolm once hoped would spread the Nation's message across the country now became an instrument actively fomenting character assassination and death threats. Bayard Rustin, Malcolm's friendly debating partner during the early 1960s, informed the *New York Times* that, although blacks rejected his solutions, they largely accepted his "analysis of the evils" perpetuated by white racism. Gloria Richardson, the Cambridge, Maryland, activist who attended Malcolm's Detroit speech, applauded his move to participate in the civil rights movement. "He can offer something that has not been offered before," she suggested. Some of the most militant civil rights activists in the country were watching Malcolm, carefully observing his political steps with an eye toward possibly joining him or gaining fresh insight from his best ideas.[10]

Two days after publicly joining the black freedom movement, Malcolm attended a conference of black political leaders in Chester, Pennsylvania, the home of King's alma mater Crozer Theological Seminary. Sixty leaders representing over forty-five local and national civil rights groups met in Chester to plot a more radical direction for the movement. Malcolm knew a lot of these activists and promised to help them in any way he could. Many, including Richardson, Chicago activist Lawrence Landry, and Brooklyn school desegregation leader Milton Galamison, eagerly accepted.[11]

In Chester, Malcolm revealed his new political direction and ideological break with the NOI. His new organization, Muslim Mosque Inc., would accept white support, but no members, since blacks needed to "unite among ourselves before uniting with them." Malcolm's willingness to accept white support in the immediate aftermath of his break with the NOI illustrates his complicated relationship with Elijah Muhammad's philosophy of racial separatism. Malcolm had joined and stayed in the NOI because of his religious devoutness. But, alongside local and national civil rights struggles, he developed political instincts that led him to privately disagree with many of the Nation's positions. Now unshackled from the organization, Malcolm publicly embraced a radical human rights agenda that had always formed the core of his political identity as a black Muslim. "If the government doesn't help us, we'll have to arm ourselves. When our people are bitten by dogs, they're within their rights to kill those dogs," Malcolm asserted to enthusiastic applause. His push for black political organizing in this speech marked a noticeable shift in his political rhetoric, one that found common ground with King.[12]

That same day, King responded. During a speech in New York City to over 2,500 teachers, King characterized Malcolm's "call to arms" as a strategy that was "ineffective and immoral." He claimed to want to personally discuss the issue of nonviolence with Malcolm. Like the Muslim leader, King vowed that "the struggle ahead will be of massive proportions," but he insisted that only nonviolence offered a clear path to black citizenship. He acknowledged the simultaneous "frustration and determination" felt among black communities protesting around the country for civil rights, and he supported the New York City school boycotts as a creative way to highlight "injustice and indignities" nonviolently. King vowed to "wear down" congressional filibusters against pending civil rights legislation, an assertion that would eventually lead him to appear at the US Senate.[13]

Malcolm also supported the boycott of New York City schools. But speaking at a rally organized by Harlem rent-strike leader Jesse Gray on West 118th Street, Malcolm refused to join picket lines, because the demonstration's commitment to nonviolence clashed with his own belief in self-defense. Malcolm made sure to note that his support was not for racial integration but ending white supremacy. "I'm aligned with everyone who will take some action to end this criminal situation in the schools," he told reporters. "I don't care what kind of action it is." Over a quarter of a million absent schoolchildren made the boycott against New York's public schools a massive success, which offered intriguing new possibilities for Malcolm. Police commissioner Michael Murphy denounced Malcolm as a dangerously subversive leader capable of inspiring citywide violence. "The greatest compliment anyone can say to me," Malcolm responded, "is to say I'm irresponsible, because by responsible they mean Negroes who are responsible to white authorities—Negro Uncle Toms."[14]

The *Los Angeles Times* reported that boycott leaders were "elated" by the dual support of Malcolm X and Martin Luther King Jr., but the historic importance of this political convergence remained lost on the wider public. Malcolm basked in the spotlight of serving as a roving ambassador to militant civil rights activists. Two days after King's speech in New York, Malcolm triumphantly walked into the Brooklyn headquarters of the school boycott, Siloam Presbyterian Church. His surprise appearance upstaged the presence of Galamison and Congressman Adam Clayton Powell Jr., attracting journalists and organizers who watched as Malcolm turned Galamison's upstairs church study into an impromptu briefing room. His aura of celebrity gave a jolt of energy to the one thousand demonstrators who came to the church in support of the boycott. "It's Malcolm!" screamed one young white woman. Malcolm spent an hour serving as a spokesman for a boycott he considered more a necessary evil than the correct strategy for defeating racial injustice. "You can propose all day," he said at one point, "what you need is action."[15]

Not everyone in the civil rights community welcomed Malcolm into its fold. A *Baltimore Afro-American* editorial, titled "Welcome Mat Missing," pointedly reminded Malcolm of his caustic attacks on civil rights leaders supporting racial integration, criticism that was as recent as it was raw and personal. If Malcolm faced skepticism from parts of the black press, he also experienced public repudiation from an older generation of black activists led by Ralph Bunche, the Howard University professor turned UN undersecretary and Nobel Prize winner, who blasted Malcolm's talk of rifle clubs and self-defense as "immoral." The Messenger also attacked him as a hypocrite who had strayed from NOI orthodoxy "to go after something that he himself has been criticizing—to the civil righters' movement." Muhammad alleged that Malcolm sought spiritual salvation through political means, and the Messenger alternated between a public stance of equanimity and fits of pique and mourning, where he expressed astonishment at a betrayal whose source he intimately understood yet refused to acknowledge.[16]

In a speech that spring at Harvard University, Malcolm continued his critique of America's political system, characterizing himself as "one of twenty-two million black people in this country who are victims of your democratic system." He explained, "Yesterday, our people used to look upon the American system as an American dream. But the black people today are beginning to realize that it is an American nightmare. What is a dream to you is a nightmare to us." Malcolm hoped to end this nightmare with black power, which he defined as voting rights, political consciousness, community control of neighborhoods, and black pride. King's dream encompassed parts of this formula in service of comprehensive political reform, but he still regarded black pride as largely a vehicle for black nationalism, which might lead to racial separatism of the kind advocated by the NOI. Malcolm disagreed. "The restoration of our cultural roots and history will restore dignity to the black people in this country," he said. He defined radical black dignity expansively, decrying racial gerrymandering in congressional districts as an evil that existed on the same spectrum as being denied knowledge "about the glorious civilization that existed" in Africa. Malcolm's prediction that a large enough black vote "would change the foreign policy as well as the domestic policy" of the country offered the clearest indication of his new political direction. In Malcolm's imagination, blacks recognized as "victims" of democracy would become its greatest architects.[17]

At Harvard, Malcolm repeatedly upheld the black vote as the key to the future of American democracy. He chided both major political parties as hypocrites, citing black power as a threat to a status quo enjoyed by politicians on both sides of the political divide. "Therefore," Malcolm argued, "the only valid approach toward revolutionizing American foreign policy" was to ensure voting rights for blacks. Malcolm rehearsed aspects of the argument he would make in one of his most famous speeches, "The Ballot or the Bullet," during this appearance at Harvard, showcasing a newfound faith in the power of social movements to bend history's arc toward black citizenship and racial justice. Elijah Muhammad had publicly repudiated Malcolm, but the Messenger had erred in accusing Malcolm of trying to join the civil rights movement. Malcolm instead wished to lead a national movement for black power, which he defined as a struggle for radical political self-determination, anti-colonialism, and human rights that intersected with a vision of local, regional, national, and global racial and economic justice. Malcolm wasn't trying to join the movement, but rather to co-opt it into a broader and more revolutionary global insurgency that would culminate in radical black dignity globally.[18]

Malcolm's speech before an audience of three thousand people at Harlem's Rockland Palace on Sunday, March 22, announced his participation in what he called a "human rights" movement that would utilize grassroots organizing, electoral politics, and self-defense to achieve racial justice in America. "It's time for you and me to let the Government know it's ballots—or bullets," Malcolm said to cheering supporters. He called for one million new registered voters, anticipating the political leverage in national and local elections that blacks would utilize after the passage of voting rights. "There will be nonviolence only with those who are not violent with us," Malcolm said. He placed himself alongside national movement leaders as a social justice warrior battling for more than civil rights. "If Adam Clayton Powell, Martin Luther King and the Rev. Milton A. Galamison can fight for human rights as Christian ministers," Malcolm reasoned, "I see no reason why I can't do the same as a Muslim minister." He promised to "form whatever is necessary—whether it's a black nationalist party or black nationalist army—to achieve black citizenship that would end police brutality, eliminate the newly instituted stop-and-frisk law, and integrate public schools. He offered a tantalizing sketch of racial unity that would lead to unprecedented black power. His speech in Harlem positioned his concept of radical black dignity against King's notion of radical black citizenship. Although Malcolm remained skeptical of American democracy, he now campaigned for voter education, grassroots agitation, and community organizing.[19]

The freedom to choose his own path broadened Malcolm's ideological horizons and took him to unexpected sites of political conflict. On Wednesday, March 25, Malcolm announced plans to visit the US Senate to observe the filibuster of the civil rights bill. "I am throwing myself into the heart of the civil rights struggle and will be in it from now on," Malcolm informed the *New York Amsterdam News*. He arrived in Washington the next day, emboldened by supporters of his efforts to internationalize the civil rights struggle. The transformation of American domestic policy loomed large, and Malcolm spent the last Thursday in March holding impromptu press conferences, stalking the halls of the Senate building, and conducting a seminar on black radicalism that jarred Washington's political equilibrium while scandalizing its sense of decorum. He questioned the Democratic Party's commitment to racial justice, pointing out the large number of southerners participating in the filibuster, and accused President Johnson of being unable to end Jim Crow "in his own home state of Texas," let alone the entire nation.[20]

Martin Luther King Jr. also roamed the halls of the Senate that day, holding a press conference after conferring with Senator Hubert Humphrey, who was leading the fight on the floor to pass the bill. Malcolm listened quietly as King vowed to continue fighting for racial justice whether the bill passed or not. Afterward, Malcolm ran into King in the Senate gallery, both men surrounded by aides and journalists. King spoke first, greeting his adversary within the movement like an old friend. "Well, Malcolm, good to see you," he said, offering a handshake. Malcolm, recognizing the gesture of fellowship, replied in kind. "Good to see you."[21]

It was their first and only meeting, and photographers snapped pictures of them smiling as they shook hands. As they strolled the corridors of the Senate, Malcolm leaned down to listen to King while a media throng surrounded them. The *Chicago Defender* ran an alternate photo of the two looking serious, above a caption describing the scene as "a bizarre union," a sentiment that obscured the political kinship between Malcolm and Martin that remained a mystery to the wider public. The *New York Journal-American* featured a photo of them beaming, their smiles projecting their shared charisma and sense of humor, below a headline that signaled a potential rapprochement: "King and Malcolm X Join in Protest Vow." The story characterized their meeting as a sign of the times, where two men, "often poles apart," found common ground in predicting a fresh round of protest as Congress continued to debate the civil rights bill.[22]

Malcolm was tall and lean, his clean-shaven face making him look younger than thirty-eight. King's statesman-like bearing made him seem taller than he was. The photographers captured both men in a moment of transition. While Malcolm was newly free of the confines of the NOI and exploring his political persona, King found himself more easily shouldering his role as a civil rights symbol. After Birmingham, he exuded the confidence of someone who regularly consulted with presidents. His lobbying efforts in support of the civil rights bill were deliberate, organized, and impactful. While legislators and activist groups wrote the details of the bill, King could rightfully claim to have popularized many of the bill's ideas. The meeting between Malcolm and Martin represented a culmination of two political leaders whose search for black citizenship and dignity found them converging at an unlikely location on the road to a shared rendezvous with destiny.

The growing momentum behind his organizing efforts and the recent glimpses of success allowed King to think more ambitiously. The Johnson administration and the upcoming presidential election created new opportunities for King and the movement. When

Malcolm and King met, King had earned a privileged position within the American establishment as the major representative of the black freedom struggle, though he remained committed to retaining his political independence as a social movement leader, pastor, and public intellectual willing to speak truth to power. King's conception of nonviolence had swelled beyond the legislative and legal battles that marked the civil rights era's heroic period. In the wake of Birmingham, Johnson's poverty war, and the prospect of passing major civil rights legislation, King began to identify more with the poor. Links between race, war, and economic justice that black radicals associated with Malcolm X would soon prove crucial to King's politics, especially after the August 1965 Watts rebellion.

Malcolm's journey made him better able to recognize the world's inherent humanity, but he hedged, finding renewed faith not in American democratic institutions but in leveraging grassroots activism to reimagine the world. Malcolm's talk of human rights found common ground with King's vision of the "world house," but the two diverged over nonviolence. Malcolm told anyone who would listen at the Senate building that any law passed would never be enforced. "Enforcing it would bring a civil war to the South and a race war to the North," he predicted. He provocatively added that, despite this bleak future, he planned to support "anything the Negro believes will help solve this problem." Malcolm's world was growing at a pace that exceeded his political grasp. His ambitions now outstripped his ability to garner the resources to implement a political revolution that could achieve black dignity that transcended domestic boundaries.[23]

At this moment, Malcolm X and Martin Luther King Jr. were starting to recognize each other's potential. King looked toward major urban centers in the North as possible sites of protest capable of expanding the freedom struggle beyond its southern roots. Malcolm looked both outward and within, signaling to American activists his willingness to enter their struggle and traveling around the world in hopes of building alliances that would empower him back home. At each step, the two men's political ambitions grew in proportion to the political challenges they faced.

Malcolm departed his meeting with King as black America's prosecuting attorney turned prime minister, a role he would play on the world stage the next month. He now publicly identified as a political and moral crusader in the mold of evangelist Billy Graham. "I will preach the gospel of Black Nationalism," he informed a group of astonished interracial clerics in Brooklyn on the second day of April. Asked by one minister if he had ever met a good white person, Malcolm replied with a quote that would become legendary: "I do not say there are no sincere white people," he replied, "but rather that I haven't met any." Malcolm's barbed wit masked a more complicated truth about his relationship with whites and his thoughts about interracial political organizing.[24]

Just a few days earlier, Malcolm had conducted an interview with the *Militant*, the official publication of the Socialist Workers Party (SWP). White socialists, most notably *Militant* editor and SWP founder George Breitman, would play a pivotal role in helping spread Malcolm's message of revolutionary black nationalism to white radicals around the nation and, over time, the world. Breitman courted Malcolm by covering his rallies, hosting forums on the "black revolution," and projecting him as an icon of a global political revolution among leftists. White interest in Malcolm's politics grew throughout the year. "Astonishing numbers of white people called," trying to join his mission, Malcolm recalled. The Nation of Islam responded with veiled death threats in *Muhammad Speaks*, character assassination, and public excommunications of Malcolm's old friends, protégés, and family members. *Muhammad Speaks* became the vehicle for spreading rumors and lies designed to incite violence against Malcolm. Elijah Muhammad, meanwhile, correctly interpreted Malcolm's apostasy as an existential threat, a fate that would reverberate back to centers of power, influence, corruption, and violence. Malcolm knew as much, confessing that "I had taught" NOI members how "to think."[25]

A culture of violence in the NOI that had been incubated in the paramilitary Fruit of Islam spread to mosques, where ministers doled out harsh punishments that included physical violence against members judged recalcitrant in work ethic, spiritual faith, or personal rectitude. Although not directly involved in these actions, Malcolm nonetheless sanctioned them while in the Nation and would be haunted by his failure to root out and eliminate the same organizational violence that now threatened him and his family. The April 10 issue of *Muhammad Speaks* cryptically announced a death sentence in a cartoon that featured Malcolm's decapitated head rolling toward a graveyard for alleged treachery against the Messenger, a gruesome threat reinforced by coverage of Malcolm's brother Philbert denouncing him as a traitor. Against the backdrop of these threats, Malcolm made plans to go on a five-week tour of Africa and the Middle East, a trip that signaled his deepening interest in orthodox Islam.[26]

Before departing for Cairo, Malcolm delivered two more versions of "The Ballot or the Bullet," an address that he expertly honed into a quintessential political stump speech. Cleveland and Detroit greeted him with rapturous crowds that included large numbers of black radicals, white Marxists, and civil rights apostates searching for new avenues of political engagement. Malcolm reimagined black radicalism, rhetorically knitting together a panoramically complex vision of black political self-determination expansive enough to appeal to broad activist constituencies. "The entire civil-rights struggles need a new interpretation, a broader interpretation," Malcolm suggested. He argued that years of seeming progress masked "more racial animosity, more racial hatred" in 1964 than had existed a decade before. Malcolm judged America for transgressions that stretched back to slavery, a period of time that produced undreamed-of wealth. "You let the white man walk around here talking about how rich this country is, but you never stop to think how it got rich so quick," he admonished. "It got rich because you made it rich. . . . Whenever you're going after something that belongs to you, anyone who's depriving you of the right to have it is a criminal."[27]

Malcolm interpreted antiblack racism as a series of historical and contemporary crimes against black dignity, citizenship, and equality. In "The Ballot or the Bullet," he documented these crimes, promoted self-defense against racial terror as legally and morally right, and called for a dramatic reinterpretation of the civil rights movement that would allow for radicals to join the fight for racial justice. He endeavored to "expand the civil rights struggle to the level of human rights" in an effort to leverage international opinion—from the United Nations to African and Third World nation-states—to finally achieve black citizenship. A worldwide struggle for black liberation underway mandated black dignity in America, Malcolm asserted. "Let it be the ballot or the bullet," he said. "By ballot I only mean freedom." Malcolm's call for massive black voter registration showcased his pragmatic side, even as his comment that the "leading Dixiecrat in Washington is in the White House" found him once again insulting a sitting president.[28]

Malcolm arrived in Africa with "one asset," his "international image," which he wielded to build global alliances. Time in Africa reinforced Malcolm's "psychological divorce from the Nation of Islam." His hajj to Mecca also proved to be revelatory personally as well politically. From the holy city, he penned a letter in the third week of April purposefully crafted to elicit shockwaves back home. Aware that his political mission required a new origin story, Malcolm gave the world one. With an eye for detail, he described the rituals of prayer that made up the holy pilgrimage, including a candid description of meeting, praying, and spiritually embracing Muslim "pilgrims" who ranged "from blue-eyed blonds to black skin Africans." The experience, Malcolm confessed, changed him. "I have never before seen sincere and true brotherhood practiced by all colors together, irrespective of their color." Honored as a guest of state by Saudi Arabia's Crown Prince Faisal, Malcolm stayed in accommodations reserved for visiting dignitaries, enjoying benefits that included air-conditioned living quarters, a guide, and a car and driver. Marveling at his good fortune, the preternaturally austere Malcolm—now going by his Muslim name, El-Hajj Malik El-Shabazz—basked in receiving "honors that in America would be bestowed upon a King—not a Negro."[29]

The royal treatment continued throughout his trip. Malcolm's bracing speeches on American racism captivated African students and revolutionaries. In Ibadan, Nigeria, Malcolm stressed the ancestral and political bonds linking continental Africans to black Americans fighting for human rights. "We are determined to change the image of Negroes in the US to a positive one," he explained to the Nigerian press, "with a view to restoring our cultural identity and build up communications between black Muslims in US and African countries." Malcolm's words captured his efforts to construct a revolutionary pan-African politics that included a global understanding of the Islamic faith. He now dreamed of becoming the leader of a political revolution steeped in the anticolonial fervor sweeping Africa, and to serve as a global ambassador of Islam, a religion that, in Malcolm's eyes, held the key to promoting racial and economic justice internationally.[30]

From Africa, Malcolm began a public-relations campaign to change his image, sending carefully worded telegrams to civil rights leaders—including friendly combatants Bayard Rustin and Milton Galamison—that were leaked to the press. The letters detailed his racial epiphany in Mecca, called for unity among civil rights leaders, and asked for "forgiveness" for words of fire deployed as recently as the previous month against black leaders. Malcolm kept a travel diary that offers profound insights into his intelligence, curious mind, and personal charm. These journal entries self-consciously document his evolution as a statesman on the world stage. Although he suspected he might have been a lawyer under different circumstances, his keen observational skills made him a deft cultural anthropologist. He documented everything from meetings with royalty in the Middle East to conversations with African students.

Nigerian students feted him as "Omowale," the Yoruba term for "the son who has come home." At virtually every stop, Malcolm met with Islamic and African scholars and intellectuals whom he impressed with his open mind, quick wit, and capacity to listen.[31]

In his diary, Malcolm recounted with pride visiting the cockpit of an airplane for the first time and meeting with Egyptian pilots. On Friday, April 17, from Saudi Arabia, he described the feeling of being comfortable around whites for the first time ever: "The white don't seem white," he wrote. "Islam actually removed differences" to allow all Muslims to relate to one another as human beings. Malcolm's contacts in the Middle East shepherded his time there in relative luxury. He stayed at Jeddah Palace in Saudi Arabia, and when he went before the hajj court to request approval to embark on the pilgrimage, he encountered an Islamic judge whom he knew from his trip in 1959. Shuttled along the route to the holy city by private chauffeur, Malcolm engaged in Muslim prayer rituals, read books about Islamic history, and stayed in comfortable rooms complete with "servants in each city that I've visited." He basked in the glory of being publicly referred to as "the Muslim from America" and especially appreciated being schooled on the particulars of the holy sites during his time in Mecca. On Tuesday, April 21, Malcolm reached Mount Arafat, the pinnacle of the hajj, located twelve mile east of Mecca. "The road to Arafat was crowded," he recalled in his diary, but the sight of hundreds of thousands of pilgrims from a variety of racial backgrounds left him inspired and breathlessly optimistic. "Islam brings together in unity all colors & classes," Malcolm wrote, exaggerating the power of any religion to dispatch racial and class hierarchies, but nonetheless offering a powerful reflection of his epiphany during the hajj.[32]

After the hajj, Malcolm toured Africa, paying attention to the relationship between black nationalism and Islam. He wrote in his diary that it would take black nationalism "to make our people conscious of doing for self & then Islam will provide the spiritual guidance." Malcolm defined racial oppression in his diary in terms that were personal, political, and religious. "For me the earth's most explosive evil is racism, the inability of God's creatures to live as One, especially in the west," he observed. Malcolm's experience on the hajj convinced him of Islam's ability to diminish racial, ethnic, and class differences among diverse groups of people. Muslim elites and members of the Saudi royal family embraced Malcolm as a visiting dignitary, treatment that he mistakenly interpreted as exemplifying Islam's lack of hierarchy. Nevertheless, the trip marked a personal watershed. It planted the seeds for an expansive political awakening that combined Malcolm's steadfast faith in the politics of racial solidarity with his newfound religious awakening and belief in the powers of Islam to transcend long-standing racial differences. Malcolm believed that pan-Africanism—black nationalism's global equivalent—held the key to organizing an international struggle for black dignity that would find spiritual sustenance in orthodox Islam. The hajj tapped Malcolm's poetic side. "A part of me, I left behind in the Holy City of Mecca," he explained in his autobiography. "And, in turn, I took away with me—forever—a part of Mecca."[33]

Ghana proved to be the most welcoming country toward Malcolm's burgeoning pan-African politics. He arrived on May 10 after four exhilarating days in Nigeria. Over dinners, tours of Accra, and ad hoc diplomatic meetings, Malcolm regaled the "Malcolm X committee" with plans to transform black freedom struggles around the world. Maya Angelou, Alice Windom, and Vicki Garvin facilitated the most important aspects of Malcolm's visit to the country. Garvin, in particular, was indispensable. A southern-born and Harlem-raised black feminist with a graduate degree in economics from Smith, Garvin defiantly spent over a decade organizing for racial justice and gender equality in trade unions. In Garvin, Malcolm encountered a seasoned political veteran who had been joining the Communist Party while he was in jail. She introduced Malcolm to Algerian, Cuban, and Chinese foreign dignitaries, who shaped his future travel plans as well as his ideology. Malcolm's humility touched the worldly Garvin. "He was not a know it all," she recalled fondly. Shirley Graham Du Bois, the second wife, political partner, and widow of the legendary civil rights leader and intellectual W. E. B. Du Bois, spoke to Malcolm for an hour at a Chinese embassy soiree in Accra. "This man is brilliant!" she announced, before adding that "I am taking him for my son." Through his newly adopted mother's intervention, Malcolm met Prime Minister Kwame Nkrumah. But Nkrumah—who had been hailed as Osagyefo, or the "redeemer of his native land"—had bumped into the ideological constraints of Cold War politics and a personal tendency toward authoritarianism, curtailing Ghana's democratic hopes in the seven years since Martin Luther King Jr.'s triumphant visit.[34]

Malcolm's time in Africa changed his mind, body, and soul. He sported a reddish-brown goatee in the manner of orthodox Muslims, eschewing the clean-shaven appearance favored by the Nation of Islam. With some physical discomfort, he acclimated himself to traditional Muslim prayer, which included positioning his arms and legs in new ways. He abandoned business suits for linen pants, tunics, and a wardrobe that reflected his embrace of a pan-African identity that would live on in posterity through photographs, pictures, and rare clips from the home movie camera he traveled with abroad. He immersed himself in the local culture, watching movies, sightseeing, eating regular lunches for the first time in many years, and enjoying small comforts, including several sips of liquor, pleasures long denied as a member of the NOI. A picture of Malcolm in local dress feasting on a simple lunch of yams, plantain, and rice was splashed across the *Ghanaian Times*. The photo was taken during one of the many marathon question-and-answer sessions Malcolm engaged in during his time in Accra, an exchange that a reporter described as one of "ideas and the physical symbol of Africanity" Malcolm now embodied. Cairo became his favorite international city.[35]

Nkrumah, the first prime minister of Ghana, greeted Malcolm from behind his long desk with a firm handshake and a warm smile. The two retreated to the couch for an hour-long discussion. As head of state, Nkrumah declined to formally endorse Malcolm's quest for black power, although he would later forge an alliance, while in exile in neighboring Guinea, with the black revolutionary Stokely Carmichael. Before departing Ghana, Malcolm addressed students at the Kwame Nkrumah Ideological Institute and grabbed dinner with black American expats at the Chinese embassy, where they watched Chinese documentaries supporting the black freedom struggle.[36]

Political opportunities discovered abroad would ultimately elevate Malcolm in the eyes of much of the world. He celebrated his thirty-ninth birthday in Algiers, his last stop before returning home. He toured the city, intently listening as cab drivers recounted stories of French atrocities during the Algerian War. The African continent intoxicated Malcolm X and informed his political dreams. He came away from the experience certain that "all Africa is seething with serious awareness of itself, its potential wealth & power, and the role it seems destined to play."[37]

He returned to Harlem on May 21 and conducted his largest press conference to date. Reporters expressed more interest in his perspective on whites than on human rights, African travails, or Islam as a religion capable of altering power relations between the Global North and South. The more he traveled, he explained, the more his perspective grew, culminating in a worldview not so much radically altered as complicated by personal development, intellectual deliberation, and religious contemplation. Reporters asked Malcolm about his transformed physical appearance. Dressed in a blue seersucker suit and carrying a walking stick, he promised to keep his beard "for a little while." Charisma practically radiated from his body. Tall, broad shouldered, and pulsing with a superhuman energy, Malcolm X embodied an aura of physical invincibility that enraptured supporters and critics. But even as it drew him deeper into the global Islamic world, his changing appearance inspired ridicule from the NOI.[38]

Malcolm backtracked on his previous condemnations of white people, which his recent experience in the Middle East had disproved. "Yes, I have been convinced that some American whites do want to help cure the rampant racism which is on the path to destroying this country!" Malcolm admitted. He divorced himself from criticism against racial oppression based on biology or genetics. Historical and political context now guided a bold indictment of racism in white society, which was guilty of crimes against black people based on behavior rather than religious prophecy. But Malcolm's new perspective did not make him a conventional racial integrationist. He scoffed at one reporter's suggestion that his views now fit comfortably in the political mainstream; Malcolm argued that his travels had exposed him to a deeper level of humanity that included some whites while excluding others. Membership in the world community encountered abroad required ending white supremacy through a belief in Islam. According to Malcolm, Islam introduced whites to a deeper understanding of themselves and others. His increased popularity in segments of the white community did not alter his views about the entrenched nature of racism in America. "No matter how much recognition whites show towards me, as far as I'm concerned as long as that same respect and recognition is not shown toward every one of our people it doesn't exist for me," Malcolm explained.[39]

Malcolm unveiled more parts of his reimagined political framework during a Chicago debate with his old friend Louis Lomax, the black journalist whose research led to *The Hate That Hate Produced* television special that introduced black Muslims to the nation. Malcolm and Lomax debated the merits of American democracy, a system Malcolm claimed to have no confidence in and that Lomax cherished as exemplifying the nation's highest ideals. During this appearance, Malcolm publicly linked the emerging Third World and the black freedom struggle in a shared rejection of "the so-called capitalistic system" for a turn "in the direction of socialism." He compared Harlem to Algeria, a country he described as a "police state" under past French occupation. During the question-and-answer session, he went further. "You can't have capitalism without racism," he remarked, noting that anti-racist forces were typically socialists. He flirted with openly embracing socialism, a political philosophy that the *Militant* frequently argued could harness the untapped revolutionary potential of the black working class. Like the young King, Malcolm found himself fascinated by nations that searched for alternatives to capitalism. But when asked what system he supported for achieving black citizenship, Malcolm hedged. "I don't know," he replied. "But I'm flexible."[40]

Malcolm's personal sincerity, uncompromising political integrity, and unapologetic love for black people the world over announced him as a global revolutionary. His human rights advocacy made him open to engagement with King's concept of radical black citizenship. Having surmised through experience that America's political system was run by "imperialists" who were also "segregationists," Malcolm now made a distinction between structures of oppression and whites who gained privileges from living in an antiblack society. He now welcomed white support of "human dignity" for black people, so long as these new allies displayed enough political integrity to "be just as active in your neighborhood as you have been in our neighborhood." Malcolm argued that racial justice required black political leadership to end racial oppression. This meant that even the most sympathetic whites could not define the scope of black citizenship.[41]

Malcolm's political thought remained animated by a deep interest in the impact of racial slavery on American society. He forcefully argued that although slavery had ended, its power between and within black and white communities remained embedded in American democracy. After over a decade bleeding for a cause he now deemed misguided, Malcolm resisted the temptation to replace old political and religious dogmas with new ones. His interest in socialism, overtures to civil rights leaders, and receptiveness to white allies dovetailed with a larger goal of promoting black liberation by any means necessary. Malcolm preferred to think of his political evolution as the by-product of an expanding perspective. "Travel broadens one's scope," he explained. "Anytime you do any traveling, your scope will be broadened. It doesn't mean you change, you broaden."[42]

On Sunday, June 28, Malcolm X officially announced the formation of the Organization of Afro-American Unity (OAAU). He addressed a group of one thousand who listened to him read a mission statement that cited the US Constitution and Declaration of Independence as "documents if put into practice represent the essence of mankind's hopes and good intentions." The OAAU mixed revolutionary ambitions with a practical understanding of American democracy. It challenged the nation to reimagine civil rights struggles, arguing that protest (including appeals to the UN) against the "continued criminal injustices" blacks faced in America required broad coalitions, grassroots organizing, and a deft understanding of the connections between local and international social movements fighting for human rights. Malcolm's opening remarks linked his new organization to Africa, a continent he praised for having achieved "more independence, more recognition, more respect as human beings than you and I have."[43]

The OAAU proved to be more important as a template for the future than as an organizing force in the present. The group's call for community control of neighborhoods, black electoral power, and freedom from the shackles of white supremacy would stimulate a vitally important path for black political radicalism. Malcolm's call for a "cultural revolution" anticipated the coming birth of a Black Arts movement, whose themes of black beauty, pride, and literary self-determination shaped much of the next decade and beyond. Malcolm proposed to bequeath Promethean fire to all willing to join the OAAU for a modest yearly membership fee of $2.[44]

Two days after the group's founding rally, Malcolm sprang into action. As if to make amends for all the years he spent ridiculing civil rights groups, he now offered his support, sending Martin Luther King Jr. a telegram in St. Augustine, Florida, which received no reply. Malcolm continued to engage in rhetorical combat during a visit to his birthplace of Omaha, Nebraska, where he addressed a local civil liberties group. In Omaha, Malcolm defined the struggle for racial equality as a national issue. "I consider anything south of Canada as the South," he quipped. "It's an American problem, and injustice in Mississippi or Alabama casts a reflection on Nebraska, New York or Oregon." Smiling broadly and frequently during an hour-long press conference, Malcolm talked of peace but prepared for war. "Today," he argued, "the Ku Klux Klan has taken off its sheets and donned a uniform—a police uniform."[45]

Before he could defend nonviolent demonstrators in the South, Malcolm set out to save his own life by leaving New York City. Revelations of Elijah Muhammad's infidelities had electrified the black press, which documented claims that "Muhammad Brought Stork to Six Teens." Salacious details included secret abortions, unfair expulsions from the NOI, and a leader who claimed divinity but practiced bare-knuckled politics to keep a grip on a teetering empire. The *Chicago Defender* published an exposé featuring the Messenger's prodigal son, Wallace Muhammed, and his apostate grandson, Hasan Sharif, who denounced Elijah Muhammad as a false prophet guilty of betraying the Muslim faithful. Chicago NOI officials traced the sordid maze of truthful allegations back to one source that needed to be silenced at all cost: Malcolm X.[46]

In the spring of 1964, Malcolm X offered a vision of revolution forged by his travels across the Third World, while Martin Luther King Jr. concentrated on domestic issues with an equal stake in shaping global affairs. Their meeting at the Senate building foreshadowed paths of political alignment between them. Malcolm's break from the NOI and five-week tour of Africa and the Middle East expanded his political consciousness even as it drew him closer to King's orbit. In many respects, Malcolm followed King throughout the first half of the year, a pattern that would continue as their political missions—seemingly worlds apart over the last decade—converged against domestic and international forces that still heralded King as a world-historic prophet of peace and regarded Malcolm as the specter of violent revolt.

CHAPTER 8

"Seeking Freedom Like Dr. King, but Faster"

T he occasion that drew Malcolm and Martin to the Senate proved to be a historic turning point. The civil rights bill, H.R. 7152, consisted of legislation that banned discrimination in employment and dramatically increased federal power to end racial discrimination in public life and file suits on behalf of racially integrated schools. The bill was first proposed by President Kennedy but evolved in the months after his assassination, aided through the legislative process by a coalition of liberal Democrats and Republicans in the Senate and House of Representative who bypassed a coalition of Dixiecrats and conservative Republicans, such as Arizona senator Barry Goldwater, to pass the bill on July 2. The combined might of grassroots pressure from below and skillful legislative maneuvering from the Johnson administration above aligned the political stars to achieve the most expansive measure of racial justice since Reconstruction.[1]

King flew to Washington to attend President Johnson's signing of the Civil Rights Act, which passed 73 to 27 in the Senate and 289 to 126 in the House. King had come from St. Augustine, Florida, where the new law would go a long way toward ensuring a measure of racial integration but would still require enforcement. Johnson addressed a group of two hundred invited guests to the White House East Room, celebrating the victory while describing the current moment as "a time of testing." King planned to continue what the president called "an unending search for justice within our own borders" by leading efforts to test out implementation of the new law, a situation that worried Johnson, as the presidential election was just four months away. In private, King listened to the president, but in public he went on the offensive, vowing to force compliance in recalcitrant southern cities and states. From the White House after the bill-signing ceremony, King promised "massive direct action programs" targeting parts of the South unwilling to immediately desegregate in the face of sweeping new legislation.[2]

One month before the passage of the civil rights bill, Malcolm X had given a surprising interview to novelist Robert Penn Warren at the Hotel Theresa, praising the goals of black dignity and respect. Compiled for a book, *Who Speaks for the Negro?*, published to great fanfare the next year (and also featuring an interview with King), Malcolm's interview confounded Warren. Warren had reached for the clichéd terms—racial separatism versus integration, nonviolence versus self-defense—that dominated the mainstream civil rights discussion. Malcolm refused to be boxed in by these binaries, which failed to recognize the full range of black political reality. He eschewed his past racial separatism as impractical, even as he decried conventional notions of racial integration as a fantasy. Self-determination offered the tools for the black dignity and political power necessary to reshape American society. Malcolm suggested "nonviolence with King is only a method" but far from his main "objective." He now recognized King as a fellow traveler on a human rights mission that conventional liberals could hardly recognize. "Well, his objective, I think, is to gain respect for Negroes as human beings," Malcolm told Warren, summoning a kind of patience that allowed for the slow unpeeling of hidden truth. "Yes," affirmed Warren. "And nonviolence is his method," said Malcolm. "Well, my objective is the same as King's." If he had spoken these words on national television, it might well have been a bombshell that made international news. Disagreements over methods, Malcolm went on, did not preclude an alliance with King "as long as we agree that the thing that the Afro-American wants and needs is recognition and respect as a human being."[3]

By this time, Malcolm no longer viewed himself as at odds with King's goals, a point Warren could hardly fathom. Finding common ground in a mutual quest for radical black dignity, Malcolm disparaged nonviolence but kept his eyes on the larger prize of black citizenship. United Press International reporter Bryce B. Miller emerged as one of the few journalists of the era to comprehend this, noting in a story that summer that Malcolm X was "Seeking Freedom Like Dr. King, but Faster." Malcolm's efforts on behalf of this goal included cultivating a relationship with Clarence Jones, the black lawyer who doubled as one of King's closest confidants. Jones and a group of black intellectuals met with Malcolm at the home of actor Sidney Poitier in New York that June to listen to him privately detail his plans to charge America with human rights violations before the United Nations. Whitney Young of the Urban League attended, as did writer John Oliver Killens and the well-known actors Ruby Dee and Ossie Davis. Jones concealed his attendance at this meeting to King but nonetheless presented himself to Malcolm as an authorized surrogate testing the waters for the potential of a more formal meeting between the two leaders in the near future. On June 30, Malcolm fired off a telegram to King, who was spending increasing amounts of time in St. Augustine, spearheading a campaign to desegregate the nation's oldest city. Racial violence against demonstrators echoed aspects of Birmingham, yet this campaign produced none of the high drama of the Magic City, turning it into less of a watershed moment than a war of attrition, marked by local thugs beating African Americans trying to integrate segregated beaches. "We have been witnessing with great concern the vicious attacks of the white racists against our poor defenseless people there in St. Augustine," began Malcolm's telegram. If the Johnson administration delayed in offering help, Malcolm noted, "just say the word and we will immediately dispatch some of our brothers there to organize self-defense unity among our people and the Ku Klux Klan will then receive a taste of its own medicine," he continued. "The day of turning the other cheek to those brute beasts is over." No doubt sincere in his offer, Malcolm's telegram received no reply from King. Nonetheless it marked the continuation of Malcolm's efforts to cultivate a dialogue between the two that would continue throughout the year.[4]

The police shooting of a fifteen-year-old black teenager from New York City drew King to Harlem as local protests swelled into a full-scale riot. Malcolm X's return to Africa at the end of June had left a temporary vacuum among black militants eager to harness the community's outrage. King's reluctance to negotiate with Mayor Robert F. Wagner proved to be well founded after four meetings produced no tangible concessions from city hall. Demands for a civilian police-review board were ignored, and Wagner placed King in the position of advocating an untenable middle ground between revolutionary calls from Harlem activists, such as rent-strike leader Jesse Gray, and the antiblack posture of police commissioner Michael Murphy, an old nemesis of Malcolm X. Characterizing Murphy as "unresponsive to the demands or aspirations" of blacks, King caught a glimpse of the particular style of white power in New York that Malcolm had spent over a decade combating. Harlem pushed King to publicly demand more police accountability—a course of action that offered a prelude to his increasing political radicalism. The mayor had invited King to New York as a peacemaker, only to discover, to his chagrin, that the apostle of nonviolence remained most comfortable as a passionate truth teller. Harlem exposed King to a deeper reality of institutional racism that made him better able to understand Malcolm X's political rage, as well as the intractable forces that remained obstacles to the revolutionary changes that true justice required.[5]

As King negotiated for peace in Harlem, Malcolm X was making diplomatic inroads in Africa. During the trip, he grappled with his political and religious identities. In correspondence with Islamic scholar Dr. Malik Badri of the American University of Beirut, he confessed the need to "wear two hats" to be an effective leader. As both a "Muslim religious leader and an Afro-American freedom fighter" he addressed two at times overlapping audiences on the world stage. World leaders more easily recognized him as a black freedom fighter, a situation he was now seeking to rectify. For political and practical reasons, Malcolm hoped to gain official recognition as a legitimate Muslim leader, in contrast to the skepticism that still surrounded the Nation of Islam abroad, and resources from the Islamic world—and, in the process, end confusion among orthodox Muslims regarding his religious leadership back home. Malcolm was convinced that his Muslim identity offered the basis to build global coalitions, so he couched his political mission in religious terms while in Cairo, urging officials to support him on a quest to spread Islam throughout the West. Writing to the Supreme Council for Islamic Affairs, Malcolm positioned himself as a moderating influence between liberal and conservative forces in the Muslim world: "My heart is in Cairo," he explained, touting the city as home to the most progressive forces in the world.[6]

But Malcolm refused to completely submerge his racial identity into a religious one. His status as a social justice leader still outshone his emerging identity as an orthodox Muslim minister with a modest group of devoted followers in the Muslim Mosque Inc., some of whom still clung stubbornly to discredited tenets of the NOI. Indeed, Malcolm's status as a radical black political activist opened more diplomatic channels than his identity as a Muslim, although news of his successful hajj found him embraced by Muslim diplomats, activists, and leaders during his travels. Malcolm sought to merge his political and religious identities by becoming a secular evangelist, one comfortable enough in his religious faith to proudly proclaim "I am a Muslim" twice during a debate at Oxford University and bold enough to argue that the key to eradicating American racism was a movement that recognized black people's inherent humanity.[7]

Malcolm had emerged from his conflict with Muhammad, local police and FBI surveillance, assassination attempts, and organizational setbacks to achieve a measure of grace that had eluded him since his years of confinement in a Massachusetts state prison. He survived the humiliating spectacle of having spent over a decade idolizing someone he now regarded as a false prophet. Now, Malcolm was seen as the embodiment of the struggle for black dignity in America and around the world.

Malcolm set his sights on conquering new political worlds just as King confronted ghosts of racial prejudice back home. King's rising political stature lent an already hectic schedule of speeches, fundraisers, and meetings the air of a political campaign. The 1964 presidential election season often found him juggling divergent, at times contradictory roles, as a political dissident, presidential ally, and national political mobilizer.

King's July 7 appearance before the Republican Party's platform committee in San Francisco, where he warned against complacency in the civil rights struggle, represented a high-profile stop on a summer filled with speeches that took him from rural hamlets in Mississippi to the streets of Harlem. King's brief tour of Mississippi in July marked his first return to the Magnolia State since Medgar Evers's funeral. Protected by FBI agents reluctantly deployed by Director Hoover at the insistence of President Johnson, King resumed direct contact with SNCC activists who continued to mock, prod, and cajole him into more radical action. Although King fielded Malcolm X's radicalism from a distance, SNCC represented a more painfully intimate source of conflict.

SNCC placed new pressure on King through the Mississippi Freedom Democratic Party (MFDP). The MFDP challenge to the state's all-white delegation set the stage for a historic confrontation at the Democratic National Convention in Atlantic City that August. MFDP delegates, led by sharecropper turned activist Fannie Lou Hamer, lobbied Democratic Party officials, civil rights leaders, and labor organizers for a literal seat at the political table. This required either acquiescence from the state's Jim Crow political machine or their expulsion. Bayard Rustin supported the MFDP challenge, but his deep ties to big labor blunted his usual go-for-broke strategies, which elicited cries of betrayal from former Rustin disciples, most notably one young activist who screamed, "You're a traitor, Bayard, a traitor!" following a speech that called for surrender under the guise of recognizing the "difference between protest and politics." Hamer's televised address on Saturday, August 22, turned a formal credentials committee hearing into riveting political drama. She recounted two years of racial terror in Mississippi, including a savage beating in tiny Winona for trying to register to vote. "I didn't try to register for you," she told the plantation owner who had evicted her entire family after her initial registration attempt. "I tried to register for myself." Hamer's failure to register to vote inspired a torrent of political will that shone through her plainspoken eloquence. Her exposure of the hidden blight in the recesses of American democracy was enough for Lyndon Johnson to launch an impromptu news conference expressly meant to interrupt her live testimony. Behind the scenes, Johnson threatened, bullied, and cajoled allies, surrogates, and his presumed running mate, Minnesota senator Hubert Humphrey, into squashing the MFDP's efforts, which he interpreted as a threat to party unity and ultimate victory in November.[8]

Martin Luther King Jr. lobbied hard on behalf of the new party, even at the risk of damaging his relationship with the president. MFDP delegates recognized Johnson's offer of two nonvoting delegates to the Democratic Convention as an insult, even as Bayard

Rustin and others advised taking the deal. The proposed compromise meant that the Democratic Party would officially recognize the segregated Mississippi party members at the convention, while only allowing the integrated MFDP delegates to observe, but not vote, during proceedings. Facing pressure from all sides, King confessed that the MFDP's acceptance of Johnson's offer would make his life easier, "but if I were a Mississippi Negro, I would vote against it." Which is exactly what the MFDP did, maintaining their political integrity in the face of small and large betrayals that spanned from United Auto Worker lawyers and political lobbyists all the way to the White House.[9]

The Atlantic City debacle cleaved one faction of SNCC activists away from the Democratic Party and mainstream politics and thrust others, most notably Fannie Lou Hamer (who would be a delegate four years later), deep into the party machinery. King departed the convention, having missed the Johnson and Humphrey acceptance speeches, in the face of withering private criticism from SNCC activists who lumped him together with Rustin as supporting the rejected compromise.[10]

On Wednesday, October 14, 1964, Coretta called King with the news that he would be awarded the Nobel Peace Prize. The news lifted King above the politics of Atlantic City and elevated his stature as a global figure. The decision to award the prize to King recognized nonviolence as a political philosophy capable of changing the world. The Nobel arrived at a critical moment for him. The youngest-ever recipient of the award at thirty-five, King dedicated the prize money, and the attached symbolism, to the movement. "I am a minister of the gospel, not a political leader," he demurred. In truth, he was both, which made him, weeks before a presidential election, a rival to Johnson on the world stage. The president recognized as much. From Air Force One, he dictated a memo congratulating King two days after the announcement. Johnson noted the award's global implications. "It signals," he said, "the world's recognition that Americans committed to a course of justice for all our people and the role that you have played in that effort. The Award is not only a tribute to you but to the Nation as well." The president's note sought to interpret the Nobel Prize as a symbol of racial progress and a peculiar kind of American exceptionalism that allowed even racially oppressed groups to garner the type of global reputation usually befitting monarchs and millionaires. King's international stature now compelled Johnson to treat him as less of an adversary, at least publicly, than a political equal.[11]

The Nobel Prize committee's decision also acknowledged Malcolm X's insistence that racial justice was a global issue that Americans could no longer ignore. Newspapers regarded King's victory as internationalizing the civil rights movement. Black editorials stressed King's personal sacrifice in the face of racial violence, while the white press lauded him for helping to burnish America's global image of racial progress. King barnstormed around the country organizing black voter turnout as his staff prepared for his December trip to Oslo to accept the prize. He blasted "Goldwaterism" during a speech before the Baptist Ministers Conference in Los Angeles, warning that the Republican Party's presidential nominee threatened "the health, morality and survival of our nation." He didn't mention his recent disappointment in Goldwater's challenger.[12]

After the election, King cited Johnson's landslide victory over Goldwater as "a definite mandate" for civil rights. Simultaneously, he promised to increase voting-rights demonstrations in Mississippi and Alabama. King's plans to organize a massive voting-rights campaign in the south dovetailed with his larger ambitions to mobilize national demonstrations that would turn political beachheads in the northern and western parts of the country into headquarters for racial and economic justice. In short, King proposed to mobilize a broad-based coalition in pursuit of an expansive vision of black radical citizenship—far beyond the political imagination of elected officials—to lift the most despised Americans from poverty, hunger, and racial segregation.[13]

The corollary to Johnson's electoral landslide could be seen in the coming Eighty-Ninth Congress, where Democrats controlled 295 of 435 seats in the House of Representatives and fell just two seats short of seventy in the one-hundred-seat Senate. This Congress would pass much of Johnson's Great Society legislation. But for King, the ideal of the Great Society fell short of the scale of social change the nation required. Its historic passing set the stage for King's transformation into a political revolutionary whose critique of American democracy found him converging with Malcolm X.[14]

When they met in the Senate, Malcolm joked to King, "Now you're going to investigated." The comment assumed that federal agents weren't already interested in King. But government and law enforcement officials kept track of both Malcolm and Martin. J. Edgar Hoover had called King the nation's "most notorious liar" and used King's connections to Stanley Levison as proof of his political bankruptcy. Hoover used evidence of King's extramarital affairs, gleaned through illegal wiretapping, to prove his moral degeneracy. King had a portfolio of surveillance all to himself, motivated by Hoover's personal enmity and sanctioned by Bobby Kennedy, the former attorney general now running for a New York state senate seat. King's growing international reputation, culminating in the Nobel Prize and his campaign for the Democratic Party in the presidential election, spurred Hoover into action. The FBI director's boldest gambit would come early in the New Year, in the form of an anonymous package authored by the FBI that threatened to reveal King's extramarital affairs. The package, initially opened by Coretta, urged King to commit suicide rather than risk public shame. King resisted the ploy but remained anxious that his private life might prove fodder for public consumption, even as he looked ahead toward mounting a voting-rights campaign in Selma, Alabama.[15]

While King's Nobel Prize helped coalesce world opinion around the importance of civil rights and racial justice, Malcolm X practiced his own brand of personal diplomacy in Africa.

In London, he met with the aides of African leaders he planned to lobby in Cairo. Malcolm's ultimate objective of having African rulers charge the United States with human rights violations against black Americans at the United Nations relied on audacious hope. "If our problem does not come up then neither South Africa, nor Angola, nor Southern Rhodesia, nor any other colonial issue should be discussed at the United Nations," he defiantly informed reporters.[16]

In Cairo, Malcolm settled into the role as black America's unofficial prime minister. He arrived in Africa brimming with confidence that he represented the majority of the black folk he characterized as "Field Negroes." In Africa, he planned to broker alliances, secure financial and organizational resources, and formalize broad based Pan-African coalitions on behalf of twenty-two million black people who Malcolm recognized as political leverage in his plans to seek international allies in the struggle for radical black dignity.

Granted permission to attend the Organization of African Unity conference in Cairo, Malcolm made the case that African countries should support his fledgling group, the OAAU, even at the risk of angering American officials. The *New York Journal-American* blasted Malcolm as a pawn in a bigger game orchestrated by communists who relished the black radical's provocative description of the United States as a "national torture chamber" on race matters. To reporters who questioned his appearance in Cairo, Malcolm answered succinctly: "I have as much right to be an observer from an oppressed area as they [white reporters] have," once again underscoring how America's system of Jim Crow mirrored colonial regimes condemned the world over. He warned journalists that "a bloodbath is on its way to America." Such provocations at times obscured Malcolm's more nuanced efforts to reveal "the true plight" of blacks in America to a global audience.[17]

The formal aid that Malcolm hoped for in Cairo would prove elusive, however, with Organization of African Unity leaders unwilling to risk a public break with America. Malcolm navigated murky political waters, where even Kwame Nkrumah, a leader he admired and thought "made the best" and most comprehensive speech in Cairo, spoke circumspectly on the subject of racial inequality. Malcolm chafed at listening to speeches where African "Heads of State seem to avoid mentioning the US & its racism." American State Department officials fretted over the consequences of Malcolm's freelance diplomacy, parsed through rumors that the Saudis were bankrolling him, and breathed a sigh of relief that no African countries were willing to publicly support the OAAU's explosive agenda. In his diary, Malcolm extolled "the importance of building bridges of communication, understanding & cooperation between Africans & Afro-Americans." This was the raison d'être of his trip to Cairo: to use international diplomacy as a political sword capable of transforming the relationship between black Americans and the federal government by leveraging the power of Africa.[18]

The OAAU memorandum that Malcolm hand delivered in Cairo offered a revised pan-African narrative that suggested Africans, not black Americans, were in a unique position to aid their "long lost Brothers and Sisters." The memo rejected strains of black nationalism and pan-Africanism (including aspects of Garveyism) that imagined Africa as a benighted continent awaiting rescue from black Western-educated elites. It described US racial politics in one sentence: "During the past ten years the entire world has witnessed our men, women and children being attacked and bitten by vicious police dogs, brutally beaten by police clubs, and washed down the sewers by high-pressure water hoses that would rip the clothes from our bodies and the flesh from our limbs." America's racial crisis, far from being a local or domestic issue, was part of a larger global crisis: "It is not a problem of civil rights, but a problem of human rights." Rather than condemn America to a violent catastrophe based in religious prophecy, as the NOI had done, Malcolm openly pleaded with African leaders for aid in forcing a UN investigation into human rights violations against black Americans. Ultimately, he failed in this goal, but on the trip he forged strong bonds with an influential coterie of African and Third World activists, intellectuals, grassroots leaders, and organizers.[19]

FBI agents, meanwhile, monitored Malcolm's international activities with keen interest. As Malcolm lobbied in Cairo, New York's special agent in charge forwarded Director Hoover a news story announcing Socialist Workers Party presidential candidate Clifton DeBerry's public endorsement of Malcolm's OAAU. The FBI also tracked down false rumors that Malcolm had already returned from Africa with plans to turn his earlier talk of rifle clubs into reality. At home and abroad, Malcolm attracted the attention of several law enforcement agencies—a level of scrutiny that would only, and perhaps surprisingly, be surpassed by that directed at Martin Luther King Jr.[20]

Malcolm's international foray cast him as a bridge between two generations of politically engaged black radicals. Langston Hughes, the poet laureate of the Harlem Renaissance who cut his teeth in anti-colonial politics alongside the Abraham Lincoln Brigade of American volunteers resisting fascism in 1937 Spain, reminded Malcolm of this long history. Hughes belonged to a generation enthralled by the actor, singer, and activist Paul Robeson's legendary solidarity with political underdogs around the world. Robeson's global fame marked him for enduring infamy during the Cold War, his illegal passport revocation symbolizing America's silencing of dissident voices after the postwar freedom surge of the 1940s. Hughes, while applauding Malcolm's efforts in Cairo, recalled two earlier efforts by the National Negro Congress and the NAACP to gain UN support for black citizenship.[21]

Malcolm's call for a human rights movement also enthralled a younger generation captivated by African decolonization, thrilled by the sit-in movement, and angered by the sight of racial violence against civil rights demonstrators. SNCC chairman John

Lewis, only dimly aware of the long history of black radicalism, was influenced by Malcolm's electrifying African tour. "I respected Malcolm," Lewis recalled. He had already begun to sympathize with Malcolm's fervent anti-racist posture before encountering him personally in Kenya during Malcolm's visit. There, Malcolm told Lewis that he planned to tour the South after returning from Africa. Malcolm impressed upon Lewis that "this was a world struggle we were engaged in here, not just an American struggle." Lewis went from viewing Malcolm as an outsider to preparing to meet him on the shared battleground of America's domestic civil rights struggle. And Malcolm now counted Lewis, one of the most devout believers in nonviolence next to King, as a political ally in expanding the black freedom struggle into a human rights movement capable of liberating America and Africa and beyond.[22]

For Malcolm, links between Harlem, Mississippi, and Africa were self-evident yet obscured by self-defeating political interests on both sides of the Atlantic. But as he toured Egypt, Saudi Arabia, Kuwait, and Lebanon, his face graced the cover of the *Saturday Evening Post* back home, which published excerpts from his forthcoming autobiography. Since 1963, Malcolm had been working with journalist Alex Haley on a memoir narrating his evolution from a criminal into a global freedom fighter. The political drama surrounding Malcolm's exit from the NOI made the book more newsworthy than ever. The *Post* touted Malcolm's "own story of crime, conversion and Black Muslims in action" to lure readers in. It framed Malcolm's prediction that "more and worse riots will erupt!" as real-life urban pulp fiction. Although Malcolm had worked to craft a reputation as a leader wielding a political sword, image makers continued to rely on his notoriety as a selling point to American audiences.[23]

Ebony magazine published an insightful profile, "Mystery of Malcolm X," that offered a tantalizingly nuanced portrait of Malcolm. Accompanied by fifteen photographs, the story portrayed him as a man of startling juxtapositions: a political activist, who once trafficked in anti-white prejudice, now insisting that "whites are human beings—as long as this is borne out by their humane treatment of Negroes." Driving around New York City in a dark navy sedan, dressed in a seersucker suit, dark-framed glasses, and sporting a reddish-blond goatee, Malcolm captivated Harlemites, who gave him presents for his newborn daughter, and curious whites, who chatted with him like an old friend, as he drove around town. A large poster of Kwame Nkrumah hung inside his East Elmhurst, Queens, home, and photographs depicted Malcolm as a loving father, devoted husband, and fierce warrior who owned a rifle for protection. Malcolm's tireless work ethic found him taking on fifteen-hour days that tested his physical stamina, exacerbated by death threats that he openly discussed with anyone willing to listen.[24]

The story presented Malcolm as a man in the process of becoming, a radical activist willing to admit that the NAACP "is doing some good" in one breath and accuse "non-violent Negroes" of needing "psychiatric care" in the next. *Ebony's* version of Malcolm X imbued him with a grounded humanity missing from many media portrayals. Malcolm leaped off the page, not so much as an icon but as a three-dimensional black man desperately trying, and at times failing, to lead a political revolution. In an American political and cultural milieu that solely acknowledged him as Martin Luther King Jr.'s violent foil, the profile daringly identified Malcolm as a radical humanist, one equally at home chatting with Harlem kids—who greeted him with "Salam Aleikum, Brother Malcolm"—and threatening to send armed guerrillas into Mississippi to protect civil rights workers.[25]

"The main difference" between himself and King, Malcolm told Ethiopian students in Addis Ababa during a lecture in early October, "is that he doesn't mind being beaten up and I do." Malcolm now identified himself as an activist seeking the same goals as King, but who chose different methods to get there. However, Malcolm's sophisticated understanding of the growing areas of political convergence between himself and King remained largely ignored by the public. After over a decade of forcefully criticizing the civil rights movement, Malcolm now recognized King's ultimate goal of achieving black citizenship as his own cause.[26]

In Dar es Salaam, Tanzania, Malcolm regaled global journalists with vivid descriptions of American racism and efforts to "make Africans hate American Negroes," a circumstance his presence on the continent helped upend. Malcolm attracted front-page attention in the local papers the *Nationalist* and the *Tanganyika Standard*. Characterizing the presidential race as a choice "between the lesser of two evils," he vowed to return to America only after the election, to prevent right-wing forces from exploiting his presence on behalf of Goldwater. Malcolm described Goldwater as a "villain that suits the American psychology" of avoiding the nation's tragic racial history.[27]

The African press cultivated Malcolm's image as perhaps the most important black freedom fighter of the era. In Monrovia, Liberia, Malcolm spoke about human rights during a lunch in his honor attended by a range of dignitaries. He applauded China's nuclear capability as a victory for the Third World, expressed skepticism over Lyndon Johnson's political sincerity toward blacks, and indicated mild disapproval of America's new Nobel Prize winner. "They should have given it to Lumumba, Nkrumah, Kenyatta, or Mandela," claimed Malcolm, offering a catalogue of martyred, living, and imprisoned African leaders more deserving than King. His love for controversy remained. "I learned that white people only understand the language of hurt, pain, and blood," he reportedly said in Liberia. "If you speak any other language you speak over their heads." Established heads of state accorded him respectful audiences, while more dissident oppositional leaders openly embraced his call for political liberation by any means necessary.[28]

Malcolm X spent the last week of his trip in Paris, speaking to a capacity crowd at the Maison de la Mutualité, where he displayed evidence of conquering old demons by speaking approvingly—"How can anyone be against love?"—of interracial marriage. He also discussed the role of black Americans in the African revolution. "In Africa I met open hearts, open arms, and open spirits," he proudly asserted. He narrated his recent nineteen-week African sojourn as a family reunion that amplified his efforts in pursuit of global radical black dignity. Malcolm contrasted the potential good American power could accomplish in the world with the brutal reality that his nation was too "morally bankrupt" to "help anybody, anywhere." No aspect of his remarks in Paris made waves in the American press, which seemed more eager to chronicle his continuing legal battle to avoid eviction from his Queens home than his international diplomacy.[29]

On November 24, 1964, Malcolm was greeted at Kennedy airport by Betty, three of his daughters, and signs reading "Welcome Back Brother Malcolm." He returned for less than a week before flying to Europe, a trip that would see one of the most important speeches of his life. He toured Manchester and Sheffield, England—rapidly deindustrializing cities brimming with long-simmering class tensions and imminent racial anxieties. Malcolm's visit coincided with Martin Luther King Jr.'s speech at St. Paul's Cathedral in London, part of an international victory lap on his way to collect his peace prize in Oslo. In London, King described racism as "a world problem," telling reporters that racial apartheid in South Africa merited an international boycott. Annoyed by what he may have interpreted as King's global recognition at the expense of his own foreign travels, Malcolm blasted King's nonviolent methods as "bankrupt," noting that jailed South African anti-apartheid leader Nelson Mandela tried a similar strategy. Malcolm explained over London radio, "He too, practiced non-violence and discovered to his dismay that it just didn't work and finally, Mandella [*sic*] resorted to violence."[30]

In a speech at Oxford Union, carried exclusively by the BBC, Malcolm called for a political revolution using the words of a man he had described as a "villain" and a "wolf": recently defeated presidential candidate Barry Goldwater. Goldwater's controversial quote formed the basis of the debate topic: "Extremism in the defense of Liberty is no vice; moderation in the pursuit of Justice is no virtue." Malcolm's performance captured the radical imagination of Oxford students, who jammed the hall unsure of exactly what to expect. His thirty-minute lecture spanned political, religious, historical, and intellectual worlds to sketch out the parameters of an unfolding revolution against colonialism, racism, and injustice. "I don't believe in any form of unjustified extremism, but when a man is exercising extremism in defense of liberty for human beings I do not consider that a vice," Malcolm argued. "When a man is moderate in defense of justice for human beings I say he is a sinner," he explained, publicly echoing aspects of King's critique of white liberals.[31]

Malcolm pleaded with "the young generation of whites, Blacks, browns" present to organize on behalf of revolutionary change. He promised they would not be alone, declaring his willingness to "join in with anyone, I don't care what color you are, as long as you want to change this miserable condition on this earth." His final "thank you" triggered rapturous applause.[32]

Four days later, Martin Luther King Jr. spoke at City Temple in London. King's discussion of the historical justification of racial slavery in America became an expansive talk about the evils of racial segregation compounded with economic injustice that included racism in labor unions and public policy. Black citizenship, King argued, would require "massive retraining programs, massive public works programs" to provide jobs, education, decent housing, and "adequate health facilities." King repudiated critics who cited high rates of poverty and crime in black communities as the reason whites resisted racial integration. "It is a torturous logic to use the tragic results of racial segregation," he observed, "as an argument for the continuation of it." In London, King explicitly tied black citizenship to a wider search for economic justice, a theme he would amplify in coming years. Toward the end of his speech, he talked about the struggle to end racial apartheid in South Africa. He compared it to racial injustice in Mississippi and called Nelson Mandela "a great leader" wrongfully imprisoned for demanding justice in an authoritarian "police state." King advocated for economic sanctions against South Africa and publicly repudiated the United States and Britain for failing to more forcefully align themselves with anti-apartheid activists. The speech defined racism as a global problem and, like Malcolm X's new rallying cry, announced black citizenship as the crown jewel of an international movement for human rights.[33]

The next day, King—along with an entourage of family, colleagues, and friends—arrived in Oslo, Norway. "We feel we have much to learn from Scandinavia's democratic socialist tradition and from the manner in which you have overcome many of the social and economic problems that still plague a far more powerful and affluent nation," King remarked. He accepted the Nobel Prize on Thursday, December 10, at Oslo University from King Olav V. He dressed formally, in an ascot, gray tailcoat, and striped pants, and was introduced as "an undaunted champion of peace."[34]

When King accepted the prize on behalf of the movement, he noted how improbable this day had seemed against the backdrop of Montgomery. His acceptance speech emphasized the intimate connection between race and poverty that would only continue to grow. "I am mindful that debilitating and grinding poverty afflicts my people and chains them to the lowest rung of the economic ladder," said King. He implicitly responded to Malcolm X's question: Why was he being given a peace prize in a time when domestic racial violence in the United States continued? The answer, he surmised, could be seen in the hope that swelled among people all over the world in the wake of Birmingham, a hope that continued in the face of the violent deaths of civil rights workers in Mississippi during Freedom Summer. "I have the audacity," King explained, "to believe that peoples everywhere can have three meals a day for their bodies, education and culture for their minds, and dignity, equality, and freedom for their spirits." This last sentence offered a blueprint for black citizenship that viewed racial and economic justice as intertwined objectives, something that King would come to consider the civil rights movement's most profound challenge and opportunity. Like Malcolm X, King's vocation as a political leader now encompassed nothing less than the fate of humanity.[35]

Two days later, Malcolm spoke to the Harlem Domestic Peace Corps, a group sponsored by HARYOU-ACT, Harlem's federally supported anti-poverty program. The speech addressed themes of black beauty, pan-African identity, and political self-determination that would shortly become the hallmark of Black Power politics. Malcolm's discussion of how the African image in the Western imagination inspired white revulsion and black self-hatred would be taken up by the Black Arts movement the following year. Historically, Malcolm said, American image makers denigrated Africa, changing course only after decolonization made the continent attractive to the nation's political and economic self-interest. "All you have to do is go to the African continent, travel from one end of it to the other, and you'll find out that the American position and influence has only replaced" those of former colonial powers. "I think there are plenty of good people in America," Malcolm reasoned, "but there are also plenty of bad people in America" who seemed to hold all the power.[36]

The State Department was presenting Africans with a rosy and moving picture of civil rights, burnished by legal cases, legislative victories, and King's Nobel Prize. US officials in Africa suggested that black Americans were on the "way to the promised land of integration." Malcolm believed American leaders were taking premature victory laps. "It is impossible to give out peace medals when the people who are oppressed don't have peace," he said, once again jabbing at King. He ended his talk to Harlem's future leaders by recalling the impact of the Second World War on racial justice. Without mentioning that he had spent the war years hustling in

Harlem and Roxbury, Malcolm praised this era as one where global events inspired a more democratic country. He resisted advocating a strategy of either self-defense or nonviolence, preferring the flexibility to resist political oppression and violence based on circumstances. The OAAU motto, "By any means necessary," proved to be more than a simple slogan. It acknowledged that combating racial oppression required moving beyond the confines of the political binaries that continued to mesmerize the press, even though they obscured the fact that most blacks occupied multiple political and intellectual identities and affiliations.[37]

On December 17, 1964, Malcolm sat in the massive audience of Harlem's 369th Regiment Armory, a place where he had spoken before as the Nation of Islam's young prince. Now, he listened to King speak in the wake of winning the Nobel. New York City embraced King as a favorite son that day. Malcolm's attendance was a deft act of diplomacy. The day before, during a lecture at Harvard University Law School, he had again criticized King without mentioning his name. "I would refuse to follow a general," he explained to the one thousand attendees in the school's Sanders Theatre, "who accepted a peace prize before the battle was won." When pressed on whom he was referring to, Malcolm demurred. "I have no comment on my good friend Dr. King," he said. Malcolm was now reunited, for the last time, with his "good friend," whom he heard speak for the first time since the March on Washington.[38]

Politicians—including New York mayor Robert F. Wagner, who as recently as July had distanced himself from King's call for civilian review of police—burst with public displays of pride following King's Nobel Prize. "I can think of none who has won a more lasting place in the moral epic of America," explained Wagner at a city hall ceremony earlier in the day where King received the Medal of Honor, the city's highest distinction. The celebration continued at a cocktail party at the Waldorf Astoria with Vice President Hubert Humphrey. The global status of the Nobel Prize made King too important for officials to ignore. Although

Malcolm criticized King for accepting a peace prize in a time of war, King was publicly supporting political self-determination for the Congo, an issue that Malcolm raised whenever he could, and calling for international sanctions against the apartheid regime in South Africa. Their political worlds and personal fates converged in a shared passion for global human rights.[39]

Harlem was, in many ways, Malcolm's political turf and organizational headquarters. But that night, the neighborhood cheered for King. Malcolm listened carefully as King basked in what he identified as a "mountaintop" moment that, however personally satisfying, required subsequent time in the "valley" to fulfill a political destiny that remained unwritten. Malcolm perked up when King spoke of the dearth of poverty in Scandinavia, images that contrasted with scenes of American economic misery that stretched from coast to coast. King's global travels paralleled Malcolm's exploits, but the Baptist preacher spoke to larger audiences than the Muslim minister. King's words that night in Harlem touched Malcolm. Four days later, in a sprawling lecture, also held in Harlem, that criticized America's economic and political system, Malcolm focused some of his most important thoughts on King. "There's one thing that Martin Luther King mentioned at the Armory the other night, which I thought was significant," Malcolm said, in a rare public tribute to the Nobel Prize winner's political brilliance. "He mentioned that while he was in some of those Scandinavian countries, he saw no poverty. There was no unemployment, no poverty. Everyone was getting education, everyone had decent housing, decent whatever they needed to exist." Why, asked Malcolm, did King "mention those countries on his list as different?" Malcolm suggested that the social democracies in western Europe offered an alternative political and economic model for black folk seeking a way out of racial injustice and economic misery.[40]

It was a failure of political will, explained Malcolm, that caused the richest nation on earth to be wracked by poverty, unemployment, and miserable living conditions. King's description of a social democratic political system capable of providing basic living standards for all of its citizens struck Malcolm's imagination. Africa, like the Scandinavian countries King lauded, was also pursuing collectivist economic strategies to end poverty, a vision that conformed to Malcolm's search for new methods to address economic and racial injustice. "What they are using to solve their problems in Africa and Asia is not capitalism," he reminded his audience.[41]

Malcolm had also recently met Fannie Lou Hamer, the SNCC organizer whose public testimony nearly upended the Democratic convention. In his lecture in Harlem, he characterized Hamer's vicious beating at the hands of Mississippi authorities as "the language of brutality." It was a language that blacks had yet to master, but one Malcolm recognized. Black liberation, in certain instances, required political violence. The program that night asked what Mississippi had to do with Harlem. Malcolm answered by blurring the regional distinctions that masked a national crisis. "It isn't actually Mississippi, it's America. America is Mississippi," he proclaimed. "There's no such thing as a Mason-Dixon line, it's America. There's no such thing as the South, it's America." After describing Hamer as one of America's "foremost freedom fighters," he went further. "You don't have to be a man to fight for freedom. All you have to do is be an intelligent human being." Malcolm's words showcased a rhetorical evolution on gender politics that remained, like King's, unfinished in his lifetime.[42]

Despite coming of political age within the patriarchal structure of the NOI, Malcolm had begun to develop a more nuanced sense of the relationship between gender, race, and power. He recognized and relied on the strength of black women, perhaps most profoundly his older half sister Ella Mae Collins, who, after leaving the NOI in part because of the group's sexism, financed his first trip to Africa and helped him organize the OAAU. In his new organization, Malcolm hoped to abandon some of the sexist tendencies that thrived in the Nation. He recruited black women who were brilliant organizers and thinkers. He cultivated a cross section of gifted black women artists and intellectuals whom he maintained an active correspondence with—perhaps most notably Maya Angelou, who served as Malcolm's surrogate in Africa. He was mentored by Shirley Graham Du Bois, a towering figure among black radicals and whose political experience surpassed his own. Singer Abbey Lincoln and writers Rosa Guy and Sarah Wright formed political friendships with Malcolm. During an interview near the end of December, Malcolm praised African and Middle Eastern nations that educated men and women, singling out Ghana and Egypt as two examples where the pursuit of gender equality produced "a more valid society, a more progressive society." The intellectual curiosity he displayed his entire life now made him more willing to question how patriarchal conventions sapped enormous potential from the black community. But Malcolm's relationships with women remained a work in progress, and he was still unable to make the gendered oppression of women an integral part of his overall political analysis.[43]

The subject of Martin Luther King Jr.'s Nobel Prize remained on Malcolm's mind during his last interview of the year. Malcolm took pains to explain that his difference with King was one of tactics, arguing that "black people shouldn't be willing to be nonviolent unless white people are going to be nonviolent." Malcolm claimed he received equal satisfaction from his efforts to raise black consciousness as King did from his Nobel Prize. "And when they show that they're fed up with this slow pace, you know, that's my reward." He predicted a storm of racial violence in the New Year; a prospect that no honorific bestowed on King would change. "King himself is probably a good man," Malcolm admitted, "but the danger is that white people use King." According to Malcolm, King's nonviolence protected the guilty as well as the innocent. His message lulled white society into believing myths about American democracy and racial progress that remained dangerously out of reach for ordinary blacks. Almost as if apologizing for the blunt nature of his criticism, Malcolm presented a brief elegy of his political career. "Whatever I do, whatever I did, whatever I've said, was all done in sincerity," he explained. "That's the way I want to be remembered because that's the way it is."[44]

Malcolm spent the next several weeks primarily on the road, a roving political evangelist preaching a message of radical black dignity. In January, he met for hours with the writer LeRoi Jones at the Waldorf Astoria, holding a political seminar that would soon transform black culture. Jones's restless intelligence fueled his brash literary work, including the Obie Award–winning play *Dutchman*, which chronicled the brutal death of a black man at the collective hands of white society. Several hours of conversation with Malcolm set Jones politically and intellectually ablaze, a fire that would culminate in a movement for black arts that identified Malcolm X, along with John Coltrane, as its political and cultural avatar.[45]

Over time, Malcolm was drawn deeper into the orbit of civil rights activism. SNCC proved to be a natural ally. He admired the group's political courage, even as he disapproved of their tactical adherence to nonviolence. In late December, he played host to a SNCC-sponsored delegation of thirty-seven young people visiting from McComb, Mississippi, at the Hotel Theresa. They listened to Malcolm express political solidarity with their efforts to bring racial justice to the Magnolia State. He told them that he "would go for nonviolence" only if everyone else did, including black people's political adversaries. "There [is] some worse segregation right here in New York City than there is in McComb, Mississippi," Malcolm said, disputing the notion that northern cities were somehow immune to Jim Crow. During the question-and-answer portion of the event, Malcolm summed up his feelings about black participation in democratic institutions. "If you were born in this country, nobody's doing you any favor when they let you vote or when they let you register," he reminded them. "They're only recognizing you as a human being and recognizing your right as a human being to exercise your right as a citizen."[46]

Malcolm's talk of human rights and disarmingly gentle demeanor could still surprise critics, interlocutors, and strangers
expecting the firebrand whose reputation preceded him. On January 6, 1965, Malcolm rode a chartered bus to Albany, New York,
as the guest of his lawyer and friend Percy Sutton, who was the
recently elected assemblyman from Harlem. Malcolm came to
watch Sutton take his seat at the start of the New York state legislative assembly and to witness anew the machinery of democracy.
On the ride, Malcolm chatted amiably with a stunned white minister, who had expected fire and brimstone only to find himself
engaged in a discussion about the environment and the pastoral
scenes witnessed on the way to the state capital. At the legisla-
ture, Malcolm sat in a front-row gallery seat close to Republican
governor Nelson Rockefeller, his unexpected appearance startling
reporters and alarming undercover state police. When asked what
he thought of Rockefeller's address, Malcolm dropped one of his
classic lines: "The message was quite long," he observed. "But the
part on civil rights was too short."[47]

Malcolm spent the rest of January giving lectures, conducting
interviews, and engaging in correspondence designed to consolidate the international inroads the OAAU had achieved through
his extensive travels. His planned itinerary barely stayed ahead of
continuing efforts by Muslims connected to the NOI to assassinate him. Just after 11 p.m. on January 22, a group of would-be
assassins stepped toward him as he opened the door to leave his
home, an attack thwarted only by their mistimed approach, which
caused them to retreat. Malcolm often traveled with bodyguards
and carried a tear-gas pen for protection, but he knew in his bones
that this would offer no defense against Muslims bent on killing
him as an apostate.[48]

Martin Luther King Jr. emerged from the endless rounds of
Nobel Prize celebrations in Selma, Alabama, which the SCLC
planned to use as its headquarters for a voting-rights campaign.
The action in Selma followed the strategic recipe utilized in Bir-

mingham, with the ultimate goal being voting rights rather than desegregation. Throughout the month of January, King and his aides organized peaceful demonstrations, where groups of blacks tried to legally register at the Selma courthouse, only to be arrested by the officers of Sheriff Jim Clark, a racist caricature who wore a button emblazoned "Never" as a response to the prospect of racial integration. "We must be willing to go to jail by the thousands," King told followers. He led by example, getting arrested on February 1 at the Selma courthouse alongside almost eight hundred demonstrators. In jail, King almost received a most unexpected visitor.[49]

On Wednesday, February 3, Malcolm spoke to three thousand students at Tuskegee University. The crowd's overwhelming size forced organizers to close the doors ten minutes before the start of his 8 p.m. lecture. Malcolm then drove to Selma's Brown Chapel AME Church the next day in a small red sports car. His unmistakable presence raised temperatures among King's staff, until the SCLC decided to cosponsor his appearance. Organizer Andy Young, who enjoyed a friendly relationship with Malcolm, slotted him between James Bevel and Coretta Scott King to inoculate the impressionable from the siren song of self-defense. They needn't have bothered. Malcolm spoke for an hour in support of black voting rights in Selma, which he described as the heart of a national struggle for black citizenship whose true contours, he insisted, were global.[50]

Sitting on the dais next to Coretta, Malcolm relayed a message that caught her off guard. "Mrs. King, will you tell Dr. King that I'm sorry I won't get to see him? I had planned to visit him in jail, but I have to leave," Malcolm explained. "I want him to know that I didn't come to make his job more difficult. I thought that if the white people understood what the alternative was that they would be willing to listen to Dr. King." Malcolm's performance in Selma reaffirmed Coretta Scott King's private regard for him, one that she recalled her husband shared. After hearing reports of

Malcolm's exemplary behavior in Selma, King made quiet plans to reach out to him after the conclusion of the voting-rights efforts in Alabama.[51]

Over the next two weeks, Malcolm continued to sketch out how black political self-determination might possibly avert a more violent revolution. Indignities and death threats paralleled these efforts. French authorities banned his February 9 appearance, barring him from a country he had spoken in less than three months before. After failing to get through customs, Malcolm boarded a flight back to London, stunned at what he considered a personal affront to his status as a radical international statesman. French officials had determined Malcolm's presence in Paris to be needlessly inflammatory; his words of fire about African decolonization mirrored the rebellious stirrings of a variety of Third World and Caribbean immigrants residing in France.[52]

Two days later, during a speech at the London School of Economics, Malcolm sought to redefine America's domestic civil rights struggle as an international human rights movement. He spoke passionately about the consequences of racial demonization of black people in America, which enabled the creation of "a police-state system" that made it "permissible in the minds of even the well-meaning white public" for law enforcement to "brutally suppress" political dissent and personal dignity. "They use the press to set up this police state," Malcolm argued, "and they use the press to make the white public accept whatever they do to the dark-skinned public." The logic of this kind of racial injustice stretched across the Atlantic, observed Malcolm. "They do that here in London right now with the constant reference to the West Indian population having a high rate of crime or having a tendency toward dirtiness," he explained.[53]

Malcolm critiqued racial progress as eliciting only token reforms while structural racism, injustice, and violence remained. He portrayed King as a leader who kept black anger in check—but not for long, since "the masses of black people in America are still living in the ghettoes and the slums, they still are the victims of inferior housing, they are still the victims of a segregated school system, which gives them inferior education." Civil rights bills and movements for radical democracy were only as powerful as their implementation. He found it incredulous that—in the aftermath of the murders of three civil rights workers in Mississippi and the political assassinations of John F. Kennedy, Medgar Evers, and the four girls blown up in Birmingham, Alabama—anyone could possibly be "talking about the 'Great Society'" coming into existence. Rather, he predicted that "1965 will be the longest and hottest and bloodiest year" in American history. But he ended on a note of optimism, telling all who identified as political underdogs to no longer think of themselves as racial or ethnic minorities but as part of global majority "crying out for action" in a struggle for citizenship, dignity, and justice.[54]

On February 13, fresh from his latest European speaking tour, Malcolm learned that he would be evicted from his home in East Elmhurst, Queens. The news came after almost a year of legal wrangling between Malcolm and the Messenger over ownership of a house that Malcolm claimed as his own and that the NOI regarded as organizational property. He had to make plans to relocate his four daughters amid fresh news that Betty was pregnant with twins. Despite the eviction order and the stress of moving a growing family, Malcolm made plans to fly to Detroit the next day for a speaking engagement. He spent the day catching up on work at the Hotel Theresa before returning home to spend time with his family, then staying up late reading in his upstairs study.

Just before 3 a.m., he awoke to the sounds of incendiary devices breaking through the windows of his home and filling it with smoke. At least three Molotov cocktails were launched at the house, but Malcolm managed to evacuate the entire family, who watched outside as their home burned down. In the face of Betty's strong protestation and the bewilderment of his four children, Malcolm kept his speaking engagement later that evening.

His appearance in Detroit proved tragically memorable, since it marked a low point in the way his allies in the Motor City would remember him. The dashing, well-dressed warrior for racial justice had disappeared. In a smoke-stained suit without a tie, Malcolm delivered his now-standard stump speech on the black freedom struggle. His appearance was overshadowed by the various threats emanating from the combined enmity of the NOI and law enforcement officials. The *New York Times* published a front-page photograph of a somber-looking Malcolm stepping out of his blue Oldsmobile wearing an overcoat, trademark black horn-rimmed glasses, and a hat. This image of a weary Malcolm captured the lack of sleep, anxiety, and depression that had stalked him for much of the time since his departure from the Nation.[55]

From Detroit, Malcolm returned to New York City on February 15, where he took a room at the Statler-Hilton Hotel. He kept a frenetic pace over the next five days, meeting with aides to discuss future organizational plans, speaking at Barnard College to over one thousand students about the scourge of "oppression and colonialism" that black revolutionaries were fighting, and scouting out possible sites for a new home with Betty on Long Island.[56]

Sunday, February 21, Malcolm woke up at the Hilton at 8 a.m., prepared to face a cold winter's day that would be highlighted by a rally at the Audubon Ballroom in West Harlem. He felt optimistic enough about the afternoon rally to call Betty and invite her to bring the children to the event. He left the hotel at 1 p.m. and drove his Oldsmobile to 146th Street and Broadway, judging this to be a safe enough distance to walk the twenty blocks north to the ballroom. Malcolm arrived on the second floor to the sight of aides passing out copies of the OAAU newspaper, *Blacklash*. He proceeded to meet with OAAU staff behind the stage in a small room, confessing to the stunned group of advisors that he felt close to a nervous breakdown. The day's shifting itinerary troubled Malcolm. Several guest speakers had canceled, and plans to formally release the OAAU's official political program were rescheduled, the latest setback tied to the firebombing of his home a week earlier. He refused to allow his staff to search attendees for weapons, despite knowing full well that NOI assassins were plotting to kill him. He vowed to continue in the face of all obstacles: "No matter what has happened to me, I can't go out there complaining about it," he reasoned. "What I say has to be said with their problems in mind."[57]

Malcolm X walked onto the stage just before 3 p.m. to rapturous applause from a crowd of four hundred. He gave the crowd the Muslim greeting "Assalamu alaikum," to which they responded, "Wa-alaikumu salam," and then a fight broke out several rows from the stage. "Hold it! Hold it!" Malcolm shouted, straining to regain order as the bodyguards posted near him moved closer to the melee. A smoke bomb went off at the rear of the ballroom, creating pandemonium and leaving Malcolm unprotected on the rostrum. Three assassins converged on him in an instant—one firing a sawed-off shotgun into Malcolm's left side, piercing his heart, and two others emptying handguns into his dying corpse. Betty covered her children amid the chaos. "They are killing my husband!" she screamed at one point, shielding her daughters with her body. By the time Betty felt safe enough to venture toward the stage, Malcolm was lying flat on his back, surrounded by several people trying to give him aid and comfort. As he lay on the floor, his shirt open, revealing seven bullet wounds, one OAAU member took snapshots that would become the major images of his death. A combination of Malcolm's aides, police officers, and OAAU members managed to place him on a stretcher and take him to Columbia Presbyterian Hospital, where he arrived at 3:15 p.m. Doctors tried frantically to revive Malcolm before pronouncing his official death at 3:30. "The gentleman you knew as Malcolm X," announced the Columbia Presbyterian physician, "is dead."[58]

Malcolm's assassination turned a cold winter's afternoon in New York City into the site of an unfolding political tragedy. One shooter would be arrested, but witnesses identified perhaps as many as four others, and rumors, conspiracy theories, and debates over who killed Malcolm X persist until this day. The chaos surrounding Malcolm's death seemed to echo aspects of Malcolm's predictions of race war, but with the ironic twist that the struggle would be fought among blacks rather than across the color line. Malcolm's lawyer, Percy Sutton, told reporters that his fallen client planned to release "the names of those who were trying to kill him" at the Audubon.[59]

More than ten thousand people attended Malcolm's funeral and more than twenty-two thousand people viewed his body in Harlem, braving frigid temperatures to pay respects to a political leader whose significance grew even larger in death than it had been in life. Eulogized by his friend, the actor Ossie Davis, as "our living black manhood" at a Christian church in Harlem, Malcolm was accorded the funeral rites of his orthodox Muslim beliefs. His corpse, draped in white robes, could be glimpsed through a glass-covered coffin surrounded by ten uniformed black police officers.[60]

The funeral service featured messages and tributes from Kwame Nkrumah, South Africa's African National Congress, and the ambassador of Jordan. The battle over Malcolm's legacy began immediately after his death. *The Autobiography of Malcolm X* became an instant classic following its October publication. The book presented him to a global audience as the most important self-made black activist of the twentieth century. Writer Alex Haley humanized Malcolm through a dramatic recounting of his improbable rise from street hustler and prison inmate to black nationalist, radical freedom fighter, and human rights crusader. Haley and Malcolm had begun working on the autobiography in 1963, and they developed an uncanny intellectual rapport, with the more-mainstream black writer drawing out the sense of carefully hidden playfulness that characterized some of Malcolm's best speeches. The book's emphasis on the Nation of Islam as a redemptive force in black politics shifted after Malcolm's tumultuous departure, and the transformed narrative found Malcolm undergoing, like Homer's Odysseus, a series of trials on a rough journey to renaissance that would remain incomplete. Haley framed Malcolm's story as an uplift saga that smoothed over the rough edges and filtered the more complicated sides of Malcolm's politics, creating a tale of a man cut short just as his political perspective grew wide enough to include whites in the global political revolution he spent much of his life committed to.[61]

The *New York Amsterdam News* countered the fast-developing hagiography around Malcolm, publishing retrospective articles and essays that aimed to rescue the man from a developing mythology that cleaved him in two. The "bad Malcolm" preached racial hatred, called whites devils, and looked to foment racial violence and wreck the civil rights movement. The "good Malcolm," after experiencing an epiphany during the hajj, embraced the multiracial nature of Islam, rejected his past promotion of racial separatism, and sought to join civil rights struggles. Such neat juxtapositions made for good storytelling but poor history; they veered toward making him a cliché rather than lauding him as an exemplar of the complicated rivers of oppression and resistance that animated the black freedom struggle. Malcolm's deft ability to straddle competing, at times contradictory, political and intellectual perspectives would be lost in favor of a linear story of a talented leader who devoted his best years to an organization he later denounced. Malcolm's final quest to promote human rights was cut short by the very political violence he had so frequently brandished like a rhetorical sword.[62]

Malcolm's death ignited debates over his legacy that continue to this day. The *New York Times* characterized his life as a Greek tragedy, the tale of "an extraordinary and twisted man" consumed by his own violent fantasies. The national paper of record claimed "World Pays Little Attention to Malcolm Slaying" in one story, while reporting "Malcolm Called a Martyr Abroad" in another—signs of the conflicting interpretations that greeted his passing. Harlem countered this opinion, with many fondly remembering "Brother Malcolm" as a teacher of profound eloquence, a political leader of unimpeachable integrity, and a husband, father, and black man whose personal sincerity helped define a new era in the world's collective racial imagination.[63]

Around the world, global expressions of grief recognized Malcolm as an international icon. Africa, where Malcolm had spent much of his final year traveling, memorialized him as a fallen son who, in Kwame Nkumah's words, lived a "life of dedication for human dignity" around the world. From Dar es Salaam, the South African National Congress issued a statement condemning Malcolm's murder, which made the front pages of the Tanzanian *Standard*. China's *People's Daily* accused the US government of orchestrating Malcolm's assassination. In Indonesia, the site of the Bandung Conference that Malcolm had considered a model for black solidarity, hundreds of demonstrators carrying banners staged a protest outside the American ambassador's official residence. London-area pan-Africanists marched while brandishing portraits of Patrice Lumumba, the martyred Congolese leader whom Malcolm revered. The Council of African Organizations traced Malcolm's murder back to a force larger than the NOI: American imperialism. In Accra, Malcolm's friends led a memorial service attended by many of the black expatriates who had welcomed him to Ghana twice during the previous year. They characterized Malcolm's death as the beginning, rather than end, of a new chapter of the human rights struggle being waged by blacks all over the world.[64]

Malcolm X's most significant black political adversary in life offered glowing tributes in death. Martin Luther King Jr.'s public statements following Malcolm's assassination—including telegrammed condolences—advanced a critically sympathetic elegy for his political and intellectual counterpart. King called Malcolm "a product of the hate and violence invested in the Negro's blighted existence in this nation." Through biographical details of Malcolm's familial tragedies and teenage juvenile delinquency, King sketched a portrait of a black genius capable of overcoming personal obstacles, only to be felled by political circumstances. "It is a testament to Malcolm's personal depth and integrity that he could not become an underworld czar," wrote King, "but turned again and again to religion for meaning and destiny." Malcolm's death represented King's first public acknowledgment of him as a man of deep religious faith. King openly wondered what he might have become. "Malcolm was still turning and growing at the time of his brutal and meaningless assassination." King offered details of Malcolm's recent trip to Selma, where he had yearned to work with civil rights groups but seemed incapable of turning the corner that would allow him to commit to nonviolence. Beneath Malcolm's words of fire were signs of a new "interest in politics as a way" of promoting black dignity and racial equality. King recognized the convergence between Malcolm's struggle for radical black dignity and his own quest for radical black citizenship. Malcolm's public and private efforts to engage in struggles for racial justice showcased a "man of passion and zeal" in search of "a program through which he could channel his talents."[65]

King's penetrating analysis of Malcolm's life and political influence reveals an intimate aspect of a professional relationship that remained strained throughout their lives. King respected Malcolm, even as he winced at the rhetorical barbs hurled his way by the only political leader who equaled his oratorical excellence. Martin had studied Malcolm's speeches and interviews enough to cite *The Hate That Hate Produced* as the television documentary that introduced Malcolm to the world and to detail autobiographical stories with ease. Malcolm's personal sincerity and political integrity impressed King, whose admiring essay suggested that, under different circumstances, the two might have become friends. Yet King faltered in his description of Malcolm as a man in search of a program. Malcolm's improvisational final year outlined multiple strategies for black freedom, distilling the struggle for black dignity at the local, national, and global levels. Lacking the resources and time to transform civil rights struggles into a human rights movement, Malcolm left a legacy of revolutionary politics that, shortly after his death, would galvanize Black Power activists. But his greatest impact may have been on Martin Luther King Jr.

CHAPTER 9

The Radical King

The winter of Malcolm X's death marked the beginning of
Martin Luther King Jr.'s political radicalization. King had
spent the previous decade expanding the boundaries of
American democracy by turning once-disruptive protests into part
of the political mainstream. After Malcolm's death, King challenged the alliance between the government and the civil rights
movement he had helped to broker by making new demands on
President Johnson's legislative and political agenda. In the beginning of the year, King tested the patience of a supportive White
House by pressing hard for voting rights. By summer, he went
further by defining rising civil unrest as a product of institutional
racism and poverty that required far more material and political
resources than ever imagined by the architects of the Great Society.

The struggle for voting rights found King back in Alabama,
the state judged by the SCLC to offer the best and most potentially dramatic illustration of black disfranchisement. The SCLC
and the SNCC both claimed Alabama as their territory. SNCC
activists burrowed into Lowndes County, located in the buckle of
Alabama's rural black belt, smack dab in the middle of Selma and
Montgomery—cities where King and the SCLC enjoyed considerable networks. Lowndes contained a particularly brutal history of

racial terror, serving as one of the main conduits of the convict-lease system that virtually re-enslaved tens of thousands of black folk after the Civil War. King and John Lewis, the leaders of the SCLC and SNCC, vowed to work toward an operational unity that had been continuously stymied by disagreements over strategies, tactics, and hurt feelings caused by the considerable attention King's presence garnered wherever he went. SNCC staff working in the rural counties of Alabama remained dedicated to the slow, grinding, and tedious work of building a movement by helping local people organize. They considered King's decision to march fifty-four miles from Selma to Montgomery to highlight the disfranchisement and police violence facing black voters as the kind of spectacle that Malcolm X had rejected with the March on Washington. Malcolm's presence in Alabama shortly before his death still lingered among some SNCC staff, especially in light of twenty-six-year-old Jimmie Lee Jackson's death at the hands of Alabama state troopers during a melee in Selma following a nighttime demonstration in Marion, a town twenty-seven miles northwest of the city.[1]

Over the first two months of the year, King led a number of demonstrations in Selma in between fundraising efforts, his church duties at Ebenezer, and bouts of ill health that doctors attributed to stress—tensions that were exacerbated by a constant barrage of credible death threats in Alabama and elsewhere. Against this backdrop, King approved, but did not participate in, the planned demonstration originating from Brown Chapel AME in Selma, where Malcolm X had spoken the month before, and destined for the state capitol of Montgomery. Six hundred demonstrators, led by SCLC aide Hosea Williams and SNCC chairman John Lewis, marched from Brown AME through Broad Street, Selma's main thoroughfare, before turning left to ascend the Edmund Pettus Bridge. Alabama state troopers in blue uniforms spread across the four-lane Highway 80 to block the procession. They were joined by more than a dozen of Sheriff Jim Clark's possemen, riding on horseback and armed with cattle prods. As Lewis and Williams advanced toward the east side of the bridge, they were given two minutes to disperse over a bullhorn wielded by Major John Cloud, the commander of the state troopers. A minute later, all hell broke loose.

A sea of white-helmeted state troopers swarmed the peaceful demonstrators—many of them outfitted in their Sunday church clothes—bashing anyone in their sights, women and men, with batons. White spectators, watching the proceedings from businesses that lined the road, cheered as if viewing a sporting event. Mounted law enforcement officers charged at scattering black Americans as if they were chasing runaway human chattel from another century. Then, tear gas turned the escalating chaos into a scene of unimaginable horror.[2]

Bloody Sunday galvanized voting-rights efforts in Selma, turning King's latest mobilization campaign into an international news story. ABC News broadcast footage of the afternoon of violence on Highway 80 later that evening, preempting a screening of *Judgment at Nuremberg*, an award-winning film depicting the aftermath of racial genocide in Europe.

On Tuesday, King led a group of two thousand determined marchers, whose hopes of traveling beyond the area of Sunday's violence were thwarted by fresh threats from law enforcement. King's decision to march just short of the hundreds of Alabama state troopers prevented a second violent confrontation but came at great cost to his reputation. SNCC activists, while still not officially endorsing the march, felt that King should have pressed on no matter what the obstacle. The "Tuesday turnaround" incensed SNCC staff, who channeled Malcolm X's voice in criticizing King's behavior as a betrayal of local people committed to securing the vote.[3]

Expressions of outrage, grief, and support for the movement poured into Selma from all parts of the country, including the White House. Thousands of Americans descended upon the city, including white liberals upset over the images of racial violence against civil rights activists. The violence in Selma pushed Lyndon Johnson to accelerate his plans to send voting-rights legislation to congress. The death of James Reeb, a white minister from Boston who had traveled to Selma to support the movement only to be murdered by racist vigilantes after the Tuesday demonstration, forced Johnson's hand, as did the sight of more than one thousand protesters outside the White House. Reeb's death in Selma—like the killing of white activists Mickey Schwerner and Andrew Goodman in Mississippi the previous summer—inspired national headlines, allowing the movement, once again, to leverage the human tragedy of white victims into a national moment of political reckoning. Johnson addressed the controversy at a press conference staged at the White House rose garden on Saturday, March 13. "What happened in Selma was an American tragedy," he observed. Johnson said the violence represented a crucible through which the United States would better perfect the union, strengthen democracy, and, in so doing, reveal "the heart and the purpose and the meaning of America itself." He suggested that racism undermined the grandeur of the American experiment and violence sullied the moral aspirations of all its citizens. "It is wrong to do violence to peaceful citizens in the streets of their town," said the president. "It is wrong to deny Americans the right to vote. It is wrong to deny any person full equality because of the color of his skin."[4]

An early morning court appearance and the obligation to deliver James Reeb's 2 p.m. eulogy forced King to promise the president that he would "be listening to your message on TV with great interest and appreciation." In perhaps the most powerful speech of his presidency, Johnson, during a March 15 special address to Congress, characterized the black citizens gathered in Selma as "long-suffering men and women" who "peacefully protested the denial of their rights as Americans." The president's vivid description recognized Selma as part of a long, unbroken chain of patriotism that stretched back to the Founding Fathers and historic battles waged in Lexington and Concord, Massachusetts, during the American Revolution. Johnson compared black demonstrators in Selma to the soldiers in the Battle of Appomattox, which signaled the end of the Civil War, making a claim for the civil rights struggle as the natural heir to Reconstruction's unfinished legacy. At stake for all Americans, the president observed, was nothing less than the "destiny of democracy," a political system that Malcolm X and Martin Luther King Jr. had publicly debated over the previous decade. Racial discrimination, Johnson argued, "lay bare the secret heart of America itself." He boiled the struggles for racial justice down to their root political and moral essence, reflected in the American creed: "To right wrong, to do justice, to serve man." By confronting the crisis in Selma, Johnson suggested, the nation would rediscover its moral purpose as liberty's surest guardian for all Americans.[5]

King listened intently as the president challenged the entire nation to understand that the treatment black citizens endured in Selma would never again be tolerated. Johnson announced plans to introduce comprehensive voting-rights legislation that evening. "And—we—shall—overcome," Johnson proclaimed, echoing the movement's unofficial anthem. Black Americans, he said, were the era's true heroes, exhibiting unwavering faith in democracy that produced historical breakthroughs. King wept at the flurry of words, which seemed the culmination of a decade spent in the trench warfare of racial struggle. SNCC chairman John Lewis, who watched the speech alongside King, felt Johnson spoke as both a president and "a poet." King called Johnson from Montgomery to offer words of praise and encouragement. The speech, according to King, "would help lead the way toward the salvation of the Negro." Johnson thanked him. "You're the leader who is making it possible," Johnson said. "I'm just following along trying to do what's right."[6]

After five days of marching that began in Selma, King resumed center stage in an unfolding national drama in Montgomery on March 25, where thirty thousand gathered to see his speech. The multiracial crowd made up the biggest civil rights demonstration ever produced on southern soil. Its defiant participants included the militant students bold enough to invite Malcolm X to Alabama. Veterans of the Montgomery bus boycott took a symbolic bow in advance of King's speech. Rosa Parks's appearance elicited rapturous applause, her vivid recollection of how Jim Crow's indignities robbed her family of land at odds with her public image as a genteel agent of change who accidentally stumbled into becoming "the first lady of the movement."[7] And for the second time in less than two years, large swaths of the American public listened to King's televised speech.

King described nonviolence as a weapon of peace "unsheathed from its scabbard" to wage struggle in a conflict between "good and evil" that spanned from Selma to the White House. He lauded President Johnson's voting-rights speech as "one of the most passionate pleas for human rights" in American history. King argued that "no wave of racism" could stop the movement for racial justice gaining momentum across the nation. He challenged those gathered to create campaigns against segregated public schools, poverty, and hunger until blacks and whites lived together "in decent, safe and sanitary housing." Predicting a "season of suffering" ahead, King found inspiration in nonviolence's capacity to change whole communities on the road toward creating a peaceful nation, "a society that can live with its conscience." He closed by rhetorically asking, "How long? How long? How long? How long?" would it take to achieve the dream of a beloved national community. "Not long," he answered. "Because the arc of the moral universe is long but it bends toward justice."[8]

Montgomery found King at the pinnacle of his power as a national civil rights leader and international statesman. He addressed the nation as a virtual political coequal of the president, a Nobel Prize recipient who marched under federal protection. Nineteen weeks and one day after his speech in Montgomery, a beaming King would accept a commemorative pen from Johnson, who had just signed the Voting Rights Act into legislation. But that spring, King was riding a rising crest of political emotion into new terrain. He wrote an essay, "Behind the Selma March," published in the April 3 issue of *Saturday Review*, outlining the radical vision that would come to grip his politics that year. "We are happy to know that our struggle in Selma has gone far beyond the issue of the right to vote and has focused the attention of the nation on the vital issue of equality in human rights," he wrote. King's emphasis on reimagining black citizenship as a human rights struggle echoed Malcolm X's efforts to do the same over the previous year. Barely noticed at the time, the essay marked a shift in King's approach to achieving radical black citizenship. Human rights encompassed more than formal legal and legislative breakthroughs. It required both the elimination of racial prejudice and economic injustice and the guarantee of justice in every aspect of black life in America. It required, in fact, nothing less than a revolution.[9]

On May 20, 1965, surrounded by Vice President Hubert Humphrey, Bayard Rustin, Atlanta mayor Ivan Allen, and liberal Republican and mayoral candidate John Lindsay, King addressed the American Jewish Committee at the Americana Hotel in New York. Buoyed by Humphrey's private reassurance that the voting-rights bill would be passed during the summer, King spoke to the 1,500 in attendance about the larger meaning of the quest for black citizenship. "The stirring lesson of this age is that mass nonviolent direct action is not a particular device for Negro agitation," King informed the assembly. "Rather it is an historically validated method for defending freedom and democracy and for enlarging the value to benefit the whole society."[10]

Civil rights, according to King, looked toward the universal through the particular experiences of black struggle. He reminded the audience to never forget that civil right struggles had led "to a broad war-on-poverty concept which ultimately will benefit more whites than Negroes." King felt increasingly comfortable publicly defining the movement as one without limits, despite critics and supporters who viewed him as only qualified to discuss racial matters. Instead, King implored the audience to reimagine the nation's entire democratic project by recognizing that, when civil rights activists demonstrated around the nation, they represented the best example of citizenship that America had ever witnessed. Then, King crept gingerly into the topic of Vietnam—not yet the political maelstrom it would become, but sensitive enough for the SCLC to decline offering an official policy on the subject. "We must work to end the war in Vietnam," King pleaded. He talked about the "inadequacies in our poverty program," hinting at a fundamental contradiction in the Great Society's dual efforts of ending poverty and escalating the war. He cited war, racism, and poverty as "three areas where there is a moral and spiritual progress." He quipped that, although "it is nice to have an integrated lunch counter," he didn't "want to find the milk served at the counter" suffering from nuclear radiation.[11]

The speech laid out clear themes of race, war, and poverty that King now embraced as his political calling. On the subject of Vietnam, King followed on the heels of Malcolm X's revolutionary criticism of the war. While Malcolm had energetically denounced the United States for its involvement on the wrong side of a worldwide "struggle against colonialism, neocolonialism, and imperialism," King took baby steps. His description of war as "obsolete" and his claim that the world "must have nonviolence or nonexistence" stopped far short of Malcolm's identification of Vietnam as the "struggle of the whole Third World." Yet King's decision to publicly criticize the war and point out the flaws in the nation's anti-poverty efforts exemplified his political courage. Although Malcolm X had accused King of timidity and student activists had charged him with vanity, King possessed tremendous courage, a strong will, and significant political resolve. His willingness to defy a president he considered to be an ally reflected the passion of a social movement leader whose vision of black citizenship and racial justice encompassed far more than ending racial segregation or securing the right to vote.[12]

On August 5, 1965, Johnson signed the Voting Rights Act in the same room where Abraham Lincoln, 104 years earlier, had signed the Confiscation Act, which helped pave the way for slavery's emancipation and freed enslaved black people serving in Confederate armies. Johnson signed a bill that contained no such half measures. Martin Luther King Jr., Roy Wilkins, James Farmer, and Rosa Parks were among the civil rights leaders that listened to Johnson discuss voting rights as "a triumph for freedom as huge as any victory that has ever been won on any battlefield." But King would have less than a week to bask in the achievement. Just five days later, unrest erupted in Watts, a predominantly black neighborhood in Los Angeles made up of working-, lower-, and middle-class residents. Police brutality against local blacks suspected of criminal activity sparked the violence, a pattern that echoed the civil disturbances the previous year in Harlem, Brooklyn, and Rochester, New York.[13]

The uprising fulfilled Malcolm X's grim prediction that political rebellions would soon grip the nation. The Los Angeles riot exposed deep fissures within the civil rights movement, the limits of the Great Society, and the depths of racial injustice. The scale of the Watts rebellion hardened civil rights opponents while radicalizing the advocates of Malcolm X's struggle for black dignity. Critics interpreted the waves of burning cars, burglarized stores, and chaos as criminal acts of lawlessness. Reports of sniper fire, widespread destruction of property, and violence were further heightened by the response of Los Angeles mayor Sam Yorty and police chief William Parker, who encouraged anxious white homeowners to purchase guns while dismissing allegations of police brutality raised by civil rights leaders and local activists.[14]

The political and cultural fallout from Watts forced King to confront the depth of black anger against ongoing racial oppression that stubbornly withstood the combined power of landmark civil rights and anti-poverty legislation. Watts also marked the beginning of the end of King's close professional relationship with Lyndon Johnson. King arrived in Los Angeles six days after the violence began amid false rumors that blamed the Nation of Islam for the riots. A rising death toll had recently secured Johnson's undivided attention on the crisis. On his second day in the city, King spoke to hundreds of residents at the Westminster Community Center, a neighborhood association in the center of ashes that made up a once-vibrant community. It was a searing, contentious, and uncomfortable conversation.[15]

King strode twin rhetorical paths, claiming belief in nonviolence and demanding reports of the effects of racial oppression palpating through Watts. Restless jeers of "Burn!" and plaintive calls for jobs and justice were drowned out by King's urgent baritone. He pleaded with the crowd to never forget white martyrs of the movement as recent as Viola Liuzzo, a housewife and mother of five killed during the Selma demonstrations. He publicly embraced the black community's ideological diversity by claiming, "Elijah Muhammad is my brother, even though our methods differ." Privately, King confided to Bayard Rustin that he now understood that blacks required not simply the opportunity "to eat hamburgers" but the financial means to buy them. King now sought a way to explicitly link the quest for black citizenship to the struggle for economic justice. He called for civilian review of the police, a suggestion angrily rejected by Chief Parker, who claimed, incredulously, that Los Angeles suffered from no racial discrimination. King's run-in with Parker and Mayor Yorty found him confronting old adversaries of Malcolm X, who had spent over a year traveling back and forth to Los Angeles in the aftermath of Ronald Stokes's killing. Following a fruitless three-hour meeting, King deflected press inquiries searching for substantive breakthroughs, while Yorty dropped all pretense of diplomacy and accused King of promoting "lawlessness" by calling for civilian review and the resignation of Chief Parker.[16]

King and Lyndon Johnson spoke by phone on Friday, August 20. Johnson bemoaned congressional cuts to a poverty war being fought circumspectly, rather than robustly, due to political calculations that King had neither the time nor the patience to seriously consider. Both men worried that political enemies would seize upon urban violence as an excuse to curtail the nation's fitful racial progress. Although Johnson conceded that the government was "not doing enough" to end poverty, the dealmaker in him preferred a compromise to a stalemate.

Sounding history's drumbeat, Johnson described black impoverishment as "losing ground every day," in desperate need of a massive political and financial commitment. "That's right, you said it right there," replied King to the president's declaration of being ahead of the curve on racial justice. King told Johnson that Los Angeles required an immediate infusion of anti-poverty funds. "The country's got to stand up and support what I'm doing," said Johnson, asking King to reinforce his leadership on issues of racial and economic justice. "We've got to have some of these housing programs, and we've got to get rid of these ghettos and we've got to get these children out from where the rats eat on them at night," Johnson said, getting himself worked up. He complained in detail about how the Senate's cuts to his poverty bill had stymied his efforts to get a handle on urban poverty and potential riots.[17]

The president implored King to mention the substance of Johnson's recent Howard University address, which discussed the need to assess racial equality by measurable outcomes and not just theoretical opportunities. Confronted by new depths of the very oppression he had eloquently described at Howard, Johnson claimed that black freedom, however important, represented a single part of a sprawling agenda. Vietnam's looming threat to the Great Society made both men wary of potential conflicts of interest between them. "They all got the impression that you're against me on Vietnam," Johnson said. King deflected by claiming that his peace advocacy stopped short of calling for a unilateral withdrawal. The conversation ended with the president teasing King that he could contact the White House at any time, even if he had to "call collect." King laughed and replied, "All right."[18]

Months later, in "Beyond the Los Angeles Riots," an essay published in the *Saturday Review*, King wrote that Watts exposed the "imperfections in the civil rights movement" and misguided "white racial policy" in American cities. He announced bold plans to confront the poverty in black urban communities that Malcolm X had spent his entire public life addressing. Without mentioning Los Angeles mayor Sam Yorty or New York mayor Robert F. Wagner by name, King criticized big-city politicians who lacked "statesmanship" and "compassion" on race matters but nonetheless personally "welcome me to their cities" and lavished King with praise until he pressed them about local race relations.[19]

Watts transformed King, who now surveyed the depth and breadth of racial segregation, poverty, and antiblack violence with new eyes. He characterized the past decade of civil rights activism as extracting uneven gains nationally. As the South freed itself from some of the worst vestiges of racial slavery and Jim Crow, the North lagged behind, plagued by institutional racism that ratcheted up black unemployment, residential and public school segregation, police brutality, and crime. He daringly interpreted violence in Watts as a "form of social protest" by residents of a region unfamiliar with nonviolence. Like Malcolm X, King now regarded violent disruptions rooted in antiblack racism as a form of political protest, one that he disagreed with but refused to cast negative judgments against. This proved to be a major turning point in King's rhetorical strategy against white supremacy and institutional racism.

The most important part of King's essay described nonviolence as an urgent, strategic tool of revolutionary social change, one that remained a "powerful demand for reason and justice." The uprising in Watts represented one direction that the black freedom struggle might pursue if nonviolence failed. Black nationalists, King argued, were skeptical of defeating "the tricks of sophisticated segregation" and impatient enough with American "hypocrisies" to embrace violence—a description that drew from Malcolm's oeuvre without mentioning his name. King described massive, disciplined, and nonviolent demonstrations as a shield against both white racism and black anger, noting how the strategic presence of one hundred thousand blacks in big cities could disrupt the political status quo and prevent even the most reactionary politicians from violent retaliation.

These were the bold maneuvers that Malcolm X had repeatedly called for in his "Farce on Washington" speeches, where he scorned the evolution of the March on Washington from a daring showcase of civil disobedience to a stage-managed demonstration where protestors marched "between two dead presidents" rather than confronting the living one. Less than two years later, and with very little fanfare, King publicly sided with Malcolm. King, now more forcefully than ever before, called for massive civil disobedience to be used as a political tool in service of a black revolution. Although he took care to assure readers that no people or property would be harmed during his proposed northern demonstrations, he described nonviolence as a "peaceful sword" that blacks needed to "firmly" wield in pursuit of justice. Watts gave King his clearest understanding to date that black citizenship required the raw power to not only change hearts and minds but fundamentally alter power relations between blacks and whites. This meant utilizing black bodies to change the status quo of American race relations and make the beloved community a reality. King framed nonviolence as creative, moral, and powerful enough to smash "the savagery of Southern segregation" and, in the process, earn the respect and "emulation" of northern activists.[20]

King's words eloquently framed the next chapter of his public career as a civil rights organizer. They also reveal Malcolm X's influence on his political worldview. It was in the aftermath of Malcolm's assassination and the Watts uprisings that King's transition began: from a Nobel Prize–winning political mobilizer—whose eloquent composure from a Birmingham jail, speech at the nation's capital, and presence in Selma placed him in the front ranks of American political royalty—into a revolutionary dissident vilified in quarters that once feted him. Watts marked a decisive shift in King's thinking about racial and economic justice, one that found him in closer alliance with Malcolm X.

In the late spring of 1966, King attended the White House's civil rights conference, organized to the last detail by the Johnson administration, on June 1 and 2, where he enjoyed perhaps his last public rapprochement with Lyndon Johnson. Intended as a public victory lap in the wake of Johnson's soaring Howard University speech and the subsequent voting-rights bill, the conference, which occurred almost one year after that shining moment, had morphed into something far different since its initial planning. Riots, Vietnam, and white backlash hovered over the entire proceedings.

During a *Face the Nation* television appearance three days before the conference, King edged closer to a complete break with the White House on the subject of war, racism, and democracy. "I know where your heart is there your money will go, and the heart of many people in the Administration and others happens to be in Vietnam," observed King. The strain between King and the president could be seen by the civil rights leader's relatively low profile throughout the conference. Johnson feared being upstaged at his own event, and he lavished praise and attention on hand-picked surrogates who doubled as political insiders: Solicitor General Thurgood Marshall and the NAACP's Roy Wilkins. Marshall, the crusading litigator behind the epic public school integration, viewed King's demonstrations as unnecessary diversions from the legal work crafted by himself and the NAACP, so his elevated position, alongside Wilkins, as a keynote speaker rankled King.[21]

Over two thousand delegates representing civil rights, business, civic, religious, and political groups attended the two-day affair. The president warmly greeted Boston Celtics basketball star Bill Russell after the outspoken athlete's talk on racial bias in employment. Vice President Hubert Humphrey opened the event with a speech decrying racism and poverty. "Slumism is segregated, inferior schooling for those who so urgently need the best," he said. Humphrey received a standing ovation from delegates for exposing "America's shame." Supporters of the president, such as the Urban League's Whitney Young, praised Johnson as determined "to right the past wrongs," arguing that "the White House Conference points the way for all of us to follow." In contrast, SNCC and other dissident groups condemned the event as a public-relations stunt. Delegates attended discussion groups centered around issues related to racial justice, equality, and citizenship where they could offer recommendations, but the entire affair turned out to be a highly controlled exercise orchestrated by Lyndon Johnson. The president—finding himself fiscally constrained by a Congress already concerned with midterm elections, fearful of growing military commitment in Vietnam, and painfully aware of how King's recent rhetoric had highlighted disappointment in the Great Society—positioned himself as a statesman capable of listening to reasonable dissenters and hovering above partisan politics.[22]

Johnson showed up unexpectedly to the Sheraton on Wednesday evening, greeting King, Roy Wilkins, and A. Philip Randolph in the hotel's banquet hall before promising "to give my days, and such talents as I have been given, to the pursuit of justice and opportunity for those so long denied them." For King, in light of the president's increased attention to Vietnam and retreat from advancing his Great Society ambitions, his words fell flat.[23]

King managed to speak at one session but was largely overlooked by Johnson, the White House, and the press. The administration's efforts to diminish King's stature were a response to his deepening criticism of the Great Society and, implicitly for the most part, Johnson's leadership. On Thursday, King retreated to his hotel room. He only appeared at the evening dinner because organizers asked Coretta to perform the national anthem before the event's closing. King departed the conference disappointed in what he correctly interpreted as a permanent breach with Johnson on core issues of justice, citizenship, and dignity—a split that would soon play out in vicious debates over the future of the Great Society and American democracy. King, who abhorred personal confrontations with friends and adversaries, complained to staff that he felt disrespected.[24]

Following the conference, King went to Mississippi, where he resumed the role of fireman, a position he once vowed to never perform again. When James Meredith, the first black student to enroll at the University of Mississippi and a strong figure in the movement, was shot by a white vigilante on June 6, King rushed to his bedside, despite Meredith's penchant for being a political wild card. Meredith's one-man march against fear across the entire state of Mississippi had received little attention until he was met with violence. The shooting drew SNCC and Stokely Carmichael to Mississippi as well. Carmichael and SNCC staff still felt residual tension from their disagreements with the SCLC and King in Selma. But Mississippi was SNCC territory, so familiar to Carmichael as to be considered a second home. No other organization could claim the extensive number of contacts or active projects in the state. Any successful march would, out of necessity, rely on SNCC's network. Carmichael instantly recognized this potential leverage and set out to take advantage of it.[25]

Carmichael and SNCC used their intimate knowledge of Mississippi to take over the spirit of Meredith march. Over the next three weeks, King walked through Mississippi alongside Carmichael in a demonstration that came to be known as the March against Fear. Media coverage provided Carmichael and SNCC a national platform that they used to redefine the black freedom struggle and articulate a vision of black political self-determination and power. King treated Carmichael like an equal. Although he felt uncomfortable with SNCC's increasing militancy, King made a concerted effort throughout the march to project a sense of political solidarity in front of reporters. He refused to distance himself from Carmichael or SNCC, whom he respected despite their political differences.

On June 7, Bobby Kennedy, King's onetime nemesis turned crusading liberal senator from New York, announced at the University of Natal in Durban, South Africa, that if racial apartheid did not end "there is going to be a major crisis not only in Africa but throughout the world." That same day, King led a press conference with fellow movement leaders before continuing James Meredith's march across Mississippi. Flanked by Carmichael and CORE leader Floyd McKissick, King addressed the reporters and television cameras that had descended on Mississippi. King lauded SNCC's "Herculean efforts" in the state and talked of plans to complete the march that Meredith began. "I am confident that this march will have as great or greater impact than the march from Selma to Montgomery," said King. "We are going all out to make this the largest march ever held in this section of the country." He continued, "We want to put President Johnson on the spot. He called a conference to 'fulfill these rights' and we want them fulfilled, but words can't stop bullets. We want action and we want it now!" King's passionate words and challenge to the president pushed him away from civil rights moderates and closer to the political radicals who, following Malcolm X, offered harsh truths as a balm for nation's searing racial wounds.[26]

After the press conference, King and movement leaders drove to Hernando, the spot where the wounded Meredith had dragged himself out of harm's way one day earlier, and began to march south on Highway 51. Mississippi state troopers warned demonstrators, including King, Carmichael, and SNCC activist Cleveland Sellers, to stay off the highway. "We walked" on the main road from "Selma to Montgomery," protested King. One trooper replied that they could walk to China but could not use the main road. After the back-and-forth, three troopers shoved King, Carmichael, and Sellers to the ground. King called after colleagues to restrain Carmichael, who attempted to pull away from the group to confront the officers. As Carmichael lunged, King held his arm and yelled, "Get Stokely, somebody, lay on him!" The maneuver worked, and King privately chided Carmichael afterward, reminding him of the "greater responsibility" imposed on him by his new leadership role. The scene captured in miniature the way the rest of the march would unfold, with Carmichael issuing words of fire reminiscent of Malcolm X and King reining him in. Debates over tactics of nonviolence versus self-defense, strategies of political self-determination versus interracial coalitions, and ideologies of black nationalism versus racial integration became sensationalized in journalistic narratives that framed the march as a generational struggle between the mature King and the youthful Carmichael. Boiled down to its essence, the debate centered on whether black citizenship could be achieved through political reforms, or if more radical changes were required to fundamentally restructure American democracy. King, unbeknownst to most people, favored the latter course.[27]

Carmichael's plan to make the march a criticism of the Johnson administration alienated Roy Wilkins and Whitney Young, who decided against supporting the demonstration. King chose to stay rather than abandon the young SNCC militants. He hoped to utilize the creative tension within the movement to craft a radical agenda that, although nonviolent, might disrupt America's racial status quo. On Wednesday, June 8, following the departure of Wilkins and Young, King read a march manifesto whose description of Mississippi as symbolizing "every evil" blacks historically faced recalled the stinging rebukes of Malcolm X. He issued a "public indictment" against antiblack racism in blunt language that matched the tenor of the times.[28]

King, Carmichael, and other organizers directed the march on a detour through the more rural parts of the delta to register voters, mobilize the poor, and raise political consciousness. The sight of King attracted curiosity seekers, journalists, and locals. SNCC's nickname for King—"De Lawd"—summed up the awe he inspired in Mississippi, where elderly women delivered food and water and even young militants walked alongside him. "I've heard so much about him," remarked a maid in the small town of Coldwater, "and I just wanted to see him." King wore new boots, sunglasses, and a yellow hat with a straw band to march from Coldwater to Senatobia that Wednesday. Between 200 and 350 demonstrators walked single file down the highway in punishing ninety-degree heat. To loud cheers, King told one group of young people to tell their parents to vote in order to "put some of these mean sheriffs out of office" and elect black candidates.[29]

Over the next three weeks, the march made its way from Memphis, Tennessee, to Jackson, Mississippi, on Highway 51. King alternated between flying to Chicago, where he spent most of the year organizing a movement to end segregation in the largest city the SCLC ever tackled, and marching in Mississippi, where his presence represented a clear draw for organizers, local people, and reporters. Carmichael filled the vacuum in King's absence. He welcomed King as a galvanizing force in service of black political self-determination. Carmichael promoted the demonstration as an opportunity to organize the entire state of Mississippi, most importantly the backwater towns and rural hamlets that had been the sight of unspeakable violence against black locals and civil rights workers. If King provided the march with the credibility of a statesman, Carmichael lent the proceedings the urgency of a radical. He rankled journalists by characterizing Mississippi as full of "a bunch of racists." As the march progressed, SNCC organizers stressed the need to recruit black demonstrators to ensure that Mississippi would not be a replay of Selma. Northern white liberals could not rescue the state, Carmichael argued; only black people could do that.[30]

On Thursday, June 16, 1966, Carmichael transformed the political imagination of the civil rights movement and America's racial consciousness by calling for "Black Power!" during an evening rally in Greenwood, Mississippi, with over six hundred attendees. Earlier in the day, Carmichael had been arrested for trying to put up an overnight camp on the grounds of a black elementary school. "This is the twenty-seventh time that I have been arrested," said Carmichael. "I ain't going to jail no more. What we gonna start sayin' now is Black Power!" he cried. "What do we want?" The crowd chanted back in the call-and-response tradition of the black church, "Black Power!" The slogan reflected SNCC's evolution, born out of a unique blend of racial integration, radical democracy, black nationalism, Gandhian nonviolence, and a black Christian ethic of love.[31]

Black nationalist elements had always existed in SNCC, their power tempered by the push toward interracial democracy, the influence of King and activists such as James Lawson and Ella Baker, and the belief that the movement contained a spiritual basis that would compel political transformation. But six years of organizing against white supremacy in the Deep South, the frustratingly inconsistent support of northern liberals, and a federal government more concerned with winning an international war than establishing domestic peace had radicalized the organization. The small towns of Sunflower, Tunica, Belzoni, Grenada, and Tallahatchie were unfamiliar to most Americans, yet SNCC and Carmichael argued these were the true laboratories of racial justice and American democracy. Black Power identified racial integration as secondary to amassing political power capable of promoting radical black citizenship and dignity. It also vociferously criticized the violence, segregation, and economic injustice emanating from white institutions. In this sense, Black Power represented a structural critique of the multiple ways that racial terror and hypocrisy informed American democracy. The solution, Black Power activists implied, lay less in entering all-white spaces than in building enough political, economic, and cultural power to decide whether or not to join the political mainstream, develop black institutions, or some combination of both.

Black Power also gave a name to the simmering tensions that plagued the White House civil rights conference, internal divisions within the black freedom struggle, and the competitive interpretations of race, war, democracy, and citizenship that critically divided Martin Luther King Jr. and Lyndon Johnson. The phrase both described the movement Malcolm X had led since the 1950s and encompassed something more. As defined by the civil rights militants turned political revolutionaries, Black Power linked a structural critique of racism, white supremacy, and war to the struggle for black dignity and black citizenship. It allowed leaders, organizations, and individuals to more ably straddle the political thought and activism of Martin and Malcolm without choosing sides. Black nationalists, integrationists, liberals, conservatives, women, men, theologians, college students, prisoners, and the poor would all find kinship and organizing ballast in Black Power.[32]

King arrived in Mississippi the day after Carmichael's Black Power speech. He played down internal differences in favor of presenting a unified front. He defined the term Black Power as simply "the ability to make the power structure say yes, when it wants to say no." The definition worried the *Los Angeles Times*, which feared that Carmichael and King were speaking in "almost one voice." King spoke to a crowd of one thousand in Greenwood, Mississippi, that Friday, standing in front of the Leflore County courthouse. Black people continued to march, King explained, "because we are tired of being beaten, tired of being murdered." Although King matched Carmichael's passion, he tried to steer energies away from any hint of violence. Andy Young, one of King's most pragmatically effective political aides, who also had known Malcolm X, stressed to reporters that the radicalism behind King's message positioned him and the SCLC in conversation with Carmichael. He portrayed Carmichael as simply filling Malcolm X's role as both a racial provocateur and visionary capable of furthering the movement by pushing black "protest as far as he can, carrying along white liberals as far as they will go." Young argued that "SNCC's position on Black Power isn't too far from ours except in style and semantics."[33]

The call for Black Power drew King closer to SNCC and especially to Carmichael. Long days marching alongside one another led to late nights debating and laughing together. For the duration of the march, King became both a national leader and a field worker in the movement. Carmichael credited the time spent in Mississippi for turning the grudging respect many in SNCC felt toward King into open admiration. He marveled at King's courage in the face of threats, hecklers, and law enforcement along the demonstration route. King's star power awed him. Black Mississippians rushed to greet King as he walked on highways, into towns, and through plantations to recruit marchers and encourage voter registration. Local people risked economic and physical reprisal to come hear him, a phenomenon that Carmichael witnessed up close after being accidentally knocked over by a group of women rushing to see De Lawd.[34]

King decided not to openly criticize the feelings behind the call for Black Power, but he remained wary of the phrase's growing association with violence and anti-white sentiment. For the duration of the march, which grew into the biggest civil rights campaign since Selma, King assumed the uncomfortable position of trying to maintain the primacy of a civil rights movement under assault by the politics of racial fatigue, Vietnam, and antiblack violence. From Atlanta, King told reporters that the term Black Power too closely mirrored black nationalism—Malcolm X's political philosophy—the growing power of which King denied in the face of overwhelming evidence. "I see no significant trend in the country toward black nationalism," King explained, four days after Carmichael's cry sounded the biggest clarion call for political self-determination since Malcolm. Carmichael's description of racial integration as "a subterfuge for white supremacy" elevated black "political and economic power" above romantic ideas of interracial brotherhood. But Carmichael was no conventional racial separatist. He cherished white colleagues, grieving over the death of Jonathan Daniels, a white volunteer martyred the previous year in Alabama, and maintaining SNCC's dwindling interracial staff even as he urged, like Malcolm X, that whites form organizing beachheads outside of racially segregated black communities.[35]

On June 18, King, along with three hundred demonstrators and dozens of reinforcements, marched down a Mississippi highway toward Belzoni. They were antagonized by a burning cross and cars teeming with racists carrying signs reading "Ku Klux Klan—Knights of the Green Forest." Marchers also passed a large placard with a photo of a young King attending Highlander Folk School's citizenship class in the late 1950s. Mississippi state officials had rebranded the program as a "communist training school." Organizers urged black residents of the delta's wide-open spaces and cotton fields to temporarily abandon their work and join them. Many did, ditching hoes used to till cotton and stepping out of humble shacks with slanted roofs to join the march, even for just a short time.[36]

King and Carmichael deepened their friendship during the Meredith march. King still abhorred confrontation, but he gently chided Carmichael in private for rhetoric that could be misinterpreted by the press and thus hurt the wider movement. King's ability to forge personal connections with everyone he encountered—young or old, black or white, educated or illiterate—impressed SNCC activists such as Cleveland Sellers, who found him "easygoing, with a delightful sense of humor."[37]

On June 21, King led a detour to the small town of Philadelphia, Mississippi, for the second anniversary memorial of James Chaney, Andrew Goodman, and Mickey Schwerner, whose 1964 deaths at the hands of a combination of racist law enforcement officials and local white terrorists less than two weeks before the passage of the Civil Rights Act made them enduring martyrs. Throughout the detour, marchers confronted as many as three hundred white locals, including Deputy Cecil Price, the folk hero, Klansman, and law enforcement officer facing federal charges in the disappearance of Chaney, Goodman, and Schwerner. King led the group down the red clay streets toward the Neshoba County courthouse, the site of a public memorial. "Oh yes," said King, recognizing Price standing in front of the courthouse, surrounded by deputies. "You're the one who had Schwerner and the other fellows in jail?" Price immediately replied, "Yes sir." King knelt on the street and prayed for the souls of the three civil rights workers.[38]

White locals jeered King, hurling insults and driving perilously close to demonstrators, as law enforcement stood by and watched. Several skirmishes broke out between white thugs and protesters who defended themselves. Bands of white youth burst through parts of the march, pushing and shoving demonstrators, knocking down reporters, and breaking television cameras. Deputy Price refused to allow protesters access to the courthouse lawn, so King, joined this day by Ralph Abernathy, conducted a prayer service surrounded by hundreds of angry whites and ten sheriff's deputies. King acknowledged the tension in the air. Amid boos and jeers, he noted Philadelphia as the site of the brutal murders two years earlier. "I believe in my heart that the murderers are somewhere around me at this moment," King remarked, to murmurs of white approval. "I want you to know that we are not afraid," he said. "If they kill three of us, they will have to kill all of us." King's face poured with sweat as he received cheers from black marchers and heckling from an outer ring of whites. "I am not afraid of any man," he said, whether they lived in Birmingham or Boston, Mississippi or Michigan. "Hey Luther!" someone yelled from the outer ring. "Come up here alone and prove it!" On Deputy Price's orders, whites tossed small fireworks near King, who continued amid thunderclaps that sounded like gunshots. Chaos interrupted his closing prayer. Rocks, bottles, and eggs were launched at demonstrators. The now-shaken King watched in horror as disorder broke out.[39]

The Philadelphia terror, raw and insistent, affected King deeply. "This is a terrible town, the worst I've seen," he relayed to reporters while leading demonstrators away from downtown back to the city's black community. "There is a complete reign of terror here." The horror continued hours after he departed, as Philadelphia's black community defended itself from four separate shooting attacks from organized bands of white terrorists. The next day's *New York Times* front page featured King, in dark sunglasses, speaking with Deputy Price as Ralph Abernathy looked on. King sent a telegram to the White House asking for federal protection in Philadelphia that same day, explaining that civil rights leaders planned a second march. After Lyndon Johnson responded with a telegram expressing "sympathy" without action, organizers filed a lawsuit in district court for an order of protection.[40]

On Thursday, June 23, in Canton, Mississippi, King found himself in the middle of more racial violence. Three thousand demonstrators marched to the town, where they had a dispute with local authorities over putting up a tent at a black school. King and the protesters stood defiant. "If necessary," remarked King, "we're willing to fill up all the jails in Mississippi." Mississippi highway patrol fired tear gas and wielded nightsticks against individuals attempting to set up tents. "This is the very state patrol that President Johnson said today would protect us," King shouted to a stunned crowd seeking refuge from the outbreak of police violence. "Anyone who will use gas bombs on women and children can't and won't protect anybody," he said, sounding more like Carmichael, who had been temporarily felled by gas. Later, Carmichael tried to help in organizing a retreat. "Don't make your stand here," he said at one point as he wandered through the chaos. "I just can't stand to see any more people get shot."[41]

Unbeknownst to reporters, the White House had messaged King roughly three hours before the violence erupted, inviting him, Carmichael, and other major civil rights leaders to a secret parley with the president. King declined, aligning himself with the local movement rather than the diplomatic mission of the White House. As far as King was concerned, he and Johnson were long past the time for negotiations. King returned to Philadelphia the next day, this time accompanied by Carmichael. Television-network camera crews traveled with bodyguards. White spectators threw eggs, bottles, and debris at the demonstrators. King, once more, headed to the courthouse. "We are here once again to pay tribute to Andrew Goodman, Michael Schwerner, and James Chaney," he proclaimed. Whites, some of whom had traveled from over forty miles away to gain a glimpse of King, yelled out "Sooie! Sooie!" in a mock rendition of a hog call meant as a derisive slur.[42]

King and Carmichael delivered competing speeches during the June 26 closing rally in Jackson, Mississippi, an event that captured long-running tensions between the SCLC and SNCC and reflected the movement's transition from a focus on political reform to a demand for more far-reaching institutional and structural change. Competing chants from SNCC organizers shouting "Black Power!" and SCLC activists yelling "Freedom Now!" marked the final day's walk from Tougaloo College to the capitol building. King's staff distributed American flags, while Carmichael's surrogates passed out stickers featuring a snarling black panther. King preached a commitment to nonviolence to an audience that was beginning to lose faith in the combined powers of moral persuasion and massive protest. In a move that might have made Malcolm X smile, King confessed that his dream of multiracial democracy "had turned into a nightmare" for African Americans.

Local people in Mississippi were "no longer afraid," King observed. He marveled over the fact that "thousands and thousands of Negroes have straightened their backs up. They realize that a man can't ride your back unless it is bent." He decried witnessing blacks suffering from poverty amid "a vast ocean of prosperity" in other parts of the nation. Nonetheless, King continued to believe "that even here in Mississippi justice will come to all of God's children." He envisioned "a new day," one where "rat-infested slums" would be relegated to history's dustbin and "the empty stomachs of Mississippi will be filled." He considered these words directly connected to the movement's future organizing, community building, and policy demands. A month spent shuttling between the White House, Chicago, and Mississippi had inspired in King a simmering indignation that fueled his political speeches and organizing ambitions.[43]

The sporadic outbreaks of violence during the final days of the march worried King, as did Carmichael's penchant for grabbing headlines at the expense of what King considered the larger purpose of securing the passage of a pending civil rights bill designed to strengthen voting-rights enforcement. Once-firm ties to the White House diminished to the point that King now communicated with the president through reporters. "I have heard nothing from President Johnson," King admitted to the press. The White House demurred from any official position on the naked brutality by law enforcement in Canton, which had matched the terror witnessed in Selma just fifteen months before.[44]

Malcolm X became the Black Power movement's avatar and intellectual North Star, a mesmerizing martyr who, depending on one's perspective, supported radical political self-determination, independent black politics, Third World socialism, an Africa-centered cultural renaissance, or some combination of all this and more. Carmichael projected Malcolm's inimitable combination of strength and vulnerability, passion for racial justice, and hunger to internationalize the black freedom struggle. He also embraced Malcolm's critique of racial oppression's structural nature. While Malcolm's autobiography had made the political uniquely personal, Carmichael's book *Black Power* introduced the term "institutional racism" almost as an act of defiance against those who remained convinced that defeating racism simply required changing hearts and minds. Carmichael's envelope-pushing rhetoric knitted multiple parts of the movement into a powerfully cohesive argument for political revolution. He advocated Malcolm's self-defense posture, regaled audiences with popular seminars on the importance of black history and the richness and beauty of African culture, and proved a vociferous enough critic of the Vietnam War to merit simultaneous investigations from the FBI, State Department, White House, and Mississippi State Sovereignty Commission (the Magnolia State's version of the secret police).

Black Power's arrival on the national scene coincided with King's campaign to end housing segregation and urban poverty in Chicago, a city ruled by the combined might of legendary mayor Richard Daley and a ruthless local Democratic Party machine. King responded to the Black Power controversy by adopting what he considered to be the movement's virtues while projecting nonviolence as the best strategy for the political struggles ahead. On July 10, King spoke at Soldier Field to a crowd of more than thirty thousand about the Chicago freedom movement and the larger black liberation struggle. He fused aspects of black nationalism and political self-determination with an unyielding commitment to peacefully disruptive protest. "We must be proud of our race," King insisted. "We must not be ashamed of being black. We must believe with all our hearts that black is as beautiful as any other color." King's words could be traced back to Malcolm X's emphasis on recognizing civil rights as a referendum on black dignity. But King, like Malcolm after the hajj, resisted the general denunciations of white racism that gripped portions of the black movement, reminding those in attendance of the practical need for interracial coalitions and the sacred bond forged with white activists who risked their lives for black citizenship. King lauded "white Americans who cherish democratic principles above privilege," even as they became less visible in the public imagination the more that black demands for justice increased.[45]

Black Power hovered over the Chicago freedom movement, where late-night sessions with gang leaders produced temporary breakthroughs that faltered against the intransigence of a big-city political machine that King distrusted. Black Power became an obsession among King's closest allies, most notably advisor Stanley Levison, whose ghostwritten statement criticizing the movement appeared in the *New York Times* under King's name. The statement distanced King from the Black Power movement's historical origins in the political and religious organizing of Marcus Garvey, Elijah Muhammad, and Malcolm X, arguing that the call for political self-determination paradoxically revealed the weakness, rather than strength, of a black community in crisis, a government in hiding, and a white majority experiencing its latest bout of racial fatigue. The statement betrayed a fundamental misreading of the most radical aspects of the black freedom struggle, especially the forces bound to Malcolm X's legacy—an interpretation that King would subsequently correct in *Where Do We Go from Here: Chaos or Community?*, his final book and most eloquently nuanced statement on Black Power.[46]

King's movement for economic and racial justice wilted amid the combined heat of political and environmental elements that summer. Bursts of spontaneous civil disorder on Chicago's predominantly black West Side produced fresh charges against King as a pied piper of violence disguised as a peace activist. The specter of white locals hurling bricks, rocks, and bottles at peaceful demonstrators in a northern city gave proof of Malcolm X's characterization of racism as a national illness not quarantined in the South. The white mobs angrily confronting open-housing activists in Chicago neighborhoods and surrounding suburbs revealed new dimensions of Jim Crow, ones that supported black radicals' demands for political power to finally break white supremacy's grip on black life.[47]

On Wednesday, August 17, King and Mayor Daley met with dozens of real-estate, political, and civic leaders for an intense round of negotiations. The conversation settled on the need for more discussion, after both sides expressed open skepticism of the other's willingness to honor verbal pledges to open Chicago's housing for all blacks in exchange for ending citywide demonstrations. "Our humble marches have revealed a cancer," explained King, likening resistance against the movement to a patient accusing a doctor of causing, rather than discovering, a malignant tumor. "We haven't even practiced civil disobedience as a movement," he said, offering a candid prelude to the bold tactics he would shortly endorse in his efforts to end racism and poverty.[48]

Stokely Carmichael's emergence as a national political leader both energized and exasperated King. Carmichael's genuine intellectual curiosity lent gravitas to his increasing national profile, including an August 21 *Meet the Press* appearance alongside King and other civil rights leaders. Before a national audience, dressed in a suit and tie, Carmichael broke new political and rhetorical ground by placing Black Power at the center of a swelling anti-war movement. Carmichael's quicksilver delivery reflected his itinerant young adulthood in Trinidad, the Bronx, and parts of the Deep South. He combined the thoughtfulness of an academic with the rapid-fire delivery of a native New Yorker, massaged through a slight Caribbean lilt topped off by a southern drawl. Carmichael trekked where King couldn't before an audience unaware of Malcolm X's anti-Vietnam denunciations. Declaring the Vietnam War to be immoral proved to be the tip of the iceberg, as Carmichael explained to his interlocutors that he planned to "urge every black man in this country not to fight in Vietnam."[49]

On the same program, appearing from a studio in Chicago, King praised nationwide protests as part of the solution to, rather than the instigator for, racial violence. At Chicago's Palmer House six days later, King and leaders of Chicago's civil rights movement accepted a written open-housing settlement with city leaders and Mayor Daley. The largely symbolic agreement promised incremental progress toward residential integration but lacked enough enforcement powers to be considered anything more than a face-saving measure for both sides.[50]

Black Power hovered over the midterm elections of 1966. Racial fatigue over civil rights, desegregation, and urban riots formed a toxic brew that found Republicans winning significant congressional gains that foreshadowed the coming presidential election. The Voting Rights Act allowed federal registrars to spot-check counties that refused to comply with the legislation's elimination of poll taxes and other processes that restricted black access. Yet voter suppression and intimidation continued to thrive in parts of the South, especially in rural areas where local officials defied civil rights laws through threats of physical violence and economic reprisal. The Meredith march in Mississippi succeeded in registering thousands of new black voters, but many more remained unable to vote or unwilling to even try. Those who made it to the polls in 1966 found a climate that differed starkly from the feel-good election two years earlier, which had taken place in the shadow of the Kennedy assassination. Political realignment between the major parties openly hinged on the willingness to offer safe harbor to racists. Moderate Republicans, like Massachusetts senatorial candidate Edward Brooke, struck gold with lines touting, "A vote for me is a vote against Stokely Carmichael." Actor turned dashing conservative spokesman Ronald Reagan swamped incumbent Edmund Brown in California's gubernatorial race with a bracingly pugnacious campaign opposing civil rights, black radicalism, and Carmichael's frequent presence in the state. Lyndon Johnson privately blamed the Democratic Party's loss of three senators and forty-seven congressmen on a seemingly ungrateful core constituency. "I think the Negroes lost it," he told aides.[51]

Martin Luther King Jr.'s radicalization took public shape against the backdrop of the political triumph of the Voting Rights Act and the violence that engulfed Los Angeles less than a week later. The radical King linked the effectiveness of voting rights to the entrenched poverty and racial segregation that marked too many urban cities. Watts amplified King's efforts to turn the civil rights struggle into a human rights movement that expansively defined black citizenship and, in the process, reimagined American democracy. King's working alliance with the Johnson administration and white liberals frayed as the Vietnam War took increasing resources, energy, and commitment away from the movement for racial justice. As Black Power tapped into the unspoken anger, pain, and pride of black people across the nation, King deeply empathized with the movement's insistence on radical black citizenship, even as he disagreed with its supporters on goals, tactics, and strategies.

King's radicalization in the eighteen months after Malcolm X's assassination found him on the precipice of losing his faith in the vision of a black freedom struggle tied to civic democracy that had sustained him over the previous decade. He found a renewed purpose and amplified sense of mission by connecting the broad sweep of the struggle for black dignity with the individual humanity of the dispossessed from all racial and ethnic backgrounds, whose lives, he argued, not only mattered but deserved a place of honor in the nation. King searched, with increasing fervor, to illustrate the universality of race, democracy, and citizenship through the particular lens of a black freedom movement that he remained convinced held the key not only to racial justice, but to an end to war, poverty, and violence in America and beyond.

CHAPTER 10

The Revolutionary King

On April 4, 1967, a crowd of almost four thousand gathered to hear Martin Luther King Jr. speak from the pulpit of New York City's Riverside Church. King denounced the Vietnam War in unequivocal terms. "I come to this platform to make a passionate plea to my beloved nation," he explained early in the speech. King's criticism of military escalation in Vietnam and the declining effectiveness of the war on poverty had severed his political alliance with President Lyndon Johnson. The Great Society's political shortcomings were now an unfolding moral disaster—"the cruel irony of watching Negro and white boys on TV screens as they kill and die together for a nation that has been unable to seat them together in the same schools." Racial apartheid's grip on American democracy, argued King, corrupted the nation in war and peace, hurling large numbers of poor black and white soldiers toward a death march in international slaughter fields. King challenged America's moral and political authority to wage war in Vietnam by comparing the military's use of force overseas to the black youth throwing Molotov cocktails to wage rebellion in urban ghettos. Both used violence in service of larger ambitions that, King suggested, represented political and moral dead ends.[1]

Riverside marked King's transition from a civil rights leader into a political revolutionary, one who refused to remain quiet in the face of domestic and international crises. The speech represented the boldest political decision of his career. Despite King's proclaimed belief in the roots of American democracy, he publicly assailed the hypocrisy behind the country's posture as liberty's surest guardian around the world. In the months before his death, Malcolm X, too, had discussed the Vietnam War, marveling at how courageous peasants, "with nothing but sneakers on and a rifle," were defying the world's greatest military power. But even as King decried America as pursuing a catastrophic trajectory rooted in greed, violence, and racism, he found optimism in the potential for democratic transformation. At Riverside, King assumed Malcolm's previous role as black America's prosecuting attorney, publicly denouncing the war in Vietnam by offering a political seminar on American imperialism, racism, and economic injustice that announced his formal break with mainstream politics.[2]

In a preemptive strike against critics who would accuse him of confusing his civil rights leadership with foreign policy expertise, King cited Langston Hughes, "the black bard of Harlem," explaining that "America never was America to me." "If America's soul becomes totally poisoned," reasoned King, "part of the autopsy must read Vietnam." King was squarely confronting American political hubris by characterizing the Vietnam War as the nation's Achilles' heel. He considered foreign-policy analysis to be a substantive part of his role as a civil rights leader. Domestic and international struggles for justice and equality were never mutually exclusive but, on the contrary, intimately connected in a manner that demanded forthright criticism. For King, America remained, at its best, a country filled with unrealized potential—as Hughes's poetry brilliantly evoked—but whose promise receded the further the nation strayed from its core values of liberty, freedom, and democracy. King characterized American soldiers in Vietnam as "the victims of our nation" and "strange liberators" who ravaged peaceful villages, killed innocents, and impoverished peasants. His anti-war criticism echoed and amplified Malcolm X's denunciations before his death, when he characterized Vietnam as "the struggle of the whole Third World" against Western imperialism.[3]

Like Malcolm X, King publicly wrestled with the grandeur and travails of American democracy. King confronted Johnson's intransigence on the war with a biting quote from his predecessor, the late John F. Kennedy: "Those who make peaceful revolution impossible will make violent revolution inevitable." Kennedy had spoken these words almost five years earlier, during the wave of demonstrations, arrests, and violent reprisals that forced a sitting US president to confront the nation's racial demons for the first time in a century. The stakes, now global in scope, had only escalated since Kennedy's time, introducing a precarious new era where the world seemed perpetually poised on a knife's edge of destruction.

King's all-encompassing solution relied on what he called a "revolution of values" led by Americans uneasy about growing economic inequality, ashamed of a bloody history of racial oppression, and embarrassed by a rush to war that tarnished a hard-earned postwar reputation as the guardian of the free world. "War is not the answer," King pleaded, although the entire world appeared on the brink of "revolutionary times." King contextualized Marxism's global appeal in America's failure to embrace its democratic potential.

In his new role as radical civil rights leader, King wielded both the rhetorical shield of his past and a political sword forged through the crucible of Watts, Black Power, urban rebellion, and Vietnam. Confronting "the fierce urgency of now" required new levels of moral and political courage, not only to defy the "cruel manipulation of the poor," but to illuminate how racial segregation, urban poverty, and burning embers in Detroit and Hanoi were inextricably linked. King displayed a rueful awareness of institutional racism's contemporary power by naming "my own government" as "the greatest purveyor of violence in the world today." Like Malcolm X, Stokely Carmichael, and Black Power activists, King now defined violence expansively, finding a common denominator in the manner in which poverty, segregation, racism, and domestic and international violence converged in a discordant, jangling symphony of oppression.[4]

And yet, the "beautiful struggle" King outlined set him on a lonely political journey. After Riverside, one poll found that 73 percent of Americans disapproved of his Vietnam stance. Sixty percent judged his peace efforts as hurting the movement. Members of the House Armed Services Committee counted themselves among King's most powerful detractors. Congressmen L. Mendel Rivers of South Carolina and F. Edward Hébert of Louisiana led the charge in an effort to convince the Justice Department to punish King, for supporting conscientious objectors against the draft, and Carmichael, for turning "Hell no, we won't go!" into a national anti-war chant. Higher-education leaders followed suit, with the dean of the Notre Dame Law School attacking King and Carmichael as "either Communists or traitors" who had betrayed the nation by opposing the war in Vietnam.[5]

King's call for peace included publicly advocating a universal cease-fire, a cessation of bombing, recognition of the National Liberation Front by the American government, and the removal of all foreign troops in Vietnam. Not even King's statesmanship could hide the fact that his speech at Riverside had brushed aside his long-standing strategic embrace of political reform. He now openly supported a human rights revolution that would turn America into a beacon of social justice and racial equality on a scale unimagined by the architects of the Great Society. But if Malcolm X had remained, until his death, eternally skeptical of American democracy's capacity to guarantee racial and economic justice, King maintained defiant faith in the capacity of massive civil disobedience to bend the will of presidents and political leaders. This faith inspired King to create new coalitions with the peace movement, New Left radicals, and Black Power activists, all of whom found common ground in rejecting the Vietnam War as an example of American hubris, racism, and injustice. While critics labeled him politically reckless, King plotted a radical course, buoyed by his unyielding belief in the power of ordinary citizens to effect lasting social change.[6]

Large segments of America interpreted King's cry for peace as an act of war. Standing ovations received inside the friendly confines of Riverside were overwhelmed by the contempt of journalists, pundits, and politicians who viciously questioned his political judgment. The Johnson administration opted to ignore King, afraid that his anti-war remarks might spread across the spectrum of civil rights leadership. Ralph Bunche, the first African American winner of the Nobel Peace Prize, who had verbally sparred with Malcolm X, now denounced King. FBI director J. Edgar Hoover, who almost a year earlier had forwarded the White House a report on potential racial unrest that cited forty-five cities on the verge of rebellion, now furnished Lyndon Johnson with the text of King's Riverside speech, which threatened to damage the president far more than any race riots could. The FBI also furnished copies of its updated negative Martin Luther King Jr. dossier to the attorney general, Secret Service, secretary of state, and secretary of defense. The document argued that King's latest speech revealed him to be a tool of American communists.[7]

King's speech made front-page headlines, competing with the White House's announcement of plans to send doctors to Vietnam to investigate allegations of napalm being used indiscriminately against civilians by the American military, an effort to cauterize the festering national wound of Vietnam. After Riverside, King became America's most well-known anti-war activist, lending a Nobel Prize–winner's moral currency to a peace movement struggling to find its voice in a political landscape where most Americans still supported the war. Riverside transformed King, who became emboldened by the diverse throngs of supporters—religious leaders, young people, and the elderly, black and white, who gave him a standing ovation at the end of his hour-long speech—while facing soured political alliances and condemning press coverage. Media outlets that once lavished praise on King after his Nobel and civil rights victories in Birmingham and Selma now harshly criticized his strategic judgment and political temperament. Urban League leader Whitney Young publicly advocated keeping issues of war and racial justice separate, perfectly aligning with the White House's efforts to inoculate the larger civil rights struggle against King's anti-war talk. Edward Brooke, the first black man elected to the US Senate in a general election, characterized King's Vietnam position as "very costly," because it sullied not only his reputation but the entire movement. Barry Goldwater accused King of inflicting "irreparable harm" on the civil rights movement. The group Jewish War Veterans characterized King's Riverside address as an "insult to the intelligence of all Americans," while his friend and longtime supporter Jackie Robinson offered the most diplomatic criticism: "Dr. King has always been my favorite civil rights leader, but I don't agree with him on this issue."[8]

The *New York Times* termed the speech "Dr. King's Error," citing it as a tragic misstep for civil rights and peace advocates that might prove "disastrous for both causes." The paper criticized King's entrée into anti-war activism as a distraction that sapped vital energies from racial hotspots in Chicago, Watts, and Harlem. Suggesting that the "moral issues" of war were far from "clear-cut," the paper attacked King for linking Vietnam and racial justice and blasted him for sowing "deeper confusion" in a country beset by growing polarization.[9]

Positive response came from old colleagues and friendly combatants. Stokely Carmichael embraced King's Vietnam address, which telescoped much of Black Power's critique of American democracy into a powerful call for peace. Critics now characterized King and Carmichael as two sides of the same political coin. King amplified his connection with Carmichael eleven days after Riverside, when they headlined the nation's largest anti-war demonstration, in New York. On Saturday, April 15, King delivered the keynote address at the Spring Mobilization to End the War in Vietnam. The Spring Mobe, as activists dubbed the event, showcased the power of growing anti-war demonstrations, attracting a mélange of radical activists—sometimes called the New Left—whose particular interests in women's liberation, environmental justice, labor activism, and civil rights were now galvanized around building a peace movement. Four hundred thousand demonstrators marched from Central Park's Sheep Meadow to the United Nations, where King personally met with UN undersecretary Ralph Bunche. King marched at the head of the demonstration, arm in arm with Stokely Carmichael, Harry Belafonte, James Bevel, and Dr. Benjamin Spock. The Spring Mobe featured a series of firsts among demonstrators, including a group of Cornell University students who burned their draft cards in a coffee can during an impromptu ceremony.[10]

Stokely Carmichael dazzled the attendees with a speech that drew stark moral and political lines between supporters and opponents of the Vietnam War. He relished trumpeting the domestic and international contours of a "struggle against white supremacy" that had led to this moment. As he spoke, supporters chanting "Black Power!" could be heard in the distance. Carmichael praised King's anti-war position, noting that his Nobel Prize conferred a global acknowledgment of "the connection between ending war and ending racism" that still mystified American critics. "We will not support LBJ's racist war in Vietnam," said Carmichael. His speech mingled issues of race, power, and imperialism before the biggest audience he had ever addressed. King followed Carmichael with an oratory simmering with political indignation. That the two could share the same stage was all the more remarkable in light of the political tensions that grew after the Meredith march. Vietnam touched evils that transcended differences over strategy and tactics, yet King remained cautious. His call for the nation to "Stop the bombing! Stop the bombing!" was tame in comparison to Carmichael's explicitly anti-imperialist rhetoric.[11]

King continued to walk a rhetorical tightrope the next morning during an interview on CBS's *Face the Nation*. He disavowed portions of the Spring Mobe that desecrated the American flag, burned draft cards, and waved Viet Cong banners. He instead urged the peace movement to organize a "massive education" campaign and for all young men to explore the legal channel of conscientious objection. Civil rights and peace represented a "double action program" required by the force of history, observed King. He defended his appearance with Carmichael as part of a wider crusade against injustice. After citing their long history of working together in the Deep South, King went on the offensive, characterizing Black Power as a "reaction to the failure of white power." He did not mention during the interview his private deliberations with advisors about appearing on stage with Carmichael, whom he knew "scared the hell out of white folks." His decision to participate rested on his feeling that the anti-war movement required the widest possible coalition. Near the end of his appearance, King rediscovered his voice in a moment of shattering eloquence. The Great Society, he argued, represented the nation's most important war casualty, "shot down on the battle fields of Vietnam." He repudiated the fantasy that America had enough guns and butter to satisfy domestic needs and foreign ambitions. "The heart of the nation is in Vietnam," he ruefully observed. "And where your heart is, there your money will go."[12]

King telephoned Carmichael just near midnight on Saturday, April 29, with a surprise invitation to hear him preach. The invitation pleased the younger activist, who, rather than accept or decline the overture, investigated further. "Something special happening?" he asked. King replied affirmatively, telling Carmichael that "tomorrow . . . I'll be making my statement on the war." After a thirty-second pause, Carmichael announced that he would be sitting "in the front row" of Ebenezer.[13]

On Sunday, April 30, King delivered his definitive anti-war speech. He ridiculed the nation's selective acceptance of nonviolence: although he was widely praised for preaching the tactic in the face of racial terror in the South, Americans were overwhelmingly willing to "curse you when you say be nonviolent toward little brown Vietnamese children." King praised Muhammad Ali's controversial draft refusal as an act of moral witness. He spoke eloquently of Ali's sacrifice "in order to stand up for what his conscience tells him is right," as if commenting on his own path. At the conclusion of King's sermon, Carmichael jumped up from the front-row pew to lead a standing ovation, the third round of applause during the sermon, which recognized the transformation of King from a preacher and movement leader into a revolutionary. Carmichael could be exasperating, moving King to private complaints to advisors that the young Black Power leader was in over his head, and King's patrician bearing amplified an almost thirteen-year age gap. But Martin loved Stokely and treated him like a younger brother. They bonded over their shared reputation as charismatic orators, mischievous sense of humor, and unapologetic love for black people. Now, King and Carmichael shared a message against the war abroad for the sake of justice at home.[14]

King's sermon at Ebenezer drew him closer still to the orbit of Black Power activists. In Atlanta, even more than at Riverside, King dramatically proclaimed that the "madness" of war, violence, and racism must end. His anti-war stance elicited support and admiration from Carmichael but distanced him from Bayard Rustin, one of his closest former advisors. Rustin had read King's break from Lyndon Johnson as a strategic mistake. Aides to King, including Stanley Levison, urged him to be "on your guard" after Rustin publicly called upon him "to re-examine his position" on Vietnam and the civil rights struggle. King watched with dismay as Rustin, the pacifist who had snuck into Montgomery with wise counsel on the depth of nonviolence, now preferred to work within the system, through both the Democratic Party and big labor, which now funded him. Rustin, after years on the margins, had found a sinecure through the creation of the A. Philip Randolph Institute in 1965, a project backed by the AFL-CIO, blessed by his mentor Randolph, and constrained by dint of its mainstream financial backers from offering robust support to the anti-war movement.[15]

Lyndon Johnson, without ever mentioning King's name, responded to Riverside from the White House at a May 8 anti-poverty reception for 450 female volunteers. "No, we are not backing off from our commitment to fight poverty," Johnson asserted, "nor will we so long as I have anything to say about it." Unnamed critics who chided the government for spending too much or too little, or for abandoning the poor "because of our commitment to the other war," were mistaken, Johnson argued. "We may never live to see an America without poverty," he admitted, "but we may see an America where a lifetime of poverty is not the inevitable fate of a child born into it." Johnson's passionate defense of his poverty program signaled that King, having courted open conflict with the president of the United States, continued to wield enough power to place the leader of the free world on the defensive. Private reelection polling judged that King might impact "between a third to one half of all Negro voters" through his simple endorsement, meaning that Johnson's White House resisted public confrontation in favor of discrediting the Nobel Prize winner via surrogates.[16]

From Atlanta, before five hundred people at a joint meeting of a local civil rights group and a black fraternity, King admitted to being "terribly afraid we are moving toward World War III." He questioned the point of racial integration efforts absent concern for "the survival of the world" that blacks were attempting to transform. He also denounced critics who claimed his anti-war stance mortally wounded the civil rights movement. "It is more alive today than ever before," he said defiantly. Calling the epic battle to end legal Jim Crow a "struggle for decency," he identified his focus on ending war, poverty, and racism as a new chapter in "a struggle for genuine equality."[17]

King set out on a nationwide tour, displacing Carmichael as America's most well-known anti-war activist. Counterdemonstrators in Louisville, Kentucky, threw rocks at him during a speech campaigning for open housing. "Upon this rock," King declared, waving one of the stones, "we're going to build an open city and the gates of injustice will not prevail against it." He promised to "stir up trouble" in cities plagued by rioting in hopes of proving that nonviolence remained the nation's "most potent" weapon of peace. King's linking of religious faith and political responsibility fueled a mission that improbably drew him closer to Black Power activists. King's public appearances now featured the kind of pugnacious repudiation of white supremacy that marked Malcolm X's persona, a fierce truth telling that made him an even bigger draw on college campuses.[18]

The radical King stood tall during a speech at the University of California at Berkeley, where he told a crowd of seven thousand students—many holding "King-Spock" signs urging him to challenge Lyndon Johnson in 1968—that the next phase of the civil rights movement would require "a radical redistribution of economic and political power," a phrase met with echoing applause. He pushed back against white liberals who opposed racial segregation in Birmingham and Selma but repudiated "genuine equality" for black Americans. King called white backlash "a new name for an old phenomenon" and indicted the nation for a policy of white supremacy that polluted its democratic aspirations and clouded hopes for black citizenship. Again, throughout the speech, King assumed the form of black America's martyred prosecuting attorney, Malcolm X, by meticulously delineating historic and present-day efforts. "The fact is," King stated bluntly, "that America has been backlashing on the question of fundamental human rights for its black citizens for more than 300 years."[19]

He linked racism and poverty to domestic riots based on unjust public policies and a war based on political immorality. He noted that, in the aftermath of the four girls martyred at the Sixteenth Street Baptist Church in Birmingham four years earlier, there were no chants of Black Power—and yet the perpetrators of this vicious crime had yet to be found. King insisted, "Black and white together we shall overcome," even as he boldly repudiated white America for its failure to fully commit to racial justice. In an effort to illustrate the shared struggles of many Americans, King talked about the wide racial spectrum of poverty in America, where blacks, whites, Mexican Americans, and Native Americans suffered in abject misery in the bosom of the world's richest nation. The Johnson administration, King argued, seemed more concerned about "winning an unwinnable war in Vietnam than about winning the war against poverty right here at home." The "gigantic miscalculation" of the war had only yielded a barren domestic crop of violence, dissidence, and recriminations. King blamed the war on the arrogance of American exceptionalism, the idea that the United States represented the world's singular moral, political, and economic power, a country content to perpetuate "white colonialism" rather than allow global peoples the right to self-governance. "It's time to come home from Vietnam," King implored to thunderous applause. He publicly endeavored to mobilize a "peace bloc" capable of challenging Johnson in the next presidential election, yet had no intention of personally heading such a third-party ticket.[20]

That summer, King published his latest book, *Where Do We Go from Here: Chaos or Community?*, to mixed reviews. In the book, he studiously avoided demonizing Black Power, praising the movement's focus on black history, culture, and racial pride. Black Power, according to King, grew out of a despair and hopelessness that made it rely on threats of violence that sapped its potential moral and political strength. Racial separatism ignored black people's need for coalitions strong enough to challenge forms of oppression that transcended race. King analyzed slave rebellions and urban

278

riots as dual examples of the futility of violence in service of revolution. "Fewer people have been killed in ten years of nonviolent demonstrations across the South than were killed in one night of rioting in Watts," wrote King. His book made no mention of Malcolm X, preferring instead to briefly analyze Frantz Fanon, the Martinican psychiatrist and Algerian War supporter whose book, *The Wretched of the Earth*, had become required reading among Black Power activists. King challenged black radicals to create the new society Fanon advocated without resorting to violence and brutality.[21]

Meanwhile, King's detractors refused to let up. In an article written in the FBI's law enforcement bulletin, J. Edgar Hoover added to the chorus of criticism against King. "To publicly pinpoint where riots and violence may occur," he said, "seems to be inconsistent with the doctrine of nonviolence." If Birmingham, the March on Washington, and the Nobel Prize had elevated King to the status of royalty, his stances on Vietnam, race, and poverty were hurtling him toward a political reckoning that found him sharing common ground with Malcolm X, Stokely Carmichael, and the Black Panthers. The Panthers imagined themselves the political heirs of Malcolm X. The Oakland, California–based group found inspiration in Malcolm's message of self-defense and anti-colonialism, took their name from SNCC's efforts to organize independent politics in Lowndes County, Alabama, and fashioned a revolutionary persona based on a ten-point program calling for a political revolution that necessitated grassroots organizing and guns. With reckless bravado, the group legally surveilled the police arresting black motorists while armed and made national headlines by descending upon the California state capitol on May 2, 1967, to protest an impending gun control bill designed to prevent them from brandishing weapons while observing the police. On the ABC program *Issues and Answers* on the third Sunday in June, King spoke passionately about the black freedom struggle entering a new phase, one that required "the government spending billions of dollars" to eradicate poverty, ghettos, and segregation. While voting rights and public accommodations "didn't cost the nation anything," black America now required a shared measure of sacrifice.[22]

Newly emboldened, King challenged Lyndon Johnson to embrace black political self-determination in terms that Malcolm X once framed, noting that African Americans were "in the stage of self-assertive manhood and there is no way for any President, no matter who he is, to avoid this problem." The next day, King amplified these radical sentiments, arguing to a national *Today* show audience why it was "necessary to disobey unjust laws because noncooperation with evil is as much a moral obligation as cooperation with good." While the press talked of "long hot summers" of racial violence, King spoke of the "long cold winter" of discontent, when Congress and the president had ignored "the conditions that create riots."[23]

Riot politics gripped the nation that summer. Black ghettos in Newark and Detroit exploded almost in unison during the second and third weeks in July. What black radicals called urban rebellions and conservatives decried as riots were most often triggered by escalating tensions between police and black residents. The conflicts were deeply rooted in poverty, unemployment, racial segregation, and neglect. After allegations of police brutality against a black taxi driver, Newark erupted just as local and national activists announced plans for a Black Power conference, which would eventually take place in the wake of citywide violence that required the National Guard to quell. LeRoi Jones, the poet and Black Arts movement activist who deeply admired Malcolm X, received a brutal beating and arrest at the hands of police during the riot, which further radicalized him. Jones (who would change his name to Amiri Baraka shortly after) became Newark's leading Black Power activist, organizing the Committee for Unified Newark (CFUN) that would help to elect the city's first black mayor just three years later. Baraka saw himself as embodying Malcolm X's radical call for political self-determination through community organizing that stressed racial unity, black dignity, and the relationship between Africa and black America. From the smoldering ashes of urban violence and racial segregation, Newark would become a case study in the local pursuit of Black Power.[24]

Detroit's violence, which dwarfed Newark's, began after a police raid on an illegal after-hours club (what authorities called a "blind pig") on Twelfth Street. The arrest of seventy people only fueled neighborhood outrage, which grew violent enough for Lyndon Johnson to receive a 3 a.m. phone call from Attorney General Ramsey Clark on July 24. Michigan governor George Romney soon called the White House with news of widespread looting, pitched battles between bottle- and rock-throwing residents and the police, and over eighty unattended fires raging across the city. The president huddled with advisors, including the young assistant attorney general Roger Wilkins, nephew of Roy, whom he dispatched from Washington to get a ground-level view of events. Two days later, with the governor unable to quell the disturbance, President Johnson federalized the Michigan National Guard and sent in troops. Detroit's chaos left over three hundred people injured and forty-three dead. At least 1,200 people were detained in felony courts, the innocent along with the guilty. President Johnson, the most vocal supporter of racial justice in the federal government, argued during a nationally televised address that Detroit's violence "had nothing to do with civil rights," while promising to restore order and punish lawbreakers. Racial violence in Newark and Detroit seemed to fulfill Malcolm X's predictions of race war and his skepticism about the ability of civil rights laws to guarantee black dignity.[25]

King was in the midst of a book tour for *Where Do We Go from Here?* when the unrest began, and he held a press conference with reporters where he revealed the contents of a telegram he planned to send to the president. He challenged Johnson's interpretation of events in Detroit, noting that nothing short of "drastic changes in the life of the poor" would lead to a much sought-after urban peace. Violence plaguing cities was rooted in structures of oppression and the political failures of a federal government unwilling or unable to grasp the full extent of the nation's racial and economic crisis. "I propose," read King's telegram, "specifically the creation of a national agency that shall provide a job to every person who needs work." Johnson never replied to King, but the president did listen carefully to J. Edgar Hoover's fresh allegations, which falsely claimed King knew of plans to burn down parts of Chicago. Stokely Carmichael, at the beginning of a five-month global tour, discussed the uprisings from Cuba as the start of an organized revolution. "We are preparing groups of urban guerrillas for our defense in the cities," he said—a statement that made King's efforts to direct the national conversation away from fears of racial rebellion more difficult.[26]

In effect, King both led and followed the revolutionary zeitgeist that captured the imagination of late 1960s America and much of the world. Amid shifting political alliances and public sentiment, King now openly cultivated aspects of black pride. "Black Is Beautiful" posters were proudly displayed at the SCLC's August convention in Atlanta, where King decried the negative associations with the word "black" in the English dictionary in a manner reminiscent of Malcolm X, noting, "They even tell us a white lie is better than a black one." In these instances, King and Malcolm found common ground in repudiating all forms of denigration against black humanity. King's call for massive civil disobedience echoed aspects of the type of nonviolent disruption that Malcolm approvingly spoke of during his criticism of the March on Washington. Malcolm had praised the calls by civil rights militants "for a march on the White House and Congress" that would paralyze the nation's capital. Now King, in effect, sought to organize the kind of nonviolent upheaval that Malcolm X had once endorsed.[27]

King was growing depressed over the widespread violence erupting in black neighborhoods during the summer. "People expect me to have answers," he confided in Coretta, "and I don't have any answers." The behavior of major civil rights leaders, such as Roy Wilkins, who seemed more eager to release statements denouncing the riots than condemning their root causes deeply disappointed him. In a conversation with Stanley Levison, King called the NAACP leader a lost cause. "He has no integrity or philosophy and is just a hopeless case," reasoned King. He also despaired over the increasingly apocalyptic rhetoric of a younger generation of black radicals, including new SNCC chairman H. Rap Brown, who had replaced Stokely Carmichael in the spring. With his southern drawl and penchant for headline-grabbing quips—"Violence is as American as cherry pie"—Brown emerged in Carmichael's absence that summer as perhaps the most widely quoted and reviled Black Power activist. Frequently arrested after his speeches, which authorities linked to violence, Brown's abilities as a speaker outran his effectiveness as an organizer. "I think nonviolence has to be stepped up to a larger scale, to be escalated so its impact would be greater than violence," King told an advisor.[28]

In early August 1967, King roamed Cleveland's Hough neighborhood, where he preached nonviolence at the exact site of urban rioting one year earlier. Reporters covering the visit marveled at his charisma and the power of his oratory yet interpreted his inability to attract large crowds in the area as a sign of his diminished appeal in the North. "He displayed all the attributes of a great leader," observed one journalist, "except followers." But King could still extract political concessions, including from Cleveland-based Sealtest food company, which agreed to hire fifty black workers that month after a successful boycott organized by the SCLC's Operation Breadbasket. During an August 13 appearance on NBC's *Meet the Press*, King discussed his plans to confront war, racism, and poverty during a mean season of discontent in American politics and society. "The tragedy is that we are today engaged in two wars and we are losing both," King explained, highlighting the connections between the war on poverty and the Vietnam War that major political leaders stubbornly ignored. "We are losing the war in Vietnam morally and politically," he said.[29]

On Tuesday, August 15, at the SCLC annual convention at Ebenezer Baptist Church in Atlanta, King put his more radical views into action, announcing plans for nonviolent civil disobedience massive enough to paralyze cities in pursuit of major federal action. He defined the urban rebellions raging across the land as proof that "inequality will now be resisted to the death." He called for a "hungry people's" demonstration at the Department of Labor and an organization of unemployed black youth. Major cities would be targeted for school boycotts, factory sit-ins, and a wide range of protests. "Mass civil disobedience can use rage as [a] constructive and creative force," King insisted. Neither President Johnson nor Congress exhibited a willingness "to seek fundamentals beyond police measures." The movement's ultimate goal would be to "drive the nation to a guaranteed annual income," he explained to some five hundred cheering delegates. King offered his most comprehensive and radical definition of black citizenship, one that viewed racial and economic justice as inseparable and castigated war as the enemy of both.[30]

King now planned to mobilize large, multiracial groups of the dispossessed to descend on Washington in order to compel elected officials into passing radical political legislation. The Poor People's Campaign pivoted on King's understanding of the systemic nature of political oppression. He joined Black Power activists, most notably welfare-rights organizers and the Black Panthers, to highlight the widening gulf between political rhetoric and America's worsening reality for the poor. The FBI and the White House noticed too, mounting efforts to damage King by publicly linking him to Carmichael. But King's heart longed for a rapprochement with black radicals, especially on the subject of peace. He did more than align with Black Power activists on Vietnam; he had amplified their structural critique of racial injustice and economic inequality.[31]

King had grown despondent over violence in Detroit. He confessed feelings of hopelessness to aides over FBI wiretaps. "There were dark days before, but this is the darkest," he lamented. Newark and Detroit embodied the limits of the Great Society, the pervasive nature of racial violence, and the systemic oppression that Malcolm X had once raged against and that King now confronted in public speeches and private deliberations. The Poor People's Campaign would leverage the power of the poor through strategic political alliances with whites, Native Americans, Latino farm workers, and black sharecroppers, who King dreamed would descend on Washington and unleash demonstrations in numbers too large to ignore.[32]

Blacks living "in the basement of the Great Society" demanded more than political reform. They required nonviolent political revolution capable of fundamentally transforming America. King now confronted the American political establishment in uncompromising terms that recalled Malcolm X's assault against racial injustice. "The tragic truth is that Congress, more than the American people, is now running wild with racism," King said, using some of the most pointed language of his career. He envisioned protests that were less aimed at hearts and minds than based on power that could be leveraged with organized, disciplined, nonviolent political soldiers. After forming such an army, he said, "we must devise the tactics not to beg Congress for favors, but to create a situation in which they deem it wise and prudent to act with responsibility and decency."[33]

The press interpreted King's speech as a major threat to democratic order. Headlines in the *New York Times* ("Dr. King Planning Protests to 'Dislocate' Large Cities") and the *Washington Post* ("King Calls for Massive Protests") sounded like warnings to a riot-weary public. King made bold plans with the painful awareness that he lacked the organizational and financial resources to implement such an ambitious agenda. He sought to merge Black Power's far-reaching structural critique of inequality and racism with the nonviolent civil disobedience that characterized the peak social and political effectiveness of civil rights struggles. He hoped to compel the president and Congress to approve massive spending at the very moment that a projected deficit of almost $30 billion found Lyndon Johnson supporting an income tax surcharge of 10 percent. King delayed providing specifics of his new organizing thrust until he met with SCLC staff, some of whom listened with a combination of awe at his ambition and dismay at the scant resources available to implement his aggressive objectives.[34]

Not everyone on the Left applauded King's evolution. King's appearance on the last day of August at Chicago's National Conference for New Politics was a case in point. The conference featured almost three thousand representatives from 372 politically progressive groups that came together after two years of planning. Conference delegates held a wide range of opinions about King, from deep admiration that included pleas for him to run for president in 1968 to militant denunciations, especially from youthful black nationalists, that he was an Uncle Tom. Hecklers booed King for lacking the political sophistication to understand that nonviolence could no longer redeem American society. King's relationship with the strain of Black Power advocating revolutionary violence remained star-crossed. While Stokely Carmichael respected King based on shared experiences in the heat of the southern civil rights struggle, a new generation of black militants accorded him no such deference. King recounted his difficulties to Stanley Levison, recorded by an FBI phone wiretap, the next day. "The black nationalists gave me trouble," said King. "They kept interrupting me, kept yelling things at me."[35]

As frustrating as his disputes with sectarian black and white radicals could be, there still remained a segment of them who could identify with King's evolving politics. "The Second Coming of Martin Luther King," published in the August 1967 issue of *Harper's*, portrayed the former *Time* Man of the Year and Nobel Peace Prize recipient as a revolutionary who "sounded like a nonviolent" Malcolm X. Reporter David Halberstam spent ten days with King, shuttling through airports, press conferences, and numerous meetings with black preachers, civil rights activists, and local people from Cleveland, Ohio, to Berkeley, California. King openly seethed at the hypocrisy of white big-city mayors "damning me now and calling me an extremist," who only three years earlier "gave me the key to the city and said I was the greatest man of the century." Three years now measured the distance of lifetimes. "I think you've got to have a reconstruction of the entire society," King told Halberstam, "a revolution of values." For King, this meant radical black citizenship that comprised a living wage, federally guaranteed income, decent and racially integrated housing and public schools, and a wholesale reconsideration of American foreign and domestic policy. It meant leveraging America's financial might on behalf of the poor, ending racism, and obliterating poverty and injustice through guaranteed economic benefits for all, especially those left out of an era of national prosperity. The very man booed in certain quarters as insufficiently radical now candidly admitted that "most Americans are unconscious racists."[36]

King confronted the nation's unconscious racism in bold, at times belligerent, strokes at the American Psychological Association meeting in Washington on Friday, September 1. There, he eloquently articulated the need for radical black citizenship to frequent applause. His speech on "The Role of the Behavioral Scientist in the Civil Rights Movement" plumbed the state of contemporary American race relations in language reminiscent of Malcolm X's scalding critique of white supremacy. "White America needs to understand that it is poisoned to its soul by racism and the understanding needs to be carefully documented and consequently more difficult to reject," proclaimed King. He told an audience of scholars, academics, and researchers that the tragic presence of racial injustice meant that "we find ourselves psychologically and socially imprisoned." He spoke in clarifying new ways about the depth and breadth of white racism. He decried white America for expressing horror at "the Negro himself" instead of the conditions that scarred black life. The more he talked, the more King sounded like Malcolm.[37]

He argued that whites seemed insistent on keeping "the walls of segregation intact" amid urban rebellions that were rooted in efforts, however misguided, to transform the nation. "The White majority unprepared and unwilling to accept radical structural change, is resisting and producing chaos while complaining that if there were no chaos orderly change would come," he said. King characterized the years between the Montgomery bus boycott and the passage of the Voting Rights Act as an era of grand delusions, where the entire nation underestimated the power of black rage and white racism. He called the riots "a distorted form of social protest" meant to awaken the nation into radical action to eradicate racial injustice. He considered urban revolts the direct by-product of white policymakers who "perpetuate unemployment, ignorance, and poverty." Black crime, he argued, reflected the "greater crimes of the White society."[38]

Like Malcolm X, King characterized white racism as a series of crimes against black communities that created ghettos and violated laws designed to aid the poor, educate children, and promote black citizenship. Bold words of truth were necessary, King insisted, "in order to deal with the great problems that we face in our society." Vietnam represented one such problem. "The bombs that fall in Vietnam exploded at home," he observed, linking urban riots to the billions of dollars being diverted in the name of international war. He expressed his determination to continue to expose the relationship between race, war, violence, and democracy, even at the cost of a diminishing reputation in circles that once welcomed and praised him. King proclaimed that he refused to "take a Gallup Poll to determine majority opinion," preferring instead to be guided by moral conviction.[39]

Throughout his address, King discussed familiar themes in radically new and unsettling language. He deployed one of Malcolm's favorite words, "hypocrisy," when discussing the gap between public concerns for black youth and the soaring rate of unemployment in this community, especially among the poor. He challenged the entire nation to support a jobs program on a bigger scale than the New Deal's Works Progress Administration, a program that had employed laborers, young people, writers, and artists from a wide segment of society. He called civil disobedience the "militant middle ground" between riots and apathy. Only "a genuine act of massive concern" could end urban rebellions, said King, once again highlighting his plans to leverage civil disobedience toward a radical domestic restructuring of society—one that had global implications, because America could not fight and win wars against both poverty and Vietnam.[40]

Delivering the moral of his address, King challenged those in attendance to produce relevant academic studies examining the impact of civil rights as a social movement. "I have not lost hope," he said. He spoke openly about his personal frustration and the difficulties he endured during these crisis days of political realignment, racial backlash, and riot politics. He placed himself in a pantheon of what he called "maladjusted" prophets, including Amos, Abraham Lincoln, and Thomas Jefferson, who sought new ways to create more just and free societies. King closed by assuming the role of the historian, discussing the relationship between slavery and the Founding Fathers, noting that blacks toiled in North America even before the Pilgrims and Jefferson arrived. King's allusion to the Pilgrims echoed Malcolm X's famous line: "We didn't land on Plymouth Rock. It landed on us." Like Malcolm, King now relished a discussion of the legacy of racial slavery. "They made Cotton King," he reminded the audience. "They built the home of their masters in the midst of the most humiliating and oppressive conditions."[41]

King's lacerating words about white racism, call for massive redistribution of wealth, and explanation of riots as rooted in antiblack political and social structures failed to grab major headlines, but the speech illustrated the ways in which major parts of his political thought paralleled Malcolm X's bold denunciation of racial oppression. The wide-ranging lecture, broken down in the *Washington Post* as "Psychologists Hear Dr. King Explain Riots," did that and much more. King's speech laid the rhetorical groundwork and intellectual rationale for radical acts of massive civil disobedience in the hope of producing revolutionary change on an unprecedented scale.[42]

Near the end of October, King spoke about the riots to a sympathetic group of Washington officials investigating the roots behind five consecutive summers of civil disorder. King's secret testimony before the Kerner Commission came on Monday, October 23, the day after a massive anti-war demonstration at the Pentagon. The commission, ordered by Lyndon Johnson to investigate the root causes of the domestic political rebellions that had rocked his presidency, deployed field teams to urban neighborhoods, interviewed the unemployed and the educated, and conferred with esteemed political leaders in a methodical search to find a solution to the escalating racial violence. King testified that the origins of the urban crisis lay in "the greater crimes of white society," which cultivated inhumane conditions in racially segregated ghettos across the nation. Unless federal power was used to address poverty in meaningful ways, King declared, Washington would cease to function. The *Washington Post* called King's plans to bring an army of the poor to the nation's capital "an appeal to anarchy" that smeared the prince of peace as a violent extremist.[43]

King and SCLC staff convened on November 26 in Frogmore, South Carolina, for a weeklong retreat to plan the intricacies of the Poor People's Campaign. The campaign represented the culmination of a lifetime of activism for King, including his early critiques of capitalism as a young seminary student. Montgomery, Birmingham, and Selma had harnessed a quest for racial equality that would, in turn, further economic justice. A campaign to eradicate poverty would also galvanize King's anti-war criticism, which argued that the war on poverty remained stymied by war in Vietnam. King's August call for massive nonviolent civil disobedience to end war and racial injustice now became further refined, at the suggestion of Marian Wright Edelman and Bobby Kennedy, under the banner of a movement to end poverty. King had spent his entire career making a case for the universal recognition of human rights through the particular experiences of black people. Now, he amplified those efforts by seeking to illustrate the ways in which poverty both transcended race, class, and culture and could represent a common denominator for a movement powerful enough to end war, violence, and racism.

At Frogmore, King presided over intense discussions about the probability of the campaign's success, the disillusionment that failure might bring, and the possibility of violence in Washington. Colleagues questioned the utility of protests at the Department of Labor and sit-ins at the Department of Agriculture. King pushed back against skepticism from some of his own advisors. In his deep baritone, he painted a portrait of a new kind of movement, one that featured the full panorama of American society joining together for equal citizenship. King envisioned delegations of the poor lobbying Congress while whites, blacks, Native Americans, and other groups walked and rode mules through some of the nation's most poverty-stricken areas toward the capital. He described these demonstrators as "custodians of hope," whose sustained nonviolent organizing, sacrifice, and courage would move the nation, however fitfully, toward a brighter future. Over the course of the retreat, King reaffirmed his commitment to nonviolence through a program of radical civil disobedience explicitly designed to leverage the will of ordinary people against entrenched political institutions. In so doing, he tapped into the same impulse that had driven Malcolm X's efforts to internationalize the civil rights movement by leveraging the United Nations and Africa on behalf of black citizenship. After flying back to Atlanta, King formally announced plans to "lead waves of the nation's poor and disinherited" to the center of American power in the coming spring. King placed the coordination of the Poor People's Campaign in the capable hands of Bernard Lafayette, a veteran activist who had taken part in the founding of SNCC, joined the Freedom Rides, and served as a soothingly stable force among Nashville students during the early days of the movement.[44]

The celebration of King's thirty-ninth birthday on January 15, 1968, marked the convergence of grueling efforts to advocate for radical black citizenship at the local, regional, and national levels. King promoted a universal vision of justice through the particular and painful experience of the black poor from coast to coast. He increasingly faced harsh and unsubstantiated criticism that his organizing efforts would accelerate the epidemic of racial violence already sweeping the nation. The campaigns in Birmingham, Selma, and Chicago had sought to create a national movement through local organizing, but now King was targeting the nation's capital in what he characterized as a last-ditch effort to prevent America from drifting into further chaos by successfully leading a far-reaching movement to end racial injustice, poverty, and oppression.

But while King huddled with advisors over the best way to consolidate anti-poverty, anti-war, and anti-racist organizing at the grassroots level, the FBI made plans to thwart his efforts. Codenamed POCAM, the bureau's anti-King agenda grew out of its sprawling counterintelligence program, COINTELPRO, which targeted black nationalists, civil rights leaders, Black Panthers, and an assortment of social justice groups deemed to be national security threats. FBI agents, working with at least one informant in the SCLC, planted false news stories and peddled unsubstantiated rumors, fomenting character assassination against King through a profile that circulated within the federal government.[45]

In February, he organized delicate negotiations with Carmichael over the Poor People's Campaign, gaining a détente from Black Power radicals skeptical of his anti-poverty movement. Carmichael met with King in Washington. Thoughts of their own mortality gripped both men. Carmichael's political risk-taking during his exhilarating five-month tour of Africa, Asia, and Europe had lingered upon his return home. He engaged in secret talks to officially join the Black Panthers, a group rooted in the Alabama black belt that now took soaring flight as leather-jacketed armed revolutionaries for a new age. King arrived in the nation's capital fresh from preaching the elegiac "The Drum Major Instinct" at Ebenezer on February 4. At once defiant and resigned, King publicly longed, in the event of his own death, to be remembered as "a drum major for justice" and a dogged warrior for peace in a land plagued by violence and addicted to war.[46]

Throughout the sermon, King had railed against the rampant materialism that gripped American society and burdened citizens with a compulsion to consume at the expense of the nation's most important moral priorities. He decried racism as a by-product of the drum major instinct: the need to be first in everything at the expense of others, "and to feel that their white skin ordained them to be first." King recounted talking to his white jailers in Birmingham about the evils of Jim Crow, only to find out that they were as poor as the local blacks protesting segregation. Instead of resting upon "the satisfaction of your skin being white," King urged his prison guards to join the movement. "You ought to be out here marching with every one of us every time we have a march," declared King. He then turned to the global implications of materialism and racism, which he characterized as "a bitter, colossal contest for supremacy." Violence, in the form of militarism and the devastating consequences of war raging around the world, formed the third part of the drum major instinct. "We have committed more war crimes almost than any nation in the world," King claimed, "and I'm going to continue to say it." Like Malcolm X often did, King spoke of divine retribution for America's political sins. "But God has a way of even putting nations in their place," he observed. King concluded by optimistically contrasting the contemporary perversion of the drum major instinct with the life of Jesus, the exemplar who "gave us a new norm of greatness." That greatness required the recognition that the "greatest among you shall be your servant."[47]

King spent the next few weeks delivering public speeches, attending fundraisers, and recruiting allies for the anti-poverty crusade. Predominantly black welfare-rights activists turned the tables on King during an early February meeting, schooling him on the intricacies of federal welfare legislation before agreeing to send representatives to Washington. A more humble King met with nearly eighty Native American, Latino, and white organizers in Atlanta the next month in an effort to shore up support for the Poor People's Campaign. He longed to expose the racial and geographic breadth of economic injustice, as well as the awesome unrealized potential of racially and economically oppressed peoples.[48]

In Los Angeles after his rainbow summit, King spoke to the California Democratic Convention but refrained from publicly endorsing any candidate. Bobby Kennedy, running as a late entry after Minnesota senator Eugene McCarthy's surprisingly robust anti-war primary campaign against Johnson, left a message for King. Bobby pleaded with him to withhold any presidential endorsement until they had a chance to meet. Kennedy's own political evolution, from the Cold War liberal who sanctioned FBI wiretaps against King to a hero of the New Left who spoke out against racism in South Africa and now ran for president as an anti-war candidate, proved to be a remarkable transition. Kennedy now sought a path to the presidency based more on King's vision of a beloved community than on the Cold War liberalism that had propelled his brother's political ascent.

King spent the weekend in Los Angeles recruiting community activists, grassroots organizations, and church leaders to the poverty campaign. "Hot summers are caused by winters of delay," he told the convention. King argued that racial violence remained rooted in collective inaction and neglect by government officials, political leaders, and ordinary citizens unwilling or unable to confront the depth of the nation's racial crisis. King spoke of "the other America," where despair reigned in ghettos and "wall to wall rats and roaches are more likely than wall to wall carpets." No wonder there existed "a great deal of bitterness, despair, and anger among the people in the other America." He resolved to live in Washington as long as necessary. "We are going to stay until we get a response from Congress," King vowed. He continued his strident criticism of white racism, noting during his time in Los Angeles that "there aren't enough white persons in our country who are willing to cherish democratic principles over privilege."[49]

King's March 18 trip to Memphis, Tennessee, tied civil rights and labor activism in powerfully invigorating ways. The visit reunited him with James Lawson, one of his oldest movement friends and an advisor on the practical application of nonviolence to political organizing. Fifteen thousand people turned out to hear King offer words of encouragement to black sanitation workers striking for a living wage. "In a few days, you ought to get together and just have a general work stoppage in the city of Memphis," King announced to massive applause. He presented the struggle for a living wage in the city as part of a larger national movement for social justice rooted in political self-determination capable of recognizing "that if one black person suffers, if one black person is down, we are all down." Buffeted by cheers, King delved deeper, tying economic justice to a fight for racial equality. By standing together, blacks in Memphis were reminding America "that it is a crime for people to live in this rich nation and receive starvation wages." He compared unemployment and poverty in the black community to the level of misery that whites last experienced during the Great Depression. King urged those gathered to recognize their struggles as part of a human rights movement. King distilled the high points of the freedom movement's last decade to this moment, declaring that "now is the time to make real the promise of democracy," a sentiment he had expressed during the March on Washington nearly five years prior. He promised to return at the end of the week to lead a march through the city.[50]

From Memphis, King traveled to Mississippi on the first stop of a five-day publicity tour for the Poor People's Campaign. It marked a return to the Magnolia State and parts of the delta that he had last walked during the Meredith march. He traveled by small plane and automobile through some of the poorest counties and towns in the nation. King's appearance in Marks, a small rural hamlet in Quitman County in northwest Mississippi, exposed the face of extreme poverty. In a ramshackle church that doubled as the town's anti-poverty center, King listened to black mothers recount the lack of food, clothes, "shoes and decent education" for their children. One hundred children attended the event, many of them barefoot and without proper clothes. Visibly moved, King wept as he listened to parents describe fruitless job searches and a brutal level of economic misery that simply overwhelmed him. Black residents of Marks offered personal stories of suffering, accounts of entire families without food or warm blankets. Andrew Young and Ralph Abernathy watched in quiet astonishment as the tears rolled down King's face. King admitted to being "deeply moved" by what he witnessed and heard, then invited all who could to come to Washington. At one point, a woman called out the president for having failed to deliver on his promises to aid the poor. "Johnson said when he came in he was going to wipe out poverty, ignorance, and disease," she said. "Now where's our money?" King vowed to take them all to the nation's capital to find out. He characterized the deplorable living conditions plaguing the entire county as "criminal" and immoral. "God does not want you to live like you are living," he assured them. King carried the pain of Marks with him through the rest of his tour, offering testimony of his experiences there from church pulpits and in interviews. He decided on the spot to originate the poverty caravan to Washington in Marks.[51]

King offered Marks, Mississippi, as an example of racial suffering that justified massive civil disobedience and would guide the Poor People's Campaign. The people of Marks reminded King of his calling as a faith leader, public intellectual, and international political mobilizer. In an interview in New York's Catskills Mountains, King recalled finding "myself weeping before I knew it" in Marks. The sight of dozens of barefoot, hungry children living with parents who "are not even getting an income" resonated deeply with him. "Some of them aren't on any kind of welfare," explained King, "and I literally cried when I heard men and women saying that they were unable to get any food to feed their children."[52]

King's efforts at galvanizing enthusiasm for the Poor People's Campaign bumped into waning staff energy and scant organizational resources. King grew increasingly depressed over the state of race relations, suffered chronic anxiety, and feared that a catastrophic reckoning would grip the nation absent a massive nonviolent movement capable of forcing a radical reimagining of American society. Friends, colleagues, and staff noticed the change in his demeanor. During his lowest moments of depression, he confided in Coretta and close friends that he dreamed of taking time off to recharge, write, and think about new liberation strategies. King still had standing offers to teach at Union Theological Seminary in New York or to assume pastoral duties at prestigious churches nationally and around the world.[53]

But King had no real intention of giving up on the movement. Instead, he returned to Memphis four weeks after the Kerner Commission released its explosive report on urban unrest, which blamed escalating racial violence on structural inequality, unfettered white racism, and poverty. The *Report of the National Advisory Commission on Civil Disorders* became an immediate best seller, but its impact faded after the public had digested the depth of its political inquiry into the national soul. Over six hundred pages of analysis detailing urban disorders in over two dozen cities crested with the candid admission that white supremacy produced residentially segregated neighborhoods, schools, and communities whose impoverishment, hostile relationship with the justice system, and glaring lack of resources made them racially combustible. Looters—who had been blasted as lawless thugs by the president, pundits, and politicians—were revealed as Americans desperate for advancement. "Rather than rejecting the American system," the report suggested, "they were anxious to obtain a place in it." The Kerner report amplified King's call for massive federal expenditures to eliminate poverty, acknowledged Carmichael's observation about black people's lack of political and economic power, and provided sociological and historical keys to unlock the specter of black rage that Malcolm X died trying to harness.[54]

King led over six thousand demonstrators through downtown Memphis on Thursday, March 28—a fulsome display of black political self-determination that was disrupted by teenagers unwilling to remain nonviolent. Within an hour of King's arrival, sporadic looting, shattered windows, and arrests along the demonstration route were reported. One sixteen-year-old boy died, the victim of a close-range shotgun blast by police that was later ruled justified. The FBI, sensing King's vulnerability, pounced by disseminating news stories to friendly outlets and journalists that branded the nation's foremost peace activist a hypocrite who inspired violent civil unrest. Newspapers followed suit, interpreting the episode of violence in Memphis as a sign of things to come in Washington.[55]

On March 31, Martin Luther King Jr. preached the Passion Sunday sermon at the National Cathedral in Washington. Three thousand people jammed inside the building and another thousand listened through loudspeakers on the chapel steps. King arrived in Washington to shore up his support among white liberals, accepting Dean Francis Sayre Jr.'s invitation to speak to an overwhelmingly white crowd of Catholics who remained receptive to his increasingly radical social justice message. He spoke in the measured, calibrated voice that he often used with white audiences. The sermon's title, "Remaining Awake through a Great Revolution," drew inspiration from the book of Revelation and explored what King characterized as a "triple revolution" unfolding around the globe. King challenged the nation to recognize how interwoven the world had become—"a neighborhood" but not yet "a brotherhood," he lamented.[56]

The "unhappy truth that racism is a way of life for the vast majority of white Americans" constituted the second great challenge the nation faced. King blamed a roll call of institutions—religious, political, and private—for failing to "get rid of the disease of racism." He railed against the popular myth that time would lead to racial progress or that blacks alone could achieve full citizenship. King offered a political seminar, one of Malcolm X's specialties, rooted in the history of racial slavery and white privilege. He gave a capsule summary of the failure of Reconstruction to repair the political, physical, economic, and psychological wounds of "a people who were kept in slavery 244 years." King contrasted the lost promise of Reconstruction with "millions of acres of land in the West and Midwest" given away to "undergird its white peasants from Europe with an economic floor." White privilege became tangible through "land-grant colleges," low-interest loans to farmers, and a plethora of federally subsidized resources that remained unavailable to black Americans.[57]

In his opening section, King connected humanity's interrelationships and the ways in which racism impeded the development of brotherhood to a discussion of poverty. King recalled, once again, his recent heartbreaking visit to Marks. Trips to Harlem and Newark had also revealed new depths to the nation's poverty, where slumlords charged high rents while "our expressways carry us away from the ghetto" so the poor remain forgotten. He described to parishioners at National Cathedral the spirit imbued in the Poor People's Campaign. "We are not coming to tear up Washington," he remarked, refuting increasingly negative press accounts that had grown worse in the wake of Memphis. "We are coming to ask America to be true to the huge promissory note that it signed years ago" in the form of the Declaration of Independence and the Constitution. The recent White House civil rights conference and President Johnson's own Kerner Commission, King noted, supported major initiatives to eradicate poverty and racism. He proudly held up his anti-war criticism and the condemnation that followed as an example of ethical leadership. "I say to you that our goal is freedom," King reminded them, "and I believe we are going to get there because however much she strays away from it, the goal of America is freedom."[58]

At a press conference following his sermon, King told reporters that he would be willing to call off the planned April 22 Poor People's Campaign if he received firm assurances that emergency anti-poverty legislation would be passed by the president and Congress. "It would have to have a positive timetable attached to it," he observed. "And I don't see that forthcoming." King offered an olive branch to Johnson, who now considered him a political adversary. "I would be glad to talk to President Johnson or anyone else," he told reporters. King also discussed plans to protest the Democratic National Convention in August if Congress failed to act. "They will have a real awakening in Chicago," he warned, while noting that Republicans might face similar pickets "at their convention in Miami." That evening, almost as if in response to the panoramic vision that King had laid out at the National Cathedral, Lyndon Johnson announced that he would not seek another term as president, a decision that greatly weakened King's chances of procuring the massive political and economic concessions he hoped for.[59]

On Wednesday evening, April 3, 1968, having returned to the South, King delivered a speech in Memphis. He preached a message of defiant hope and resolute political radicalism at the Mason Temple to a crowd seeking physical shelter from a tornado and spiritual sustenance in a long struggle for black dignity. The local movement, where sanitation workers on strike proudly carried signs reading "I Am a Man," reflected a cresting national wave loudly proclaimed by Black Power proponents as the dawn of a revolution. Amid the tense crowd, King upheld nonviolence as a bulwark. "The issue is injustice," he told more than a thousand people. "All we say to America is, 'Be true to what you said on paper.'" The "greatness of America is the right to protest for right!" King extolled Black Power's call for community control over economic resources in black neighborhoods by advocating for a boycott of several companies; he urged the audience to patronize local black banks, foundational institutions of the city of Memphis. He offered a forward-looking vision of a social and political revolution he might not live to see, while triumphantly recalling how Birmingham's struggles continued to shape the contemporary "human rights revolution." "We've got some difficult days ahead," King conceded, speaking as much about the domestic and international political landscape as the local one in Memphis. He concluded his speech by bearing witness to his dual roles as a political and religious leader. He thanked God for allowing "me to go up to the mountain" and then acknowledged further gratitude for having "seen the promised land." King's admission that "I may not get there with you" would, retrospectively, lend this speech its prophetic power.[60]

King awoke on Thursday, April 4, feeling rested after a good night's sleep. He stayed, along with Ralph Abernathy, in room 306 at the Lorraine Motel in Memphis. Much work remained to be done ahead of the poverty campaign. In the short term, King dispatched aides to court to fight an injunction barring the SCLC from a planned downtown march in support of garbage workers on Monday, April 8. Meanwhile, King lunched on fried catfish and convened strategy sessions with SCLC staff and local civil rights activists about how to organize nonviolent training classes over the weekend. He spent much of the day fielding business calls and making plans to bolster the movement in Memphis before returning his attention to the broader concerns of the Washington campaign. He shuttled between rooms 306 and 201, where SCLC staff gathered throughout the day for bull sessions. His plans for the evening revolved around attending an early dinner with staff at the home of local minister Reverend Billy Kyles, before preaching at a mass meeting later that evening. Andy Young came back from testifying at the court hearing, and King exhibited his playful side by engaging in a pillow fight with his lieutenant, whom he chided for failing to tell him of his whereabouts during the day. The tense mood of the previous weeks seemed to lift. King prepared himself for dinner by joking with Reverend Kyle about his expanding waistline.[61]

Just before 6 p.m., King made final preparations to decamp for dinner back in the room he shared with Abernathy. After shaving and splashing on some cologne, King ventured out on the balcony to check the temperature, which had cooled down to the midfifties from an earlier high in the seventies. He surveyed the Lorraine Motel's parking lot and bantered from the second-story balcony with several of his aides awaiting his departure below. He teased Jesse Jackson for sporting a turtleneck and having no tie on for dinner. He asked Ben Branch, the leader of the SCLC musical band, to play "Precious Lord" for him later that night at the mass meeting. "Sing it real pretty," requested King. In an instant, a thunderclap interrupted the scene as a bullet hit King's face, severing his spinal cord, and hurtling him toward the balcony floor. Emergency services arrived within five minutes of the shot. Police officers, part of a special surveillance unit to monitor the garbage strike, arrived on foot immediately. An ambulance rushed King to St. Joseph Hospital in downtown Memphis, where doctors announced his official time of death as 7:05 p.m.[62]

The death of the civil rights icon triggered a national crisis, sparking violent upheavals in dozens of cities. Police searched for an assassin described as a white male by witnesses and eventually apprehended James Earl Ray, an escaped convict whose guilty plea did little to end unproven speculation of government involvement in King's assassination. Rumors that Black Power militants would use King's death to launch an all-out race war ran wild, fueled by reckless speculation by law enforcement officials, incendiary words from political radicals such as Stokely Carmichael, and public anxiety. Carmichael warned the nation that a race war might erupt as a consequence of an assassination he blamed on America's collective racist consciousness. "White America has declared war on black people," observed Carmichael.[63]

Large parts of urban communities seemed to agree with him. One hundred and twenty-five American cities erupted into open political rebellion after King's assassination, turning the spring of 1968 into a national test of democratic resolve. The presence of four thousand military and National Guard reservists outside the White House demonstrated the scope and reach of violence that King had spent his life decrying. Riots that broke out along Washington's U Street corridor paralleled the civil disorders in Chicago and provoked the imposition of curfews across the country. The *Washington Post* characterized King as "a militant activist" who "burned with indignation" against racial injustice. In Los Angeles, hundreds of young people marched along Van Nuys Boulevard carrying signs that read "End White Racism," while 2,500 gathered inside of the Second Baptist Church on Griffith Avenue to listen to a tape recording of a King speech. Five thousand mostly white residents of the New York City suburbs traveled to the Bronx to sign up for an effort to clean up blighted neighborhoods in honor of King two days after his assassination. Seventy black soldiers were joined by five white marines for a memorial service for King in Da Nang, Vietnam, where the chaplain called him "America's voice for the wisdom of nonviolence." American flags flew at half-staff at military command, and China Beach, the recreational facility just outside the city, closed in honor of King's death.[64]

Bobby Kennedy heard the news in Indianapolis, the latest stop in his presidential campaign. Despite the news, Kennedy continued plans to address a rally in the city's black neighborhood, where he came the closest he ever would to offering a public apology for his past mistreatment of King. In an extemporaneous speech, Kennedy reflected on the crisis of race and democracy in American society, an era of "great polarization" marked by racial hatred between blacks and whites. Then he suggested an alternative American future, one that Martin Luther King Jr. exemplified, "to understand and to comprehend, and to replace that violence, that stain of bloodshed that has spread across our land, with an effort to understand with compassion and love." King's death ended one part of Kennedy's political career and ushered in his final chapter, one that lasted barely two months, as a political crusader whose disarmingly vulnerable speeches drew multiracial and multigenerational crowds right up until his assassination on June 5, 1968, in California. Too much political history and too many personal wounds prevented King and Kennedy from ever establishing a warm, intimate relationship—yet, by the end of their lives, they had drawn closer to each other through a shared commitment to social justice.[65]

Black Americans mourned King privately and collectively. Major black political and cultural figures, from Stokely Carmichael to James Baldwin, attended King's Atlanta funeral. Baldwin had last met King during an affair at Carnegie Hall in New York City for which he had purchased a new dark suit, one that he wore, weeks later, to his friend's funeral. King's death personally rocked Baldwin, who staggered toward the end of the decade weighed down by the murders of King, Malcolm X, and Medgar Evers. Four years later, in "Malcolm and Martin," published in *Esquire*, Baldwin wrote a beautiful elegiac essay that sought to reconcile the fates of two political icons he considered to be close friends. "By the time each met his death," Baldwin observed, "there was practically no difference between them."[66]

Baldwin characterized Malcolm X as a gentle soul, who, even at his fiercest, possessed infinitely more humanity than the majority of his critics. "What made him unfamiliar and dangerous was not his hatred of white people but his love of blacks, his apprehension of the horror of the black condition and the reasons for it, and his determination so to work on their hearts and minds that they would be enabled to see their condition and change it for themselves." The world recognized Malcolm primarily as a honed political sword, cutting a wide swath through America's racial wilderness, whereas Baldwin remembered him as a master teacher who believed in black dignity even when most Negroes would not dare to. King's greatest act of self-creation, Baldwin contended, could be traced back to the demands he placed on a still-evolving country. He believed in the idea of America more than the nation did. Both men sealed their mutual fates through dual, posthumously converging, efforts at promoting radical black dignity and radical black citizenship as the keys to fulfilling America's democratic promise.[67]

One hundred and twenty million Americans watched King's funeral broadcast over the three major television networks. Children stayed home from school, unions shuttered ports, and stores closed, as much to honor King's memory as to prevent outbreaks of potential violence. Lyndon Johnson's absence from King's April 9 funeral reflected the depth of personal hurt between the two. Johnson's White House, like Hoover's FBI, had recognized King's peaceful sword as a political threat, one ironically rendered more, rather than less, dangerous by nonviolent appeals still capable of attracting domestic allies and global sympathy. But Johnson circumspectly responded to King's death with acts of presidential kindness and dignity. Behind the scenes, the president assembled an emergency cabinet meeting the morning after the assassination that was attended by major civil rights leaders, including King's sometimes-nemesis Roy Wilkins, who sat alongside Vice President Hubert Humphrey, Democratic and Republican congressional leaders, and Supreme Court justice Thurgood Marshall. Johnson gave the room a modified version of his famous "treatment"— the president's signature use of his six-foot, four-inch frame to plead, cajole, and at times intimidate political foes and friends into

305

submission. Johnson radiated mournful empathy to those gathered as he avowed that, despite the well-documented conflicts between himself and King, "on the issue of human dignity, there was no difference between us." Johnson asked civil rights leaders to help heal a wounded nation, provided updates to them on the investigation into finding King's assassin, and promised to step up national anti-poverty and civil rights efforts.[68]

Johnson's televised address featured a president who had only recently announced his bombshell decision to not seek another term, calling for national resolve on the civil rights issues that King died for. The president designated Palm Sunday, April 7, as a national day of mourning. In Washington, all government offices would remain unopened, flags lowered to half-mast, for the next three days—homage to a man who, just a few days earlier, much of the nation feared.[69]

The Legacy of Malcolm X and Martin Luther King Jr.

"I don't think that any black person can speak of Malcolm and Martin without wishing that they were here."[1]

—JAMES BALDWIN

Perhaps no other person spent more time, respectively, with Malcolm and Martin than James Baldwin. In "Malcolm and Martin," an incisive 1972 essay for *Esquire*, Baldwin offered a revelatory interpretation of the two deceased icons through his own personal relationship with each. Baldwin had heard the news of King's death as he was working feverishly on a screenplay for an ill-fated Malcolm X film. He remained fascinated by the complex human beings they both were, rather than the romantic clichés they were becoming. "Malcolm and Martin, beginning at what seemed to be very different points," increasingly shared a revolutionary political vision that bound them together less as adversaries than as colleagues whose initial conflict gave way to a shared destiny. Baldwin's intrepid analysis proved ahead of the times, since the legacies of the two men would be claimed in American and African American political culture as contrasting examples of the pursuit of social justice, equality, and citizenship.[2]

Martin Luther King Jr. became an enduring global icon. Fifteen years after his assassination, the passage of a national holiday in his honor cemented him as a permanent facet of American political and popular culture. The holiday helped to turn King—one of the most eloquent critics of racism, economic injustice, and war the nation ever produced—into the most important symbol of racial progress in American history. Ironically, it was President Ronald Reagan, the smooth-talking conservative who publicly admitted to having disagreements with the civil rights leader, who signed his holiday into law on November 2, 1983. Surrounded by members of the Congressional Black Caucus and Coretta Scott King, Reagan signed national legislation in honor of a man whom, while living, Reagan considered the symbol of political radicalism. The day after King's assassination, then governor Reagan spoke to the Women's National Press Club, where he traced King's death back to "our first acceptance of compromise with the laws of the land." He placed the blame for King's murder partially on the civil rights activist's insistence that immoral laws required people of conscience to disobey them. Reagan identified King's advocacy of insurgent protest as creating the atmosphere that led to his assassination and imagined civil disobedience as the moral equivalent of those who practiced racial segregation in the first place. Reagan's signature on the holiday exemplified the contested national memory of the civil rights era, where a politician who opposed King's dream of radical democracy could be compelled to praise him while also co-opting parts of his legacy.[3]

The holiday did more than simply recognize King's individual accomplishments. It celebrated the civil rights movement's successful inclusion of racial justice and human rights as fundamental principles of American democracy. But Martin Luther King Jr. Day allowed America to bask in his dream, even as the nation stood further from fulfilling its mandate. King would not recognize himself in the uncomplicated, largely timid figure that much of the nation and the world celebrate today. The radical King, who gathered an army of the poor to descend upon the nation's capital in defiance of critics, is airbrushed from history. The risk-taking King, who defied a sitting president to protest war, is missing from our popular memory. The revolutionary King, who marched shoulder to shoulder with garbage workers, locked arms with Black Power militants, and lived in Chicago ghettos in an effort to stimulate social change, is forgotten. The King who proclaimed that America's greatness remained "the right to protest for right" has all but vanished, replaced by generic platitudes about freedom and justice.[4]

The national holiday magnified King's personal and political frailties. Biographers uncovered that he had plagiarized portions of his Boston University doctoral dissertation and used uncredited passages in speeches and other writings. The vast corpus of his published work, like that of presidents and other high-level political officials, was largely ghostwritten, a circumstance that ignited fierce debate in certain quarters regarding his intellectual and scholarly legacy. Personal revelations, aided by illegal FBI wiretaps, of King's extensive and habitual extramarital affairs stirred prurient interest and discussion over whether his illicit behavior tarnished the power of his legacy. The civil rights movement's heroic period, which spans the time from the Supreme Court's 1954 desegregation decision until King's assassination in 1968, transformed King into an unofficial Founding Father, burnishing his credentials as an architect of a new American republic and turning him into a political titan whose moral power surpassed American presidents and global political leaders. Yet King's national recognition as a civil rights champion served to obscure his more radical ideas and activism.[5]

Martin Luther King Jr. Day, a hard-won victory organized by veterans of the civil rights era alongside black elected officials, became a crucial part of a new national consensus on racial equality in the post–civil rights era. In the shadow of continued racial inequality, the rise of mass incarceration, and the political realignment of the two major political parties, the holiday represented America's rhetorical acceptance of civil rights as a moral and political symbol. King now became embraced by conservatives and liberals as an enduringly unique example of American exceptionalism. But the elevation of King too often came at the expense of wrestling with his moral outrage at the nation's racism, violence, and inequality. Politicians from both major political parties crafted milquetoast versions of King suitable for mass consumption—easily digestible platitudes that ultimately ignored his political radicalism. What King characterized as the "great wells of democracy" became a metaphor for a panoramic movement for social justice that reshaped every corner of American society and inspired presidents Kennedy and Johnson to make his cause their own. Yet the core of King's philosophy has become malleable enough to be embraced by subsequent presidents who opposed his political vision and radical policy agenda, rendering their rhetorical advocacy hollow.

King's most important legacy is his conception of radical black citizenship as not simply the absence of racial oppression but the beneficial good found in a living wage, decent housing, safe neighborhoods, health care, and racially integrated public schools and communities. The radical King waged struggles for economic justice in Chicago, spoke out against the Vietnam War, organized alongside welfare-rights activists, and attempted to lead a poor people's movement whose multiracial makeup formed one strand of a global community that King characterized as the "world house." Over the course of his tenure as a major civil rights leader, King grew increasingly bold as he confronted systemic challenges to his dream of multiracial democracy, what he called a "beloved community." The proliferation of urban violence, rural poverty, institutional racism, and war forced him to reconsider his faith in political reform. Yet the radical King never abandoned his faith in America's capacity for social and political transformation. Near the end of his Riverside speech, he spoke of the "long and bitter— but beautiful—struggle for a new world" he proudly engaged in.[6]

Malcolm X shared King's passion for racial justice but not his patience with American democracy's imperfections. While King imagined blacks participating in a multicultural American "dream," Malcolm witnessed a "nightmare" of racial segregation, police brutality, and misery that he distilled into a ferocious-yet-elegant stump speech that made him Harlem's hero and, over time, an icon of the Black Power movement. But after spending a dozen years in the black freedom struggle, Malcolm was convinced that political coalitions, including the type that King extolled, might offer a shield of protection for a movement capable of guaranteeing radical black dignity and citizenship. Malcolm X's legacy proved more controversial and unwieldy but no less magnetic than King's. Black activists to the left of the civil rights movement embraced Malcolm as the patron saint of black radicalism in the decades following his assassination. By the 1990s, Malcolm had reentered the mainstream of American political culture through rap lyrics, music videos, the Spike Lee–directed film *Malcolm X*, and even a portrait on a US postage stamp. His image remains an indelible figure of political defiance against racial injustice.

Malcolm emerged as black America's revolutionary truth teller, a formerly incarcerated street hustler transformed into a working-class hero capable of eviscerating the political, intellectual, and cultural totems of white supremacy. He's best remembered as black America's prosecuting attorney who defiantly placed Jim Crow on trial and channeled the anger, rage, humor, and pain of African Americans living on the margins. Malcolm's most famous catchphrase, "By any means necessary," succinctly announced his willingness to defend black life and lead a political revolution at any cost. Malcolm insisted that black lives mattered and demanded that blacks plumb the depths of their history in order to rediscover a racial identity that transcended slavery and segregation in an era where black excellence and accomplishment were considered freakish aberrations. Hailed as an oracle of untapped black ambition, progress, and political radicalism, Malcolm came to redefine the contours of African American political culture. His legacy endures in contemporary movements for systemic racial justice and human rights around the world.

Martin Luther King Jr.'s promotion of nonviolence as a shield against Jim Crow's denial of black citizenship sharpened Malcolm's political sword, placing them in a conversation that would continue beyond death. As political antagonists, they verbally sparred over democracy's redemptive capacity. King's diplomatic temperament suited him for the role of black America's defense attorney, a scholar-preacher who defended black humanity to whites with an unmatched depth of compassion and supple intelligence. He assumed the same role before black folk, defending white capacity for individual and collective transformation as the hallmark of democratic progress rooted in his profound faith in Christianity, the black Social Gospel, and the black church.

At various points, Martin Luther King Jr. and Malcolm X each utilized the political sword and shield. Together, they represent two at times overlapping and intersecting strains of revolutionary black activism that continue to animate contemporary black freedom struggles. Malcolm and Martin collectively grew to define the fight for black dignity as part of an expansive human rights movement promoting racial equality, economic justice, and an end to war and violence globally. Malcolm's promotion of self-defense to protect black lives against racial oppression both enlarged the ideological scope of the civil rights movement and obscured his larger political message. He argued that the crisis of race and democracy necessitated a dramatic, collective response to unspeakable political conditions.

In contrast, King's commitment to nonviolence masked his philosophy's revolutionary potential and strategic advantages. In a world shadowed by racism, poverty, and violence, King's use of nonviolence seemed to many, especially Malcolm, weak or even cowardly. But many of his enemies and critics knew better, recognizing the aspects of coercive strength and power contained in each collective display of civil disobedience and every act of individual defiance that might lead to nonviolent revolt. King's revolution of values staked its national claim and international reputation on the moral high ground of changing hearts and minds. At the ground level, King, alongside thousands of grassroots activists and organizers, practiced hardball politics that leveraged mass demonstrations, protests, boycotts, sit-ins, and jail-ins to start to bring the walls of racial segregation and inequality tumbling down brick by painful brick. While never reconciling their disagreement on the issue of self-defense and violence, over time Malcolm and Martin came to share views on important issues.

Malcolm X and Martin Luther King Jr. found common ground and a measure of unacknowledged political convergence through their respective advocacy of black dignity and black citizenship. Their lone joint appearance at the US Senate building illustrates their shared belief in the capacity for mass movements to transform democratic institutions. They both came to define America as an empire whose political economy seemed to thrive on racial violence, exploitation of the poor, and war. King's academic study and global travels armed him with an intellectual understanding of world affairs that grew more radical over time. Vietnam turned him into the nation's sharpest and most vocal critic of American imperialism. Like a man possessed, King raged against the triple evils of militarism, racism, and materialism in a style that shocked critics and might have made Malcolm proud. By the end of their lives, both Malcolm and Martin had sought to leverage international opinion, global political and intellectual networks, and the world stage in an increasingly convergent struggle for black dignity and citizenship.

Malcolm and Martin's enduring influence continues to shape America's contemporary racial and political landscape. Malcolm's ability to connect with black folk mired in urban ghettos and struggling for survival grew out of his intimate knowledge of racial tragedy, economic injustice, and poverty. He came to understand his time as a hustler, thief, and prisoner as a search for political identity, religious understanding, and personal dignity in America's searing racial wilderness. Malcolm found his vocation as a political organizer, religious preacher, and public intellectual but always remembered his time in the bowels of urban America, which included stints as a day laborer, Pullman car porter, and factory worker. Before the age of Black Lives Matter, Malcolm X promoted a global movement for Black Power that recognized the transcendent dignity of the struggle for black citizenship in America and beyond.

By the end of their lives, Malcolm and Martin had added critical new dimensions to their political and intellectual repertoire. Malcolm X, the most electrifying political combatant for racial justice of his generation, found a state of grace through identification with human rights struggles capable of shielding black people from sprawling regimes of racial oppression that stretched from America to Africa and beyond. Martin Luther King Jr., the national conscience on race and democracy, took up the peaceful sword of nonviolence to aggressively call for an end to racism, militarism, and poverty. King, like Malcolm, charged America with political crimes from church pulpits across the nation—allegations that pushed him off the list of the nation's most admired citizens, ratcheted up FBI plots to destroy him, and ended his relationship with the president.

The two men's stature has grown exponentially over the last half century. While Malcolm secured official status as a political folk hero through literary and cultural adoption by generations born after the Black Power era, King became enmeshed in the very discourse of American democracy, enshrined as one of the nation's founders through an annual federal holiday, a memorial in the nation's capital, and global commemorations of his legacy. However, their ubiquitous presence in American popular and political culture flattens a deeper understanding of their legacies. Framing them as simplistic dueling opposites obscures the ways in which each served as the alter ego of the other. By the end of his life, Malcolm viewed himself as working in tandem with King, even when he disagreed with the civil rights leader's tactics. And Malcolm's swashbuckling internationalism, which included public criticism of the Vietnam War, offered a framework for King's radical peace efforts three years later.[7]

Malcolm and Martin publicly debated and privately wrestled over large questions about radical black dignity and citizenship. Malcolm's scalding critique of American democracy asked why blacks needed to protest for the citizenship rights constitutionally guaranteed after slavery. "Whenever a Negro fights for 'democracy,'" he reminded the world, "he's fighting for something he has not got never had and never will have." Where Malcolm identified democratic failure, King saw untapped potential. At the March on Washington, King urged the nation to make real "the promise of democracy." He repeated this phrase in Memphis just before his death. Malcolm found tentative hope in the prospects for black political power through democratic institutions, but he hedged, offering words of fire—"the ballot or the bullet"—if black citizenship was not immediately achieved. King grew increasingly frustrated with the possibility of radical democratic reform, a pessimism that transformed him into a firebrand who publicly questioned the fealty of America's political leaders and citizens to the nation's founding principles. American strength, King argued, required the nation to actively embrace democratic ideals and not simply congratulate itself for having once expressed them.[8]

Martin and Malcolm loved black folk sincerely and unapologetically. Harlem celebrates Malcolm's memory well into the twenty-first century based on this love, which has been bequeathed to generations of blacks who remain enthralled by his broad smile, confident oratory, and wicked sense of humor. King's personal ease with the black poor impressed even his adversaries, who recognized the sincerity of his interaction with the elderly, unemployed, and children who flocked to his sermons, political speeches, and public appearances. Spending time with impoverished black folk in places like Mississippi, Chicago, and Alabama buoyed King, lifting his spirits as his presence captivated poor people who regarded him as a living prophet.

Malcolm and Martin continue to offer the world powerful legacies of radical social and political transformation. Contemporary movements for social justice have helped to resurrect the historical Malcolm and Martin, challenging the pop-culture icons that each has become. The roiling demonstrations against structural racism in the nation's criminal justice system in the twenty-first century have coupled the large-scale acts of civil disobedience personified by King's legacy with a defiant critique of the systemic nature of racial oppression that became Malcolm's calling card. These new movements both stand upon and expand on Malcolm and Martin's political legacies, offering an intersectional analysis of race, class, gender, sexuality, and the environment and their connections to black dignity and citizenship. Through demonstrations, protests, and policy agendas, social justice activists have forcefully argued that America's criminal justice system, persistently segregated and underfunded public schools, and discriminatory finance and housing practices represent a gateway to a sprawling system of racial inequality and economic injustice that has grown, not diminished, since the 1960s.

There is no way to understand the history, struggle, and debate over race and democracy in contemporary America without understanding Malcolm X and Martin Luther King Jr.'s relationship to each other, to their own era, and, most crucially, to our time. The presidency of Barack Obama, in many ways, helped to frame the limits of a liberal democratic framework rejected by Malcolm X and vociferously criticized by the radical King. Obama's election offered a romantic, although unearned, conclusion to the civil rights and Black Power movements without having to examine the underside of the American dream that helped end the lives of Malcolm and Martin. The killings of Sandra Bland, Tamir Rice, Korryn Gaines, Trayvon Martin, Eric Garner, Freddie Gray, and Michael Brown represent only the tip of contemporary racial injustice. America has innovated new forms of racial oppression in criminal justice, public schools, residential segregation, and poverty that scar much of the black community. What Michelle Alexander has dubbed the "new Jim Crow"—the continuation of a racial caste system through the justice system's disparate treatment of black prisoners—touches virtually every facet of black American life.[9]

Malcolm X and Martin Luther King Jr. matter now more than ever. The deaths of Gray and Brown triggered urban rebellions in Maryland and Missouri, recalling the spasms of racial unrest that gripped the nation over fifty years ago. Malcolm and Martin argued that the future of American democracy depended on the wholesale recognition of black dignity and citizenship, struggles that are still ongoing and remain vitally connected to the social movements of the 1960s they helped to define. Malcolm promoted a bold struggle against white supremacy as the corollary to a passionate crusade for black dignity. He did more than hurl general accusations. He prosecuted his case through historical methodology that meticulously recounted the litany of crimes perpetrated against black people. Malcolm's rhetorical sword evolved from brandishing punishing truths about racial injustice into inspiring community pride by offering unmerited grace to all who identified themselves as human rights activists.

Martin Luther King Jr. marshaled his love for black lives through a strategic rebellion that left room for compromise. King's hopes for racial rapprochement with both the architects and beneficiaries of racial oppression faltered in the face of war, racism, and white supremacy. His defense of black humanity pivoted on a belief in mutual redemption for the descendants of both enslaved blacks and plantation owners, a faith overwhelmed by a harsh reality of state-sanctioned violence, poverty, and war.

Malcolm X and Martin Luther King Jr. sought a moral and political reckoning with America's long history of racial and economic injustice. Urban rebellion, entrenched poverty, and the tragic resiliency of Jim Crow forced King to confront uncomfortable truths about the depths of American racism. Having successfully climbed previously insurmountable political mountains, King set his sight on scaling the political equivalent of Mount Everest. Whereas Malcolm's philosophy of self-defense grew to include forays into global diplomacy and recognition of the importance of formal voting rights, King's visions of peace acknowledged the need for a nonviolent political war that would be waged by ordinary citizens seeking universal truths through the particular struggles of the poor and racially oppressed. By the end of their lives, Malcolm X and Martin Luther King Jr. each drew closer to the political philosophies of the other—the sword and the shield no longer reflecting divergent worldviews but dual, at times intersecting and even complementary, strategies that continue to shape movements for racial justice, dignity, and citizenship in America and around the world.

Acknowledgments

In the course of writing *The Sword and the Shield*, my life went through a series of extraordinary personal and professional transformations that have made the completed book all the better. In many ways, the seeds of this book have been germinating for decades, the product of my mother and first history teacher Germaine Joseph's uncanny ability to recount her firsthand experience with the traumas and joys of the 1950s and 1960s, the decades that saw Malcolm X and Martin Luther King Jr. come to prominence, and that paralleled her own remarkable sojourn from Haiti to New York City. As a native New Yorker, I came to revere Malcolm X from an early age, a fascination that only accelerated with the release of the *Eyes on the Prize* documentary series that, over the course of fourteen parts, inflamed an already ignited passion for the study of history. *Eyes on the Prize*'s diligent, nuanced, and spectacularly grounded rendition of history let me, even in junior high school, understand both Malcolm and Martin as radical thinkers and activists whose deep commitment to black liberation and human rights outlasted their own prematurely brief lives.

I would like to thank all of the research libraries, archives, and research assistants who have helped me over the course of the project, especially the Schomburg Center for Research in Black Culture in New York.

Two decades as a professional historian and an even longer time as a lifelong student has allowed me space to better appreciate the many people, family, friends, colleagues, students, archivists, administrators, and activists who have helped inspire me to continue to teach, write, research, and speak truth to power through scholarship and activism. Yohuru Williams, a brilliant scholar, historian, and friend, has, for more than twenty years, been like a brother to me. Ricky Jones is a fearless critic, intellectual provocateur, and good friend. The late Manning Marable, author of a Pulitzer Prize–winning biography of Malcolm X, proved to be a generous mentor and an exemplary scholar of the black radical tradition. Manning's generosity toward me as a young scholar will never be forgotten, and I have modeled my own mentoring efforts after his example. Numerous scholars, colleagues, friends, and writers continue to inspire me. On this score thanks goes to Pero Dagbovie, Derek Musgrove, Michelle Alexander, Jeanne Theoharis, Rhonda Y. Williams, Khalil Muhammad, Alondra Nelson, and Michael Ezra.

Thanks to Professor Clayborne Carson for his amazing and continuous work on the Martin Luther King Papers, which planted seeds for this project. Clay's work is an intellectual model of careful research, scholarship, and analysis in service of the public good. Clay has also done extraordinary work on Malcolm X, which influenced my own thinking in tackling this subject.

Thanks to Cornel West for his insistence that scholars and the larger general public recognize Martin Luther King Jr.'s radical political essence.

Michael Eric Dyson's work on Malcolm X and Martin Luther King Jr. has critically shaped the intellectual terrain of studies of both figures, offering new and important insights into how each relates to contemporary social movements and activists.

Almost a decade spent in Boston proved indispensable to my personal and professional development. Thanks to the many friends who became my second family while living there. Former Tufts colleagues turned friends Liz Foster, Dennis Rasmussen, and Kendra Field were enormously helpful and inspiring during my time there. Two years' worth of fellowships at Harvard introduced me to a wonderful set of colleagues and friends. Skip Gates is a towering scholar, outstanding institution builder, and a generous friend and dazzling intellectual interlocutor. Skip's vast contributions as an intellectual leader and visionary have opened up new doors and opportunities for multiple generations of African American scholars. Brandon M. Terry's work on King's political philosophy offered crucial insights that made this book better. Laurence Ralph is my much smarter younger brother whose unabashed humility allows me to enjoy his brilliance that much more. Patrick Sylvain is one of the most talented and gifted thinkers, poets, and critics of his generation and a good friend.

Robin D. G. Kelley has been an intellectual North Star from the moment I first read his work over twenty-five years ago, and he has proved to be the kindest soul in person. Many thanks to Robin for his intellectual acuity and political integrity and for remaining so loyal and available to a former student.

In 2015, I joined the faculty at the University of Texas at Austin as the Barbara Jordan chair in political values and ethics at the LBJ School of Public Affairs and professor of history. Jeremi Suri, my brilliant colleague in history and at the LBJ School, is a world-class scholar, a talented intellectual leader, and an even better friend. Thanks to the entire Suri-Alter clan—Alison, Natalie, and Zachary—for welcoming me and my family to Austin. The University of Texas has proved to be a fertile ground for intellectual collaboration and institutional building. As the founding director of the LBJ School's Center for the Study of Race and Democracy, I have had the opportunity to work with extraordinary colleagues. Robert Hutchings, the former dean of the LBJ School, offered critical support for my coming to Austin. Jacqueline Jones, the chair of the history department, is an amazing academic leader, peerless scholar, and an inspiration to continue to write, research, and engage with students and the mission of higher education throughout one's career. I instantly recognized Daina Ramey Berry's extraordinary gifts as a historian while still in graduate school, and her talent has only grown in the intervening years. Len Moore's excellence as a scholar and university administrator is only exceeded by his personal integrity and passion to build an ethic of care and support for black students at the University of Texas that rivals that of our nation's leading HBCUs (Historically Black Colleges and Universities). Thanks to Richard Reddick, Brandon Jones, Devin Walker, and colleagues and students connected to the Division of Diversity and Community Engagement, the department of history, and the LBJ School of Public Affairs.

Thanks to Asilee Parkinson, the Center for the Study of Race and Democracy's former administrative associate. Kudos to Chloe Latham Sikes, who served as a graduate research assistant for the center and helped assist on this book project all while finishing a PhD in education at UT. I would like to thank all of my graduate and undergraduate students for inspiring me and wrestling with the ideas in this book, especially Brandon Render, a University of Texas history doctoral student destined to make an indelible mark as a scholar in the near future.

A generation of Black Power studies scholars continue to shape and inspire my own work, most notably but not limited to: Robyn Spencer, Komozi Woodard, Scot Brown, Fanon Wilkins, James Smethurst, Clarence Lang, Keith Mayes, Kimberly Springer, Ula Taylor, Jeffrey Ogbar, Stephen Ward, Matt Countryman, Premilla Nadasen, Tom Sugrue, Hasan Jeffries, Heather Ann Thompson, Tim Tyson, Waldo Martin, and Akinyele Omowale Umoja.

A new generation of black studies scholars have become a new and welcome set of interlocutors and collaborators over the past several years. Thanks to Keisha N. Blain, Ibram X. Kendi, Ashley Farmer, Christopher Lebron, Vesla Weaver, Dan Berger, Nico Slate, Keeanga-Yamahtta Taylor, Ruha Benjamin, and Shirletta J. Kinchen for their intellectual leadership, critical analysis, and commitment to scholar-activism in the best tradition of black intellectualism.

Some fellow authors, some whom I know personally, others only by their work, deserve mention for the way in which their books inspired me. Bryan Stevenson, David Blight, Monique Morris, James Forman Jr., Craig Wilder, Carol Anderson, Roxane Gay, Patrisse Cullors, Asha Bandele, Herb Boyd, Tommy Orange, Lawrence P. Jackson, Manisha Sinha, and Jeff Chang all helped to light the path toward the completion of this book.

Many thanks to the students, scholars, researchers, filmmakers, poets, artists, dancers, singers, actors, archivists, and griots, too numerous to mention in full, who have spent decades examining the lives and legacies of Malcolm X and Martin Luther King Jr. Their vast corpus of work—including books, films, essays, articles, anthologies, songs, and stories—has helped to make this book possible.

My agent Gloria Loomis is a font of wisdom, faith in the importance of this book and in my voice as a writer, and fearless determination in protecting the integrity of the stories that I long to tell. Special thanks to Sonia Sanchez for introducing me to Gloria and for being such a brilliant mentor and guide since my days at Temple University. Lara Heimert, publisher of Basic Books, welcomed this project with her customary grace, enthusiasm, and brilliance. Brian Distelberg's critical and painstakingly nuanced readings greatly improved the entire project. Katie Lambright's excellent line edits helped to bring us home.

Thanks to my good friend Darryl Toler for being such a committed and passionate interlocutor and debating partner over the years. Femi Vaughan continues to be a great mentor, friend, and intellectual guide. Many thanks to Larry Hughes, Priest, Curtis Byrd, Michael Williams, Sal Mena, and Chris and Ina Pisani for their supportive friendship.

My daughter Ayelet changed everything for the better and represents one-half of this book's dedication. Aya has made her

daddy's heart grow wider, deeper, and larger each day while impart-
ing endless lessons about patience, compassion, humor, and love.
Aya's piercing intelligence, wide-eyed curiosity, and robust sense of
humor make every minute an adventure, and I wouldn't have it any
other way. My mother continues to offer the love, support, and ad-
vice that helped me embrace my vocation as a historian, writer, and
teacher. My brother, niece, and sister-in-law, Kerith, Caitlin, and
Dawn, remain steadfast and loving supporters of me and my work.

My partner Laura is truly miraculous, and this work could not
have been completed without her. Laura helped me to see the world
with new eyes that enabled me to better recognize the beauty, love,
and infinite wonder found in the spectacular as well as the mun-
dane. Laura's intelligence, compassion, and empathy for humanity
is marvelous and animates her vocation as a women's health advocate and healer, her love of art and culture, and devotion to family,
friends, health, and wellness. Our love has produced a bountiful
harvest of blended and extended family and friends. Vivienne and
Saylor have made me officially a father of three and in possession
of all the more joy and love for it. My father-in-law David is a
man after my own heart with a wicked sense of humor to boot.
My late mother-in-law Lucy loved history and politics and would
have relished discussing the story this book tells. My thanks to
Julia, Sandy, Jeff, Quinn, June, Ginny, Tom, Gracie, Fletcher, the
Jahangiris, and all of my in-laws and outlaws for welcoming me
into the family.

Archives Sourced

Malcolm X Papers, Schomburg Center for Research in Black Culture, New York Public Library

The King Center for Nonviolent Social Change and Archives

James Baldwin Papers, Schomburg Center for Research in Black Culture, New York Public Library

Clayborne Carson Collection, Martin Luther King Jr. Research and Education Institute, Stanford University

The Papers of Martin Luther King Jr. Volumes I-VI, Martin Luther King Jr. Research and Education Institute, Stanford University

Pacifica Radio Archives, KPFA, Los Angeles

Special Collections, Charles E. Young Library, UCLA

Miriam Matthews Collection of Los Angeles Newspapers on African Americans

Mississippi Sovereignty Commission Papers, Mississippi Department of Archives and History

Stokely Carmichael–Lorna D. Smith Collection, Green Library, Stanford University

Taylor Branch Collection in the Southern Historical Collection, Wilson Library, University of North Carolina at Chapel Hill

Ralph J. Bunch Oral History Collection, Moorland-Spingarn Research Center, Howard University

Robert Penn Warren Papers, Beinecke Rare Book and Manuscript Library, Yale University

FBIMX File No. 100-399321 (Malcolm X)
NYFBIMX File No. 105-8999 (Malcolm X New York)
FBIOAAU File No. 100-442235 (Organization of Afro American Unity)
FBIMMI File No. 100-441765 (Muslim Mosque Incorporated)
FBISNCC File No. 100-147963 (Student Non-violent Coordinating Committee)
FBIKT File No. 100-446080 (Kwame Ture/Stokely Carmichael)

Lyndon Baines Johnson Presidential Library
Lyndon Johnson Papers
Kerner Commission Federal Records
Tape WH6508.07 (Conversation with Martin Luther King, August 20, 1965).

NEWSPAPERS

Atlanta Constitution
Atlanta Daily World
Austin American-Statesman
Baltimore Afro-American
Baltimore Sun
Boston Globe
Chicago Defender
Chicago Tribune
Christian Science Monitor
Cleveland Call and Post
Daily Times (Nigeria)
Detroit Free Press
East African Standard
Ebony
Ethiopian Herald
Esquire
Freedomways
Ghanaian Times
Hartford Courant
Harvard Crimson
Hilltop (Howard University)
Jet

Liberator
Liberian Star
Liberian Age
Life
Los Angeles Sentinel
Los Angeles Times
Louisville Courier-Journal
Militant
Morning Post (Nigeria)
Movement
Muhammad Speaks
Nationalist (Tanzania)
National Guardian
New York Amsterdam News
New York Journal-American
New York Newsday
New York Times
New York Tribune/Herald Tribune
Nigerian Daily Express
Norfolk Journal and Guide
Philadelphia Inquirer
Philadelphia Tribune
Pittsburgh Courier
St. Louis Post-Dispatch
Tanganyika Standard
Time
US News and World Report
Wall Street Journal
Washington Post
West African Pilot (Nigeria)

FILM AND TELEVISION

CBS News Special Report: "The March in Mississippi," June 26, 1966
CBS Reports: "Black Power, White Backlash," September 27, 1966
Eyes on the Prize, PBS, 1987, 1990

Notes

INTRODUCTION: BEYOND DREAMS AND NIGHTMARES

1. Alex Haley and Malcolm X, *The Autobiography of Malcolm X* (New York: Ballantine Books, 1999), 415, 418.

2. *New York Times*, March 27, 1964, 10. *Austin American-Statesman*, March 26, 1964, A8.

3. Taylor Branch, *Pillar of Fire: America in the King Years, 1963–65* (New York: Simon and Schuster, 1998), 267. *Boston Globe*, March 27, 1964, 7.

4. *New York Times*, March 27, 1964, 10. *Austin American-Statesman*, March 27, 1964, A8.

5. David J. Garrow, *Bearing the Cross: Martin Luther King, Jr., and the Southern Christian Leadership Conference* (New York: Quill, 1999), 319. *New York Newsday*, March 27, 1964, 67.

6. *New York Newsday*, March 27, 1964, 67. *Austin American-Statesman*, March 27, 1964, A8.

7. Branch, *Pillar of Fire*, 268.

8. Manning Marable, *Malcolm X: A Life of Reinvention* (New York: Viking, 2011), 302.

9. Clay Risen, *The Bill of the Century: The Epic Battle for the Civil Rights Act* (New York: Bloomsbury, 2015), 245–246, 250.

10. Robert H. Wilson, Norman J. Glickman, and Laurence E. Lynn Jr., eds., *LBJ's Neglected Legacy: How Lyndon Johnson Reshaped Domestic Policy and Government* (Austin: University of Texas Press, 2015). Elizabeth Hinton, *From the War on Poverty to the War on Crime: The Making of Mass Incarceration in America* (Cambridge, MA: Harvard University Press, 2016).

11. John Edgar Wideman, "Malcolm X: The Art of Autobiography," in Joe Wood, ed., *Malcolm X: In Our Own Image* (New York: Anchor Books, 1994), 102.

12. Peniel E. Joseph, *Waiting 'til the Midnight Hour: A Narrative History of Black Power in America* (New York: Henry Holt, 2007). Brenda Gayle Plummer, *Rising Wind: Black American and U.S. Foreign Affairs, 1935–1960* (Chapel Hill: University of North Carolina, 1996). Penny von Eschen, *Race against Empire: Black Americans and Anticolonialism, 1937–1957* (Ithaca, NY: Cornell University Press, 1997). Nikhil Pal Singh, *Black Is a Country: Race and the Unfinished Struggle for Democracy* (Cambridge, MA: Harvard University Press, 2004).

13. Danielle L. McGuire, *At the Dark End of the Street: Black Women, Rape, and Resistance—a New History of the Civil Rights Movement from Rosa Parks to the Rise of Black Power* (New York: Alfred A. Knopf, 2010). Rhonda Y. Williams, *The Politics of Public Housing: Black Women's Struggles against Urban Inequality* (New York: Oxford University Press, 2004). Deborah Gray White, *Too Heavy a Load: Black Women in Defense of Themselves 1984–1994* (New York: W. W. Norton, 1999). Beverly Guy-Sheftall, ed., *Words of Fire: An Anthology of African-American Feminist Thought* (New York: New Press, 1995). Paula Giddings, *When and Where I Enter: The Impact of Black Women on Race and Sex in America* (New York: Bantam Books, 1984).

14. See, for example, Jeanne Theoharis, *A More Beautiful and Terrible History: The Uses and Misuses of Civil Rights History* (Boston: Beacon Press, 2018). Peniel E. Joseph, "The Black Power Movement: A State of the Field," *Journal of American History* (December 2009): 751–776. Peniel E. Joseph, "The Black Power Movement, Democracy, and America in the King Years, *American Historical Review* (October 2009): 1001–1016. Peniel E. Joseph, "Rethinking the Black Power Movement," *Journal of Southern History* (August 2009): 707–716. Peniel E. Joseph, "Black Liberation without Apology: Rethinking the Black Power Movement," *Black Scholar* 31, nos. 3–4 (2001): 2–17.

15. James M. Washington, ed., *A Testament of Hope: The Essential Writings and Speeches of Martin Luther King, Jr.* (New York: HarperCollins, 1991), 617–633.

CHAPTER 1: THE RADICAL DIGNITY OF MALCOLM X

1. Adam Ewing, *The Age of Garvey: How a Jamaican Activist Created a Mass Movement and Changed Global Black Politics* (Princeton, NJ: Princeton University Press, 2014), 83–91, 114.

2. Marable, *Malcolm X*, 17–23. Peniel E. Joseph, *Dark Days, Bright Nights: From Black Power to Barack Obama* (New York: Basic Books, 2010), 35–36. Ula Yvette Taylor, *The Veiled Garvey: The Life and Times of Amy Jacques Garvey* (Chapel Hill: University of North Carolina Press, 2002). Steven Hahn, *A Nation under Our Feet: Black Political Struggles in the Rural South from Slavery to the Great Migration* (Cambridge, MA: Belknap Press: 2004). Mary G. Rolinson, *Grassroots Garveyism: The Universal Negro Improvement Association in the Rural South, 1920–1927* (Chapel Hill: University of North Carolina Press, 2007). Robert A. Hill, ed., *The Marcus Garvey and Universal Negro Improvement Association Papers*, 10 vols. (Berkeley: University of California Press, 1983). (Volumes 11–13 have been published by Duke University Press.) See also Jeffrey B. Perry, *Hubert Harrison: The Voice of Harlem Radicalism, 1883–1918* (New York: Columbia University Press, 2009).

3. Marable, *Malcolm X*, 27.

4. Marable, *Malcolm X*, 29–31. Haley and Malcolm X, *Autobiography*, 13.

5. Manning Marable and Garrett Felber, eds., *The Portable Malcolm X Reader* (New York: Penguin Books, 2013), 23–24. Marable, *Malcolm X*, 23–33.

6. Marable, *Malcolm X*, 60–61, 64–69.

7. Robin D. G. Kelley, *Race Rebels: Culture, Politics, and the Black Working Class* (New York: Free Press, 1994), 163–173. Marable, *Malcolm X*, 39–47.

8. Marable, *Malcolm X*, 51–52. FBIMX 100-399321-16, "Minister Malcolm X," May 23, 1955, 4.

9. Marable, *Malcolm X*, 59–60.

10. Marable, *Malcolm X*, 68.

11. Haley and Malcolm X, *Autobiography*, 166–167.

12. Haley and Malcolm X, *Autobiography*, 169. Marable, *Malcolm X*, 73–74.

13. Marable, *Malcolm X*, 75–79.

14. Marable, *Malcolm X*, 88–90.

15. Haley and Malcolm X, *Autobiography*, 169–173. Marable, *Malcolm X*, 73–79.

16. Marable, *Malcolm X*, 74–78, 91–92.

17. Marable. *Malcolm X*, 93–99. Marable and Felber, *Malcolm X Reader*, 40–41.

18. Marable and Felber, *Malcolm X Reader*, 43.

19. Marable, *Malcolm X*, 69, 141–146. Ula Yvette Taylor, *The Promise of Patriarchy: Women and the Nation of Islam* (Chapel Hill: University of North Carolina Press, 2017).

20. Haley and Malcolm X, *Autobiography*, 201.

21. *Life*, March 20, 1964.

22. Haley and Malcolm X, *Autobiography*, 196. Karl Evanzz, *The Messenger: The Rise and Fall of Elijah Muhammad* (New York: Vintage, 2001), 162–163. Claude Andrew Clegg III, *An Original Man: The Life and Times of Elijah Muhammad* (New York: St. Martin's, 1998), 107–108. Marable, *Malcolm X*, 102.

23. Haley and Malcolm X, *Autobiography*, 204–205.

24. Haley and Malcolm X, *Autobiography*, 199.

25. Joseph, *Waiting 'til the Midnight Hour*, 16–18. Taylor, *Promise of Patriarchy*, 74–78.

26. Haley and Malcolm X, *Autobiography*, 206. Malcolm X to Beatrice X, March 5, 1955, 2, Box 3, F3, Malcolm X Collection, Schomburg Center for Research in Black Culture, New York Public Library.

27. Ferruccio Gambino, "The Transgression of a Laborer: Malcolm X in the Wilderness of America," *Radical History Review* 55 (1993): 23. Marable, *Malcolm X*, 95, 103–104.

28. Gambino, "Transgression," 23. For W. E. B. Du Bois's signature statement on anti-colonialism, see W. E. B. Du Bois, *Color and Democracy: Colonies and Peace* (New York: Harcourt, Brace, and Company, 1945). See also Paul Robeson, *Here I Stand* (Boston: Beacon Press, 1988).

29. *New York Amsterdam News*, August 20, 1960, 4. Peter Goldman, *The Death and Life of Malcolm X* (New York: Harper and Row, 1973), 135.

30. Gambino, "Transgression," 4.

31. Marable, *Malcolm X*, 112–114. Joseph, *Waiting 'til the Midnight Hour*, 17.

32. Marable, *Malcolm X*, 63–164. Joseph, *Waiting 'til the Midnight Hour*.

33. Joseph, *Waiting 'til the Midnight Hour*, 1–8. David Levering Lewis, *When Harlem Was in Vogue* (New York: Penguin Books, 1997). "Malcolm K. Little," May 23, 1955, 9–11, in MXFBI 100-399321-11.

34. Sohail Daulatzai, *Black Star, Crescent Moon: The Muslim International and Black Freedom beyond America* (Minneapolis: University of Minnesota Press, 2012), 2.

35. Daulatzai, *Black Star, Crescent Moon*, 120.

36. Haley and Malcolm X, *Autobiography*, 245.

37. Marable, *Malcolm X*, 134.

38. Taylor, *Promise of Patriarchy*, 90–91. Marable, *Malcolm X*, 144–147.

39. *Pittsburgh Courier*, June 15, 1957, 10. See also *New York Amsterdam News*, June 15, 1957, 25.

40. *New York Amsterdam News*, May 4, 1957, 32.

41. Haley and Malcolm X, *Autobiography*, 255. James L. Hicks, "Sick of It All," *New York Amsterdam News*, July 2, 1960, 10. Marable, *Malcolm X*, 128. Joseph, *Waiting 'til the Midnight Hour*, 10.

42. Hinton received the then largest police brutality settlement ($70,000) in New York City history by an all white jury in the event's aftermath. See Haley and Malcolm X, *Autobiography*, 255, and Joseph, *Waiting 'til the Might Hour*, 11. See also *New York Amsterdam News*, November 9, 1957, 1.

43. After the Hinton case, Malcolm became the point person for publicizing police brutality cases against black New Yorkers, including Muslims. He negotiated with high-level NYPD officials, including deputy police commissioner Walter Arm in 1959, but he had a tense relationship with police commissioner Stephen Kennedy. See, for example, "Moslems Didn't Get to See Commissioner," *New York Amsterdam News*, June 27, 1959; "Boro Ired by Cop's Promotion," *New York Amsterdam News*, January 24, 1959; "Say NY Cops KKK Members," *New York Amsterdam News*, September 12, 1959, 1, 9; and "Muslim Charges Police Brutality," *New York Amsterdam News*, August 19, 1961, 18, 26.

44. Haley and Malcolm X, *Autobiography*, 255–256. *New York Amsterdam News*, May 11, 1957, 1, 21.

45. Haley and Malcolm X, *Autobiography*, 258. *New York Amsterdam News*, July 6, 1957, 3.

46. Marable, *Malcolm X*, 102–114.

47. Marable, *Malcolm X*, 123.

48. *New York Amsterdam News*, August 3, 1957, 22. *New York Amsterdam News*, July 12, 1958, 11. Marable, *Malcolm X*, 123–144. Haley and Malcolm X, *Autobiography*. *New York Times*, April 29, 1957, 12.

CHAPTER 2: THE RADICAL CITIZENSHIP OF MARTIN LUTHER KING

1. Clayborne Carson, ed., *The Papers of Martin Luther King, Jr.*, vol. 1, *Called to Serve, January 29–June 1951* (Berkeley: University of California Press, 1992), 30–31.

2. Harvard Sitkoff, *King: Pilgrimage to the Mountaintop* (New York: Hill and Wang, 2008), 8–9.

3. Stephen B. Oates, *Let the Trumpet Sound: A Life of Martin Luther King, Jr.* (New York: Harper Perennial, 1993), 12. Clayborne Carson, "Introduction," in *Papers of Martin Luther King, Jr.*, 1:33. Clayborne Carson, ed., *The Autobiography of Martin Luther King, Jr.* (New York: Grand Central Publishing, 1998), 5.

4. Oates, *Let the Trumpet Sound*, 11. Haley and Malcolm X, *Autobiography*, 36.

5. Carson, *Autobiography of Martin Luther King Jr.*, 10.

6. Carson, *Autobiography of Martin Luther King Jr.*, 12.

7. Carson, *Autobiography of Martin Luther King Jr.*, 15–16. Oates, *Let the Trumpet Sound*, 16. Taylor Branch, *Parting the Waters: America in the King Years 1954–63* (New York: Simon and Schuster, 1988), 66.

8. Martin Luther King Jr., "Kick Up Dust," in *Papers of Martin Luther King, Jr.*, 1:121. Patrick Parr, *The Seminarian: Martin Luther King Jr. Comes of Age* (Chicago: Lawrence Hill Books, 2018), 11.

9. "Introduction," in *Papers of Martin Luther King, Jr.*, 1:42. Carson, *Autobiography of Martin Luther King Jr.*, 14. Branch, *Parting the Waters*, 61–68.

10. Branch, *Parting the Waters*, 73–74.

11. Carson, *Autobiography of Martin Luther King, Jr.*, 21–24.

12. Clayborne Carson, "The Biography Branch Might Have Written," *American Historical Review* 114, no. 4 (October 2009): 993. Martin Luther King Jr., "Preaching Ministry," in Clayborne Carson, ed., *The Papers of Martin Luther King, Jr.*, vol. 6, *Advocate of the Social Gospel, September 1948–March 1963* (Berkeley: University of California Press, 2007), 72.

13. Martin Luther King Jr. to Alberta Williams King, October 1948, *Papers of Martin Luther King, Jr.*, 1:161. Parr, *The Seminarian*, 38–43. Carson, *Autobiography of Martin Luther King, Jr.*, 23.

14. Branch, *Parting the Waters*, 81–87.

15. Parr, *The Seminarian*, 29–31, 119–121, 151–154.

16. Parr, *The Seminarian*, 102–104, 116. Martin Luther King Jr., "Notes on American Capitalism," in *Papers of Martin Luther King, Jr.*, 1:435–436. Garrow, *Bearing the Cross*, 46.

17. Oates, *Let the Trumpet Sound*, 41–42. Branch, *Parting the Waters*, 94–96, 101.

18. Jeanne Theoharis, *The Rebellious Life of Mrs. Rosa Parks* (Boston: Beacon Press, 2013). Garrow, *Bearing the Cross*, 11–82. Branch, *Parting the Waters*, 143–205. Sitkoff, *King*, 25–55.

19. Oates, *Let the Trumpet Sound*, 59–60.

20. Oates, *Let the Trumpet Sound*, 78. Garrow, *Bearing the Cross*, 1–18. See also McGuire, *At the Dark End of the Street*.

21. Branch, *Parting the Waters*, 161–166.

22. Branch, *Parting the Waters*, 173–180.

23. Branch, *Parting the Waters*, 185.

24. "Chronology," in Clayborne Carson, ed., *The Papers of Martin Luther King, Jr.*, vol. 3, *Birth of a New Age, December 1955–December 1956* (Berkeley: University of California Press, 1997), 43.

25. "Introduction," in *Papers of Martin Luther King, Jr.*, 3:17–20, 27–28.

26. "Introduction," in *Papers of Martin Luther King, Jr.*, 3:32.

27. Martin Luther King Jr., "The Death of Evil upon the Seashore," in *Papers of Martin Luther King, Jr.*, 3:261, 283.

28. *Papers of Martin Luther King, Jr.*, 3:305–308.

29. *Papers of Martin Luther King, Jr.*, 3:337.

30. *Papers of Martin Luther King, Jr.*, 3:453.

31. *Papers of Martin Luther King, Jr.*, 3:454–461. Branch, *Parting the Waters*, 196.

32. Clayborne Carson, ed., *The Papers of Martin Luther King, Jr.*, vol. 4, *Symbol of the Movement, January 1957–December 1958* (Berkeley: University of California Press, 2000), 139. Branch, *Parting the Waters*. George Barrett, "Jim Crow, He's Real Tired," *New York Times*, March 3, 1957, 68, 74.

33. Carson, *Autobiography of Martin Luther King, Jr.*, 111–114. Clayborne Carson, "Introduction," in *Papers of Martin Luther King, Jr.*, 4:9.

34. "Introduction," in *Papers of Martin Luther King, Jr.*, 4:10. Martin Luther King Jr., "The Birth of a New Nation," in *Papers of Martin Luther King Jr.*, 4:156.

35. King, "Birth of a New Nation," in *Papers of Martin Luther King Jr.*, 4:164.

36. Martin Luther King Jr., *"In a Single Garment of Destiny": A Global Vision of Justice*, ed. Lewis V. Baldwin (Boston: Beacon Press, 2012).

37. *Atlanta Daily World*, January 2, 1957, 1, 4.

38. William P. Jones, *The March on Washington: Jobs, Freedom, and the Forgotten History of Civil Rights* (New York: W. W. Norton, 2013).

39. Martin Luther King Jr., "Give Us the Ballot," in *Papers of Martin Luther King Jr.*, 4:211. *Atlanta Daily World*, June 9, 1957, 1.

40. Garrow, *Bearing the Cross*, 98. Robert A. Caro, *Master of the Senate: The Years of Lyndon Johnson* (New York: Alfred A. Knopf, 2002), 1003–1005.

41. David Halberstam, *The Fifties* (New York: Villard Books, 1993), 687–688. Branch, *Parting the Waters*, 222–224.

42. "MLK to Dwight D. Eisenhower," September 25, 1957, in *Papers of Martin Luther King, Jr.*, 4:278. "Dr. King Asks Non-Violence in Little Rock School Crisis," in *Papers of Martin Luther King, Jr.*, 4:279.

43. "Interview by Martin Agronsky for 'Look Here,'" in *Papers of Martin Luther King, Jr.*, 4: 294, 296.

44. Branch, *Parting the Waters*, 231–233.

45. Garrow, *Bearing the Cross*, 107, 141.

46. Martin Luther King Jr., "His Influence Speaks to World Conscience," January 30, 1958, in *Papers of Martin Luther King, Jr.*, 4:354–355.

47. Garrow, *Bearing the Cross*, 113–114. Clayborne Carson, "Introduction," in Clayborne Carson, ed., *The Papers of Martin Luther King, Jr.*, vol. 5, *Threshold of a New Decade, January 1959–December 1960* (Berkeley: University of California Press, 2005), 4–6, 8.

48. Nico Slate, *Colored Cosmopolitanism: The Shared Struggle for Freedom in the United States and India* (Cambridge, MA: Harvard University Press, 2012), 222–224.

49. Martin Luther King Jr., "My Trip to the Land of Gandhi," July 1959, in *Papers of Martin Luther King, Jr.*, 5:237–238.

CHAPTER 3: THE WORLD STAGE

1. Evanzz, *The Messenger*, 193–194. Marable, *Malcolm X*, 165.

2. FBIMX 100-399321 (Part 21), Sub A, *Pittsburgh Courier*, August 15, 1959, C1.

3. FBIMX 100-399321 (Part 21), Sub A, *Pittsburgh Courier*, August 15, 1959, C1. Marable, *Malcolm X*, 167.

4. *New York Amsterdam News*, August 22, 1959, 10.

5. FBIMX 100-399321-39, Malcolm K. Little, November 17, 1959, 38. Evanzz, *The Messenger*, 197. Marable, *Malcolm X*, 161–162.

6. Marable, *Malcolm X*, 123.

7. Martin Luther King Jr., "Address at the Thirty-Fourth Annual Convention of the National Bar Association," August 20, 1959, in *Papers of Martin Luther King, Jr.*, 5:267.

8. King, "Address at the Thirty-Fourth Annual Convention," 267–269.

9. Robert F. Williams, "'For the Positive' Williams Says 'We Must Fight Back,'" *Southern Patriot*, reprinted in *Papers of Martin Luther King, Jr.*, 5:300.

10. Martin Luther King Jr., "The Social Organization of Nonviolence," October 1959, in *Papers of Martin Luther King, Jr.*, 5:299–305. "From the Negative: King Sees Alternative in Mass Actions," *Southern Patriot*, reprinted in *Papers of Martin Luther King, Jr.*, 5:300.

11. *Muhammad Speaks*, June 7, 1963, 12. Huey P. Newton and Bobby Seale, the future cofounders of the Black Panther Party for Self-Defense, would prove to be perhaps the newspaper's most enterprisingly avid readers. Newton and Seale listened to Malcolm in person during his Bay Area appearances and would tout their organization as his political heirs during the Black Power era. Jeffrey O. G. Ogbar, *Black Power: Radical Politics and African American Identity* (Baltimore: Johns Hopkins University Press, 2004), 82. Joseph, *Waiting 'til the Midnight Hour*, 176.

12. *Time*, August 1, 1959, 24–25.

13. *New York Times*, January 25, 1960, 1, 18.

14. "Barry Gray Interview: WMCA-FM, New York City, New York," March 10, 1960, in Sandeep S. Atwal, ed., *Malcolm X: Collected Speeches, Debates and Interviews* vol. 1, *1960–1965* (self-published, 2015), 16, 20, 23.

15. Peniel E. Joseph, *Stokely: A Life* (New York: Basic Books, 2014), 45–61.

16. Joseph, *Waiting 'til the Midnight Hour*. Joseph, *Stokely*.

17. Martin Luther King, Jr., "Statement to the Press at the Beginning of the Youth Leadership Conference," April 15, 1960, in *Papers of Martin Luther King, Jr.*, 5:426–435.

18. *New York Amsterdam News*, May 21, 1960, 2. *New York Amsterdam News*, June 4, 1960, 11. Marable, *Malcolm X*, 171.

19. Haley and Malcolm X, *Autobiography*, 248–249, 251. Marable, *Malcolm X*, 169–171.

20. *New York Amsterdam News*, June 17, 1961, 1. *New York Amsterdam News*, July 1, 1961, 37.

21. *New York Amsterdam News*, July 30, 1960, 1, 5, 11.

22. Joseph, *Waiting 'til the Midnight Hour*, 35–38.

23. Joseph, *Waiting 'til the Midnight Hour*, 35. Ralph D. Matthews, "Going Upstairs—Malcolm X Greets Fidel," *New York Citizen-Call*, September 24, 1960, reprinted in *Malcolm X Reader*, 173–174.

24. *New York Amsterdam News*, September 24, 1960, 1, 31. Joseph, *Waiting 'til the Midnight Hour*, 37.

25. Evanzz, *The Messenger*, 222. Marable, *Malcolm X*, 173.

26. "Malcolm X Explains Wee-Hour Visit to Castro at Theresa," *Pittsburgh Courier*, October 1, 1960, in *Malcolm X Reader*, 169. Joseph, *Waiting 'til the Midnight Hour*, 36.

27. *New York Amsterdam News*, October 8, 1960, 1, 11. *New York Times*, October 6, 1960, 18. *Baltimore Afro-American*, October 15, 1960, 3.

28. August Meier and Elliott Rudwick, *CORE: A Study in the Civil Rights Movement, 1942–1968* (New York: Oxford University Press, 1973), 5–22, 204, 206–207, 332.

29. James Hicks, "Patrice Lumumba," *New York Amsterdam News*, February 18, 1961, 8.

30. Joseph, *Waiting 'til the Midnight Hour*, 39–42.

31. James Baldwin, "A Negro Assays the Negro Mood," *New York Times Magazine*, March 12, 1961, 25.

32. Baldwin, "A Negro Assays the Negro Mood," 42.

CHAPTER 4: A WORLD ON FIRE

1. Garrow, *Bearing the Cross*, 143–144.

2. Branch, *Parting the Waters*, 412–414.

3. *Papers of Martin Luther King, Jr.*, 5:28–29.

4. Martin Luther King Jr. to Jackie Robinson, June 19, 1960, in *Papers of Martin Luther King, Jr.*, 5:477.

5. Branch, *Parting the Waters*, 362–370. Steven Levingston, *Kennedy and King: The President, the Pastor, and the Battle over Civil Rights* (New York: Hachette Books, 2018), 87–105.

6. James Baldwin to Martin Luther King Jr., May 26, 1960, in *Papers of Martin Luther King, Jr.*, 5:460–461. James Baldwin, "The Dangerous Road before Martin Luther King," *Harper's*, February 1, 1961, 34, 42.

7. Sitkoff, *King*, 72–73. Branch, *Parting the Waters*, 351–378.

8. Branch, *Parting the Waters*, 314.

9. Branch, *Parting the Waters*, 368–369.

10. Oates, *Let the Trumpet Sound*, 166–168.

11. Levingston, *Kennedy and King*, 64. Branch, *Parting the Waters*, 344.

12. Martin Luther King Jr., "Equality Now: The President Has the Power," in Clayborne Carson, ed., *The Papers of Martin Luther King, Jr.*, vol. 7, *To Save The Soul of America, January 1961–August 1962* (Berkeley: University of California Press, 2014), 139–140.

13. MLK to John F. Kennedy, March 1, 1961, in *Papers of Martin Luther King, Jr.*, 7:171–172.

14. Oates, *Let the Trumpet Sound*, 171. Garrow, *Bearing the Cross*, 152.

15. Branch, *Parting the Waters*, 405–407. Garrow, *Bearing the Cross*, 154. Levingston, *Kennedy and King*, 129–130.

16. Garrow, *Bearing the Cross*, 153.

17. Garrow, *Bearing the Cross*, 156. Branch, *Parting the Waters*, 419–420.

18. Garrow, *Bearing the Cross*, 158.

19. Garrow, *Bearing the Cross*, 158. Branch, *Parting the Waters*, 460, 464–468.

20. Branch, *Parting the Waters*, 467. Raymond Arsenault, *Freedom Riders: 1961 and the Struggle for Racial Justice* (New York: Oxford University Press, 2006), 249–251.

21. Branch, *Parting the Waters*, 475. Garrow, *Bearing the Cross*, 159–160. Arsenault, *Freedom Riders*, 274–275.

22. Branch, *Parting the Waters*, 468–469.

23. Arsenault, *Freedom Riders*, 431. Martin Luther King Jr., "'The Time For Freedom Has Come,'" *New York Times Magazine*, September 10, 1961, SM25.

24. Garrow, *Bearing the Cross*, 169–170.

25. "Press Conference after Meeting with John F. Kennedy," October 16, 1961, in *Papers of Martin Luther King, Jr.*, 7:309. Branch, *Parting the Waters*, 476.

26. Joseph, *Stokely*, 41. Marable, *Malcolm X*, 186–187.

27. *Chicago Defender*, November 11, 1961, 8.

28. *Chicago Defender*, November 11, 1961, 8. Joseph, *Stokely*, 42.

29. Stokely Carmichael and Ekwueme Michael Thelwell, *Ready for Revolution: The Life and Struggles of Stokely Carmichael (Kwame Ture)* (New York: Scribner, 2003), 257.

30. John D'Emilio, *Lost Prophet: The Life and Times of Bayard Rustin* (Chicago: University of Chicago Press, 2003), 324.

31. David P. Cline, *From Reconciliation to Revolution: The Student Interracial Ministry, Liberal Christianity, and the Civil Rights Movement* (Chapel Hill: University of North Carolina Press, 2016), 90–95. For a firsthand account of black women in the Albany Movement see Faith S. Holsaert et al., eds., *Hands on the Freedom Plow: Personal Accounts by Women in SNCC* (Urbana: University of Illinois Press, 2012), 91–155.

32. "Address Delivered at Albany Movement Mass Meeting at Mt. Zion Baptist Church," December 15, 1961, in *Papers of Martin Luther King, Jr.*, 7:344. Garrow, *Bearing the Cross*, 173–189.

33. *Baltimore Afro-American*, February 3, 1962, 16. "Bayard Rustin Debate," February 15, 1962, in *Malcolm X: Collected Speeches*, 1:157.

34. "Bayard Rustin Debate," 157–158, 159.

35. "Separation or Integration," *Dialogue*, May 1962, 14. Joe Matasich, "2 Negroes with Opposing Views Debate Segregation-Integration," *Ithaca Journal*, March 8, 1962, in *Malcolm X Reader*, 194–198.

36. "Separation or Integration," 14.

37. "Separation or Integration," 14.

38. "Separation or Integration," 16–17.

39. "Separation or Integration," 16. Matasich, "2 Negroes," 194–198.

40. James Farmer, *Lay Bare the Heart: An Autobiography of the Civil Rights Movement* (Fort Worth: Texas Christian University Press, 1998), 223–227.

41. Marable, *Malcolm X*, 207.

42. Isabel Wilkerson, *The Warmth of Other Suns: The Epic Story of America's Great Migration* (New York: Random House, 2010). Gerald Horne, *Fire This Time: The Watts Uprising and the 1960s* (New York: Da Capo Press, 1997). Hinton, *War on Poverty*.

43. Louis E. Lomax, *To Kill a Black Man* (Los Angeles: Holloway House, 1968), 96–97. Goldman, *Death and Life*, 97–98.

44. Branch, *Pillar of Fire*, 10.

45. *Los Angeles Times*, May 5, 1962, 19. See also, Branch, *Pillar of Fire*, 3–13, and Marable, *Malcolm X*, 206–210.

46. *Philadelphia Tribune*, May 1, 1962, 1. *New York Amsterdam News*, July 28, 1962, 33. The Harlem rally led by Malcolm X, with 2,500 in attendance, became a more commonplace occurrence in the aftermath of the Stokes shooting. Malcolm led a rally of five thousand in Boston, where Ronald Stokes was originally from, on July 29, 1962, in an appearance that further augmented his stance as a national political leader. See *Boston Globe*, July 30, 1962, 1, 4. Malcolm X, "The Crisis of Racism," May 1, 1962, in *Malcolm X: Collected Speeches*, 1:172.

47. Malcolm X, "The Crisis of Racism," 175–176.

48. Malcolm X, "The Crisis of Racism," 179, 186. Marable, *Malcolm X*, 215–216.

49. *New York Times*, May 14, 1962, 1, 32. *New York Times*, May 28, 1962, 31. Marable, *Malcolm X*, 216–217, 227–228.

50. Carson, "Introduction," in *Papers of Martin Luther King, Jr.*, 7:28–36.

51. Martin Luther King Jr., "Fumbling on the New Frontier," March 3, 1962, in *Papers of Martin Luther King, Jr.*, 7:413.

52. King, "Fumbling on the New Frontier," 414.

53. King, "Fumbling on the New Frontier," 414.

54. Branch, *Parting the Waters*, 631. *New York Times*, August 18, 1962, 44.

55. Martin Luther King Jr., "My Talk with Ben Bella," *New York Amsterdam News*, October 27, 1962, 13.

56. King, "My Talk," 225.

CHAPTER 5: BIRMINGHAM'S RADICALS

1. Branch, *Pillar of Fire*, 182.

2. Garrow, *Bearing the Cross*, 239, 244–245. *Baltimore Afro-American*, April 20, 1963, 1. See also Diane McWhorter, *Carry Me Home: Birmingham, Alabama: The Climactic Battle of the Civil Rights Revolution* (New York: Simon and Schuster, 2001).

3. Carson, *Autobiography of Martin Luther King, Jr.*, 192, 196–197.

4. Carson, *Autobiography of Martin Luther King, Jr.*, 192, 196–197.

5. Garrow, *Bearing the Cross*, 248–249.

6. Garrow, *Bearing the Cross*, 262–264. Kelley, *Race Rebels*, 87–91. Joseph, *Waiting 'til the Midnight Hour*, 80.

7. *New York Times*, March 10, 1963, 1. Joseph, *Dark Days, Bright Nights*, 64–65.

8. Kelley, *Race Rebels*. *Chicago Defender*, May 25, 1963, 9. *New York Times*, March 11, 1963, 9.

9. *New York Times*, March 11, 1963, 77. *New York Times*, May 17, 1963, 14.

10. Haley and Malcolm X, *Autobiography*, 231–234. *Chicago Daily News*, February 27, 1963, 43, and *Washington Post*, February 28, 1963, 17, in FBIMX 100-399321-A.

11. Malcolm X, interview by Alex Haley, *Playboy*, May 9, 1963, in *Malcolm X: Collected Speeches*, 1:367.

12. Malcolm X, interview by Alex Haley, *Playboy*, May 9, 1963, in *Malcolm X: Collected Speeches*, 1:365.

13. "Malcolm X on a Mission," *New York Herald Tribune*, May 10, 1963, 16, in FBIMX 100-399321-A. "Muslim Leader Poses Political Action Issue," *Militant*, April 29, 1963, 3, in FBIMX 100-399321-A.

14. *Newsweek*, May 27, 1963, 27–28. *Chicago Defender*, June 5, 1963, 13. Marable, *Malcolm X*, 253.

15. Branch, *Parting the Waters*, 809–813.

16. Joseph, *Waiting 'til the Midnight Hour*, 69–73.

17. Michael Eric Dyson, *What Truth Sounds Like: RFK, James Baldwin, and Our Unfinished Conversation about Race in America* (New York: St. Martin's Press, 2018), 39–41.

18. *Washington Post*, May 26, 1963, A6.

19. *New York Times*, June 3, 1963, 1, 19.

20. Dyson, *What Truth Sounds Like*, 49, 51. Branch, *Parting the Waters*, 813. Garrow, *Bearing the Cross*, 268–269.

21. Crowd estimates for the Freedom Rally ranged from thirty thousand reported by the *Los Angeles Times*, to thirty-five thousand reported by the Associated Press, and fifty thousand by the *Los Angeles Sentinel*. See "30,000 at Rally Hear Plea for Civil Rights," *Los Angeles Times*, May 27, 1963, 2; "Los Angeles Rally Draws 35,000," *Chicago Tribune*, May 27, 1963, A11; "Kingly Tribute," *Los Angeles Sentinel*, May 30, 1963, A6; "Greatest Freedom Rally Here Nets Heroes Over $75,000," *Los Angeles Sentinel*, May 30, 1963, A1. *Los Angeles Times*, May 27, 1963, 2. Martin Luther King Jr., "We Want to Be Free," Freedom Rally, May 26, 1963, PRA BB4745a-b.

22. Martin Luther King Jr., "We Want to Be Free," Freedom Rally, May 26, 1963, PRA BB4745a-b.

23. *Chicago Tribune*, May 27, 1963, A11.

24. Branch, *Parting the Waters*, 825. See also "Race Crisis Action Put Up to JFK," *Washington Post*, May 30, 1963, A1, A7; "Coeds Dragged to Paddy Wagon," *Norfolk Journal and Guide*, June 1, 1963, 1; "Johnson Signals Drive," *Christian Science Monitor*, June 1, 1963, 1; "Negro Violence in North Feared," *New York Times*, May 27, 1963, 19; "Warns of Negro 'Breaking Point,'" *Boston Globe*, May 29, 1963, 4; "Black Muslims Are Waiting in the Wings," *New York Newsday*, 32; "James Baldwin Rejects Despair Despite Race 'Drift and Danger,'" *New York Times*, June 3, 1963, 1, 19. Marable, *Malcolm X*, 242.

25. Peniel E. Joseph, "Kennedy's Finest Moment," *New York Times*, June 11, 2013, A23. Theoharis, *A More Beautiful and Terrible History*.

Matthew Delmont, *Why Busing Failed: Race, Media, and the National Resistance to School Desegregation* (Berkeley: University of California Press, 2016).

26. John F. Kennedy, "Report to the American People on Civil Rights," CBS, June 11, 1963, www.jfklibrary.org/asset-viewer/report-to -the-american-people-on-civil-rights-11-june-1963.

27. Branch, *Parting the Waters*, 828.

28. *Washington Post*, June 15, 1963, 1, 10. *Boston Globe*, June 15, 1963, 1–2. *Washington Post*, June 15, 1963, 10.

29. Garrow, *Bearing the Cross*, 272. Oates, *Let the Trumpet Sound*, 246.

30. Garrow, Parting the Waters, 272. Oates, *Let the Trumpet Sound*, 246.

31. Garrow, *Bearing the Cross*, 273.

32. Branch, *Parting the Waters*, 843.

33. *Chicago Defender*, June 20, 1963, 28. PBS, "Malcolm X on 'The Negro and the American Promise,'" *American Experience*, aired January 18, 2004, www.pbs.org/video/american-experience-malcolm-x-on-the -negro-and-the-american-promise/.

34. *Boston Globe*, June 25, 1963, 7. Martin Luther King Jr., interview by Kenneth Clark, *The Negro and the American Promise*, WGBH, June 24, 1963, http://openvault.wgbh.org/catalog/V_0DE798F473F D45E98E451C0FAA8CB2AE.

35. *New York Times*, June 25, 1963, 13. *Chicago Tribune*, June 25, 1963, 6. *Chicago Defender*, June 25, 1963, 13.

36. *Cleveland Call and Post*, June 29, 1963, 7A. *New York Amsterdam News*, June 29, 1963, 6.

CHAPTER 6: "NOW IS THE TIME TO MAKE REAL THE PROMISE OF DEMOCRACY"

1. William W. Sales Jr., *From Civil Rights to Black Liberation: Malcolm X and the Organization of Afro-America Unity* (Boston: South End Press, 1994), 127–128. Joseph, *Waiting 'til the Midnight Hour*, 108. Joseph, *Stokely*, 40–43. Marable, *Malcolm X*, 303, 411–412. Rhonda Y. Williams, *Concrete Demands: The Search for Black Power in the 20th Century* (New York: Routledge, 2015), 104.

2. Transcript of Cleveland Sellers interview with Peniel Joseph, December 14, 2009, 25–27.

3. *New York Times*, August 6, 1963, 19.

4. *New York Times*, August 11, 1963, 61. Marable, *Malcolm X*, 254. *Chicago Defender*, August 10, 1963, 2.

5. Goldman, *Death and Life*, 104–105. Marable, *Malcolm X*, 257. Branch, *Parting the Waters*, 872–873.

6. James H. Cone, *Martin & Malcolm & America: A Dream or a Nightmare* (Maryknoll, NY: Orbis Books, 1991), 83–84. *New York Times*, August 29, 1963, 1, 17.

7. Garrow, *Bearing the Cross*, 284. Carson, *Autobiography of Martin Luther King, Jr.*, 225–226.

8. Branch, *Parting the Waters*, 883.

9. Joseph, *Dark Days, Bright Nights*, 71.

10. Joseph, *Waiting 'til the Midnight Hour*, 84–85.

11. Joseph, *Waiting 'til the Midnight Hour*, 86–87.

12. Branch, *Parting the Waters*, 883. McWhorter, *Carry Me Home*, 450.

13. James Baldwin Debate, September 5, 1963, in *Malcolm X: Collected Speeches*, 1:449–450.

14. James Baldwin Debate, 450.

15. James Baldwin Debate, 450.

16. *New York Amsterdam News*, September 7, 1963, 6.

17. Branch, *Parting the Waters*, 893–894. Garrow, *Bearing the Cross*, 303–304.

18. *Chicago Defender*, November 21, 1963, 16. Joseph, *Waiting 'til the Midnight Hour*, 88–89.

19. Joseph, *Waiting 'til the Midnight Hour*. Malcolm X, "Message to the Grass Roots," in *Malcolm X Reader*, 265–273.

20. Malcolm X, "Message to the Grass Roots." Haley and Malcolm X, *Autobiography*, 306.

21. *Chicago Defender*, November 21, 1963, 16. *New York Amsterdam News*, November 23, 1963, 1. Joseph, *Waiting 'til the Midnight Hour*, 91–92.

22. Garrow, *Bearing the Cross*, 307.

23. Malcolm X, *The End of White World Supremacy: Four Speeches by Malcolm X*, ed. Benjamin Karim (New York: Arcade Publishing, 1971), 124, 130.

24. *New York Times*, December 2, 1963, 21. Branch, *Pillar of Fire*.

25. Joseph, *Dark Days, Bright Nights*, 74–75.

26. *Chicago Defender*, December 5, 1963, 1, 3. *Boston Globe*, December 5, 1963, 22. *Chicago Tribune*, December 5, 1963, 22. *New York Times*, December 5, 1963, 22.

27. Garrow, *Bearing the Cross*, 307. Branch, *Parting the Waters*, 918.

28. Garrow, *Bearing the Cross*, 308–309. Martin Luther King Jr., "What Killed JFK?," *New York Amsterdam News*, December 21, 1963, 12.

29. King, "What Killed JFK?," 12.

CHAPTER 7: "WHAT IS A DREAM TO YOU IS A NIGHTMARE TO US"

1. "President's Speech: 'Peace and Abundance for All,'" *Atlanta Constitution*, January 9, 1964, 6.

2. Branch, *Pillar of Fire*, 210.

3. Garrow, *Bearing the Cross*, 310.

4. Garrow, *Bearing the Cross*, 312.

5. Clegg, *An Original Man*, 84, 92, 120, 175. Marable, *Malcolm X*, 139. Haley and Malcolm X, *Autobiography*, 281–282.

6. *New York Post*, March 10, 1964, 5, in FBIMX 105-8999-4453.

7. "Statement to the Press by Malcolm X," March 8, 1964, 1, and "Text of Telegram from Malcolm X to Honorable Elijah Muhammad," March 11, 1964, 1, in MXP, Reel 13, Folder 1. Joseph, *Waiting 'til the Midnight Hour*, 97.

8. Karim, *End of White World Supremacy*, 132. *Norfolk Journal and Guide*, March 14, 1964, 1–2. "Malcolm X Press Conference Statement," March 12, 1964, 2, in MXP, Reel 13, Folder 2. Joseph, *Dark Days, Bright Nights*, 76–77. *New York Times*, March 14, 1964, 10. *Life*, March 1964, in MXP, Reel 16, Folder 2.

9. *Baltimore Afro-American*, March 21, 1964, 1–2. *Militant*, March 23, 1964, 6, in MXP, Reel 16, Folder 1. "Malcolm X Press Conference Statement," March 12, 1964, 4, in MXP, Reel 13, Folder 1.

10. Joseph, *Dark Days, Bright Nights*, 81. *New York Times*, March 15, 1964, 46.

11. *Washington Post*, March 15, 1964, A4. Joseph, *Waiting 'til the Midnight Hour* and *Dark Days, Bright Nights*.

12. *Philadelphia Tribune*, March 17, 1964, 1–2.

13. *New York Times*, March 15, 1964, 46.

14. *Los Angeles Times*, March 16, 1964, 27. *New York Times*, March 16, 1964, 1, 26. *Chicago Defender*, March 17, 1964, 1, 22. *Los Angeles Times*, March 17, 1964, B8.

15. *New York Times*, March 17, 1964, 25. Joseph, *Waiting 'til the Midnight Hour*, 99.

16. *Baltimore Afro-American*, March 21, 1964, 4. *Norfolk Journal and Guide*, March 21, 1964, 8. *New York Times*, March 22, 1964, 106. Joseph, *Waiting 'til the Midnight Hour*, 99–100.

17. Malcolm X, "Leverett House Forum," Harvard University, March 18, 1964, in *Malcolm X: Collected Speeches* 1:642–643.

18. Malcolm X, "Leverett House Forum," 646.

19. *New York Times*, March 23, 1964, 18. *Chicago Tribune*, March 23, 1964, 22. *Militant*, March 30, 1964, 1, in MXP, Reel 16, Folder 1.

20. *New York Amsterdam News*, March 28, 1964, 50. *Pittsburgh Courier*, March 28, 1964, 1.

21. *New York Journal-American*, March 27, 1964, 4, in MXP, Reel 16, Folder 2. Branch, *Pillar of Fire*, 268.

22. *Chicago Defender*, April 4, 1964, 9. *New York Journal-American*, March 27, 1964, 4. *Eyes on the Prize*, episode 7, "The Time Has Come," written and directed by James A. DeVinney and Madison D. Lacy, aired January 18, 1990, on PBS.

23. *New York Journal-American*, March 27, 1964, 4.

24. *New York Times*, April 3, 1964, 23.

25. Marable, *Malcolm X*, 302. George Breitman, "New Force Can Bring Major Rights Gains," *Militant*, March 30, 1964, 3, in Malcolm X Papers, Reel 16, Folder 1, SCFRBC. Haley and Malcolm X, *Autobiography*, 323.

26. Marable, *Malcolm X*, 242–243, 301. Branch, *Pillar of Fire*, 269.

27. Malcolm X, "The Ballot or the Bullet," in *Malcolm X Reader*, 319–321.

28. Malcolm X, "The Ballot," 322. *Chicago Defender*, April 14, 1964, 7.

29. Haley and Malcolm X, *Autobiography*, 316. Malcolm X, "Letter From Mecca," April 20, 1964, in *Malcolm X: Collected Speeches*, 1:687, 689.

30. *Nigerian Daily Express*, May 11, 1964, 6. Marable, *Malcolm X*, 360–374. Edward E. Curtis IV, "'My Heart is in Cairo': Malcolm X, the Arab Cold War, and the Making of Islamic Liberation Ethics," *Journal of American History* 102, no. 3 (December 2015): 775–798.

31. *New York Times*, May 19, 1964, 28. Haley and Malcolm X, *Autobiography*, 357. Malcolm X, "We Are All Blood Brothers," *Liberator*, July 1964, 4–6.

32. El-Hajj Malik El-Shabazz, *The Diary of Malcolm X*, eds. Herb Boyd and Ilyasah Al-Shabazz (Chicago: Third World Press, 2013), 5, 9, 14–16. Haley and Malcolm X, *Autobiography*, 374.

33. El-Shabazz, *Diary*, 19, 23. Haley and Malcolm X, *Autobiography*, 380.

34. El-Shabazz, *Diary*, 42–42. Dayo F. Gore, *Radicalism at the Crossroads: African American Women Activists in the Cold War* (New York: New York University Press, 2011), 148. Gerald Horne, *Race Woman: The Lives of Shirley Graham Du Bois* (New York: New York University Press, 2000), 189.

35. *Ghanaian Times*, May 18, 1964, 5. Marable, *Malcolm X*, 363. Jan Carew, *Ghosts in Our Blood: With Malcolm X in Africa, England, and the Caribbean* (Chicago: Lawrence Hill Books, 1994).

36. Marable, *Malcolm X*, 317. Joseph, *Waiting 'til the Midnight Hour*, 106. Joseph, *Dark Days, Bright Nights*, 88–90.

37. Haley and Malcolm X, *Autobiography*, 367. El-Shabazz, *Diary*, 55.

38. *New York Times*, May 22, 1964, 22. Joseph, *Waiting 'til the Midnight Hour*, 107. Joseph, *Dark Days, Bright Nights*, 85–86. Haley and Malcolm X, *Autobiography*, 367–370. Marable, *Malcolm X*, 319. Branch, *Pillar of Fire*, 256–257.

39. Haley and Malcolm X, *Autobiography*, 369. Malcolm X, "Return from Mecca Press Conference," May 21, 1964, in *Malcolm X: Collected Speeches*, 1:701.

40. Malcolm X, "The Harlem Hate Gang Scare," Militant Labor Forum, May 29, 1964, in *Malcolm X: Collected Speeches*, 1:712–713.

41. Malcolm X, "Harlem Gang Scare," 714.

42. Malcolm X, "Harlem Gang Scare," 715.

43. Marable, *Malcolm X*, 350–351. Joseph, *Dark Days, Bright Nights*, 90–91.

44. Malcolm X, "OAAU Founding Rally," June 28, 1964, in *Malcolm X: Collected Speeches*, 1:758.

45. *Evening World-Herald*, June 30, 1964, 1–2. MXP, Reel 16, Folder 1.

46. Joseph, *Waiting 'til the Midnight Hour*, 109–110. Marable, *Malcolm X*, 355, 358. *Chicago Defender*, July 9, 1964, 4.

CHAPTER 8:"SEEKING FREEDOM LIKE DR. KING, BUT FASTER"

1. Risen, *Bill of the Century*. Todd S. Purdum, *An Idea Whose Time Has Come: Two Presidents, Two Parties, and the Battle for the Civil Rights Act of 1964* (New York: Henry Holt, 2014).

2. *Boston Globe*, July 3, 1964, 1–2.

3. Malcolm X, "Robert Penn Warren Interview," June 2, 1964, in *Malcolm X: Collected Speeches*, 1:729.

4. Branch, *Pillar of Fire*, 345. Marable, *Malcolm X*, 342–343. Malcolm X to Dr. Martin Luther King Jr., June 30, 1964, MXP, Reel 14, Folder 2.

5. *New York Times*, July 29, 1964, 1–2. Branch, *Pillar of Fire*, 422–423.

6. Malcolm X to H.S. Muhammad Taufik Oweida correspondence, November 30, 1964, 2, MXP, Reel 3, Folder 4.

7. Saladin Ambar, *Malcolm X at Oxford Union: Racial Politics in a Global Era* (Oxford: Oxford University Press, 2014), 65.

8. Joseph, *Stokely*, 76. Branch, *Pillar of Fire*, 459. Branch, *Parting the Waters*, 466–474. Barbara Ransby, *Ella Baker and the Black Freedom Movement: A Radical Democratic Vision* (Chapel Hill: University of North Carolina Press, 2003), 336–344.

9. Garrow, *Bearing the Cross*, 349.

10. Garrow, *Bearing the Cross*, 350–351.

11. Garrow, *Bearing the Cross*, 353. *Los Angeles Sentinel*, October 15, 1964, 1, 5. *New York Times*, October 15, 1964, 14. Lyndon Johnson to Martin Luther King Jr., October 16, 1964, Martin Luther King Jr., 1963-1964 Folder, LBJ Archives, Lyndon Johnson Presidential Library.

12. "Evangel of Nonviolence," *New York Times*, October 15, 1964, 38. "Why They Picked Dr. King," *Boston Globe*, October 17, 1964, 6. "King and Nobel Prize," *Chicago Defender*, October 19, 1964, 11. "The Nobel Peace Prize," *Baltimore Afro-American*, October 24, 1964, 4. "A Citation for Non-Violence," *Cleveland Call and Post*, October 24, 1964, 8B. "King in a Pantheon of Greatness," *Norfolk Journal and Guide*, October 24, 1964, 8. *Los Angeles Sentinel*, October 29, 1964, A1.

13. *New York Times*, November 5, 1964, 1. Garrow, *Bearing the Cross*, 353–354, 358.

14. For the significance of the Eighty-Ninth Congress to the implementation of the Great Society see Julian Zelizer, *The Fierce Urgency of Now: Lyndon Johnson, Congress, and the Battle for the Great Society* (New York: Penguin Books, 2015).

15. Branch, *Pillar of Fire*, 268. Garrow, *Bearing the Cross*, 372–373. Nick Kotz, *Judgment Days: Lyndon Baines Johnson, Martin Luther King, Jr., and the Laws That Changed America* (Boston: Mariner Books, 2005), 246–249.

16. *Chicago Defender*, July 13, 1964, 3.

17. Joseph, *Waiting 'til the Midnight Hour*, 112. Marable, *Malcolm X*, 363–364. See also Victor Riesel, "Malcolm X and the Red Chinese,"

New York Journal-American, August 5, 1964, 7, in FBIMX 105-8999-4823. *Chicago Defender*, July 14, 1964, 3. *Chicago Defender*, July 14, 1964, 3. *Baltimore Afro-American*, July 18, 1964.

18. El-Shabazz, *Diary*, 85–86. Joseph, *Waiting 'til the Midnight Hour*, 112–113. Marable, *Malcolm X*, 362.

19. All quotes from OAAU Press Release addressed to "First Ordinary Assembly of Heads of State and Governments Organization of African Unity," July 17, 1964, in FBIMX 105-8999-4974.

20. Airtel to Director Hoover from New York SAC, July 21, 1964, FBIMX 100-399321-135, and Teletype to Director Hoover, July 21, 1964, FBIMX 100-399321-137. Bruce Perry, *Malcolm: The Life of a Man Who Changed Black America* (Barrytown, NY: Station Hill Press, 1991), 313. *Ghanaian Times*, July 30, 1964, 4.

21. Langston Hughes, "Malcolm in Cairo," *New York Post*, 32, in FBIMX 105-8999-4742. Joseph, *Dark Days, Bright Nights*, 80.

22. John Lewis, *Walking with the Wind: A Memoir of the Movement* (San Diego, CA: Harvest, 1998), 205, 324. Joseph, *Waiting 'til the Midnight Hour*, 113. Joseph, *Dark Days, Bright Nights*, 80.

23. Marable, *Malcolm X*, 367–370. *Saturday Evening Post*, September 12, 1964.

24. Hans J. Massaquoi, "Mystery of Malcolm X," *Ebony*, September 1964, 38–46.

25. Massaquoi, "Mystery," 39–40, 46.

26. Joseph, *Dark Days, Bright Nights*, 93.

27. *Tanganyika Standard*, October 13, 1964, 1. *Nationalist*, October 12, 1964, 1.

28. *Liberian Age*, November 9, 1964, 1–2. *Liberian Star*, November 9, 1964, 5. For example, reporter M. S. Handler's nuanced coverage of Malcolm's efforts in Cairo was buried in the *New York Times*. See M. S. Handler, "Malcolm X Seeks U.N. Negro Debate," *New York Times*, August 17, 1964, 22, in FBIMX 105-8999-4873. For critical articles on Malcolm's foray into Africa, see Victor Riesel, "Malcolm X Gives Africa Twisted Look," *New York Journal American*, July 25, 1964, 20, in FBIMX 105-8999-4789, and Charles Bartlett, "In Search of Armageddon," *Chicago Sun-Times*, July 29, 1964, 32, in FBIMX 105-8999-4779.

29. Marable, *Malcolm X*, 386. Ambar, *Malcolm X at Oxford Union*, 28–30. Malcolm X, "The AfroAmerican in Face of the African Revolution," November 23, 1964, 1, 3, in "Transcripts: Malcolm X Speaks at the Maubert Mutalite," trans. Carlos Moore and Emile Saint Lo, Carlos Moore Papers, Box 7, Folder 2, UCLA Ralph Bunche Center for

African American Studies. In France, he reunited for the last time with Chester Himes, by now universally acknowledged as a cynically astute race-relations sage whose bitter literary screeds against American racism offered daringly gratified French audiences an unvarnished look at the kind of hypocrisy Malcolm made a career of exposing. In their final meeting, Malcolm and Himes traded barbed war stories about Harlem in between sober conversations about the political future. Himes's recent, dispiriting foray in Egypt made him skeptical of the revolutionary alliances Malcolm touted. See Lawrence P. Jackson, *Chester B. Himes* (New York: W. W. Norton, 2017), 449–452.

30. *New York Courier*, December 5, 1964, 9, in FBIMX 105-8999-5221. Joseph, *Dark Days, Bright Nights*, 95. Garrow, *Bearing the Cross*, 364. *Pittsburgh Courier*, December 19, 1964, 10. Branch, *Pillar of Fire*, 539.

31. Ambar, *Malcolm X At Oxford Union*, 3–5, 7. "Millions of Britons See Malcolm X in TV Broadcast of Debate at Oxford," *Voice*, January 2, 1965, MXP, Reel 16, Folder 1.

32. Ambar, *Malcolm X at Oxford Union*, 118. Marable, *Malcolm X*, 391. *Daily Telegraph and Morning Post*, December 4, 1964, 17, in MXP, Reel 3, Folder 15. *Sheffield Telegraph*, December (?), 1964, in MXP, Reel 3, Folder 15.

33. Martin Luther King Jr. Speech in London, December 7, 1964, PRA KZ4492, Pacifica Radio Archives.

34. Garrow, *Bearing the Cross*, 364.

35. Martin Luther King Jr., "Nobel Prize Acceptance Speech," in *A Testament of Hope*, 224, 226.

36. James Smethurst, "Malcolm X and the Black Arts Movement," in *The Cambridge Companion to Malcolm X*, ed. Robert E. Terrill (Cambridge: Cambridge University Press, 2010), 78–89. Joseph, *Waiting 'til the Midnight Hour*, 118–123. Malcolm X, "HARYOU-ACT Forum Speech," December 12, 1964, in *Malcolm X: Collected Speeches*, 1:869.

37. Malcolm X, "HARYOU-ACT Forum Speech," 869–870.

38. "Malcolm X Suggests King Accepted Prize Too Early," *Harvard Crimson*, December 17, 1964, 1, in MXP, Reel 16, Folder 1.

39. *Washington Post*, December 19, 1964, A2.

40. *New York Times*, December 18, 1964, 37. Branch, *Pillar of Fire*, 546–547. Garrow, *Bearing the Cross*, 368. Malcolm X, "By Any Means Necessary," December 20, 1964, in *Malcolm X: Collected Speeches*, 1:916. This is the transcript from the evening OAAU Rally at the Audubon,

the second event Malcolm held with Hamer and the SNCC Freedom Singers that day.

41. Malcolm X, "By Any Means Necessary."

42. Malcolm X, "By Any Means Necessary," 927.

43. Joseph, *Waiting 'til the Midnight Hour*. Maya Angelou, *The Heart of a Woman* (New York: Random House, 1981). Jerrie Norris, *Presenting Rosa Guy* (Boston: Twayne Publishing, 1988), 16–20. Historian Ruth Feldstein offers the most insightful portrait of black women artists and intellectuals during this era. See Feldstein, *How It Feels to Be Free: Black Women Entertainers and the Civil Rights Movement* (New York: Oxford University Press, 2013). Malcolm X and Bernice Bass Interview, December 27, 1964, in *Malcolm X: Collected Speeches*, 1:934.

44. Malcolm X and Claude Lewis Interview, December 31, 1964, in *Malcolm X: Collected Speeches*, 1:943, 945, 950.

45. Author's interview with Amiri Baraka, July 7, 2004. Komozi Woodard, *A Nation within a Nation: Amiri Baraka (LeRoi Jones) and Black Power Politics* (Chapel Hill: University of North Carolina Press, 1999), 59–64.

46. "Speech to SNCC Civil Rights Workers," January 1, 1965, in *Malcolm X: Collected Speeches*, 1:955, 957, 965.

47. Goldman, *Death and Life*, 226. *New York Times*, January 7, 1965, 21.

48. Marable, *Malcolm X*, 409.

49. David Levering Lewis, *King: A Biography* (Urbana: University of Illinois Press, 2013), 268.

50. "Malcolm K. Little," February 8, 1965, 1, in FBI MX 105-8999-239.

51. Henry Hampton and Steve Fayer, eds., *Voices of Freedom: An Oral History of the Civil Rights Movement from the 1950s through the 1980s* (New York: Bantam, 1990), 221–222. Goldman, *Death and Life*, 231–232. Lewis V. Baldwin, *To Make the Wounded Whole: The Cultural Legacy of Martin Luther King, Jr.* (Minneapolis, MN: Fortress Press, 1992), 38–42.

52. Moshik Temkin, "Malcolm X in France, 1964–1965: Anti-Imperialism and the Politics of Travel Control in the Cold War Era," in *Decolonization and the Cold War: Negotiating Independence*, eds. Leslie James and Elisabeth Leake (London: Bloomsbury Academic Press, 2015), 219–238.

53. Malcolm X, "The Oppressed Masses of the World Cry Out for Action against the Common Oppressor," February 11, 1965, in *Malcolm X Collected Speeches*, 1:1067.

54. Malcolm X, "The Oppressed Masses," 1079–1080.

55. Marable, *Malcolm X*, 411, 415–417. Joseph, *Waiting 'til the Midnight Hour*.

56. Marable, *Malcolm X*, 418–422.

57. Marable, *Malcolm X*, 430, 435.

58. "400 See Malcolm X Assassinated," *Boston Globe*, February 22, 1965, 4. Marable, *Malcolm X*, 432–441.

59. The late historian Manning Marable, Malcolm X's most authoritative biographer, attempts to solve this mystery in *Malcolm X*, 423–449. "Malcolm X Shot to Death at Rally Here," *New York Times*, February 22, 1965, 10.

60. *New York Times*, February 28, 1965, 1, in FBIMX 105-8999-5963.

61. Ossie Sykes, "The Week that Malcolm X Died," *Liberator*, April 1965, 6. *New York Herald Tribune*, February 22, 1965, 5, in FBIMX 105-899-5869. *Chicago Daily News*, February 23, 1965, 4, in FBIMX 105-8999-5882.

62. Joseph, *Waiting 'til the Midnight Hour*, 115–117.

63. Joseph, *Waiting 'til the Midnight Hour*, 116. *New York Times*, February 27, 1965, 75, and February 26, 1965, in FBIMX 105-8999-5944 and 105-8999-5923.

64. Joseph, *Dark Days, Bright Nights*, 98–99. *Standard* (Tanzania), February 23, 1965, 1. *Liberian Star*, February 25, 1965, 2. *Ghanaian Times*, March 2, 1965, 4. *Daily Times* (Nigeria), February 26, 1965, 9. *Ghanaian Times*, February 26, 1965, 2.

65. Martin Luther King Jr., "The Nightmare of Violence: Regarding the Death of Malcolm X," in *Martin Luther King, Jr., Malcolm X, and the Civil Rights Struggle of the 1950s and 1960s: A Brief History with Documents*, ed. David Howard-Pitney (Boston: Bedford/St. Martin's, 2004), 125–126.

CHAPTER 9: THE RADICAL KING

1. Joseph, *Stokely*, 82–83. Taylor Branch, *At Canaan's Edge: America in the King Years, 1965–68* (New York: Simon and Schuster, 2006), 25–26. Branch, *Pillar of Fire*, 593–594. Garrow, *Bearing the Cross*, 391–393. For Lowndes's role in the convict-lease system, see Douglas A. Blackmon, *Slavery by Another Name: The Re-Enslavement of Black American from the Civil War to World War II* (New York: Anchor Books, 2009), 271–274.

2. Garrow, *Bearing the Cross*, 397–399.

3. Branch, *Pillar of Fire.*

4. Garrow, *Bearing the Cross*, 407.

5. Martin Luther King Jr. to the President, March 15, 1965, Martin Luther King Jr. (1965) Folder, LBJ Archives, LBJ Presidential Library. "President Johnson's Special Message to the Congress: The American Promise," March 15, 1965, LBJ Presidential Library, www.lbjlibrary .org/lyndon-baines-johnson/speeches-films/president-johnsons -special-message-to-the-congress-the-american-promise.

6. Joseph, *Stokely*, 83–84. Kotz, *Judgment Days*, 312. Kotz, *Judgment Days*, 312.

7. Theoharis, *Rebellious Life*, 188.

8. Martin Luther King Jr., "Our God Is Marching On!," in *A Testament of Hope*, 228–230.

9. Martin Luther King Jr., "Behind the Selma March," *Saturday Review*, April 3, 1965, 16.

10. *Chicago Defender*, May 25, 1965, 5. *New York Newsday*, May 21, 1965, 15.

11. *New York Newsday*, May 29, 1965, 7.

12. Marable, *Malcolm X*, 340. *New York Newsday*, May 29, 1965, 7.

13. Eric Foner, *The Fiery Trial: Abraham Lincoln and American Slavery* (New York: W. W. Norton, 2010), 174–175. Kotz, *Judgment Days*, 336. Joseph, *Waiting 'til the Midnight Hour*, 111. David C. Carter, *The Music Has Gone Out of the Movement: Civil Rights and the Johnson Administration, 1965–1968* (Chapel Hill: University of North Carolina Press, 2009), 170.

14. Joseph, *Waiting 'til the Midnight Hour*, 121–123. Branch, *At Canaan's Edge*, 293–299. Thomas F. Jackson, *From Civil Rights to Human Rights: Martin Luther King, Jr., and the Struggle for Economic Justice* (Philadelphia: University of Pennsylvania Press, 2009), 243–244.

15. Branch, *At Canaan's Edge*, 293–294.

16. Branch, *At Canaan's Edge*, 297–298. Jackson, *From Civil Rights*, 240–241. Garrow, *Bearing the Cross*, 439.

17. Branch, *At Canaan's Edge*, 234. LBJ Presidential Library Oral History Archives, tape no. 65708.07, August 20, 1965.

18. Branch, *At Canaan's Edge*, 308–309.

19. Martin Luther King Jr., "Beyond the Los Angeles Riots," *Saturday Review*, November 13, 1965, 33.

20. Joseph, *Dark Days, Bright Nights*, 71. King, "Beyond the Los Angeles Riots," 33.

21. Branch, *At Canaan's Edge*, 470, 472–472. Oates, *Let the Trumpet Sound*, 395. Garrow, *Bearing the Cross*, 473. Kotz, *Judgment Days*, 359.

22. *New York Times*, June 3, 1966, 21. Whitney Young, "Interracial Confrontations Needed to Solve Nation's Race Problem," *Baltimore Afro-American*, June 4, 1966, 12. *Boston Globe*, June 3, 1966. *Philadelphia Tribune*, June 4, 1966, 8.

23. Branch, *At Canaan's Edge*, 472.

24. Branch, *At Canaan's Edge*, 473. Aram Goudsouzian, *Down to the Crossroads: Civil Rights, Black Power, and the Meredith March Against Fear* (New York: Farrar, Straus, and Giroux, 2014), 6. Branch, *At Canaan's Edge*, 473.

25. Goudsouzian, *Down to the Crossroads*, 6. *Eyes on the Prize*, season 2, Southern Regional Council, "Will the Circle Be Unbroken?" collection, Emory University, 6–8.

26. *Philadelphia Inquirer*, June 8, 1966, 1. *New York Times*, June 8, 1966, 26. *Boston Globe*, June 8, 1966, 2.

27. Joseph, *Stokely*, 106. Branch, *At Canaan's Edge*, 577. Goudsouzian, *Down to the Crossroads*, 33–34. Carmichael and Thelwell, *Ready for Revolution*, 503.

28. Joseph, *Stokely*, 108.

29. Goudsouzian, *Down to the Crossroads*, 83. Joseph, *Stokely*, 82. *Boston Globe*, June 9, 1966, 3.

30. Goudsouzian, *Down to the Crossroads*, 57.

31. Joseph, *Stokely*, 114–115. Joseph, *Waiting 'til the Midnight Hour*, 142. Branch, *At Canaan's Edge*, 477.

32. Peniel E. Joseph, ed., *The Black Power Movement: Rethinking the Civil Rights–Black Power Era* (New York: Routledge, 2006). Peniel E. Joseph, ed., *Neighborhood Rebels: Black Power at the Local Level* (New York: Palgrave MacMillan, 2010).

33. Joseph, *Stokely*, 116. Paul Good, "A White Look at Black Power," *Nation*, August 8, 1966, 115.

34. Carmichael and Thelwell, *Ready for Revolution*, 513.

35. *New York Times*, June 21, 1966, 30. Austin C. Wehrwein, "Dr. King Disputes Negro Separatist," *New York Times*, May 28, 1966. Joseph, *Stokely*.

36. *Chicago Tribune*, June 19, 1966, 5. *Boston Globe*, June 19, 1966, 30–31. *Los Angeles Times*, June 19, 1966, J4.

37. Joseph, *Stokely*, 110.

38. Goudsouzian, *Down to the Crossroads*, 171. *Time*, July 1, 1966, 12.

39. Goudsouzian, *Down to the Crossroads*, 174–176.

40. *New York Times*, June 22, 1966, 1, 25. Goudsouzian, *Down to the Crossroads*, 190.

41. *Time*, July 1, 1966, 12. *New York Times*, June 24, 1966, 20. *New Yorker*, July 1966, 24.

42. Goudsouzian, *Down to the Crossroads*, 191. *Washington Post*, June 25, 1966, A4. Joseph, *Stokely*, 119.

43. *Los Angeles Times*, June 27, 1966, 13. *New York Times*, June 27, 1966, 29. *New York Times*, June 27, 1966, 29. Goudsouzian, *Down to the Crossroads*, 243.

44. Branch, *At Canaan's Edge*, 495.

45. Garrow, *Bearing the Cross*, 492.

46. Garrow, *Bearing the Cross*, 497.

47. Garrow, *Bearing the Cross*, 498–500. Branch, *At Canaan's Edge*, 508–509.

48. Garrow, *Bearing the Cross*, 513.

49. Joseph, *Stokely*, 137.

50. Branch, *At Canaan's Edge*, 519, 521–522. Garrow, *Bearing the Cross*, 519–524. Sitkoff, *King*, 203–204.

51. Joseph, *Stokely*. Branch, *At Canaan's Edge*, 548–549.

CHAPTER 10: THE REVOLUTIONARY KING

1. Martin Luther King Jr., "A Time to Break Silence," in *A Testament of Hope*, 232–233.

2. Malcolm X, "The Oppressed Masses of the World Cry Out for Action against the Common Oppressor," London School of Economics, February 11, 1965, in *Malcolm X: Collected Speeches*, 1:1071.

3. Atwal, *Malcolm X: Collected Speeches*, 1:234–236. Marable, *Malcolm X*, 340.

4. King, "A Time to Break Silence," 233, 243.

5. King, "A Time to Break Silence," 243. *New York Times*, May 6, 1967, 1, 6. *New York Times*, May 7, 1967, 127.

6. Garrow, *Bearing the Cross*. Michael Eric Dyson, *I May Not Get There with You: The True Martin Luther King, Jr.* (New York: Free Press, 2000). Jackson, *From Civil Rights*. Branch, *At Canaan's Edge*. Martin Luther King Jr., *The Radical King*, ed. Cornel West (Boston: Beacon Press, 2015). Sylvie Laurent, *King and the Other America: The Poor People's Campaign and the Quest for Economic Equality* (Oakland: University

of California Press, 2018). Brandon M. Terry and Tommie Shelby, eds., *To Shape a New World: Essays on the Political Philosophy of Martin Luther King, Jr.* (Cambridge, MA: Harvard University Press, 2018).

7. "Racial Unrest and Violence Potential in the United States," June 14, 1966, 41pp, FBI, Office Files of Mildred Stegall, Box 71B, 2 of 2, LBJ Library. Gerald McKnight, *The Last Crusade: Martin Luther King, Jr., the FBI, and the Poor People's Campaign* (Boulder: Westview Press, 1998), 15–16.

8. *Boston Globe*, April 6, 1967, 1. *Boston Globe*, April 5, 1967, 1. *Los Angeles Times*, May 13, 1967, 12. *Chicago Defender*, May 15, 1967, 8. *New York Times*, April 6, 1967, 10.

9. "Dr. King's Error," *New York Times*, April 7, 1967, 36.

10. Joseph, *Stokely*, 186–190. Stewart Burns, *To the Mountaintop: Martin Luther King Jr.'s Sacred Mission to Save America 1955–1968* (San Francisco: Harper San Francisco, 2004), 309. Branch, *At Canaan's Edge*, 598.

11. Joseph, *Stokely*, 187–188. *New York Times*, April 16, 1967, 2. Branch, *At Canaan's Edge*, 600.

12. Martin Luther King Jr., interview on *Face the Nation*, April 16, 1967, transcript, 16pp, King Center Box 121, 1, 3, 7, 13. Branch, *At Canaan's Edge*, 599.

13. Joseph, *Stokely*, 190.

14. Joseph, *Stokely*, 190. *New York Times*, May 1, 1967, 1.

15. *Washington Post*, May 1, 1967, A13. Adam Fairclough, *To Redeem the Soul of America: The Southern Christian Leadership Conference and Martin Luther King, Jr.* (Athens: University of Georgia Press, 2001), 339. D'Emilio, *Lost Prophet*, 396–397, 444–448.

16. *New York Times*, May 9, 1967, 1, 24. *Washington Post*, May 12, 1967, A24. Branch, *At Canaan's Edge*, 613.

17. *Los Angeles Times*, May 11, 1967, 5. *New York Times*, May 11, 1967, 18.

18. *Chicago Defender*, May 13, 1967, 2. *Washington Post*, May 26, 1967, A2. Gene Roberts, "Civil Rights: King Sees a Dual Mission," *New York Times*, May 7, 1967, 224.

19. Martin Luther King Jr., "America's Chief Moral Dilemma," speech at University of California at Berkeley, May 17, 1967, KPFA archives BB1195.

20. King, "America's Chief Moral Dilemma."

21. Martin Luther King Jr., *Where Do We Go from Here: Chaos or Community?* (Boston: Beacon Press, 1968), 58. For an illuminating

discussion of King's efforts at critique and rapprochement with Black Power activists, see Brandon M. Terry, "Requiem for a Dream," in *To Shape a New World*, in Brandon M. Terry and Tommie Shelby, eds. (Cambridge, MA: Harvard University Press, 2018), 290–324.

22. *Los Angeles Times*, June 1, 1967, 6. *Austin American-Statesman*, June 19, 1967, 2.

23. *New York Times*, June 19, 1967, 36. *Austin American-Statesman*, June 20, 1967, 16. *New York Times*, June 20, 1967, 25.

24. Joseph, *Waiting 'til the Midnight Hour*, 183–185.

25. Joseph, *Waiting 'til the Midnight Hour*, 185–186. Lyndon Baines Johnson, *The Vantage Point: Perspectives of the Presidency 1963–1969* (New York: Holt, Rinehart, and Winston, 1971), 167–172.

26. Garrow, *Bearing the Cross*, 570. Branch, *At Canaan's Edge*, 634. Joseph, *Stokely*, 204–205.

27. Branch, *At Canaan's Edge*, 635. *Chicago Defender*, October 10, 1963, A28.

28. Garrow, *Bearing the Cross*, 571.

29. *Washington Post*, August 6, 1967, B4. *Philadelphia Tribune*, August 15, 1967. Branch, *At Canaan's Edge*, 634. Garrow, *Bearing the Cross*, 573.

30. *Washington Post*, August 16, 1967, A1, A4. *Washington Post*, August 17, 1967, A8. Branch, *At Canaan's Edge*, 635–637. Garrow, *Bearing the Cross*, 573–574.

31. Branch, *At Canaan's Edge*, 629. Joseph, *Stokely*, 196.

32. Garrow, *Bearing the Cross*, 569. Michael K. Honey, *To the Promised Land: Martin Luther King and the Fight for Economic Justice* (New York: W. W. Norton, 2018). Michael K. Honey, *Going Down Jericho Road: The Memphis Strike, Martin Luther King's Last Campaign* (New York: W. W. Norton, 2008). Laurent, *King and the Other America.*

33. *Washington Post*, August 16, 1967, A1, A4. *Washington Post*, August 17, 1967, A8. Branch, *At Canaan's Edge*, 635–637. Garrow, *Bearing the Cross*, 573–574.

34. Branch, *At Canaan's Edge*, 634, 636–637. *New York Times*, August 16, 1967, 1, 29.

35. Branch, *At Canaan's Edge*, 638.

36. David Halberstam, "The Second Coming of Martin Luther King," *Harper's*, August 1967, 42, 48.

37. *Philadelphia Inquirer*, September 2, 1967, 3. Martin Luther King Jr., "The Role of the Behavioral Scientist in the Civil Rights Movement," *Journal of Social Issues* 74, no. 2 (2018): 214.

38. King, "Behavioral Scientist," 215–216.

39. King, "Behavioral Scientist," 216–217.

40. King, "Behavioral Scientist," 217.

41. King, "Behavioral Scientist," 222–223. *New York Post*, April 10, 1964, 49.

42. *Washington Post*, September 2, 1967, D12.

43. Steven M. Gillon, *Separate and Unequal: The Kerner Commission and the Unraveling of American Liberalism* (New York: Basic Books, 2018). Garrow, *Bearing the Cross*, 579. Branch, *At Canaan's Edge*, 648. Stokely Carmichael Interview Transcript, November 7, 1988, 1, *Eyes on the Prize*, season 2, Southern Regional Council, "Will the Circle Be Unbroken?" collection, Emory University.

44. Branch, *At Canaan's Edge*, 652–656, 661. Branch, *Pillar of Fire*, 54–55.

45. Kotz, *Judgment Days*, 387–388.

46. Joseph, *Stokely*, 237–238. Branch, *At Canaan's Edge*, 686.

47. Washington, *A Testament of Hope*, 263–265.

48. Branch, *At Canaan's Edge*, 686–687, 715–716.

49. *Los Angeles Sentinel*, March 21, 1968, A3, 8D. Garrow, *Bearing the Cross*, 604.

50. Martin Luther King Jr., *"All Labor Has Dignity,"* ed. Michael K. Honey (Boston: Beacon Press, 2012), 171–172, 176. Branch, *At Canaan's Edge*, 719.

51. *New York Times*, March 20, 1968, 18. Branch, *At Canaan's Edge*, 720–721. Oates, *Let the Trumpet Sound*, 472.

52. Martin Luther King Jr., *The Last Interview and Other Conversations* (New York: Melville House, 2017), 113.

53. Garrow, *Bearing the Cross*, 602–603, 607–608.

54. The black *Los Angeles Sentinel* newspaper announced the Kerner report as a national admission of guilt: "White Community Blamed for Riots." *Los Angeles Sentinel*, February 29, 1968, 2A. Joseph, *Dark Days, Bright Nights*, 178–179.

55. Honey, *Promised Land*.

56. *Baltimore Sun*, April 1, 1968, A1. Washington, *A Testament of Hope*, 269.

57. Washington, *A Testament of Hope*, 270–271.

58. Washington, *A Testament of Hope*, 274–277.

59. *Baltimore Sun*, April 1, 1968, A7. *New York Times*, April 1, 1968. 20. Branch, *At Canaan's Edge*, 746–749.

60. Steve Estes, *I Am a Man! Race, Manhood, and the Civil Rights Movement* (Chapel Hill: University of North Carolina Press, 2005).

Honey, *Jericho Road*, 338. Martin Luther King Jr., "I See the Promised Land," in *A Testament of Hope*, 279–286.

61. Branch, *At Canaan's Edge*, 759–766.

62. Joseph Rosenbloom, *Redemption: Martin Luther King Jr.'s Last 31 Hours* (Boston: Beacon Press, 2018), 156, 158. *Washington Post*, April 6, 1968, A3.

63. Branch, *At Canaan's Edge*, 769. Rosenbloom, *Redemption*, 169. Joseph, *Stokely*, 258.

64. Clay Risen, *A Nation on Fire: America in the Wake of the King Assassination* (New York: Wiley, 2009). Jason Sokol, *The Heavens Might Crack: The Death and Legacy of Martin Luther King Jr.* (New York: Basic Books, 2018). *Washington Post*, April 6, 1968, A12. *Los Angeles Times*, April 7, 1968, EB. *New York Times*, April 7, 1968, 1, 59. *Los Angeles Times*, April 8, 1968, 28.

65. Risen, *A Nation on Fire*, 49–50.

66. James Baldwin, "Malcolm and Martin," *Esquire*, April 15, 1972, 94.

67. Baldwin, "Malcolm and Martin," 196, 201.

68. Risen, *A Nation on Fire*, 88, 205. Branch, *Bearing the Cross*, 597.

69. Risen, *A Nation on Fire*, 108–111. Sokol, *The Heavens*, 44–47.

EPILOGUE: THE LEGACY OF MALCOLM X AND MARTIN LUTHER KING JR.

1. Baldwin, "Malcolm and Martin," 201.

2. Baldwin, "Malcolm and Martin," 201.

3. David L. Chappell, *Waking from the Dream: The Struggle for Civil Rights in the Shadow of Martin Luther King, Jr.* (Durham, NC: Duke University Press, 2016), 119–120. *Los Angeles Times*, April 6, 1968, 3. Sokol, *The Heavens*, 102.

4. Dyson, *I May Not Get There with You*. Michael Eric Dyson, *April 4, 1968: Martin Luther King, Jr.'s Death and How It Changed America* (New York: Basic Books, 2009). King, *The Radical King*. Chappell, *Waking from the Dream*. Sokol, *The Heavens*. Terry and Shelby, *To Shape a New World*.

5. Clayborne Carson, *Martin's Dream: My Journey and the Legacy of Martin Luther King Jr.* (New York: Palgrave Macmillan, 2013). Chappell, *Waking from the Dream*, 148–174.

6. Jackson, *From Civil Rights*. Dyson, *I May Not Get There*. Dyson, *April 4, 1968*. King, *Radical King*. King, "A Time to Break Silence," 243.

7. Graeme Abernathy, *The Iconography of Malcolm X* (Lawrence: University Press of Kansas, 2013). Dyson, *April 4, 1968*.

8. Joseph, *Dark Days, Bright Nights*, 34.

9. Michelle Alexander, *The New Jim Crow: Mass Incarceration in the Age of Colorblindness* (New York: New Press, 2010).

Index

Credit: Kelvin Ma

Peniel E. Joseph is the Barbara Jordan Chair in Ethics and Political Values at the LBJ School of Public Affairs, where he serves as founding director of the Center for the Study of Race and Democracy, and professor of history at the University of Texas at Austin. He has written several previous books on African American history, including *Stokely: A Life*. He lives in Austin, Texas.